MATLAB and Simulink In-Depth

Model-based Design with Simulink and Stateflow, User Interface, Scripting, Simulation, Visualization and Debugging

Priyanka Patankar

Swapnil Kulkarni

www.bpbonline.com

Copyright © 2022 BPB Online

All rights reserved. No part of this book may be reproduced, stored in a retrieval system, or transmitted in any form or by any means, without the prior written permission of the publisher, except in the case of brief quotations embedded in critical articles or reviews.

Every effort has been made in the preparation of this book to ensure the accuracy of the information presented. However, the information contained in this book is sold without warranty, either express or implied. Neither the author, nor BPB Online or its dealers and distributors, will be held liable for any damages caused or alleged to have been caused directly or indirectly by this book.

BPB Online has endeavored to provide trademark information about all of the companies and products mentioned in this book by the appropriate use of capitals. However, BPB Online cannot guarantee the accuracy of this information.

Group Product Manager: Marianne Conor
Publishing Product Manager: Eva Brawn
Senior Editor: Connell
Content Development Editor: Melissa Monroe
Technical Editor: Anne Stokes
Copy Editor: Joe Austin
Language Support Editor: Justin Baldwin
Project Coordinator: Tyler Horan
Proofreader: Khloe Styles
Indexer: V. Krishnamurthy
Production Designer: Malcolm D'Souza
Marketing Coordinator: Kristen Kramer

First published: August 2022

Published by BPB Online
WeWork, 119 Marylebone Road
London NW1 5PU

UK | UAE | INDIA | SINGAPORE

ISBN 978-93-55511-997

www.bpbonline.com

Dedicated to

My loving mothers:
Sandhya Patankar & Veena Bagul
My husband:
Pratik Jayraj Bagul
&
*My newborn **daughter***
In memory of:
Chandrakant Omkar Patankar
—*Priyanka Chandrakant Patankar*

My beloved Parents:
Mrunalini *and* **Mukund Devidas Kulkarni**
&
Prajakta Pradeep Pujari
&
My wife **Swarupa**
In memory of:
Pradeep Shrikrishna Pujari
—*Swapnil Mukund Kulkarni*

About the Authors

- **Priyanka Patankar** is a Technical Project Manager in the automotive industry with over 11+ years of extensive experience in Software development with MATLAB using model-based engineering approach. She has completed her M.Tech in Software Systems from Birla Institute of Technology and Science, Pilani. Since the beginning of her career, she has had opportunities to work with leading carmakers on body and comfort ECU software development. After landing her dream job with a world-leading German carmaker, she has been consistently delivering work products for upcoming luxury cars and sharing the knowledge with her team. Through this book, she wants to bring her experience to the application by inspiring the readers to learn MATLAB and reduce the knowledge gap between industry needs and education. She spends her free time learning German language as well as exploring novel aspects of motherhood. She also loves to travel to new destinations, where she clicks photographs and shares them on her travel blog.

- **Swapnil Kulkarni** is working as a Technical Project Manager in the automotive industry. He has more than 12 years of strong experience working in MATLAB. He has worked in several domains, such as Body controllers, climate control modules and Infotainment systems for various car manufacturers. He is also leading a team for patterns and architecture, where he is responsible for validating different types of model architectures and creating new patterns with reusable libraries. He has accomplished several assignments on Tool development and model architecture design with a leading carmaker in Germany. Besides working, he regularly plays lawn tennis, table tennis, and cricket. He also holds a special interest in Hindustani Indian classical music.

About the Reviewer

- **Suraj Prakash Tallur** is a Senior Technical Lead Engineer in Body Comfort Domain with 8 years of automotive experience in model based software development. He is extensively involved in MATLAB Simulink modeling, DSPACE Target Link Auto code generation, TPT MIL/ SIL testing and Canoe Virtual Integration testing for embedded ECUs in automotive applications.

  His area of work involves Cluster leadership, Stakeholder coordination and providing technical solutions to requirements of different stakeholders for various automotive applications via Model based design and development.

  He has worked with Japanese clients like Nissan, JATCO in Tata Consultancy Services for 3 years and currently working in renowned German OEM since past 5 years. He is Six-Sigma Green Belt and ISTQB Foundation Level testing certified. He has a B.E. in E&E from KLESCET VTU University Belgaum.

Acknowledgement

○ It is our great pleasure to avail this opportunity to thank everyone who has helped us write this book directly or indirectly.

First and foremost, we want to express our gratitude towards the Almighty for enabling us to acquire and share this knowledge. We would like to thank our family members for staying patient, encouraging and supportive throughout the development journey of this book.

We are inclined towards expressing our gratefulness to this book's technical reviewer Mr. Suraj Tallur. His review comments bearing in mind a reader's perspective have been helpful in refining the content. In addition, we would like to rightfully acknowledge the prompt support and tool licenses received from MathWorks Book program team. We are thankful towards The MathWorks, Inc. and Mr. Joachim Loew for permitting usage of their images in the book.

Our heartfelt gratitude goes to the BPB Publications team for being considerate, supportive, and comprehensible with us during each development stage of this book.

Preface

We are delighted to share our book 'MATLAB for Model-based design and Simulation' with our readers. Aptly suggested by the title, this book aims to highlight basics of Model-based design and Simulation by establishing MATLAB, Simulink and Stateflow core concepts. MATLAB, which stands for Matrix Library, is a powerful solution provided by MathWorks Inc. that has the capability to express matrix and array arithmetic efficiently. MATLAB is a numerical computing tool, whereas Simulink and Stateflow are Graphical Programming tools. This book is an extensive guide to learning the fundamentals of MATLAB, Simulink and Stateflow. It creates a solid foundation of techniques widely used for model-based development. MATLAB is expansively used in many industries such as Automotive, Aviation and Aerospace, Health Care, Medical devices industry, Financial, Information and Technology. MATLAB, when combined with Simulink as well as Stateflow, offers multi-domain simulation, automatic code generation, with testing and verification of embedded systems. With the help of MATLAB and its toolboxes, the development and evaluation of algorithms become considerably fast.

MATLAB is an enormous tool with several toolsets embedded within it. When one wants to start MATLAB modelling by relying on information available on the Internet or different community websites, it results in information overload, which raises questions such as where to start from, how to proceed, what are the key concepts of MATLAB, Simulink and Stateflow, etc. In this book, we have addressed most of these questions with some real-world examples.

As a novice reader, you will begin MATLAB learning journey by setting up the Tool environment in the system. Then you will get familiar with the History and Significant features of MATLAB. You will be acquainted with MATLAB's desktop user interface and basic commands, and you will learn data visualization as well. Further, you will explore Simulink with its key features, configuration settings, and libraries. You will go through the stepwise approach to create and simulate a simple Simulink model. You will explore advanced modelling techniques such as custom libraries, model referencing and subsystems. You will also learn about test environment creation and model simulation. Later, you will explore Stateflow concepts such as flow graph, hierarchical model, conditions, actions, transitions, etc.

A person who is new to MATLAB and Simulink or wants to quickly refresh her/his knowledge shall find this book useful. Students, teachers, researchers as well as professionals shall benefit from it. This book has been designed specifically for beginners to help them understand the core features of MATLAB, Simulink and Stateflow. After reading this book, the reader shall have a strong foundation of fundamental concepts of the topics, from where she/he can continue towards attaining an advanced level of expertise. Though it is not mandatory, having basic programming skills will make the learning process more efficient and enjoyable.

This book has been derived from our extensive knowledge and strong experience working with industry leaders. The reader shall be able to kick off the journey of MATLAB model-based design and Simulation with this book due to its simple and engaging language. This journey becomes more exciting with the problem-based practical examples and useful tips covered in the book. Additionally, this book will certainly be a great help to crack interviews and exams based on MATLAB model-based development with Simulink, and Stateflow.

The book is distributed among three key sections- MATLAB, Simulink and Stateflow. It comprises of total 15 chapters covering various topics under these sections, explained as follows:

Section 1: MATLAB

Chapter 1 Introduction to MATLAB takes readers through the history and origin of MATLAB. This chapter sets the context of MATLAB applications. It also describes its various industry products and toolboxes used for them. It provides detailed information on the scope of the book, the installation procedure of MATLAB and its toolboxes. It also explains how to do an Environmental setup. Readers shall also understand the benefits of choosing MATLAB over traditional programming methods.

Chapter 2 MATLAB Desktop Interface deals with the MATLAB desktop interface and its functions. It makes the readers familiar with different layouts, Windows, Workspaces, toolbars, and introduces to some key shortcuts and settings.

Chapter 3 MATLAB basics covers the fundamental concepts and core elements of MATLAB. It covers variables, arrays, constants, datatypes, functions, etc. to establish a strong foundation of building blocks.

Chapter 4 Programming Basics, Control flow and Visualization introduces readers to various visualization possibilities available in MATLAB. It covers multidimensional Plots, Graphs, and Scopes, Images etc. as well.

Section 2: Simulink

Chapter 5 Introduction to Simulink introduces the basic features of Simulink, which are essential to begin Model development. This chapter narrates a stepwise approach to creating a simple Simulink model using basic blocks. It shall explain the difference between traditional and Model based design. Here the reader shall learn how to create a blank model, how to design and implement a simple logic, how to update the model, and how to simulate the model using commonly used sources and sinks.

Chapter 6 Simulink Editor with Environment informs the reader about Simulink graphical editor, its toolstrip and menus as well as overall basic set-up. It shall explain model creation with a simple example. This chapter also deals with different approaches to creating an environment/wrapper for the developed model. In this chapter, the reader shall learn techniques that are helpful to simulate and test the model.

Chapter 7 Library browser overview provides detailed information about the classification of Simulink block sets. Important library blocks shall be explained in brief with few examples, such as Sources, Sinks, Math Operations, Logic & bit Operations, Continuous, Discrete, Signal routing and Lookup tables.

Chapter 8 Configuration Parameter settings talks about model configuration parameters and the options available under different sub-panes- such as Solver settings, Data Import/Export, Math and Datatypes Pane, and Diagnostics Pane. Before beginning with the model development, it is helpful for the reader to be familiar with the model configuration settings to be fully aware of the capabilities of Simulink.

Chapter 9 Advanced modelling techniques-I explains advanced modelling techniques that ease the model design process. In this chapter, the reader shall understand custom libraries, usage of masking for library development and some other custom approaches towards efficient model development.

Chapter 10 Advanced modelling techniques-II explains additional advanced modelling techniques that ease the model design process even further. In this chapter, the reader shall understand in detail the topics such as Subsystems, model referencing Pane, Hardware Implementation Pane and Signal bus.

Section 3: Stateflow

Chapter 11 Getting started with Stateflow introduces vital features for model development using Stateflow. It informs about advantages and use cases where Stateflow is preferred over Simulink. In this chapter, the reader shall get familiar with Stateflow graphical editor, its properties and advantages over Simulink.

Chapter 12 Flow graph explains a stepwise approach to creating a simple flow graph model using transitions and junctions. It shall explain the nodes and connections used to implement a flow graph with the help of logic-driven design examples.

Chapter 13 Statecharts and Hierarchical state model explores Statecharts and its features. In this chapter, the reader shall get to know about state machines, control flow and data flow between state machines, characteristics and hierarchy of the State model.

Chapter 14 event based execution describes event-based execution in Stateflow. In this chapter, the user shall understand different types of events and functions. We will clarify the usage of these events, function calls, functions, and truth table with the help of examples.

Chapter 15 Stateflow parsing and debugging narrates the parsing and debugging techniques applicable to Stateflow. In this chapter, we will be talking about different types of debugging options and the possibilities of deploying Breakpoints. The reader shall learn how to use animation and observe data during simulation to simplify debugging.

In this book, we have tried our best to provide information as accurate as possible. However, we understand that "To err is human", hence we wish to ask for readers' forgiveness in case of any shortcomings. We request the readers to provide their valuable feedback and suggestions on the book and we will incorporate them in subsequent editions.

—*Priyanka Chandrakant Patankar*

—*Swapnil Mukund Kulkarni*

Coloured Images

Please follow the link to download the
Coloured Images of the book:

https://rebrand.ly/omh0c8c

We have code bundles from our rich catalogue of books and videos available at **https://github.com/bpbpublications**. Check them out!

Errata

We take immense pride in our work at BPB Publications and follow best practices to ensure the accuracy of our content to provide with an indulging reading experience to our subscribers. Our readers are our mirrors, and we use their inputs to reflect and improve upon human errors, if any, that may have occurred during the publishing processes involved. To let us maintain the quality and help us reach out to any readers who might be having difficulties due to any unforeseen errors, please write to us at :

errata@bpbonline.com

Your support, suggestions and feedbacks are highly appreciated by the BPB Publications' Family.

Did you know that BPB offers eBook versions of every book published, with PDF and ePub files available? You can upgrade to the eBook version at www.bpbonline.com and as a print book customer, you are entitled to a discount on the eBook copy. Get in touch with us at :

business@bpbonline.com for more details.

At **www.bpbonline.com**, you can also read a collection of free technical articles, sign up for a range of free newsletters, and receive exclusive discounts and offers on BPB books and eBooks.

Piracy

If you come across any illegal copies of our works in any form on the internet, we would be grateful if you would provide us with the location address or website name. Please contact us at **business@bpbonline.com** with a link to the material.

If you are interested in becoming an author

If there is a topic that you have expertise in, and you are interested in either writing or contributing to a book, please visit **www.bpbonline.com**. We have worked with thousands of developers and tech professionals, just like you, to help them share their insights with the global tech community. You can make a general application, apply for a specific hot topic that we are recruiting an author for, or submit your own idea.

Reviews

Please leave a review. Once you have read and used this book, why not leave a review on the site that you purchased it from? Potential readers can then see and use your unbiased opinion to make purchase decisions. We at BPB can understand what you think about our products, and our authors can see your feedback on their book. Thank you!

For more information about BPB, please visit **www.bpbonline.com**.

Table of Contents

Section I: MATLAB 1

1. Introduction to MATLAB 3
    Introduction 3
    Structure 4
    Objectives 4
    History and origin 5
        The inception of classic MATLAB 5
        First version development 5
        From classic to commercial MATLAB 6
        MathWorks and PC-MATLAB debut 7
    Different MATLAB versions 7
    Applications and key users of MATLAB 10
    MATLAB products and toolboxes in brief 12
        Products for model-based design, development, and validation 13
            Simulink 13
            Stateflow 13
            AUTOSAR blockset 14
            Fixed-point designer 14
            Embedded coder 14
            Simulink coverage 14
            Popular MATLAB toolboxes 14
    MATLAB modeling vs. traditional programming approach 15
        Advantages 15
        Challenges 16
    System requirements 16
    MATLAB installation 18
        License options 18

Installation procedure 19
    Steps to get the installer 19
    Steps to install the products on Windows OS 20
  Steps to activate the products 21
    Online activation 21
    Offline activation 22
Important links 23
Conclusion 25
Points to remember 25
Multiple choice questions 26
Questions 27
Answers 27

2. MATLAB Desktop Interface 29
Introduction 29
Structure 29
Objectives 30
MATLAB desktop 30
Panels 32
  Command Window panel 32
  Current folder browser panel 33
    Details panel 33
  Command history panel 34
  Editor 34
  Live editor 35
  Workspace browser panel and variables editor 35
Toolbars 35
  Toolstrip 35
    Home tab 36
    Plots tab 43
    Apps tab 44

	Editor tab...45
	Live Editor tab..45
	View tab...46
Quick access toolbar..46
Current folder browser toolbar 47
Workspace browser 47
The concept of workspace..47
Access variables using command window..49
	Create variable 49
	Delete variable 49
	Modify variable 50
Access variables using workspace browser 51
	Create variable..51
	Delete variable 52
	Modify variable 53
	Modify variable using open selection 54
	Workspace durability..54
MATLAB search path setting..57
Important links..61
Conclusion 61
Points to remember 61
Multiple choice questions..62
Questions 63
Answers 64

3. MATLAB Basics..65
Introduction...65
Structure...65
Objectives...66
Command window shortcuts 66
Variables...69

- Variable naming convention ... 69
- Variables classification ... 69
  - Classification based on types or classes ... 70
  - Strings and character arrays ... 73
  - Classification based on sizes ... 78
  - Matrices and operators ... 85
  - Matrix concatenation ... 87

Built-in functions and commands ... 89
- Environment commands ... 89
  - System commands ... 89
  - Session commands ... 94
  - Help commands ... 97
- Vectors, matrices, and arrays functions ... 98
  - Create array functions ... 98
  - Combine array functions ... 104
  - Grid functions ... 105
  - Array size, shape, order functions ... 106
  - Array reshape, resize functions ... 108
  - Linear algebra matrix functions ... 109
- String and character array functions ... 111
  - Type and properties functions ... 114
  - Find, replace and remove functions ... 114
- Operators ... 116
  - Arithmetic operations ... 116
  - Rounding and division operations ... 117
  - Relational operations ... 117
  - Logical operations ... 118
  - Operator precedence ... 118

Important links ... 119
Conclusion ... 119

Points to remember 119

Multiple choice questions.. 120

Questions 122

Answers 122

4. Programming Basics, Control Flow and Visualization **123**

Introduction.. 123

Structure.. 124

Objectives 124

Scripts and functions... 124

Scripts *125*

Functions *127*

Debug MATLAB program *128*

Live scripts *129*

Control programming flow 131

"if", "else", and "elseif" statements... *131*

"switch", "case", and "otherwise" statements *132*

"try" and "catch" statements *133*

"for" loop *134*

while loop... *135*

"break", "continue" and "return" statements.. *136*

Visualization... 139

Plots *139*

Functions method *139*

Images *163*

Conclusion 168

Points to remember 168

Multiple choice questions... 169

Questions 170

Answers 171

Section II: Simulink 173

5. Introduction to Simulink 175
  Introduction 175
  Structure 176
  Objectives 176
  Simulink overview 176
    Highlights of Simulink 177
      Simulation and modeling 177
      Verification, validation, and testing 177
      Automatic code generation 178
  Types of mathematical models 178
    Linear models 179
    Nonlinear models 179
    Static models 179
    Dynamic models 179
    Explicit models 180
    Implicit models 180
    Discrete models 180
    Continuous models 180
    Deterministic models 180
    Stochastic (random) models 180
  Traditional system design vs. model-based design 181
  Traditional system design 181
    Traditional design workflow 181
    Model-based design 182
      Advantages of model-based design 183
      Model-based design workflow 183
      Model-based design process steps 184
        Derive the system requirements 185
        Define the system 185

Design the system architecture 186
Define the Simulink model behavior 186
Simulate and verify model results 186
Generate production code automatically 186
Verification and validation 187
Model-based simulation methods 187
Getting started with modeling 188
Create a simple Simulink model 188
Start Simulink 189
Open Simulink Editor 190
Open Simulink Library browser 191
Add blocks to model 192
Configure the block parameters 195
Connect the blocks 196
Define model configuration parameters 198
Run Simulation 198
Conclusion 200
Points to remember 201
Multiple choice questions 202
Questions 203
Answers 204

6. Simulink Editor with Environment 205
Introduction 205
Structure 205
Objective 206
Introducing Simulink Editor 206
Toolstrip 209
Simulation 209
Modeling 214
Format 220

Debug 220
Model example: PID controller 224
Signal loading, visualization, and logging techniques 229
　　　Signal loading techniques 230
　　　　　Using Simple Source blocks 230
　　　　　Using Dashboard blocks 231
　　　　　Using From Workspace block 231
　　　　　Using From File block 232
　　　　　Using From Spreadsheet block 233
　　　　　Using Signal Editor 233
　　　　　Using Root Inport mapper 234
　　　Signal visualization and logging techniques 236
　　　　　Using scope 236
　　　　　Using To Workspace block 237
　　　　　Using To File block 237
　　　　　Using Signal logging 238
　　　　　Using Simulation Data Inspector 239
　　　　　Using Dashboard blocks 240
　　　　　Using Outport 240
　　Simulink modeling shortcuts 241
　　Conclusion 243
　　Points to remember 243
　　Multiple choice questions 244
　　Questions 245
　　Answers 245

7. **Library Browser Overview** 247
　　Introduction 247
　　Structure 248
　　Objectives 248
　　Simulink Library Browser 248

- Sources 250
  - Model and subsystem inputs 251
- Sinks 256
  - Model and subsystem outputs 256
  - Data viewers 258
  - Simulation control 260
- Math operations 261
  - Sum, add, subtract, and the sum of elements ... 262
  - Gain, slider gain 262
  - Product, divide, a product of elements, and dot product ... 262
- Logic and bit operations 264
- Continuous 267
  - Integrators 268
  - PID controllers 279
  - Delays 279
- Discrete 282
  - Discrete-time integrator example 284
  - Delay block example 285
- Signal routing 285
- Ports and subsystems 288
- Lookup tables 288
  - 1-D Lookup Table 289
- Conclusion 291
- Points to remember 292
- Multiple choice questions 292
- Questions 294
- Answers 294

8. Configuration Parameter Settings 295
- Introduction 295
- Structure 295

- Objectives 296
- Introducing model configuration parameters 296
- Solver settings 297
  - *Simulation time* 298
  - *Solver selection* 298
    - Type 299
  - *Solver details* 300
  - *Variable type and its parameter set* 301
    - Variable step Solver 302
    - Max step size 303
    - Min step size 304
  - *Advanced settings* 305
- Example to realize the difference between Fixed step solver and Variable step Solver 306
- Data Import/Export 308
  - *Load from workspace* 309
  - *Save to workspace or file* 310
  - *Simulation data inspector* 310
  - *Additional parameters* 311
  - *Advanced parameters* 311
    - Dataset signal format 311
- Math and data types 312
  - *Math* 313
  - *Data types* 314
  - *Advanced parameters* 315
- Diagnostics 315
  - *Solver* 316
    - Algebraic loop 316
    - Minimize algebraic loop 317
    - Block priority violation 318
    - Min step size violation 319

        Consecutive zero-crossing violation 319
        Automatic solver parameter selection 320
        Extraneous discrete derivative signals 320
        State name clash 320
        Operating point interface checksum mismatch 320
    Advanced parameters 320
    Sample Time pane 323
    Data validity pane 325
        Signals sub-pane 325
        Parameters sub-pane 328
        Advanced parameter sub-pane 332
        Type Conversion pane 334
        Connectivity pane 336
        Compatibility pane 338
        Diagnostic model referencing pane 340
        Diagnostic Stateflow pane 342

Hardware implementation pane 342
Model referencing pane 342
Simulation Target pane 342
Conclusion 342
Points to remember 343
Multiple choice questions 343
Questions 345
Answers 346

9. Advanced Modeling Techniques-I 347
Introduction 347
Structure 347
Objectives 348
Basics of custom library creation 348
Creating Simulink logic 349

- Creating Simulink library 352
- Library link 358
- Creating custom libraries with mask options 362
  - Creating library mask 362
  - Mask editor options 368
    - Icon & Ports 368
    - Parameters & Dialog 370
    - Initialization 372
    - Documentation 374
  - Model callbacks 374
  - Block callbacks 377
- Conclusion 380
- Points to remember 381
- Multiple choice questions 381
- Questions 383
- Answers 384

10. Advanced Modeling Techniques-II 385
- Introduction 385
- Structure 385
- Objectives 386
- Subsystem 386
  - The execution order of the blocks 386
  - Virtual subsystems 388
  - Non-virtual subsystems 390
  - Conditionally executable subsystems 392
  - Model referencing 393
  - Variant subsystem 395
  - Variant model 397
- Model referencing pane 397
- Signal bus 400

Virtual signal bus	*401*
Non-virtual signal bus	*402*
Signal conversion block	*404*
Hardware implementation pane	405
Conclusion	407
Points to remember	407
Multiple choice questions	408
Questions	409
Answers	410

Section III: Stateflow 411

11. Getting Started with Stateflow 413

Introduction	413
Structure	413
Objectives	414
Introducing Stateflow	414
Key features of Stateflow	*415*
Designing control logic	*415*
Chart execution and debugging	*416*
Developing reusable logic with Stateflow	*416*
Validation and code generation	*417*
Stateflow Editor	417
Title bar	*418*
Drawing area	*419*
Object palette	*419*
Model browser	*419*
Explorer bar	*419*
Status bar	*420*
Toolstrip	*420*
Simulation	*420*
Modeling	*425*

   Debug *430*

   Format *433*

  Symbols pane *434*

  Property inspector *436*

   Chart properties *436*

   Data properties *440*

 Model Explorer 442

 Stateflow diagnostics parameters 444

 Conclusion 446

 Points to remember 446

 Multiple choice questions 447

 Questions 449

 Answers 449

12. Flow Graph **451**

 Introduction 451

 Structure 451

 Objectives 452

 Overview of a flow graph 452

  Example: simple if-else condition *452*

   Implementation *453*

   Data definition *456*

   Simulation *457*

 Transitions 459

  Transition label notation *460*

  Default transition *461*

 Patterns 461

  Add predefined pattern *462*

   Add decision pattern *462*

   Add loop pattern *463*

   Add switch pattern *465*

      Save as pattern *467*

      Add custom pattern *468*

  Graphical function 468

  Conclusion 469

  Points to remember 470

  Multiple choice questions 470

  Questions 471

  Answers 472

13. Statechart and Hierarchical State Model 473

  Introduction 473

  Structure 473

  Objectives 474

  Overview 475

      Chart *475*

          Example: State transition diagram *475*

      State *476*

  State labels 480

      State name *480*

      State actions *481*

      Example: Vehicle exterior light control *482*

  State hierarchy 488

      Example: Tax calculator *489*

      Example: Vehicle exterior light control with state hierarchy *490*

  State decomposition 492

      OR (exclusive) decomposition *492*

      AND (parallel) decomposition *492*

      Example: Water dispenser *493*

  Transitions 495

      State transition *496*

          Example: state transition *496*

- Default transition 497
- Self-loop transition 498
- Inner transition 498
  - Example: inner transition 498
- Supertransition 499
  - Example: supertransition 499
- Junctions 500
  - Connective junction 500
  - History junction 501
    - Example: history junction 501
- Group and subchart 502
  - Group state 502
  - Subchart 503
- Conclusion 504
- Points to remember 505
- Multiple choice questions 506
- Questions 508
- Answers 508

14. Event-Based Execution 509
- Introduction 509
- Structure 509
- Objectives 510
- Events 510
  - Implicit events 510
  - Explicit events 512
  - Temporal logic 516
- Stateflow functions or graphical functions 521
- Simulink function 523
- MATLAB function 526
- Truth table 527

  Simulink state 530

  Calling external "C" function from statechart 533

  Conclusion 535

  Points to remember 535

  Multiple choice questions 536

  Questions 538

  Answers 538

15. Stateflow Parsing and Debugging 539

  Introduction 539

  Structure 539

  Objectives 540

  Stateflow parsing 540

    Update Chart 540

    Live Parsing 542

  Debugging options in Stateflow 542

    Breakpoints 542

      Breakpoint on transition when transition condition is valid 543

      Breakpoint on transition when transition condition is tested 545

      Breakpoint on state 547

    Stateflow animation 548

    Data display 549

  Conclusion 550

  Points to remember 550

  Multiple choice questions 550

  Questions 552

  Answers 552

Index 553-572

Section - I
MATLAB

CHAPTER 1
Introduction to MATLAB

Introduction

> **You don't have to be great to start, but you have to start to be great.**
> *- Zig Ziglar.*

A good start is an essential part of the success of great learning. The journey of model-based design and Simulation commences with the fundamental knowledge of MATLAB. This chapter is written as the very first piece of the MATLAB puzzle. At first, this chapter introduces the reader to the exciting history of MATLAB, and the chapter then traverses various possibilities to begin with, such as software versions, areas of application, multiple products, and the dissimilarities between the model-based and traditional programming approaches. For novice readers, who are curious to understand where to begin, this chapter introduces several possible ways to get the software license and install the software using the suitable method. The reader, who already has some prior knowledge of MATLAB, can refer to this chapter to gain some interesting insights into the history and origin of MATLAB and its diverse applications.

Structure

In this chapter, we are going to cover the following topics:

- History and origin
    - The inception of classic MATLAB
    - First version development
    - From classic to commercial MATLAB
    - MathWorks and PC-MATLAB debut
- Different MATLAB versions
- Applications and key users of MATLAB
- MATLAB products and toolboxes in brief
    - Products for model-based design, development, and validation
- MATLAB modeling vs. traditional programming approach
- System requirements
- MATLAB installation
    - License options
    - Installation procedure
    - Steps to activate the products
- Important links

Objectives

After studying this chapter, the reader will be able to:

- Get some interesting information about the origin of MATLAB.
- Understand the chronology of MATLAB versions.
- Be informed about different applications and products of MATLAB.
- Define the factors to decide whether to use MATLAB for the project.
- Choose a suitable system configuration.
- Determine product license.
- Install and activate MATLAB on a single computer.

History and origin

MATLAB, which stands for **MATrix LABoratory**, is a proprietary programming language developed by *MathWorks Inc.* and has been revolutionary in different fields of science and engineering. Since its commercial launch in 1984, MATLAB has continuously gained popularity among scientists and engineers as a computing software for numeric computation, algorithm development, data analysis, and visualization. With its wide range of 100+ products, more than 4 million users worldwide use MATLAB.

The inception of classic MATLAB

Today MATLAB is a full-fledged technical computing environment, but would you believe if someone inform you that MATLAB was born just as a primitive matrix calculator without any intention of making it a commercial product? It all started in the 1970s and early 1980s, when *Cleve Moler*, then Professor of Mathematics and then of Computer Science at the University of New Mexico in Albuquerque, was teaching Linear Algebra and Numerical Analysis. He wished his students had easy access to *EISPACK* and *LINPACK* functions without having to write *FORTRAN* programs. A group of researchers developed EISPACK and LINPACK at Argonne National Laboratory. EISPACK was created to support numerical computation of eigenvalues and eigenvectors of matrices, whereas LINPACK was designed to perform numerical linear algebra on digital computers. EISPACK and LINPACK are the software libraries developed in FORTRAN, so to use them, one must write a program in FORTRAN. And not only that, every time, the students must perform remote batch processing followed by `Edit | Compile | Link | Load | Execute` process on the university campus central mainframe computer. The solution had to be an interactive interpreter that could operate in the time-sharing systems of that time.

First version development

Cleve Moler had some ideas to develop a software or a programming language; by using that, EISPACK and LINPACK library operations could be used with ease. To learn how to parse programming languages, he studied a book by *Niklaus Wirth*: "*Algorithms + Data Structures = Programs*". Following the approach of the book, Moler came up with software in FORTRAN that could perform interactive matrix calculations. This software had 71 essential functions and commands, some of which shall be covered in upcoming chapters. *Figure 1.1* shows the start-up screen for the MATLAB 1981 software version, where these 71 functions are also displayed:

```
       < M A T L A B >
      Version of 05/12/1981
   <>

   The functions and commands are...
   ABS   ATAN  BASE  CHAR  CHOL  CHOP  COND  CONJ
   COS   DET   DIAG  DIAR  DISP  EIG   EPS   EXEC
   EXP   EYE   FLOP  HESS  HILB  IMAG  INV   KRON
   LINE  LOAD  LOG   LU    MAGI  NORM  ONES  ORTH
   PINV  PLOT  POLY  PRIN  PROD  QR    RAND  RANK
   RAT   RCON  REAL  ROOT  ROUN  RREF  SAVE  SCHU
   SIN   SIZE  SQRT  SUM   SVD   TRIL  TRIU  USER
   CLEA  ELSE  END   EXIT  FOR   HELP  IF    LONG
   RETU  SEMI  SHOR  WHAT  WHIL  WHO   WHY
```

Figure 1.1: 1981 MATLAB start-up screen (reprinted with permission of The MathWorks, Inc.)

The historic MATLAB did not have any graphics, toolboxes, **Fast Fourier Transform (FFT)**, or **Ordinary Differential Equation (ODE)**. To add a new function, the students had to request Moler for the source code, edit it and add a FORTRAN-based subprogram. It supported some useful operators and commands such as backslash (\), colon (:), and why. This is how the first version of MATLAB came into existence because of Cleve Moler's hobby to learn a new aspect of programming and his strong will to create something beneficial to his students that could ease their efforts. At that time, he did not have any business aspect in his mind.

For a detailed historic MATLAB user guide, visit:

https://blogs.mathworks.com/cleve/2018/02/05/the-historic-matlab-users-guide/

From classic to commercial MATLAB

During the year 1979–80, Cleve taught a graduate course in Numerical Analysis at Stanford. There he presented MATLAB to the class. Students who were studying control theory and signal processing found MATLAB immensely useful due to the importance of Matrices in Mathematics. Jack Little, also a graduate engineering student at Stanford, was introduced to MATLAB by his friend. Jack started using MATLAB for his control systems work. In 1983, Little explained his idea of commercializing MATLAB. Little wanted to work on MATLAB, so in 1983, he left his job to make some modifications and improvements and developed MATLAB in C under Moler's guidance and with the help of a friend *Steve Bangert*. *Jack Little*, *Cleve Moler*, and *Steve Bangert* came up with a PC-based MATLAB version.

MathWorks and PC-MATLAB debut

Little, Moler, and Bangert established MathWorks in 1984 in California. PC-MATLAB was introduced to the world in December 1984 at the IEEE Conference on Decision and Control in Las Vegas, and MATLAB started its journey in the commercial world. Day by day–year by year, many toolboxes for different utilities were added to MATLAB to fulfill the requirements of scientists, engineers, and mathematicians. First, PC-MATLAB had a cover face, as shown in *figure 1.2*:

Figure 1.2: *MathWorks 1985 PC-MATLAB cover face (reprinted with permission of The MathWorks, Inc.)*

Different MATLAB versions

MathWorks follows a practice of releasing two MATLAB versions per year. The first release in March is referred to as an *"a"* release, whereas the second release in September is referred to as a *"b"* release, where the naming convention indicates a bi-yearly release cycle. Release "a" and release "b" terminologies came into existence for MATLAB in 2006. Sometimes there are supplementary versions released other than release "a" and release "b"; these releases are named **Service Pack** (**SP**) releases. Commonly, SP releases are bug-fix releases. *Table 1.1* describes some of the important release events in chronological order until release *R2022a*:

Year	MATLAB version or release name	Key features
1978	Classic MATLAB	Matrix calculator with the option of 71 different types of operations such as ABS, DIAG, INV, and CHAR.
1981	Classic MATLAB	Publication of the first MATLAB user guide
1984	MATLAB 1 PC-MATLAB	Scripts, Functions, and ".m" file format have been introduced. Addition of new functions such as Elementary math functions, Attributes, Array Manipulations, and Signal processing filters.
1986	MATLAB 2 PRO-MATLAB	MATLAB for Unix and Workstations introduced
1987	MATLAB 3	MATLAB for Apple Macintosh launched
1990	MATLAB 3.5	DOC compatible version with 386 Processor and math Coprocessor introduced
1992	MATLAB 4	Version compatible with Windows 3.1x
1996	MATLAB 5.0 Volume 8	Unified release for all platforms
2001	MATLAB 6.1 – R12.1	This was the last release of Windows 95
2003	MATLAB 6.5.1 – R13SP1 MATLAB 6.5.2 – R13SP2	R13SP2 was the last release for Windows 98, Windows ME, IBM/AIX, Alpha/TRU64, and SGI/IRIX
2004	MATLAB 7 – R14 MATLAB 7.0.1 – R14SP1	Anonymous and Nested functions were introduced
2005 2005	MATLAB 7.0.4 – R14SP2 MATLAB 7.1 – R14SP3	Support for "Memory Mapped Files" was introduced first in SP2. SP3 was the first 64-bit version available for Windows XP 64-bit.
2006	MATLAB 7.2 – R2006a MATLAB 7.3 – R2006b	HDF5-based MAT-file support was introduced in the R2006b release
2008	MATLAB 7.6 – R2008a MATLAB 7.7 – R2008b	R2008a had significant enhancement concerning object-oriented programming abilities with new syntaxes for the "Class" definition. At the same time, R2008b was the last release for processors w/o SSE2. The new MAP data structure was introduced in R2008b; also, there were some updates on random number generators in R2008b.

Year	MATLAB version or release name	Key features
2009	MATLAB 7.8 – R2009a MATLAB 7.9 – R2009b	R2009a was the first release for Windows 7 32-bit and 64-bit OS. However, R2009b was the first release for Intel 64-bit Mac.
2011	MATLAB 7.11.1 – R2010bSP1 MATLAB 7.11.2 – R2010bSP2 MATLAB 7.12 – R2011a MATLAB 7.13 – R2011b	R2010bSP1 and R2010bSP2 were the bug fix releases for R2010b. In the R2011a version new "rng" function was introduced for the calculation of random numbers. R2011b had Access-change parts of variables directly in MAT-files, without loading into memory.
2012	MATLAB 7.14 – R2012a MATLAB 8 – R2012b	R2012a was the last version for 32-bit Linux. Toolstrip interface and MATLAB apps were redesigned in release R2012b, along with the documentation system.
2013	MATLAB 8.1 – R2013a MATLAB 8.2 – R2013b	The new unit testing framework was added in R2013a. Furthermore, a new data type as "table" was introduced in R2013b.
2014	MATLAB 8.3 – R2014a MATLAB 8.4 – R2014b	Several features have been added in R2014a, such as USB webcam support and a simplified compiler setup for mex files. R2014b had even more key highlights, such as a new class-based graphics engine, tabbing function in GUI, new objects for time-date manipulations, big-data abilities, and a new package for Python.
2016	MATLAB 9.0 – R2016a MATLAB 9.1 – R2016b	Several exciting features were introduced in R2016a, such as a Live script, interactive documents to combine text, code and outputs, and new development environment for building apps. Whereas R2016b also came up with more features like a definition of local functions and automatic expansion of dimensions.
2017	MATLAB 9.2 – R2017a MATLAB 9.3 – R2017b	MATLAB Online with cloud-based MATLAB desktop access using a Web browser was first introduced in R2017a. R2017a also contained some other sensational features such as double-quoted strings, a new memorize function for Memorization, and expanded object properties validation.

Year	MATLAB version or release name	Key features
2019	MATLAB 9.6 – R2019a MATLAB 9.7 – R2019b	MATLAB projects are made available for the first time in version R2019a. "arguments" block for input validation and enabling dot indexing into function outputs are added in the R2019b release
2020	MATLAB 9.8 – R2020a MATLAB 9.9 – R2020b	Mupad has been removed in R2020a Performance improved for AMD CPUs; Simulink online is available from this version
2021	MATLAB 9.10 – R2021a MATLAB 9.11 – R2021b	Browsing chart types in scripts is enabled with Create Plot Live Editor Task. Simulink Code Importer helps build a Simulink library out of a custom C/C++ code library. Class Diagram Viewer can be used to author, document, and implement a family of related classes. New capabilities for code refactoring and block editing with the support of code suggestions and debugger introduced. Setting up and running multiple simulations in parallel is enabled with multiple Simulations Panel from Simulink Editor.
2022	MATLAB 9.12 – R2020a	3 New Apps—Data Cleaner, Hardware Manager, and Code Compatibility Analyzer added. Improved python performance support with Editor syntax highlighting, name=value syntax, and list-tuple conversion. MATLAB app generation, Modification, and Deployment for Simulink Model are possible.

Table 1.1: *MATLAB version history*

For detailed release notes on each MATLAB version, please visit https://www.mathworks.com/help/matlab/release-notes.html

Applications and key users of MATLAB

Over the years since its launch, MATLAB has been adapted to be used in plenty of industries. Sensing the market needs and an ability to respond to them quickly has fetched success in many industrial applications. *Table 1.2* mentions some significant applications and the uses of MATLAB and Simulink product families:

Application	Used for
Embedded systems	Designing, coding, and verification of embedded systems
Computational biology	Analysis, visualization, and modeling of biological data and systems
Control systems	Designing, testing, and implementing control systems
Signal processing	Analyzing signals and time-series data. Modeling, designing, and simulating signal processing systems
Image processing	Acquiring, processing, and analyzing images and video, algorithm development, and designing system
Data science	Exploring data, performing predictive analytics, and developing machine learning algorithms
Deep learning	Preparing data, designing, simulating, and deploying deep Neural networks
Machine learning	Training models, tuning parameters, and deploying to the production
Power electronics control design	Designing and implementing digital controls for motors, power converters, and battery systems
Robotics	Converting the robotics ideas and concepts to autonomous systems
Wireless communications	Creating, designing, testing, and verification of wireless communications systems
Internet of things	Connecting different embedded devices and gaining insights

Table 1.2: Applications of MATLAB

MATLAB is used in many industries due to the wide span of capabilities, such as model-based system engineering, agile system development, embedded and HDL code generation, algorithm development, continuous integration, cloud, parallel, and GPU computing, mathematical and physical modeling, discrete-event and real-time, system design and simulations, data analysis and acquisition, report generation, verification, validation and testing, and Web and desktop deployment.

In the following image are some of the industries where MATLAB and Simulink are extensively used:

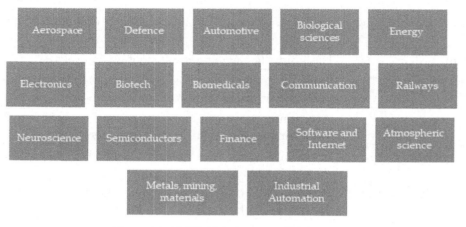

Figure 1.3: MATLAB industry applications

For detailed information on MATLAB applications, please visit https://www.mathworks.com/solutions.html

MATLAB products and toolboxes in brief

MATLAB has a vast product family containing almost 100+ products. These products are distributed mainly into the MATLAB family, Simulink family, and product applications, as indicated in *table 1.3*:

MATLAB family	Simulink family	Product applications
• Parallel computing • Math and optimization • AI, data science, and statistics • Code generation • Application deployment • Database access and reporting	• System composer • Event-based modeling • Physical modeling • Real-time Simulation and testing • Code generation • Application deployment • Verification, validation, and test • Simulation graphics and reporting	• Signal processing • Image processing and computer vision • Control systems • Test and measurement • RF and mixed-signal • Wireless communications • Autonomous systems • FPGA, ASIC, and SoC development • Automotive

MATLAB family	Simulink family	Product applications
		• Aerospace • Computational finance • Computational biology • Code verification

Table 1.3: MATLAB product family

Products for model-based design, development, and validation

Model-based design is a procedure where a model is at the center of the overall development process during every phase—requirements analysis, design, implementation, and testing. MathWorks offers the following MATLAB products that are used largely for model-based design, development, and validation in many industries:

Simulink

Millions of users worldwide use MATLAB and Simulink. Simulink is used extensively for model-based development and Simulation, early testing, and automatic code generation. Simulink models are deployed in a wide range of industries, as mentioned in *figure 1.3*. Simulink comes with different block sets for various industries. For example, Aerospace block sets are used in the Aerospace industry, and AUTOSAR block sets are used in the automotive industry. Users can purchase these block sets based on their specific requirements. Simulink has its default Simulink block sets; in the book, we have explained these default block sets and contained library blocks in *Chapter 7: Library Browser Overview*. It is possible to use the default block sets and create a Simulink model for any kind of algorithm development and validation.

Stateflow

Stateflow enables an effective graphical representation of state-based logic. Stateflow consists of states, transitions, flowcharts, and truth tables. Stateflow is used as a block within a Simulink model or executed as an object in MATLAB. It is used to design and develop supervisory control, task scheduling, and fault management. It is also convenient to model combinational and sequential logic in Stateflow. Graphical animation helps while debugging. In this book, we have explained Stateflow in detail in Chapters 11–15.

AUTOSAR blockset

Automotive Open System Architecture (AUTOSAR) blockset provides apps and blocks for the development of both AUTOSAR Classic and Adaptive software using Simulink models. One shall be able to design and map Simulink models to software components using the AUTOSAR Component Designer app. On the other hand, by importing software components and composition descriptions from **AUTOSAR XML (ARXML)** files, the users can generate new AUTOSAR Simulink models.

Fixed-point designer

Fixed-point designer provides data types and tools to optimize and implement the fixed-point and floating-point algorithms on embedded hardware. It combines fixed-point, floating-point data types and target-specific numeric settings. This designer enables target-aware simulation, which is bit-true for fixed-point. It is possible to test and debug quantization effects, for example, overflows and precision loss way before the design is implemented on hardware.

Embedded coder

Embedded coder offers possibilities to generate readable, compact, and fast C and C++ code for embedded processors used for mass production. Embedded coder enhances MATLAB Coder and Simulink Coder with the help of advanced optimizations for precise control of the generated functions, files, and data. They improve the efficiency of code and enable integration with legacy code, data types, variables, and parameters. It is possible to use a third-party development tool to build an executable for turnkey deployment on either an embedded system or a rapid prototyping board.

Simulink coverage

Simulink coverage analyzes model and code coverage and measures test completeness in models and generated code. It uses industry-standard metrics: decision, condition, modified condition/decision coverage (MC/DC), and relational boundary coverage for model simulation testing, **software-in-the-loop (SIL)**, and **processor-in-the-loop (PIL)**. Later this missing coverage data can be referred to find the gaps in testing, missing requirements, or unreachable functionalities.

Popular MATLAB toolboxes

These are some of the most popular MATLAB toolboxes as follows:

- Control system toolbox
- Curve fitting toolbox

- DSP system toolbox
- Image processing toolbox
- Instrument control toolbox
- Optimization toolbox, parallel computing toolbox
- Signal processing toolbox
- Statistics and machine learning toolbox
- Symbolic math toolbox

MATLAB modeling vs. traditional programming approach

Here, we have listed the advantages and limitations of MATLAB modeling over conventional programming. Based on the below-mentioned points, the user can make an informed decision about the appropriate programming approach.

Advantages

The following list describes the advantages of the MATLAB modeling approach:

- Interactive development using MATLAB is more convenient than the traditional approaches, as the graphical representation of the logical program is more comfortable to develop and simulate iteratively.
- Due to the possibility of immediate debugging and Simulation without recompilation, the development and verification time before the market is significantly reduced.
- With the extensive support of MATLAB help and a vast community of libraries with thousands of functions, examples, codes, and tutorials, one can make the most of its toolset.
- A wide selection of toolboxes is available for industry-specific purposes.
- MATLAB allows mixed-language programming, too, for example, C, C++, C#, Python, Java, .NET, and FORTRAN.
- MathWorks provides highly efficient post-purchase technical support.
- Products are always up-to-date as there are two releases in a year, which include new releases, bug-fixes.

Challenges

The following points describe the challenges of MATLAB-based programming:

- MATLAB desktop application requires high system configuration. Detailed information is available in the *System requirements* section.

- MATLAB code could not be deployed directly on target boards. Generally, the C code needs to be generated from the MATLAB model, which sometimes proves to be less readable and efficient.

- MATLAB, being an interpreted language, could take more time to execute when compared to the compiled languages.

- License costs could be considered high. Nevertheless, there are also some reduced cost provisions and special prices.

System requirements

Until now, you must already have been able to identify the desired MATLAB products and their release versions. So naturally, the next step shall be the installation process. However, before we begin installing these products, we need to answer any of these questions: *Does MATLAB work on my machine?* or *Which machine should I choose to install MATLAB?* We shall answer these questions by verifying the feasibility of several system configuration aspects.

Operating systems

Before installation, it is recommended to verify the operating system requirements for the specific version to ensure that it is supported by the target OS. MATLAB 9.7 (R2019b) can be installed in the following operating systems:

- Microsoft® Windows® operating system (64-bit)
    - Windows 10, 7 Service Pack 1
    - Windows Server 2019 /2016
- Linux® operating system (64-bit)
    - Ubuntu 19.04, 18.04, 16.04 LTS
    - Debian 10, 9
    - Red Hat Enterprise Linux 8, 7 (min 7.3), 6 (min 6.7)
    - SUSE Linux Enterprise Desktop/Server 15, 12 (min SP2)
- macOS operating system
    - macOS Catalina (10.15), Mojave (10.14), High Sierra (10.13.6)

Similarly, a newer version of MATLAB 9.12 (R2022a) can be installed in the following operating systems. We can observe that the support for older OS versions is discontinued for the newer version:

- Microsoft® Windows® operating system (64-bit)
    - Windows 11, 10 (Windows 7 is not supported)
    - Windows Server 2019 (Windows Server 2016 is not supported)
- Linux® operating system (64-bit)
    - Ubuntu 20.04, 18.04 LTS
    - Debian 10
    - Red Hat Enterprise Linux 8 (min 8.1), 7 (min 7.6)
    - SUSE Linux Enterprise Desktop/Server 15, 12 (min SP2)
- macOS operating system
    - macOS Monterey (12), Big Sur (11), Catalina (10.15)

Processors

The minimum requirement for the processor is Intel or AMD x86-64 processor. Any before-mentioned processor with four logical cores and AVX2 instruction set support is recommended.

Disk space

MATLAB requires a minimum of 3.6 GB of HDD space. A typical installation needs around 5–8 GB. Full installation of MATLAB products can occupy up to 31.5 GB for Windows and Linux OS and 24 GB for Mac OS. SSD is recommended.

RAM

A minimum of 4 GB RAM shall be required. 8 GB RAM is recommended.

Graphics

No specific graphics card is required as such, but a hardware-accelerated graphics card supporting OpenGL 3.3 with 1 GB GPU memory is recommended.

> **The preceding information is for reference, and it could be different for the released versions. Therefore, before proceeding any further, please confirm the details on** https://www.mathworks.com/support/requirements/matlab-system-requirements.html

MATLAB installation

In this section, we shall discuss the various aspects of MATLAB installation, such as available licenses, installation steps based on software versions, and activation steps. You may skip this section in case the software is already available to you.

License options

Once you have acquired a system that meets the minimum criteria, the next step shall be choosing from license options available at https://www.mathworks.com/store/. However, before confirming any option, kindly set the appropriate region, as few options might be applicable only for specific regions. Apart from a new purchase, the store also offers an option to get a product trial, request a quote, and enroll in software maintenance service.

MathWorks provides these four basic license purchase options for single users:

- **Standard**: For single end-users at government, commercial, or other organizations
- **Education**: These licenses are available purely for teaching and academic research purpose.
    - **Academic use—Individual**: For the faculty, staff, or researcher at a degree-granting institution
    - **Campus-wide use**: For students, faculty, and researchers of degree-granting institutions. This license allows MATLAB to be installed on students' computers too. To check the availability of a license at your university, please visit https://www.mathworks.com/academia/tah-support-program/eligibility.html
- **Student**: For students of the degree-granting institution who needs MATLAB and its add-on products to meet course requirements and for academic research. You may purchase any of the following options if you do not have the availability of an Education license from your university.
    - **Student suite**: MATLAB and Simulink with ten widely used add-on toolboxes and additional add-on purchases are possible.
    - **Student license**: MATLAB and Simulink with the possibility of add-on purchase
- **Home**: For personal use only. You may opt for the standard option in case this license is unavailable in your region.

Besides the purchasing options, MathWorks provides an opportunity of getting a 30-day trial license for the latest as well as previous release versions of 80+ products.

You may request the trial license at https://www.mathworks.com/campaigns/products/trials.html

- **There could be a change in the MathWorks offerings at a later point in time. So before proceeding toward the next steps, please confirm the latest information published on the MathWorks website** `https://www.mathworks.com`
- **If you are a start-up in business for five years or fewer, you may be eligible for MATLAB and Simulink support for the start-up. Please visit for eligibility and application** https://www.mathworks.com/products/startups/startup-form.html

Installation procedure

After availing of the license option of your choice, let us move to the installation process. There are two primary installation options available for end-users with a single computer:

- **Online installation**: Installation using an internet connection. This method is to be followed for a single computer when you have an active internet connection on this computer. For installation, you will require a MathWorks account, a license, or a file installation key.
- **Offline installation**: Installation without an internet connection. This method is to be used for a single computer when it does not have an internet connection. For installation, you will require the file installation key and license file.

Steps to get the installer

The following steps are required to get the installer:

1. Visit https://www.mathworks.com/, and on the top right corner, log in to the MathWorks account used for license try or buy requests. In my software section, you can see the license assigned to your account. In case you want to link an additional license, or application for a trial license, you may place the request.

2. Click once on the blue download arrow next to the license number.

3. In the next window, select the release version to be downloaded, and you are prompted to choose the OS type.

4. Choose the appropriate option, and the installer is downloaded.

5. For offline mode: At the computer with an internet connection, run the installer and choose **Download only** or **Advanced** option in the installer **I want to download without installing**, whatever is applicable. Later, copy these files to the destination computer. For detailed information, please visit

   https://www.mathworks.com/help/install/ug/download-without-installing.html

Steps to install the products on Windows OS

The following steps show the installation procedure for Windows OS. The steps mentioned here are for MATLAB 2019b version, but they shall stay somewhat similar for older and newer versions. Kindly refer help documentation for accurate information:

1. Run the installer. It will start self-extractor. Please note that you will require administrator access for this process, so click on yes whenever asked.

2. Select the installation method.
   - **For Online mode**: Select **Log in with a MathWorks account** (default option). For detailed steps, visit https://www.mathworks.com/help/install/ug/install-products-with-internet-connection.html
   - **For Offline mode**: Select **Use a File installation key**. For detailed steps, visit https://www.mathworks.com/help/install/ug/install-using-a-file-installation-key.html

3. Accept the terms and conditions.

4. Login/File installation key
   - **For online mode**: Log in to your MathWorks account using your email ID and password. The account should be the same to which our license is linked.
   - **For offline mode**: Enter the 25-digit file installation key. The administrator can get this release-specific key from the advanced options of the license center at https://www.mathworks.com/licensecenter/
   - Alternatively, if you choose to activate first, you will receive the File installation Key along with the license download option when you submit the Manual activation form.

5. License details
    - **For online mode**: Select the license that has the products to be installed. In the case of multiple licenses, the administrator can suggest the correct license number. You may also mention the activation key in case there is an unlinked license for an add-on product.
    - **For offline mode**: Select the license file that can be downloaded from the license center. This license file has information about the available products linked to the license.
6. Select the destination location for the installation.
7. Tick the checkbox for the products to be installed. By default, licensed products are selected. Add if required.
8. In installation options, you may add a shortcut to the desktop or start menu.
9. Verify the summary of options. Click install to confirm the installation. Installation begins.
10. Leave the box checked for the option: `Activate MATLAB after installation is complete`.

The installation is complete. It is recommended to activate products using an internet connection immediately.

Steps to activate the products

There are two methods to activate the installed MATLAB products.

Online activation

This process is relatively easy. As we have chosen Activate MATLAB option during installation, the activation client pops up. These are the steps of the online activation process:

1. The user is prompted to provide a computer operating system username. By default, it shows the administrator's username. Change this username only if some other account is going to use the tool, or else keep this field unchanged.
2. Users can identify the operating system username by running the command set username on the command prompt.
3. There will be a confirmation screen that mentions licenses and products.
4. Verify the details and click `Finish`.

5. Alternatively, the user can run MATLAB. Go to the **Resources** section in the **Home** tab. Here select **Help | Licensing | Activate software** option.

OR

In case you cannot open MATLAB, manually run the activation client application from a given path in the installation location

`C:\Program Files\MATLAB\R20XXx\bin\winXX\activate_matlab.exe`

Offline activation

The user is required to activate MATLAB manually when the user does not have internet access to the target computer. Nevertheless, the user still needs to login into the MathWorks account from any computer to download the license file. The following steps are to be followed for offline product activation.

1. Login to your MathWorks account and visit the license center at https://www.mathworks.com/licensecenter. Click on the license number and go to the **Install and activate** tab.

2. Select **Activate to retrieve license file** or **Activate software** under **Related tasks**.

3. Fill in the required details in the **Manually Activate Software** on a Computer. Please note that these details are of the computer where activation is required.

4. Select the software release to be installed, for example, **R2019b,** from a drop-down menu, which has options between R2008a and the latest version.

5. Now you need to describe a computer on which software is to be activated.

6. Select operating system: Windows/Mac/Linux

7. Provide Host ID. The Host ID is usually the Volume Serial Number of the **C:** drive in the case of an individual computer. Run **vol c:** in command prompt.

8. If your computer has a **B:** drive or if you have a network license, your Host ID shall be the Mac address of the network adapter. Run the **getmac** command on the command prompt.

9. Mention the user details of the software. By default, they are administrator details.

10. Provide computer login name. In case you are not aware of the login name, type the set username command in the command prompt.

11. Provide an activation label for your reference and click on continue.

12. Download or email the license file specific to the Host ID.

13. Copy the 25-digit File Installation Key if the installation is to be done and mention it during installation when prompted.

14. Store the license file at path `C:\Program Files\MATLAB\R20XXx\licenses`

    OR

    If you do not have administrator access, place the license file at `%AppData%\MathWorks\MATLAB\R20XXx_licenses` path.

15. Run MATLAB. Go to the **Resources** section in the **Home** tab. Here select **Help | Licensing | Activate software** option.

    OR

    In case you cannot open MATLAB, manually run the activation client application from a given path in the installation location:

    `C:\Program Files\MATLAB\R20XXx\bin\winXX\activate_matlab.exe`

16. In the activation application, select the option **Activate manually without the Internet** and click **Next**.

17. Browse to the license file and select.

18. Once the Activation client reaches the last step, click **Finish**.

For detailed information on manual activation with or without the internet, please visit https://www.mathworks.com/help/install/ug/activate-matlab-installation-manually.html.

> The section Installation procedure has been simplified for understanding of the process, and some of the steps could be different based on OS and release versions. So, please use it only as a reference and follow the complete steps from Installation help published on the MathWorks website at https://www.mathworks.com/help/install/index.html.

Important links

These are the important links specified in this chapter:

- For all kinds of information, visit the MathWorks website:

    https://www.mathworks.com

- The historic MATLAB's user guide:

  https://blogs.mathworks.com/cleve/2018/02/05/the-historic-matlab-users-guide/

- List of MATLAB solutions- applications, industries, disciplines, and capabilities:

  https://www.mathworks.com/solutions.html

- Detailed release notes for each MATLAB version:

  https://www.mathworks.com/help/matlab/release-notes.html

- Complete steps from Installation help:

  https://www.mathworks.com/help/install/index.html

- MATLAB system requirements:

  https://www.mathworks.com/support/requirements/matlab-system-requirements.html

- License options offered by MathWorks:

  https://www.mathworks.com/store/

- Check availability of license at your university:

  https://www.mathworks.com/academia/tah-support-program/eligibility.html

- Request for trial license:

  https://www.mathworks.com/campaigns/products/trials.html

- Check eligibility for start-up and apply for a license:

  https://www.mathworks.com/products/startups/startup-form.html

- Offline installation setup download:

  https://www.mathworks.com/help/install/ug/download-without-installing.html

- Online installation steps using Internet Connection

  https://www.mathworks.com/help/install/ug/install-products-with-internet-connection.html

- Offline installation using file installation key:

  https://www.mathworks.com/help/install/ug/install-using-a-file-installation-key.html

- Activate the license and get the File Installation Key:

  https://www.mathworks.com/licensecenter/

- Manual installation activation guide:

  https://www.mathworks.com/help/install/ug/activate-matlab-installation-manually.html

Conclusion

Before starting to learn the technicalities of a new topic, it is fruitful to understand the history and reason behind it. This approach makes the user aware of the various available product options, advantages as well as limitations of the said technology. In this chapter, we have familiarized ourselves with several essential yet widely unknown characteristics of MATLAB. At first, we educated ourselves with some interesting facts about the history of MATLAB. We have learnt the significance of the different MATLAB versions and the key features of all the release versions. Then we have gained knowledge of the various industries and applications as well as a brief overview of the product and toolboxes used for model-based design, development, and validation. We have also discussed the challenges and advantages of the MATLAB modeling approach. For the readers who do not have any knowledge of the software offered by MATLAB, we have simplified the process for them to choose the correct license type, pick a suitable installation method based on the available system as well as activate the products. In the upcoming chapter, we shall be familiarized with the MATLAB desktop interface. We shall learn about various panels, toolbars, windows, and browsers.

Points to remember

- MATLAB, an acronym of Matrix Laboratory, is a proprietary programming language launched by MathWorks Inc. in 1984 that is used in many fields of engineering and science.

- MATLAB consists of 100+ products, which are used by more than 4 million users worldwide.

- Cleve Moler, an American mathematician, is the father of MATLAB. Jack Little, an electrical engineer, is the father of MathWorks Inc.

- MATLAB releases two software versions every year: version a and version b.

- Many products and toolboxes, such as Simulink, Stateflow, AUTOSAR, Embedded coder, Fixed-point designer, and so on, are used for MATLAB model-based design, development, and validation.

- Only R2015b and older versions support both 32-bit and 64-bit operating systems. The newer release versions support only 64-bit operating systems. MathWorks offers various types of licenses for single users as well as enterprises. It also offers discounted licenses for students. There is also an option to get 30 days trial license.

- The software installation can be done online using a license file or installation key, whereas offline installation requires a file installation key and license file.

- It is possible to activate the MATLAB products online with an internet connection, or it is done manually when the system does not have an internet connection.

Multiple choice questions

1. Which programming language was initially used to develop LINPACK and EISPACK libraries?

    a. Pascal

    b. COBOL

    c. Algol

    d. FORTRAN

2. **True or False: MathWorks releases a maximum of two versions of MATLAB software.**

    a. True

    b. False

3. **During which version release was the Live script introduced for the first time?**

    a. R2019a

    b. R2014b

    c. R2016a

    d. R2011b

4. Can Stateflow be used independently of Simulink?

    a. Yes

    b. No

5. True or False: It is not possible to install MATLAB without an internet connection.

    a. False

    b. True

Questions

1. Describe the origin of classic MATLAB.
2. How and when was commercial MATLAB created?
3. Explain the applications of MATLAB in different industries.
4. Explain in brief the MATLAB products used for model-based design and development.
5. Describe three points each for the advantages and challenges of using MATLAB over conventional programming techniques for programming.
6. What is the minimum RAM requirement for the installation of the MATLAB R2019b version?
7. Explain the different MATLAB activation methods.

Answers

1. d
2. b
3. c
4. a
5. a

CHAPTER 2
MATLAB Desktop Interface

Introduction

MATLAB desktop is a self-contained yet straightforward interface, which is a collection of various panels, windows, toolbars, and menus. After the installation and activation process, this chapter acts as a quick start-up guide for novice MATLAB users. This chapter makes the reader familiar with the essentials of the MATLAB desktop interface. It explains, in brief, all extensively used options available for the panels, toolbars, menus, editors, and workspace browser. It also explores in detail the workspace variables and several operations on them. This chapter also thoroughly explains the MATLAB search path settings.

Structure

In this chapter, we shall discuss the following topics:

- MATLAB desktop
- Panels
    o Command Window panel
    o Current folder browser panel
    o Command history panel

- Editor
- Live editor
- Toolbars
  - Toolstrip
  - Quick access toolbar
  - Current folder browser toolbar
- Workspace Browser
  - The concept of workspace
  - Access variables using command Window
  - Access variables using workspace browser
- MATLAB search path setting
- Important links

Objectives

After studying this chapter, the reader will be able to:

- Get familiar with the MATLAB desktop environment.
- Understand the primary usage of available panels and windows.
- Learn to run a few basic commands and scripts.
- Understand operations from toolstrip, quick access, and current folder toolbar.
- Learn in detail how to create, modify, delete, save, and load workspace variables using workspace browser.
- Understand the MATLAB search path and the reason to update the search path.

MATLAB desktop

MATLAB desktop is a simple and user-friendly interface that introduces the user to several possibilities of design, development, data exchange, visualization, programming, and so on in an interactive environment. MATLAB desktop interface starts when the user opens the MATLAB application. A user can open a MATLAB application in several ways, such as double-clicking the MATLAB icon on the desktop or running the MATLAB application from the Start menu in windows OS.

After initialization, the MATLAB desktop window becomes visible. The default desktop layout looks similar to *figure 2.1* based on the user software version.

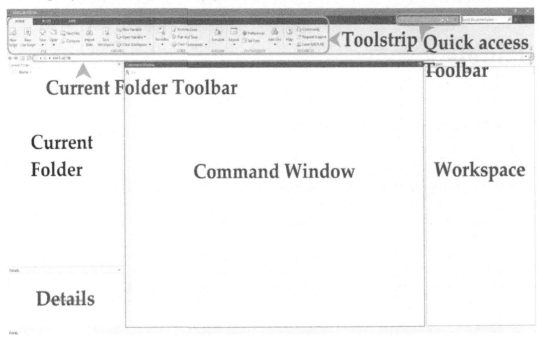

Figure 2.1: *MATLAB 2019b desktop interface*

Upon starting MATLAB, the desktop opens with a default layout. Desktop similar to *figure 2.1* is available in MATLAB release 2019b and newer releases. Release 2012a and older releases have an old desktop with the same panels but a reduced number of menu options.

The default layout consists of the following three main panels:

(1) **Current Folder browser**: To navigate and access the files and folders on your computer.

(2) **Command Window**: To execute the commands.

(3) **Workspace**: To create, modify, and explore the data.

Additionally, there are different toolbars available.

- **Toolstrip**: Toolstrip has three tabs: Home, Plots, and Apps. Each tab contains different sections for performing operations.

- **Quick access toolbar**: This customizable toolbar includes some of the frequently used operations.

- **Current folder browser toolbar**: It shows the current folder full path.

The default layout can be restored from the **Layout** | **Default Layout** option. We will learn these topics in detail in the upcoming sections.

Panels

The panels in MATLAB desktop are explained here in brief.

Command Window panel

The command Window panel is an essential part of the MATLAB desktop. It allows the user to write individual commands and monitor the results. Command Window accepts the command after the command prompt symbol **>>**. A statement is written in the command line after the **>>** symbol. Let us try a basic command. Next to the command prompt, type **ver** and press *Enter*. Soon MATLAB will show installation information: software installation number, license number, operating system, Java version, and a list of all installed products and their respective versions. In *figure 2.2*, a small example of a sum operation is depicted in the command Window panel:

```
Command Window
>> a=1

a =

     1

>> b=2;
>> a+b

ans =

     3

>> c=a+b

c =

     3

fx >> |
```

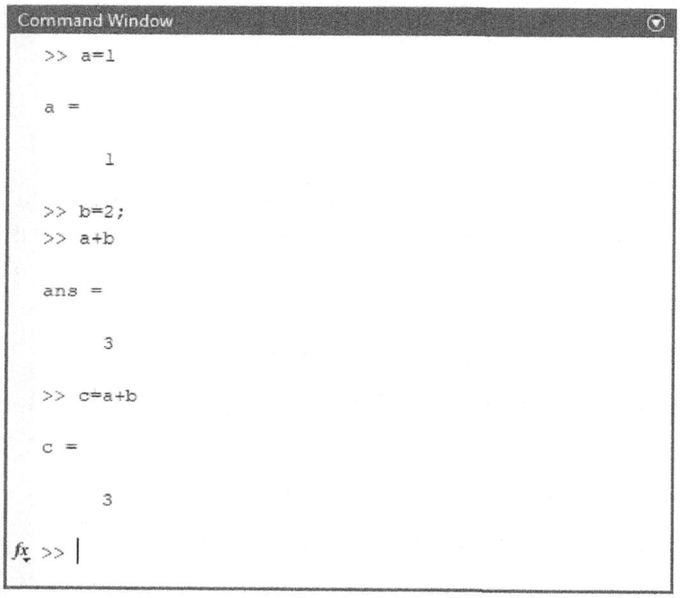

Figure 2.2: *Command Window panel*

By default, the results of the input statement are again displayed as an output unless followed by a semicolon. If no variable is used for the result, by default, MATLAB uses the output variable as **ans**. It is also possible to combine multiple statements in a single line. In the command Window, we can run numerous MATLAB commands.

To clear the command Window, right-click on the command window and select the option `Clear Command Window` or type `clc` command. A detailed explanation of how to execute statements is available in *Chapter 3: MATLAB Basics*.

Current folder browser panel

As the name suggests, this panel displays the list of all files and folders available in the current folder. With the help of the current folder browser toolbar's navigation keys, we can easily navigate among various folders located on the computer. It is also possible to perform operations, such as add new, cut, copy, paste, rename, move, find, compare, group, sort, and sp on, by right-clicking on the file or folder names. If the option "Indicate files not on path" is enabled, the locations unavailable in the MATLAB search path are greyed out. A right-click operation provides the opportunity to add the folders and subfolders to the search path. More details related to the search path are available in the MATLAB search path section. *Figure 2.3* shows the current folder panel with the current folder browser tool and the details panel:

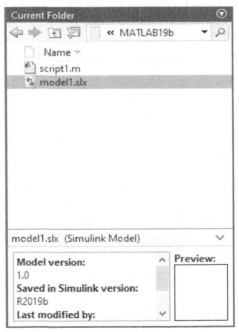

Figure 2.3: *Current folder panel and details*

Details panel

This panel is available as a part of the current folder panel. It shows some details of the selected file, for example, file name, file type, version, saved product version, last modified by, and a preview of the file.

Command history panel

Command history panel is not part of the default layout. However, we can enable or disable it from **Layout | Command History | Docked/Pop up/Closed** command. This window is usually docked below the Workspace. This panel shows the date, time, and then the list of statements run. It retains the history even when the application is closed unless explicitly cleared. To clear the **Command History**, right-click and select clear command history operation. By default, MATLAB saves the last executed 25,000 statements. This number can be adjusted with the help of preferences. Through right-click options, it is also possible to evaluate the commands and create scripts and functions out of the selected commands. *Figure 2.4* shows the command history panel displaying previously executed commands:

Figure 2.4: Command history panel

Editor

An editor window generally opens above the Command Window panel. A sequence of commands, which we run in the command window, could be created, modified, and saved as a .m file with editor. Later we can load and run this file. *Figure 2.5* shows a simple script with display command, and the results in the command window after the script is executed:

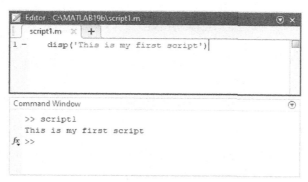

Figure 2.5: Editor window

The editor is useful to create new scripts, files, functions, classes, system objects, and so on. In the preceding image, a simple `disp` command is executed in the script. While editing, the editor highlights suggestions and possible syntax errors. It is also possible to open multiple files in the editor window.

Live editor

Figure 2.6 shows a simple live script in a live editor window with the results displayed on the right side:

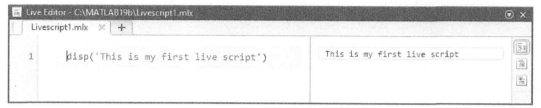

Figure 2.6: *Live editor window*

Live editor window supports the user to create, modify, and execute live scripts and functions. A live editor looks similar to the editor, except it allows seeing live results for each line in the editor itself. `.mlx` is the file extension of live scripts. Moreover, the live script provides an opportunity to run the command and observe the output in the live editor itself. For the live scripts, the live editor has three icons on the right side, which has the option to display output on the right, display output inline or hide code and display only the output.

Workspace browser panel and variables editor

Workspace panel is available in the default layout. The variables editor window opens above the command window when we right-click on any variable from the workspace panel. These topics are thoroughly explained in the workspace browser section.

Toolbars

There are different types of toolbars available on the MATLAB desktop.

Toolstrip

The toolstrip has a comprehensive collection of operations. It is located at the top of the desktop. The toolstrip could be either minimized or restored using right-click or with the help of the small arrow icon on the right side. As mentioned earlier, the toolstrip has three tabs: **HOME**, **PLOTS**, and **APPS**. In this section, we have tried to cover some of the widely used operations. Hovering on these icons provides a short introduction. Please refer to the help documentation for detailed information.

Home tab

The **HOME** tab is the default tab of the toolstrip. It consists of six different sections: **FILE**, **VARIABLE**, **CODE**, **SIMULINK**, **ENVIRONMENT**, and **RESOURCES**, as indicated in *figure 2.7*:

Figure 2.7: Toolstrip home tab

Here is a short introduction of the sections before discussing their operations in detail:

- **FILE**: File section has operations to create new files or open the existing ones.
- **VARIABLE**: This section provides options to perform workspace operations.
- **CODE**: This section offers operations for code, for example, favorite commands or code analysis.
- **SIMULINK**: As the name suggests, the Simulink operation navigates to the Simulink start page, which is the same as the **New** operation in the **FILE** menu.
- **ENVIRONMENT**: This section includes **Layout** settings as well as preferences.
- **RESOURCES**: It has the resources in case of any further information is needed, for example, help, community, request support, and tutorial.

Here is the brief information on the crucial sections and respective operations:

File

These are the various operations offered in the **FILE** section as follows:

- **New script**: When we click **New** script, it opens a new blank script file in an editor window. The default datatype of the file is **.m** (MATLAB code file). A script is a series of commands. It does not have any input and output arguments. Along with the editor, three more tabs: **Editor**, **Publish**, and **Open,** become visible in the toolstrip. Once we write the commands in the script, we can save it using **Save** operation in the **FILE** section of the **Editor** or **Publish** tab.
- **New Live script**: Similar to the **New script** operation, the New Live script opens a new blank live script file in a Live Editor window. The default datatype of the file is **.mlx** (MATLAB live code file). As the name suggests,

a live script is an interactive document that bundles MATLAB code with formatted text, equations, and images in a Live Editor. New tabs: **Live Editor**, **Insert**, and **View** are visible once we open a live script.

- **New**: This operation provides us with multiple options to create a new file type. This list suggests file types, windows, and basic options for creation.
    - **Script**: Same as preceding
    - **Live Script**: Same as preceding
    - **Function**: **.m**, Editor, function name, inputs, outputs
    - **Live Function**: **.mlx**, Live Editor, function name, inputs, outputs
    - **Class**: **.m**, class name, properties, method, function, object, arg
    - **System Object**: **.m**, Basic/ Advanced/ Simulink extension
    - **Project**: Blank/ from folder/Git/SVN/Simulink template
    - **Figure**: **.fig**, figure window, figure name, value, properties, and so on.
    - **App**: **.mlapp**, App designer, blank/2-Panel/3-Panel app
    - **Stateflow Chart**: **.sfx**, Stateflow Editor, State, Junction, Symbols
    - **Simulink model**: **.slx**, Simulink Editor, model/subsystem/library

Figure 2.8 shows all the options from the **New** operation:

Figure 2.8: *New operation*

- **Open**: This operation provides the possibility to browse and open the file. It also suggests some recently opened files and projects.
- **Find Files**: The user can search for specific files by providing the name, file type, file path, or particular text in the file.
- **Compare**: When we select two files and the appropriate compare option between text and binary compare, this operation provides the result of whether the files are identical or have any difference.

Variable

This list provides operations available in the variable section as follows:

- **Import Data**: This operation allows the user to browse and select the data file and import the data into Workspace. Some of the recognized data file format types are audio, video, image, graphics, MATLAB data, spreadsheet, text, icon, and so on.
- **Save Workspace**: We can save the Workspace variables in a file for future use. The possible file types are **.mat** (MATLAB data file) and **.m** (MATLAB script file). We can run the file next time we open MATLAB, and it loads the variables Workspace.
- **New Variable**: This operation opens a new variable in the Variables editor window. There is also a new tab **VARIABLE**, where some options such as new variable creation from selection, rows, columns, insert, delete rows and columns, transpose, and sort operations are available.
- **Open Variable**: Opens an existing variable for editing in variables editor.
- **Clear Workspace**: Based on the selection, this operation clears all workspace variables or workspace variables and functions.

Code

- **Favorites**: This option allows the user to create a set of frequently used commands. *Figure 2.9* shows the **Favorite Command** editor window:

MATLAB Desktop Interface ■ 39

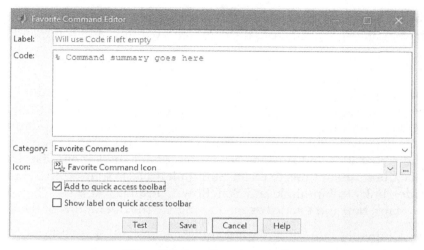

Figure 2.9: *Favorite command editor*

These are the fields to be filled in the favorite command Editor to create a new favorite command as follows:

- **Label**: Any name of choice
- **Code**: write the set of commands of drag and drop from the command window or history. Example: clear; `clc;`
- **Category**: Favorite Commands/Examples
- **Icon**: Available options are favorite command, MATLAB, Simulink, Help icon, as well as Alphabets and numbers
- Tick box to add to quick access Toolbar

- **Analyze code**: This option prepares a code analyzer report for all the files present in the current folder. This report displays the messages with potential errors and inefficiencies in the code. The report opens in the MATLAB Web browser and shows all folder files with or without problems. Once we click on the file name or error message, the corresponding file opens in Editor. The error areas are highlighted in red and warnings in yellow. Hovering suggests an option to see a detailed error or warning explanation and offers an automatic fix if possible. The automatic fix areas are highlighted in orange.

- **Run and Time**: This operation runs code and analyzes execution time. After clicking on this icon, a profiler window pops up. Once we click start profiling and then stop profiling, a profile summary is generated that includes details such as the number of calls, total and self-time in seconds, and total time plot for respective functions.

- **Clear commands**: By executing this command from the drop-down, the user can clear all commands from the command window and command history.

Simulink

Clicking the Simulink icon opens the Simulink Start page of the Simulink product family. The same page is visible while selecting the Simulink Model from the new drop-down list. The Simulink start page offers different possibilities to start working on Simulink. Left side, there are options to browse and open existing files and projects. The recent files and projects are visible under the **Recent** list. Under the **Projects** list, there are options to create Simulink Projects from source control; and learn provides links to Simulink and Stateflow On-ramp tutorials. The start page includes two tabs, **New** and **Examples**. Following are the operations of these tabs:

- **New**: Under this tab, there are standard templates available for Simulink products: Simulink, Embedder Coder, Simscape, and Stateflow. These are the template options available for Simulink and Stateflow.
    - **Simulink**: The available template options are Blank model, Blank subsystem, Blank library, code generation, and project creation templates.
    - **Stateflow**: The Stateflow available templates are Blank Chart, Simple Stateflow chart, Hierarchical chart, State transition table, and Moore Chart.
- **Examples**: Under the examples tab, users can find Simulink Documentation, Release notes, and references to Simulink blocks help. There are also different examples of Simulink products based on various industry real-life use cases. Open Example opens the example, and the user can simulate and observe the output results.

Environment

These are the operations available under the **ENVIRONMENT** section as follows:

- **Layout**: This option is helpful to adjust the MATLAB desktop layout as per user preference. As shown in *figure 2.1*, the default layout is a layout with three columns. There are other options available with fewer panels. The Layout offers the possibility to save the desired Layout and organize them. The current folder Workspace, panel title, and toolstrip could be enabled or disabled. The user could also choose what to do with **Command History**, quick access toolbar, and current folder toolbar.
- **Set Path**: Set Path allows the user to add a folder or a folder with subfolders to the MATLAB search path. It also allows changing the order of search. Detailed information is available in a later section.

- **Preferences**: The user can specify the preferences for MATLAB, Simulink, and other related products for different windows and toolbars, images, text, shortcuts, projects, code, and so on. It also supports to adjust the toolbars and panel default settings. Figure 2.10 shows the preferences window, including the windows or toolbars in the left browser. Further options are revealed once clicked on the list options.

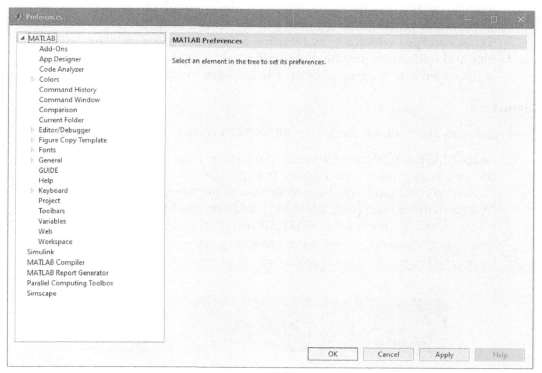

Figure 2.10: *MATLAB preferences*

- **Add-Ons**: A click on colorful Add-On icon takes us to the Add-On Explorer window. Now, Add-On explorer introduces us to the opportunities available with our MATLAB software. It helps the user to stay updated. In case the computer has an older MATLAB version, there is a link to the latest software version in Add-On Explorer. Moreover, Add-on explorer shows an extensive collection of MathWorks products such as MathWorks toolboxes and products, Hardware support packages, MathWorks options features, as well as community solutions such as toolboxes, Apps, Simulink models, functions, and collections.

- **Manage Add-Ons**: After clicking on this option from the drop-down menu, the **Add-On** manager window pops up. Under the **Installed** tab, one can see all installed toolboxes, installation date, documentation, and uninstall button. Under the **Updates** tab, one can see if any updates available for their products.

- **Package Toolbox**: An option to package a toolbox project file into a MATLAB toolbox. Detailed information is available in later chapters.

- **Package App**: This option packages the user-created app into a single installation file. It helps the user to share the app with other users. The initial step for this process is to provide a Main function file (MATLAB executable file **.m**, **.mlapp**), which acts as a starting point of the program. Then additional files and folders are provided. After the user inputs app description, the app is packaged into a signal package file (**.mlappinstall**).

Resources

These resources are available under the **RESOURCES** section as follows:

- **Help**: MATLAB help is an extensive database with the documentation of all the essential products and areas. It is possible to get detailed information about any command, function, toolbox, and blockset, or installation topic just by browsing or searching a few keywords on the MATLAB documentation page. *Figure 2.11* shows the MATLAB help main page:

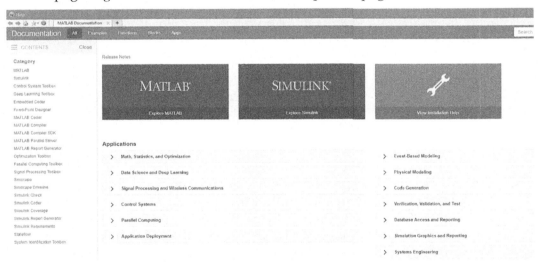

Figure 2.11: *MATLAB help*

- **Examples**: It opens the examples section on the MATLAB documentation page, where different MATLAB and Simulink examples are available as references.

- **Support website**: MATLAB supporting website has references to the support resources for MathWorks products and services. One can browse through various Help topics: documentation, examples, functions, blocks, apps, videos, answers, and bug reports. Additionally, there are links available on the support page to download products, get Installation help, and learn MATLAB through informative tutorials. There are community solutions to connect to other enthusiasts. The link to the support page is https://www.mathworks.com/support.html.

- **Licensing**: Licensing provides options to update and manage the existing licenses, activate and deactivate the software

- **About MATLAB**: This option launches a window where the user gets information about the software full release version number, License number, Activation date, and License type.

- **Community**: This option opens a Webpage of MATLAB central open exchange community for MATLAB and Simulink users. MATLAB Central offers various alternatives for the user to contribute to the community through MATLAB Answers, File exchange, Cody, Blogs, Topics, and so on. The link to the MATLAB central is https://www.mathworks.com/matlabcentral/.

- **Request support**: The user can request for assistance. To avail the support, one needs to login into the MathWorks account.

- **Learn MATLAB**: This icon navigates to the MATLAB academy Webpage, where several training modules are made available by MathWorks. There are options of self-paced or Instructor-led courses as well as certification by MathWorks. Based on the requirements, training sessions could be arranged at a user facility. The link to the MATLAB Academy is https://matlabacademy.mathworks.com/.

Plots tab

Figure 2.12 is the screenshot of the plots tab from the toolstrip.

Figure 2.12: Plots tab

After learning about the operations performed through the **HOME** tab, we will move to the second tab, which is known as the Plots tab. The plots tab offers a catalog of plots depending on the type of the selected variable. The variable could be chosen from the workspace, which is to be plotted. From the drop-down menu in the plots option, one can choose between the possible plot varieties for the selected variable or all. Some of the popular plot types are line, stem, bar, scatter, graph, pie, contour, and so on. Each type has further subtypes.

Once a plot type is selected, a figure window is launched with the plotted variable values. There is an option to create a new figure every time or reuse the existing figure. There is a catalog button in the drop-down menu, which launches a **Plot catalog** window. The left side of the window lists all the types of the plots, and only the applicable ones are highlighted, whereas others are greyed out. Next to this column, there is a list of subtypes based on the selection. A selection of any of these subtypes displays documentation for this selection. *Figure 2.13* shows the plot catalog window with plot types and subtypes of line plots:

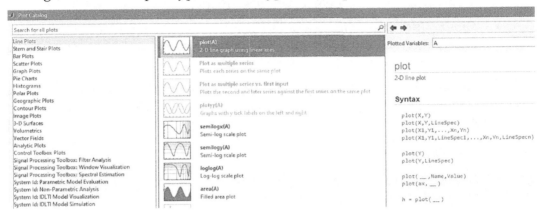

Figure 2.13: *Plot catalog*

Apps tab

Figure 2.14 shows the icons available in the **Apps** tab:

Figure 2.14: *Apps tab*

The apps tab offers several solutions for app management. The options available in **FILE** section are **Design App**, **Get More Apps**, **Install App**, **Package App** into a single file, and so on. In the apps, some of these options are available in other tabs too; for example, **Design App** is available in the **HOME** tab under **New** icon, which launches app designer window. **Get More Apps** launches Add-On Explorer, and Package App operation is the same as Add-Ons drop-down in **HOME** tab. The drown-down list in the apps section displays multiple toolbox solutions such as Machine Learning, Math, Control system, Code generation, Signal processing, and so on. Even though these solutions are visible, they open only when a valid license is available for the toolbox; else, they throw a license error.

Apart from these three permanent tabs, there are some additional supporting tabs with specific operations. These tabs become visible only when the respective window, such as Editor is open. The following are some of these tabs and their operations in brief.

Editor tab

Figure 2.15 is the Editor tab that becomes visible when a MATLAB file is open in the Editor window:

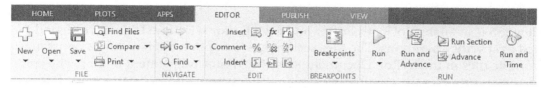

Figure 2.15: Editor tab

The file section offers operations from the **HOME** tab such as **New**, **Open**, **Find**, **Compare**, and along with these, it offers script-specific options such as **Save**, **Save as**, **Save all**, and so on. Navigate has an option to go to a line, set or clear bookmarks, and file and replace. The **EDIT** section contains options to insert section, function or fixed-point data, datatype, or behavior. Using comment, we can comment or uncomment. Indentation could be adjusted using Indent icons. We can set, clear, enable, and disable the breakpoints. The **RUN** section has multiple options to run and pause the file execution.

Live Editor tab

Similar to Editor Tab, Live Editor tab becomes visible when a live script or function is open in the Live Editor window. *Figure 2.16* shows the live editor tab:

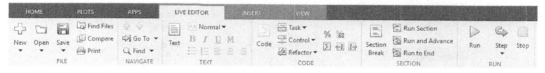

Figure 2.16: Live Editor tab

This tab includes the operations from **Editor** tab, and additionally, there are operations specific to the live script. A live Editor has an option to add text, task, control, and section breaks. Using **Refactor**, selected code is converted to a function or a local function. While running, there is an additional option of running the code line at a step.

View tab

Figure 2.17 shows the view tab that is visible for the editor window.

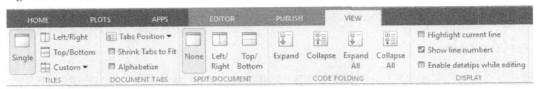

Figure 2.17: View tab

View tab is available for both Editor and Live Editor window. They have shared as well as specific operations. The tiles section has the option to view Single or arrange multiple files in the Editor. Document tabs offer visual adjustment of tabs. The split document provides the possibility to split the document into two parts. Code folding from the Editor supports in expanding and collapsing folds in code. The display section shows line numbers, datatips, and full-screen options.

Output option that is available only in Live Editor clears all outputs, whereas view offers output display options: display output on the right or in line with the code, or hide all code.

Quick access toolbar

Figure 2.18 shows a quick access toolbar with a drop-down option as well as icons available on the toolbar in the default layout:

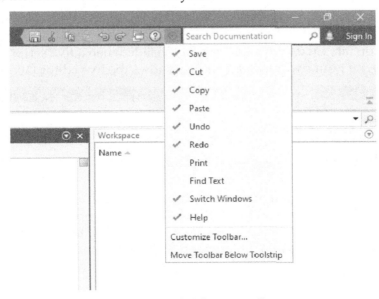

Figure 2.18: Quick access toolbar

Quick access toolbar is a small toolbar usually located at the top right corner above toolstrip. It provides easy access to some of the most widely used operations. The enabled operations in the default layout are: save, cut, copy, paste, undo, redo, Switch windows, and Help. User can enable the operations print and find text operations. There is an option to `Customize Toolbar...`. It launches the preferences window, where we can add, remove, or adjust the operation icons. Other than preferences, a user can add any operation to this toolbar by right-clicking any icon and selecting the `Add to Quick Access Toolbar` option. It is also possible to move the toolbar below toolstrip.

Current folder browser toolbar

The current folder browser toolbar is generally located below the toolstrip. *Figure 2.19* shows the current folder browser toolbar:

Figure 2.19: Current folder browser toolbar

The toolbar helps in navigating to the desired folder on the computer. It has back, forward, up one level, and browse to folder keys. Next to these navigation keys, there is an address field, where the full path of the current folder is visible. The drop-down list has some of the recently visited locations. A user can also copy or paste a complete path in the address field. Additionally, the find button enables search operation for the provided text in folders and subfolders. Right-click operation suggests an option to move this toolbar inside the current folder browser panel.

Workspace browser

Workspace browser manages the workspace content. Before going into the details of the Workspace browser, let us first understand the concept of workspace.

The concept of workspace

The workspace is used to store variables. MATLAB workspace is categorized mainly into two groups, base workspace and mode workspace. We will get into the details of these workspaces in further chapters.

As mentioned earlier, workspace contains variables. These variables are part of user-defined programs. Variables are the key content of any program without which none of the programs can run successfully. MATLAB provides a user interface to deal with these variables. This user interface is known as workspace browser.

It is easy to monitor the variables using the workspace browser. Workspace browser has a provision not only to maintain variable values but also to facilitate some other vital aspects of variables such as:

- Value
- Size (number of elements in matrix format),
- Bytes (Memory used to store the variable),
- Class (Type of data, for example, Double, Integer, char, and so on)
- Min (Minimum value among all elements of variable)
- Max (Maximum value among all elements of variable)
- Range
- Mean (Average of all elements of variable)
- Median
- Mode
- Var
- Std

Min, Max, Range, Mean, Median, Mode, Var, and Std are not applicable for character strings. Similarly, Mean, Median, Mode, Var, and Std are not suitable for integer types of data.

In *figure 2.20*, we can see that there are four types of variables. **Temp_Var**, a single variable with a class **double**, **Temp_Var1**, which is a character array with class **char**, **Temp_Var2**, which is an array of eight elements with a class **double**, and **Temp_Var3**, which is an array of eight elements with class **unit8**.

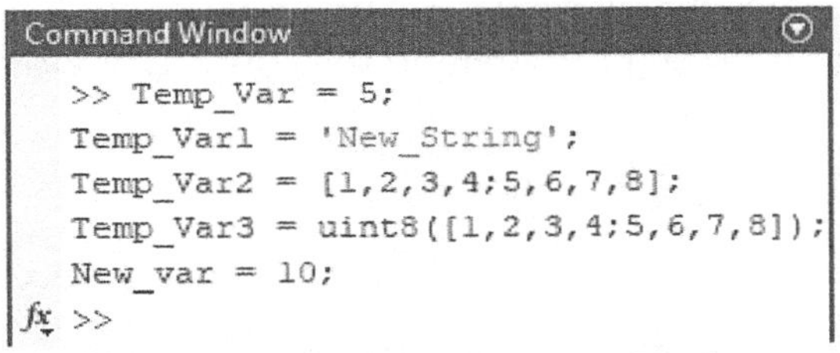

```
Command Window
>> Temp_Var = 5;
Temp_Var1 = 'New_String';
Temp_Var2 = [1,2,3,4;5,6,7,8];
Temp_Var3 = uint8([1,2,3,4;5,6,7,8]);
New_var = 10;
fx >>
```

Name	Value	Size	Bytes	Class	Min	Max	Range	Mean	Median	Mode	Var	Std
New_var	10	1x1	8	double	10	10	0	10	10	10	0	0
Temp_Var	5	1x1	8	double	5	5	0	5	5	5	0	0
Temp_Var1	'New_String'	1x10	20	char								
Temp_Va...	[1,2,3,4;5,6,7,8]	2x4	64	double	1	8	7	4.5000	4.5000	1	6	2.4495
Temp_Va...	[1,2,3,4;5,6,7,8]	2x4	8	uint8	1	8	7					

Figure 2.20: Workspace

Variables can be created using several ways. Here, in *figure 2.20*, these variables have been created using the command window. Workspace Browser also gives several options to create, delete or modify variables. Let us learn more about different options to create, delete or alter variables using command window and workspace browser.

Access variables using command window

We have explained steps with examples to create, delete and modify variables using the command window.

Create variable

Simply type an assignment command in the command window to create a variable and then press an enter key to execute the command.

For example, `Temp_Var = 5;`

The preceding command creates a variable with the name `Temp_Var` in workspace and assigns value 5 to it. Unlike "C" language, MATLAB does not need a prior declaration of variables. *Figure 2.21* shows how to create variables using the command window:

Figure 2.21: Create variable using the command window

Delete variable

Any variable can be deleted from workspace using `clear` command. Type clear and followed by a variable name:

For example, `clear Temp_Var;`

The preceding command deletes the variable `Temp_Var` from workspace.

> The `clear` should be used cautiously. If the variable name to be deleted is not mentioned in the command and only clear is executed, then it deletes the whole Workspace, that is, all variables from Workspace will be deleted. The command `clear` also supports regular expressions. Suppose all variables starting from `Temp` are required to be removed, then it is possible executing `clear Temp*;`.

Figure 2.22 explains how to delete variables using the command window:

Figure 2.22: *Delete variable from Workspace using the command window*

Figure 2.23 displays the content of Workspace before the delete operation using regular expressions:

Name	Value
New_var	10
Temp_Var	5
Temp_Var1	'New_String'
Temp_Var2	[1,2,3,4;5,6,7,8]
Temp_Var3	[1,2,3,4;5,6,7,8]

Figure 2.23: *Content of Workspace before the clear command*

Figure 2.24 illustrates how to delete a set of variables from workspace using regular expressions in the command window and to the content of workspace after a delete operation:

Figure 2.24: *Command to delete all variables starting their name from Temp, and then the content of update workspace*

Modify variable

The process to modify a variable is the same as creating a variable. Since MATLAB does not need a prior declaration of a variable, a similar assignment operation with the modified value could be used. For example, variable **Temp_Var** is already created in the Workspace with value 5, but now it is required to assign value 10 in **Temp_Var** then similar command that we used at the time of variable creation could be used. That is **Temp_Var = 10;**

> **Process for variable creation and modification is precisely the same, so while creating a variable, it is essential to check any existing required variable is not being modified unintentionally.**

Figure 2.25 displays the content of workspace before modification operation:

Figure 2.25: *Content of workspace before modify command*

Figure 2.26 shows how to modify the value of a variable using the command window and content of Workspace after modification:

Figure 2.26: *Value of Temp_Var modified from 5 to 10*

Access variables using workspace browser

We have given steps with examples to explain how to create, delete, and modify variables using workspace browser.

Create variable

This process is to be followed:

1. Right-click on workspace area, then click on **New**. Alternatively, you may press *Ctrl + N*. Step 1 to create a variable operation is shown in *figure 2.27*:

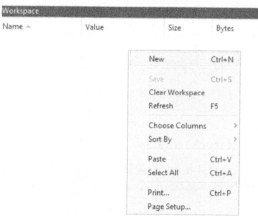

Figure 2.27: *Create variable Step 1*

2. New variable with the name **unnamed** will appear in the workspace. Then rename **unnamed** to the desired name. Here, **unnamed** is renamed to **First_Var**. Step 2 to create variable operation is shown in *figure 2.28*:

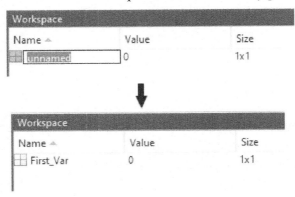

Figure 2.28: Create variable Step 2

3. By default, value **0** is assigned to **First_Var**, and it could be modified. Right-click and then select **Edit Value**, then the value field becomes editable and then desired value can be assigned to **First_Var**. Step 3 to create variable operation is shown in *figure 2.29*:

Figure 2.29: Create variable Step 3

Delete variable

Any variable can be deleted from workspace as follows:

- Right-click on the variable and select "Delete" option from the menu, or select the variable from workspace and then directly press "Delete" key.

- For deleting more than one variable, the same process can be followed after selecting all those variables that are required to be removed.

- To delete all variables from Workspace, Right-click on the empty workspace area and select "Clear Workspace". *Figure 2.30* explains the steps to delete variables from Workspace using the workspace browser.

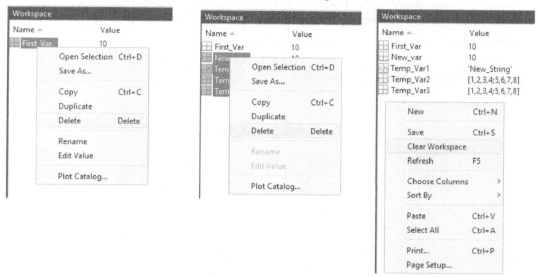

Figure 2.30: Delete variable

Modify variable

Any variable can be modified directly from workspace as follows:

- Right-click on the variable, then select **Edit Value**, then the value field becomes editable, and then the desired value can be assigned to the selected variable. This process is the same as Step 3 from **Create Variable**. *Figure 2.31* shows the steps to modify variables using the workspace browser:

Figure 2.31: Modify variable

Modify variable using open selection

In *figure 2.32*, we can see how using an open selection option from the workspace browser, we can modify variables. It shows the content of workspace before modification, then Variables Editor views with the content of workspace after modification:

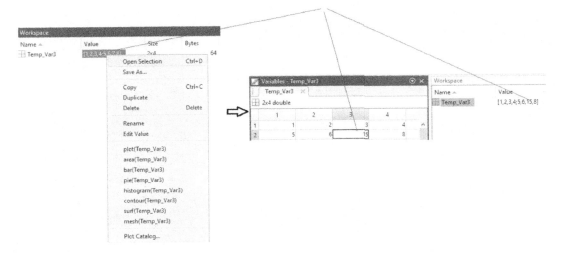

Figure 2.32: Modify variable using open selection

If the variable to be modified is a huge array, and one element of this array is needed to be modified, then it may not be feasible to use **Edit Value** option. In this case, the required variable could be opened in **Variables Editor** window. The selected variable will be shown in the **Variables Editor** window in a Matrix format. In this format, it is easier to modify the elements of the variable.

Workspace durability

Workspace data is valid and durable only until the MATLAB instance is active. It is not maintained across all MATLAB instances. So, whenever an active MATLAB instance is quit, then the content of Workspace gets cleared. If the current content of Workspace is required for future activities after closing MATLAB, then it is necessary to save content into a MAT file, which is a binary data container file format accessible in MATLAB. It is essential to load this MAT file again in MATLAB Workspace when a new instance of MATLAB is opened. Save and Load of Workspace variables could be done using the command line as well as using the Workspace Browser.

Save Workspace Variable

Workspace variables can be saved in the MAT-File using command window as well as workspace browser. We have explained the steps to save variables in the following points:

- Using command window: Simply by executing command **save('Desired Filename');** all Workspace variables could be stored in MAT-file. *Figure 2.33* shows how to save Workspace in the MAT-File using the command window:

Figure 2.33: Save MAT-file all variables

It is also possible to save only specific variables in MAT file; for example, if all variables starting from **Temp** are required to be stored in MAT file, then it could be done using save command as **save('MyTempVars','Temp*');**. *Figure 2.34* explains how to save a specific set of variables in the MAT-File using a regular expression.

Figure 2.34: Save MAT-file-specific variables

- Using workspace browser: To save all workspace variables, right-click on the empty workspace area, and select the save option. Then a pop-up will appear to enter the desired filename and select the desired file path. After that, click on the **Save** button. In *figure 2.35*, it is explained how to save Workspace variables in the MAT-File using Workspace Browser.

Figure 2.35: Save MAT file all variables using workspace browser

To save only specific variables in MAT-file. Select all those variables that are required to be saved, then right-click and select the option **Save as**, then similar pop-up browser window opens to enter the desired filename and file path, and at the last click on **Save** button. *Figure 2.36* shows how to save a specific set of variables in the MAT-File using workspace browser:

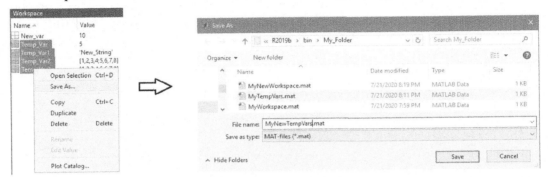

Figure 2.36: Save MAT-file-specific variables using workspace browser

Load MAT-file

Figure 2.37 shows how to load MAT-File back to workspace:

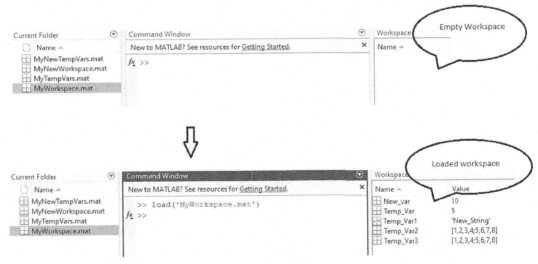

Figure 2.37: Load MAT-file

MAT-file could be loaded in several ways, such as dragging and dropping MAT-file in the command window, double-clicking on the respective MAT-file, or using **load** command.

MATLAB search path setting

Let us consider an example. Suppose there are certain **math** functions, which are defined in folder **math**, which are required to be used in folder **work**. *Figure 2.38* shows the content of folder **math**:

Figure 2.38: Math user-defined functions (*these functions are created just for an example similar case applicable for every MATLAB supported file type.)

For using these functions outside of folder **math**, it is required to add folder **math** in the MATLAB search path. Without adding folder **math** into the MATLAB search path, if we try to access any of these functions **add**, **subtract**, or **mul** outside of **math** folder, then MATLAB gives an error.

Figure 2.39 shows an error message when we try to access files that are not included in the MATLAB search path:

Figure 2.39: Error when function from the math folder is accessed from the work folder without adding "math" folder into the MATLAB search path

To solve this error, it requires to add **math** folder to the MATLAB search path. For this, right-click on **math** folder and then select **Add to Path**. Suppose the selected folder has subfolders, which are also required to be added to the path, then select **Selected Folders and Subfolders;** else, select **Selected Folders**. *Figure 2.40* shows how to add a folder in the MATLAB search path using the current folder browser:

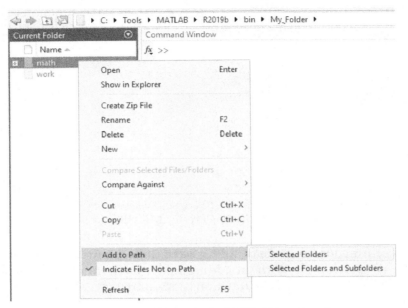

Figure 2.40: *Add folder in the MATLAB search path*

If the option **Indicate Files Not on Path** is already selected, then once folder **math** gets added to the MATLAB search path, its text color changes to black, as indicated in the following image. *Figure 2.41* displays current folder browser view before and after adding folder **math** in the MATLAB search paths:

Figure 2.41: *"math" folder added to the search path*

Once **math** folder is added to the MATLAB search path, then functions inside **math** folder become accessible from any other location. In *figure 2.42*, we can see that, after adding folder **math** in the MATLAB search path, we can access functions from folder **math** in the folder **work** without any error:

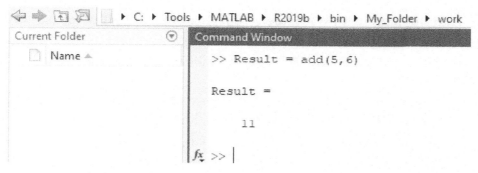

Figure 2.42: function from "math" folder executed in the work folder

If files/functions from **math** folders are no more required, then the **math** folder can be removed from the search path. For this, right-click on **math** folder and select **Remove from Path**. If the selected folder is required to be removed with its subfolders, then click on any of the options from *figure 2.43* **Selected Folders and Subfolders** or **Selected Folders**..

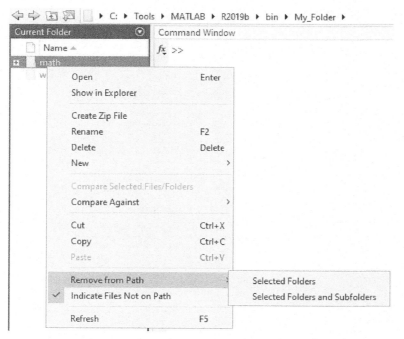

Figure 2.43: Remove folder from the MATLAB search path

Add to Path and **Remove from Path** can be done using the command window. These commands can be executed in the MATLAB command window.

- Add to path: `addpath('C:\Tools\MATLAB\R2019b\bin\My_Folder\math');`
- Add to path with subfolders: `addpath(genpath('C:\Tools\MATLAB\R2019b\bin\My_Folder\math'));`
- Remove from path: `rmpath('C:\Tools\MATLAB\R2019b\bin\My_Folder\math');`
- Remove from path with subfolders: `rmpath(genpath('C:\Tools\MATLAB\R2019b\bin\My_Folder\math'));`

Changes done in the MATLAB search path by adding/removing folders are valid only until the current MATLAB instance is active. Once the MATLAB instance is closed, then added/deleted paths in the MATLAB search path are erased, and these changes will not be visible in the newly opened MATLAB instance. It is required to *save path* to make changes done in the MATLAB search path setting to be visible in all MATLAB instances when a new instance of MATLAB is opened. This operation can be done using the utility **Set Path**. For this, first, click on **Set Path**, as highlighted in *figure 2.44*:

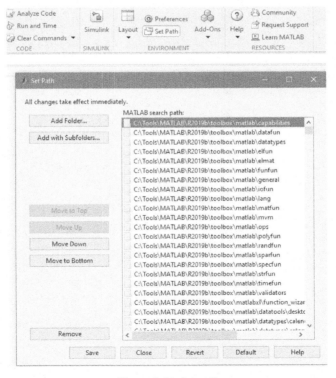

Figure 2.44: *Set path*

The **Set Path** utility provides a handy approach to make MATLAB search path settings. All options available are self-explanatory. As mentioned earlier, the **Save** option is used to save search path settings. Command **savepath**; also could be used to save a current search using command window.

Important links

These are the important links specified in this chapter:

- MathWorks support page:

    https://www.mathworks.com/support.html

- MATLAB central community page:

    https://www.mathworks.com/matlabcentral/

- MATLAB learning Academy:

    https://matlabacademy.mathworks.com/

Conclusion

Learning any new tool first entails acquaintance with the means to use the tool correctly, and MATLAB here is not any different. With this chapter, we have enabled the user to understand all the essentials of the MATLAB Desktop interface. Of course, complete knowledge is gained over the period through regular practice. Still, with this chapter, the reader has gained enough experience to take further steps toward learning the core elements. The reader now understands different panels and toolbars from the default layout. She or he is also aware of possible operations and adjustment options. The reader knows to use Workspace variables and MATLAB search path settings. Based on this chapter, the upcoming chapter further enlightens the basics of MATLAB. It shall introduce the reader to different types of variables, classes, commands, user-defined functions, scripts, and workspace.

Points to remember

- MATLAB desktop is a vibrant and user-friendly interface.
- The default layout contains various panels such as current folder browser, Command Window, and workspace browser.
- This default view can be further extended to different windows such as Command History, Editor, and so on.
- The default layout eases the user operation with these toolbars: Toolstrip, quick access toolbar, and current folder browser toolbar.

- MATLAB provides extensive help through detailed documentation, community support, request support, training, tutorials, and examples.
- The variables can be accessed using the command window as well as the Workspace browser.
- When it is required to access different folders, then with the help of search path settings, it is possible to access them.
- When there is no way forward, always seek MATLAB help, and it will never disappoint you.

Multiple choice questions

1. Which of the following window is not available in the default layout of the MATLAB desktop interface?

    a. Command Window

    b. Workspace

    c. Command History

    d. Current Folder Browser

2. Which command displays the installation information?

    a. clc

    b. disp

    c. show

    d. ver

3. It is not possible to see folders added in MATLAB search path in the current folder browser.

    a. True

    b. False

4. How many maximum numbers of statements are stored in command history?

    a. 2,500

    b. 25,000

    c. 2,50,000

    d. None of the above

5. .mlx is the file format of which file type?
    a. Live script
    b. Live app
    c. Script
    d. Simulink model

6. Which of the following section of the home tab contains the Preferences menu?
    a. Code
    b. Environment
    c. Resources
    d. None of the above

7. Using which of the following methods is it possible to access variables?
    a. Using command Window
    b. Using Workspace Browser
    c. Both A and B
    d. None of the above

Questions

1. What is a MATLAB desktop interface?
2. Explain different panels from the default layout.
3. How to change any layout to a default layout?
4. What is the difference between a script and a live script?
5. What are the different file types possible to be created with new operation?
6. Explain various methods to create, modify and delete variables.
7. Why is it required to add a folder to the search path?

Answers

1. c
2. d
3. b
4. b
5. a
6. b
7. c

Chapter 3
MATLAB Basics

Introduction

In the previous chapter, we have already familiarized ourselves with the MATLAB Desktop layout and the usage of different panels, windows, and toolbars. This chapter progresses toward getting comfortable with the core operational elements of MATLAB, which are Variables, classes, and Commands. In this chapter, the user shall learn the different types of variables based on their classes and sizes. This chapter introduces the reader to scalars, vectors, matrices, and arrays with some examples. MATLAB has a vast database of built-in functions, and the chapter tries to cover necessary MATLAB built-in commands, functions, and operators along with their syntax variations and examples where applicable. The reader shall not only learn about the essential functions but shall also get hands-on training in parallel. This learning method is going to establish a robust foundation for further topics.

Structure

In this chapter, we shall discuss the following topics:

- Command window shortcuts
- Variables
    - Variable naming convention

- Variables classification
- Built-in functions and commands
   - Environment commands
   - Vectors, matrices, and arrays functions
   - String and character array functions
   - Operators

Objectives

After studying this chapter, the reader will be able to:

- Learn some helpful command window shortcuts and tips.
- Understand the rules to name the variables.
- Classify the variables based on their types and sizes.
- Get knowledge of array and matrix operators.
- Be familiar with different MATLAB built-in functions.
- Execute essential MATLAB functions independently.

Command window shortcuts

In this chapter, we shall acquire the knowledge of variables and classes, scalars, vectors, matrices, and arrays, as well as built-in functions, commands, and operators with several examples. So, before we begin learning and executing the samples in parallel, it would help us to learn a few command window shortcuts. In this section, we have mentioned some of the helpful working tips to keep in mind:

- **Execute a statement in the command window**: As mentioned in the earlier chapter, the command window has a command prompt >>. Write a statement next to the command prompt and press *Enter*. The statement is executed, and the output is displayed by default.

- **Execute multiple statements in a single command line**: Next to the command prompt, a comma (,) or a semicolon (;) can separate more than one statement. When a comma is used, the outputs are displayed by default.

- **Suppress the display of the output on the command window**: When the statement ends with a semicolon, MATLAB executes the statement but does not display the output.

- **Re-execute the previous statement in the command window**: Using the up and down arrow key, we can access the previous statements. You may revisit the earlier statements by pressing the Up key at an empty command line, making modifications if required, and pressing *Enter* key. You may also select any previous statement in the command window and press *Enter*. The selection shall execute.

- **Write multiple statements without a single execution**: After writing the first statement, press the Shift+ Enter keys; you may now write another statement in the next command line without executing the previous one.

- **Write a single lengthy statement in multiple lines**: Include ellipsis (…) at the end of the first line, and press *Enter*. The statement shall not execute, and now you may write the next line.

- **Stop the command execution**: Press *Ctrl + C* or *Ctrl + Break* keys, and the execution shall abort. Press *Esc* to discard a statement without execution.

- **Verify the syntax**: While typing the commands or variable names, confirming the colors before execution helps to avoid syntax errors. We can observe/alter default color settings from MATLAB **Toolstrip** | **Home** | **Environment** tab | **Preferences** | **Colors** page. By default, the color of keywords is blue, the character vectors look purple, and the unterminated character vectors shall appear maroon. In the case of multiple delimiters, MATLAB also highlights the paired delimiter, such as parentheses, brackets, and so on, so we can confirm that the matching delimiters are present. *Figure 3.1* shows MATLAB default color setting options along with samples:

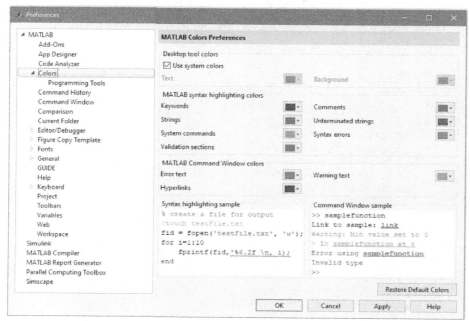

Figure 3.1: *MATLAB colors preferences*

- **Command and function syntax**: In MATLAB, due to function-command duality, many functions can be used as commands too. The difference lies in their syntax. In the command, the arguments are separated with space, and it does not have any parentheses as the inputs are passed as character vectors. Due to this, it cannot pass variable values or strings as an argument. The standard command syntax is **FunctionName Input1.... InputN**. In contrast, the standard function syntax specifies the output arguments too, and the variable values, character vectors, or strings are passed as input to the function. The standard Function syntax is **[Output1,… N]=FunctionName(Input1,…N)**

  Therefore, we can use simple commands where applicable; otherwise, we should use functions in the cases, as mentioned previously. The following are simple examples of function and command:

  `iskeyword command`

  `iskeyword('function')`

- **Find the function in command window:** On the left side of the command prompt, there is an f_x button, as shown in *figure 3.2*. The f_x button can be enabled from **Toolstrip | Home | Environment** tab | **Preferences | Command Window** page | **Display settings | Enable tick box- Show Function Browser** button. After clicking the button, the function browser opens. It is possible to search for the function or command syntax, required arguments, and description by searching for keywords in the search window. There are product-wise folders available in the browser window:

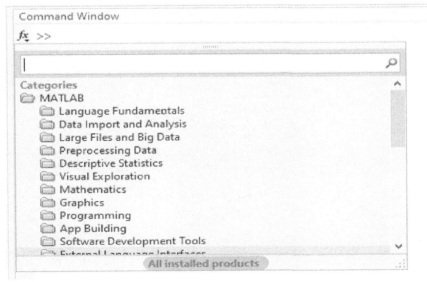

Figure 3.2: *Function browser*

Variables

In the previous chapter, we have learnt how to create, delete and modify variables and the basic concept of Workspace. In this chapter, let us understand the variables and their classification in detail. Before we begin, first, we shall have a look at the variable naming convention.

Variable naming convention

MATLAB allows a variable name to start only with a letter, and then letters, digits, or underscores can follow it. Variable names are case sensitive; that is, variables **x** and **X** are treated as different variables. Variable-length more than **namelengthmax** is not allowed. **namelengthmax** is a MATLAB command which returns the value for the maximum length allowed for the variable name. The value returned by **namelengthmax** may vary according to the MATLAB release. In MATLAB 2019b **namelengthmax** returns value 63, so variable-length more than 63 is not allowed in MATLAB 2019b. Besides, we cannot define a variable name, which is the same as the existing MATLAB command. The command **iskeyword** is used to identify whether the variable is already used for the existing command or not. *Figure 3.3* shows different examples of valid as well as invalid variable names:

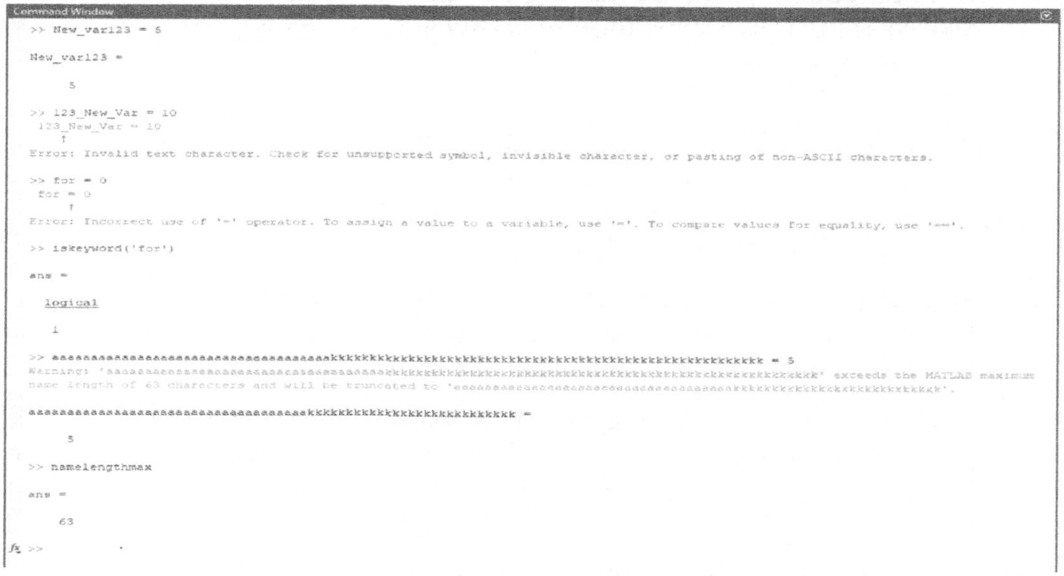

Figure 3.3: *Variables naming convention*

Variables classification

In MATLAB, we can distinguish variables based on their classes (**DataType**) and based on their sizes.

Classification based on types or classes

The variables are classified based on the classes as follows:

- Numeric
- Strings and character arrays
- Logical
- Cell arrays
- Structure

Numeric

Numeric types represent integers and floating-point numbers. Integers are classified further into signed and unsigned integers, whereas floating-point numbers are further classified into single-precision and double-precision floating-point numbers. The requirement of memory to store variables varies according to the numeric type. By default, MATLAB stores any variable initialized with a numeric value into a double-precision floating-point number. The numeric types are classified in detail as follows:

- **Double (double-precision floating-point):** The variables of type "double" take 64-bit, that is, 8-byte, to store their value. The range of the number of type double is between -1.79769×10^{308} and 1.79769×10^{308}, whereas the resolution of class double is 22507×10^{-308}.

- **Single (single-precision floating-point):** The variables of type `single` take 32-bit, that is, 4-byte, to store their value. The range of the number of type single is between -3.4×10^{38} and 3.4×10^{38}, whereas the resolution of the class single is $2.8025969 \times 10^{-45}$

- **uint8 (8-bit unsigned integer):** The variables of type `uint8` take 8-bit, that is, 1-byte, to store their value. The range of the number of type `uint8` is between 0 and 255 (2^8-1), whereas the resolution of the class `uint8` is 1.

- **uint16 (16-bit unsigned integer):** The variables of type `uint16` take 16-bit, that is, 2-byte, to store their value. The range of the number of type `uint16` is between 0 and 65535 ($2^{16}-1$), whereas the resolution of the class `uint16` is 1.

- **uint32 (32-bit unsigned integer):** The variables of type `uint32` take 32-bit, that is, 4-byte, to store their value. The range of the number of type `uint32` is between 0 and 4294967295 ($2^{32}-1$), whereas the resolution of the class `uint32` is 1.

- **uint64 (64-bit unsigned integer):** The variables of type `uint64` take 64-bit, that is, 8-byte, to store their value. The range of the number of type `uint64` is between 0 and 18446744073709551615 (2^64–1), whereas the resolution of the class **uint64** is 1.

- **int8 (8-bit signed integer)**: The variables of type **int8** take 8-bit, that is, 1-byte, to store their value. The range of the number of type **int8** is between −128 (−2^7) and 127 (2^7–1), whereas the resolution of the class **int8** is 1.

- **int16 (16-bit signed integer)**: The variables of type **int16** take 16-bit, that is, 2-byte, to store their value. The range of the number of type **int16** is between −32768 (−2^15) and 32767 (2^15–1), whereas the resolution of the class **int16** is 1.

- **int32 (32-bit signed integer):** The variables of type **int32** take 32-bit, that is, 4-byte, to store their value. The range of the number of type **int32** is between −2147483648 (−2^31) and 2147483647 (2^31–1), whereas the resolution of the class **int32** is 1.

- **int64 (64-bit signed integer)**: The variables of type **int8** take 64-bit, that is, 8-byte, to store their value. The range of the number of type **int64** is between −9223372036854775808 (−2^63) and 9223372036854775807 (2^63–1), whereas the resolution of the class **int64** is 1.

By default, variables are created with a class **double**, so just an assignment operation is sufficient to create the variable of a class **double**. However, to create the variable with a numeric class other than double, the desired class must be used while creating variables with assignment operation. Command **whos** is used to get the properties of the variable. We can use the commands **cast** and **typecast** to convert the variables into different numeric classes. Command **cast** converts variable to the desired **datatype** and assigns value, which is most suitable according to the desired class, whereas command **typecast**, converts variable into the desired class without changing underlying data. For example, the variable **New_var** has value −1 and class int8. The command **cast(New_var,'unit8')** returns value 0. 0 is the most suitable value for −1 when it is converted to uint8. The command **typecast(New_var,'unit8')** returns 255. The datatype uint8 has a range of 0–255, and int8 has a range of −128 to 127. When the conversion happens without changing underlying data, then −1 of **int8** is represented as 255 in unit8, −2 of **int8** is represented as 254, and so on. The following set of commands explains how to create a variable of different numeric classes:

```
New_var=5                                     %Input command
  New_var =                                   %command output
      5
whos New_var                                  %Input command
  Name          Size      Bytes    Class    Attributes    %command output
```

```
  New_var         1x1              8  double
New_var=uint32(5)                              %Input command
  New_var =                                    %command output
   uint32
     5
whos New_var                                   %Input command
  Name           Size         Bytes  Class     Attributes  %command output
  New_var        1x1              4  uint32
New_var=uint8(-5)                              %Input command
  New_var =                                    %command output
   uint8
     0
New_var=int8(-5)                               %Input command
  New_var =                                    %command output
   int8
    -5
whos New_var                                   %Input command
  Name           Size         Bytes  Class     Attributes  %command output
  New_var        1x1              1  int8
```

The following code explains how to use commands **cast** and **typecast** to convert variables between different numeric classes:

```
New_var=int8(-1)                               %Input command
  New_var =                                    %command output
   int8
    -1
cast(New_var,'uint8')                          %Input command
  ans =                                        %command output
   uint8
     0
typecast(New_var,'uint8')                      %Input command
  ans =                                        %command output
   uint8
    255
```

Strings and character arrays

Character array and strings represent and store the text data. Character arrays or strings are nothing but a sequence of characters, which can be stored in a variable. Whenever we need to deal with textual data while writing the programs, we must use character arrays or strings. Even though Strings and Character arrays satisfy the same purpose, but in MATLAB, they have their separate existence and are not identical. Before MATLAB version R2016b, string class was not available, and all textual operations were possible using only character arrays. In the MATLAB version, the R2016b **string** class was introduced. Character arrays are created using single quotes, and strings are constructed using double quotes. Character arrays are created with class **char**, whereas strings are created with class **string**. A string is considered as a scalar, whereas a Character array is regarded as a vector of characters. The following code explains how to create a string and character array. It also explains the differences in-between the variable properties:

```
New_var='Hello World'          %Input command to create a character array
 New_var =                     %command output
    'Hello World'
whos New_var                   %Input command
  Name          Size        Bytes  Class    Attributes    %command output
  New_var       1x11          22   char
New_var="Hello World"          %Input command to create a string
 New_var =                     %command output
    "Hello World"
whos New_var                   %Input command
  Name          Size        Bytes  Class    Attributes    %command output
  New_var       1x1          166   string
```

Logical

Logical type represents variables, which contain the logical value, that is, **true** or **false**. There are multiple ways to create variables of logical type. We can directly assign **true** or **false** to the variable, or we can use logical keywords while creating the variable. The following commands show how to create variables of logical type:

```
New_var=true        %Input command to create a logical variable
 New_var =          %command output
  logical
   1
```

```
New_var=false              %Input command to create a logical variable
 New_var =                 %command output
  logical
   0
New_var=logical(1)         %Input command to create a logical variable
 New_var =                 %command output
  logical
   1
New_var=logical(0)         %Input command to create a logical variable
 New_var =                 %command output
  logical
   0
whos New_var               %Input command
  Name        Size        Bytes  Class      Attributes    %command output
  New_var     1x1             1  logical
```

Cell arrays

Until now, we have comprehended numeric, string, char, and logical types. Suppose we need a variable that contains the data of all of these types. For example, a school needs to store the following data of students. **Roll number**, **Name**, and **Fees Paid**. Where **Roll number** is of numeric type, **Name** is on string type and **Fees Paid** is of logical type. To store this information, we need an additional type that can be used to store the data of different types. MATLAB gives handy options to solve this problem. A variable of the class **cell** can be created to store the data of different types in array form.

To add an element in the cell array, we need to use curly braces "**{}**". The following commands explain how to create cell arrays and how to access data from cell arrays:

```
Student_Info=[{1234},{'ABC XYZ'},{true}];    %command creates cell array
whos Student_Info                                      %Input command
  Name              Size        Bytes  Class    Attributes
  Student_Info      1x3           359  cell                  %command output
ArrayElement_1=Student_Info{1}       %copies cell array element 1
 ArrayElement_1 =                          %command output
      1234
```

```
whos ArrayElement_1                                 %Input command
  Name                  Size        Bytes   Class     Attributes
  ArrayElement_1        1x1           8     double              %command output
ArrayElement_2=Student_Info{2}       %copies cell array element 2
  ArrayElement_2 = %command output
    'ABC XYZ'
whos ArrayElement_2                       %Input command
  Name                  Size        Bytes   Class     Attributes
  ArrayElement_2        1x7          14     char
ArrayElement_3=Student_Info{3}         %copies cell array element 3
  ArrayElement_3 =                     %command output
    logical
     1
whos ArrayElement_3                                 %Input command
  Name                  Size        Bytes   Class     Attributes
  ArrayElement_3        1x1           1     logical   %command output
```

Structure

Similar to cell arrays, structures are also used to store heterogeneous data of different types into one variable. The fields of various types are required to be created first using the dot "**.**" operator. The fields could be created using the syntax **StructureName.FieldName**. Let us take a similar example of **StudentInfo**, which contains roll number, name, and fees paid information. Once the structure is created and data is added to the structure, simply by typing the structure name and then pressing enter shows the signature of the structure. The following image shows how to create structures with their fields and how to retrieve the data from structures:

```
Student_Info.Roll_Number=1234       %creates Student_Info Structure with
                                          Roll_Number
  Student_Info =                    %Returns the struct Student_Info with
                                          fields
    struct with fields:
      Roll_Number: 1234
Student_Info.Name='Abc Xyz'         %Adds Name field to Student_Info
                                          Structure
  Student_Info =                    %Returns the struct Student_Info
    struct with fields:
```

```
       Roll_Number: 1234
              Name: 'Abc Xyz'
Student_Info.Fees_paid=true      %Adds Fees_paid field to Student_Info
                                  Structure
 Student_Info =                  %Returns the struct Student_Info
   struct with fields:
     Roll_Number: 1234
            Name: 'Abc Xyz'
       Fees_paid: 1
whos Student_Info                %Input command
   Name              Size        Bytes    Class     Attributes     %command output
   Student_Info      1x1           551    struct
Roll_Number=Student_Info.Roll_Number %assigns Roll_number field value to
                                      variable
 Roll_Number =                   %Returns the Roll_Number
      1234
whos Roll_Number                 %Input command
   Name            Size     Bytes    Class     Attributes     %command output
   Roll_Number     1x1          8    double
Name=Student_Info.Name           %assigns Name field value to
                                  variable
 Name =                          %Returns Name
    'Abc Xyz'
whos Name                        %Input command
   Name        Size          Bytes    Class     Attributes     %command output
   Name        1x7              14    char
Fees_paid=Student_Info.Fees_paid %assigns Fees_paid field value to
                                  variable
 Fees_paid =                     %Returns Fees_paid
   logical
    1
whos Fees_paid                   %Input command
   Name           Size      Bytes    Class     Attributes     %command output
   Fees_paid      1x1           1    logical
```

MATLAB gives field suggestions after writing a dot "." in front of the Structure name and then pressing the *Tab* button on the keyboard. The content of the field also could be retrieved using the command **getfield(<StructureName>,<'FieldName'>)**. *Figure 3.4* explains how does the field suggestion look like and the use of the **getfield** command:

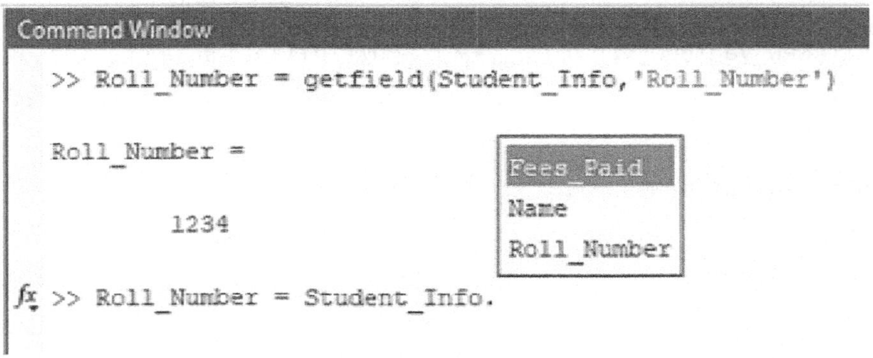

Figure 3.4: Field Suggestion and the "getfield" command

Here we have explained the most commonly used data types. There are some more datatypes supported by MATLAB; for more information, please visit https://www.mathworks.com/help/matlab/data-types.html.

Classification based on sizes

The Variables in MATLAB are classified based on their sizes into the following groups:

- **Scalars**: Variables with one row and one column.
- **Arrays**: The arrays are those variables with one row and multiple columns or one column and multiple rows.
- **Matrices**: Variables with multiple rows and multiple columns.

Scalars

Scalars are variables that have only one element; that is, the size of these variables is one, with one row and one column. Most of the variables involved in arithmetic operations or logical operations are most of the times scalars. Scalars are created using a simple assignment operation. The following code shows how to create scalars and how arithmetic operations are performed using scalars:

```
New_var=5;New_var_1=10;            %Input command to create variables
Add_result=New_var+New_var_1       %Addition operation
```

```
    Add_result =                        %Addition result output
       15
Sub_result=New_var-New_var_1            %substraction operation
    Sub_result =                        %Subtraction result output
       -5
Mul_result=New_var*New_var_1            %Multiplication operation
    Mul_result =                        %Multiplication result output
       50
Div_result=New_var/New_var_1            %division operation
    Div_result =                        %division result output
       0.5000
whos New_var                                         %Input command
    Name           Size        Bytes   Class    Attributes
    New_var        1x1             8   double              %command output
whos New_var_1                                       %Input command
    Name           Size        Bytes   Class    Attributes
    New_var_1      1x1             8   double              %command output
whos Mul_result                                      %Input command
    Name           Size        Bytes   Class    Attributes
    Mul_result     1x1             8   double              %command output
```

Arrays

An array in MATLAB is a single-dimensional vector. A variable is classified as an array when it has either one row and multiple columns or one column with multiple rows.

Creation of arrays and arithmetic operation on arrays

The comma "," operator or space operator " " is used to create an array with one row and multiple columns. A variable of an array type is created merely using assignment operation and numbers enclosed with square braces [ ]. The following code explains how to create an array variable having one row and multiple columns:

```
New_var=[1,2,3]                          %Input command
 New_var =                               %command output
     1     2     3
New_var=[1 2 3]                          %Input command
 New_var =                  %command output, same as above command
     1     2     3
whos New_var                             %Input command
  Name            Size        Bytes  Class       Attributes
  New_var         1x3            24  double              %command output
```

The semicolon "**;**" operator is used to create an array with one column and multiple rows. The following image explains how to create an array variable having one column and multiple rows:

```
New_var=[1;2;3]                          %Input command
 New_var =                               %command output
     1
     2
     3
whos New_var                             %Input command
  Name            Size       Bytes  Class     Attributes   %command output
  New_var         3x1           24  double
```

The arithmetic operation can be performed on arrays also, but for that, the arrays participating in the arithmetic operation have to be of the same dimensions. MATLAB performs arithmetic operations within elements with the same indexes and returns the result. The result is also an array with the same dimensions; for example: the variables **New_var** and **New_var1** are the arrays of three elements, that is, one row and three columns. Let us suppose the content of **New_var** is **[1,2,3]** and content of **New_var1** is **[4,5,6]** then operation **New_var + New_var1** returns an array with elements [5,7,9] that is, [1+4, 2+5, 3+6]. *Figure 3.5* shows how to perform arithmetic operations on arrays:

```
Command Window
>> New_var = [1,2,3]
New_var =
     1     2     3
>> New_var1 = [4,5,6]
New_var1 =
     4     5     6
>> Add_result = New_var + New_var1
Add_result =
     5     7     9
>> Sub_result = New_var - New_var1
Sub_result =
    -3    -3    -3
>> Mul_result = New_var .* New_var1
Mul_result =
     4    10    18
>> Div_result = New_var ./ New_var1
Div_result =
    0.2500    0.4000    0.5000
>> whos Div_result
  Name           Size          Bytes  Class     Attributes

  Div_result     1x3              24  double
fx >>
```

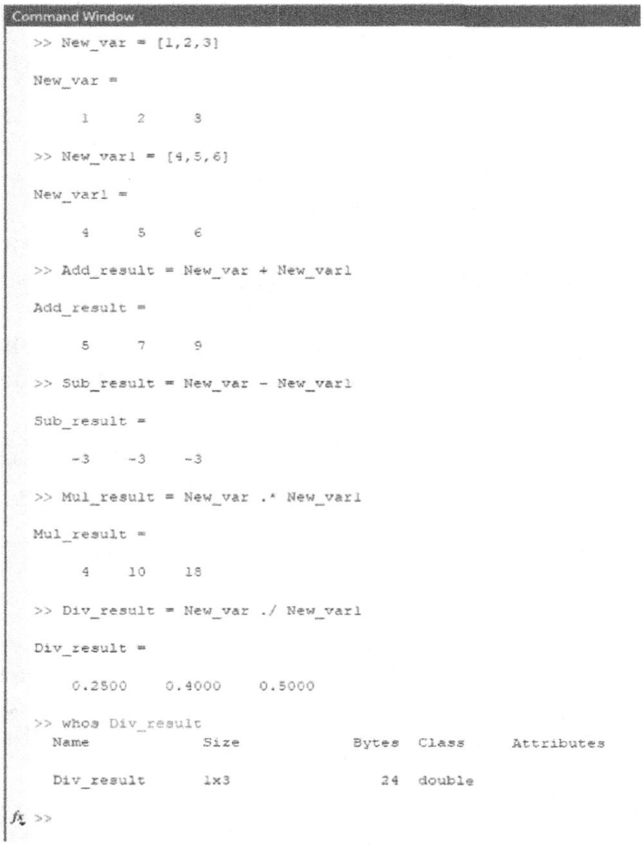

Figure 3.5: Arithmetic operations on arrays

The following code snippet shows the array commands from previous image:

```
New_var= [1,2,3];                       %create array New_var
New_var1=[4,5,6];                       %create array New_var1
Add_result=New_var+New_var_1;           %array addition
Sub_result=New_var-New_var_1;           %array subtraction
Mul_result=New_var.*New_var_1;          %array multiplication
Div_result=New_var./New_var_1;          %array division
```

We need to use .* operator to perform element-wise multiplication operation and similarly ./ for element-wise division operation on arrays. The operator * and / are used to perform matrix operations.

Figure 3.6 displays the error information when arithmetic operations are performed on arrays that are not of the same dimensions:

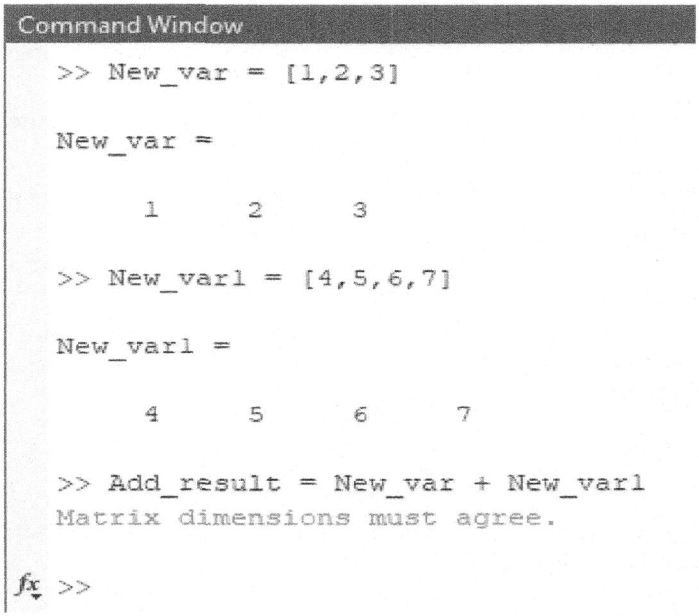

```
Command Window
>> New_var = [1,2,3]

New_var =

     1     2     3

>> New_var1 = [4,5,6,7]

New_var1 =

     4     5     6     7

>> Add_result = New_var + New_var1
Matrix dimensions must agree.

fx >>
```

Figure 3.6: Error when array dimensions are not matching

Access elements of arrays

The elements of an array can be easily accessed or retrieved using indexes. It is noteworthy to mention that MATLAB applies 1-based indexing in contrast to other programming languages that usually follow 0-based indexing. The syntax to get an element using an index is **variable(index)**. Suppose variable **New_var** has 15 elements and an element at index 10 is required to be accessed, then it could be done by executing command **New_var(10)**. MATLAB provides an option to retrieve multiple elements using an array of the index. Suppose we need to access 4th, 8th, and 10th elements from array **New_var**; then we can create an array of the indexes **Index_Arr = [4,8,10]**, and by executing **New_var(Index_Arr)**, we get an array of three elements, and those elements are nothing but 4th, 8th, and 10th elements from array **New_var**. The following code explains how to access variables by using a single index and index array:

```
New_var= [9,5,7,8,97,56,34,75,90,10,400,785,420,3,2];   %create array
whos New_var                                            %Input command
  Name          Size           Bytes   Class    Attributes %command output
  New_var       1x15             120   double
```

```
New_var(10)              %input command to return the 10th element of New_var
 ans =                   %command output
   10
Ind_Arr=[4,8,10];        %Index array variable
New_var1=New_var(Ind_Arr) %create new array from given index elements
                                of New_var
 New_var1 =              %returns the new array with three elements
    8    75    10
whos New_var1            %Input command
  Name          Size          Bytes  Class      Attributes
                                                %command output
  New_var1      1x3           24     double
```

Matrices

A matrix in MATLAB is a two-dimensional vector. A variable is classified as a matrix when it has multiple rows and multiple columns.

Creation of matrix and arithmetic operation on matrices

The comma "`,`" operator, and the semicolon "`;`" operators are used to create a matrix. Similar to the array variable matrix variable is also created only using an assignment operation and numbers enclosed with square braces "`[ ]`". The following code snippet explains how to create a simple matrix variable:

```
New_var=[1,2,3;4,5,6;7,8,9]                    %Input matrix
 New_var =                                     %Matrix output
    1    2    3
    4    5    6
    7    8    9
whos New_var                                   %Input command
  Name         Size         Bytes  Class      Attributes
  New_var      3x3          72     double     %command output
```

Similar to the arrays, elementwise arithmetic operations can be performed between two matrices of same dimensions. The following code demonstrates how to perform an arithmetic operation on matrices:

```
New_var= [1,2,3;4,5,6;7,8,9]                   %Input Matrix 1
 New_var =                                     %Returns Matrix 1
```

```
     1     2     3
     4     5     6
     7     8     9
New_var1= [11,12,13;14,15,16;17,18,19]            %Input Matrix 2
  New_var1 =                                      %Returns Matrix 2
    11    12    13
    14    15    16
    17    18    19
Add_Result=New_var+New_var1                       %Result Matrix
  Add_Result =                                    %Returns Add_Result matrix
    12    14    16
    18    20    22
    24    26    28
```

Access elements of a matrix

The user can easily access and retrieve the elements of a matrix using the following techniques:

- **Using row number and column number**: The syntax to get an element from the matrix using row number and column number is **variable(Row_number, Column_Number)**. Suppose variable **New_var** is a matrix of 3×3, that is, 3 rows and 3 columns and element at 3rd row and 2nd columns are required to be accessed then it could be done by executing command **New_var(3,2)**.

- **Using index number**: Similar to the array, an element from the matrix shall be accessed using the index number. MATLAB assigns indexing column-wise. That is, the element at Index 1 is the same as an element at Row 1 and Column 1, an element at Index 2 is the same as an element at Row 2, Column 1, and so on. Suppose **New_var** is a matrix of dimensions 3×3, then the element at Index 4 is the same as an element at Row 1 and Column 2.

- **Using an index array to retrieve multiple elements**: Similar to the array, multiple elements can be accessed from a matrix by creating an array of indexes.

- **Using colon ":" operator to retrieve rows and columns**: MATLAB provides an option to retrieve rows or columns from the matrix using the colon ":" operator. Suppose **New_var** is a matrix of dimensions 3×3, and we need to access all elements from the second row, then we need to run **New_var(2,:)** command. So the syntax is **variable(Row_Number,:)**. Here, the ":"

operator represents all column numbers. Similarly, if we need to access all elements from the second column, then we need to run the **New_var(:,2)** command. So the syntax is **variable(:,Column_Number)**. Here, ":" operator represents all row numbers. The following example shows how elements are retrieved from the matrix using different ways:

```
New_var=[9,5,7;8,97,56;34,75,90]      %creates a 3x3 Input matrix
 New_var =                            %returns the matrix
     9     5     7
     8    97    56
    34    75    90
Element_2_3=New_var(2,3)              %access element at 2nd row
                                          and 3rd column

 Element_2_3 =                        %returns the element
    56
Element_4=New_var(4)                  %access the 4th element of
                                          the matrix

 Element_4 =                          %returns the element
     5
Array_Index=[4,6,9];                  %create index array of 3
                                          elements

Elements=New_var(Array_Index)         %access index elements of
                                          matrix

 Elements =                           %returns the array with given
                                          elements
     5    75    90
Row_2=New_var(2,:)                    %access all elements of 2nd
                                          row

 Row_2 =                              %returns 2nd row
     8    97    56
column_2=New_var(:,2)                 %access all elements of 2nd
                                          column

 column_2 =                           %returns 2nd column
     5
    97
    75
```

Matrices and operators

MATLAB supports several operators to perform operations between matrices. These operators are classified mainly into two groups, arithmetic array operations, and matrix arithmetic operations.

Arithmetic array operations on matrices

Other than addition (**+**), subtraction (**-**), element-wise multiplication (**.***), and element-wise division (**./**), there are some more operators supported by MATLAB. *Table 3.1* explains about arithmetic array operators. All operators are explained, assuming X and Y are two matrices with the same dimensions.

Operator	Operation	Description
+	Element-wise addition	(X+Y) performs element-wise addition of X and Y
-	Element-wise subtraction	(X-Y) performs element-wise subtraction between X and Y
-	Unary operator minus	(-X) performs negation all elements of matrix X
.*	Element-wise multiplication	(X.*Y) performs element-wise multiplication between X and Y
./	Element-wise division	(X./Y) performs element-wise division between X and Y
.^	Element-wise power	(X.^Y) performs element-wise power operation between X and Y
.'	Transpose operation	(X.') performs transpose operation of X

Table 3.1: Arithmetic array operators

Matrix operations

MATLAB supports different types of matrix operation using operators. The *Table 3.2* describes different matrix arithmetic operators:

Operator	Operation	Description
*	Matrix multiplication	(X*Y) performs linear algebraic multiplication between X and Y. The number of columns in X must be identical to the number of rows in Y.

\	Matrix left division	(Z = X\Y) gives the solution of the matrix equation (XZ = Y). The number of rows must be identical in X and Y. For example, X is 3×3 matrix that contains $\begin{bmatrix} 8 & 1 & 6 \\ 3 & 5 & 7 \\ 4 & 9 & 2 \end{bmatrix}$ and Y is 3×1 matrix that contains $\begin{bmatrix} 15 \\ 15 \\ 15 \end{bmatrix}$, then Z= X\Y gives Z = $\begin{bmatrix} 1 \\ 1 \\ 1 \end{bmatrix}$. If we perform matrix multiplication X*Z that is, $\begin{bmatrix} 8 & 1 & 6 \\ 3 & 5 & 7 \\ 4 & 9 & 2 \end{bmatrix} * \begin{bmatrix} 1 \\ 1 \\ 1 \end{bmatrix}$. This multiplication returns Y = $\begin{bmatrix} 15 \\ 15 \\ 15 \end{bmatrix}$.
/	Matrix right division	(Z = Y/X) gives the solution of the matrix equation (ZX = Y). The number of columns must be identical in X and Y. For example, X is 3×3 matrix that contains $\begin{bmatrix} 8 & 1 & 6 \\ 3 & 5 & 7 \\ 4 & 9 & 2 \end{bmatrix}$ and Y is 1×3 matrix that contains then Z= Y\X gives Z = [1 1 1]. If we perform matrix multiplication Z*X that is , [1 1 1] * $\begin{bmatrix} 8 & 1 & 6 \\ 3 & 5 & 7 \\ 4 & 9 & 2 \end{bmatrix}$, the multiplication gives returns Y= [15 15 15].
^	Matrix power	X^Y performs X to the power "Y," that is, (XY). For example, Y is a scalar then; for other values of Y. eigenvalues and eigenvectors are considered.
'	Complex conjugate transpose	X' performs linear algebraic transpose of X.

Table 3.2: Arithmetic matrix operators

Matrix concatenation

MATLAB provides a straightforward way to perform matrix concatenation. The matrix concatenation is possible either row-wise or column-wise.

Row wise concatenation

The comma ",", operator, or space " " operator performs row-wise concatenation of matrices. For that, it is required to have the same row dimensions across all matrices taking part in the concatenation operation. Suppose matrices **New_var** and **New_var1** are of dimensions 2×2, then matrix concatenation can be done by running command **Concat_Result = [New_var,New_var1]** or **Concat_Result = [New_var New_var1]**. The following example shows the row-wise matrix concatenation:

```
New_var=[9,5;7,8]                              %creates array 1
  New_var =                                    %returns array 1
      9    5
      7    8
New_var1=[97,56;34,75]                         %creates array 2
  New_var1 =                                   %returns array 2
      97   56
      34   75
Concat_Result=[New_var,New_var1]               %Row-wise concatenation
  Concat_Result =                              %concatenation result
      9    5    97   56
      7    8    34   75
Concat_Result=[New_var New_var1]               %Row-wise concatenation,
  Concat_Result =                              %concatenation result, same
                                                  as above
      9    5    97   56
      7    8    34   75
whos Concat_Result                             %Input command
  Name              Size         Bytes    Class    Attributes
                                                   %command output

  Concat_Result     2x4          64       double
```

Column wise concatenation

The semicolon ";" operator performs column-wise concatenation of matrices. Fort that, it is required to have the same column dimensions across all matrices taking part in concatenation operation. Suppose matrices **New_var** and **New_var1** are of dimensions 2×2, then matrix concatenation can be done by running command **Concat_Result = [New_var;New_var1]**. The following code shows the column-wise matrix concatenation:

```
New_var=[9,5;7,8]                           %creates array 1
  New_var =                                 %returns array 1
      9    5
      7    8
New_var1=[97,56;34,75]                      %creates array 2
  New_var1 =                                %returns array 2
     97   56
     34   75
Concat_Result=[New_var;New_var1]            %Column-wise
                                               concatenation
  Concat_Result =                           %concatenation result
      9    5
      7    8
     97   56
     34   75
whos Concat_Result                          %Input command
  Name            Size         Bytes  Class  Attributes
                                                %Command output
  Concat_Result   4x2             64  double
```

Built-in functions and commands

Built-in functions are the predefined functions provided by MATLAB executables. MATLAB offers a wide range of these functions to make the programming more efficient. The functions are explained in MATLAB documentation, but there is no source file available for reference. These functions are executed either as a command or as a function using their syntaxes. Based on their utility, these functions are distributed into various categories and their subcategories. The chapter introduces some of the commonly used commands and functions with their syntax and examples when required. We recommend the readers to try these commands while learning them. The following sections cover some of the popular commands specific to the desktop environment:

Environment commands

The following commands are helpful to start and close the MATLAB session, to get information about the system and session, and to manage the ongoing session.

System commands

The following commands help the user to manage the system effectively:

- **matlab**: When this command is executed on the OS command prompt, it launches the MATLAB desktop app. The basic syntax for the command is as follows:

    `C:\>matlab              %starts MATLAB desktop application`

    This command also provides the possibility to provide command-line arguments as options to MATLAB. The command syntax to include the desired options is:

    `C:\>matlab option1...optionN    %multiple options are specified with - or /`

    Some examples of these command-line options for Windows platforms are as follows:

    `C:\>matlab -noFigureWindows %disables figure windows`

    `C:\>matlab -nosplash        %skips the splash screen during startup`

    `C:\>matlab -sd folder       %sets the work folder as the given path as a folder`

    `C:\>matlab -logfile name    %copies the command window results to name the file`

    `C:\>matlab -wait            %returns the existing status on the command prompt`

- **matlabroot**: This command, when run in the MATLAB command window, displays the full path of the MATLAB installation on the computer, as per the following example. It removes the dependency on knowing the exact installation path while programming.

    `matlabroot         %returns the string of full installation path`

    `ans = 'C:\Tools\MATLAB\R2019b'`

- **quit**: The command terminates the current MATLAB session. The command can be extended with further options. The syntax and options are:

    `quit        %closes MATLAB session, same as pressing the X button on the desktop`

    `quit force  %closes MATLAB immediately without executing finish.m script`

    `quit cancel %cancels quit operation, for script use`

    `quit(code)  %returns the MATLAB exit code as per the suggested value`

For a Windows-based system, a signed integer exit value is returned for—wait for option on start. For other OS, the exit code is returned by default between 0 and 255.

- **exit**: Same as quit, this command terminates the current MATLAB session. The options applicable for the quit command are applicable for the exit too. The syntax is as follows:

```
exit   %closes MATLAB session, same as quit or pressing X button on the desktop
```

- **startup**: startup is used to execute a user-defined script when MATLAB starts. For this, a **startup.m** script, which contains the series of commands to be executed during startup, is added to the folder available on the MATLAB search path. The command syntax is:

```
startup           %executes the startup.m file from MATLAB search path
which startup     %displays the startup.m file path, if found
 'startup' not found   %message is returned if no file is found
```

- **finish**: finish is used to execute a user-defined script when MATLAB terminates. For this, a **finish.m** script is placed in a folder available on the MATLAB search path. This script is used to perform a series of commands when the user executes the quit or exit command or presses **X** button. The command syntax is:

```
finish              %executes the finish.m file from MATLAB
                        search path
which finish        %displays the finish.m file path, if found
 'finish' not found   %this message is returned if no file is
                        found
```

- **version**: The command provides the version number and releases information for the MATLAB application where it is executed. When executed with one of the options, it provides information on the option. These options are:

```
version                    %displays the full release version with
                               release number
 ans = '9.7.0.1319299 (R2019b) Update 5'
version('-versionOption')          %function returns value of the
                                       version option
version -versionOption   %same as above, the following are the
                               version options
version -java or -release or -date or -description
```

- **ver**: This command is useful to know the version number of the installed MATLAB products and toolboxes. Execution of this command first displays MATLAB release version number, license number, Operating system version, and Java version and then lists all installed MATLAB products with their respective version numbers and release numbers. The different command options are as follows:

    ver   %displays the detailed version information of
                           MATLAB products

    MATLAB Version: 9.7.0.1319299 (R2019b) Update 5

    MATLAB License Number: xxxxxxxx

    Operating System: Microsoft Windows 10 Enterprise Version 10.0 (Build 17763)

    Java Version: Java 1.8.0_202-b08 with Oracle Corporation Java HotSpot(TM)

    64-Bit Server VM mixed mode

    MATLAB   Version 9.7   (R2019b)
    Simulink   Version 10.0   (R2019b)
    Stateflow   Version 10.1   (R2019b)

    ver product   %displays the version information for the mentioned
                          product name
    ver('Stateflow')   %function displays the version information of Stateflow

- **license**: This command provides the license number in use. It also has the option to display the list of licenses in the current session. The command syntax is as follows:

    license   %displays the license number
    license('inuse')   %function displays the list of licenses
                                 currently in use

- **pwd**: This command returns the current folder path as a character string, as shown in the following example:

    pwd %displays the current folder path, as seen in the current
             Folder browser
        ans ='C:\MATLAB19b' %example response, can be stored in a
                                  variable, e.g. currentfolder

- **path**: This command returns the list of folders on the MATLAB search path and provides to update the path as well. This search path is stored in a file named pathdef.m. As indicated in *Chapter 2: MATLAB Desktop Interface*, the paths are accessible through the **Set Path** dialog box available either in the **Environment** section of **Home** tab or using the command **pathtool**. The commands and various function options are as follows:

```
path                      %displays a list of all folders on the MATLAB
                              search path
path(newpath)             %MATLAB search path changes to the given
                              'newpath' path
path(oldpath,newfolder)   %'newfolder' folder is added at
                              the end of the existing search
                              path
addpath(folder1…folderN)  %adds multiple folders to the
                              search path
pathtool                  %launches the Set Path dialog box
```

- **cd**: This command returns the current working folder and gives the option to change the current folder too. The command syntax is as follows:

```
cd              %displays the current working folder path
 C:\MATLAB19b   %example response, can be stored in a variable
                    currentfolder
cd newfolder    %changes the current working folder to the
                    'newfolder' folder
```

- **dir**: This command displays the list of all files and folders in the current directory. It is also possible to get details of a particular directory. The syntax is as follows:

```
dir  %displays the list of all files and folders of the current
         working folder
dir mydir       %displays the list of all files and folders of
                    'mydir' folder
```

- **what**: This command displays the list of all files in the current working folder based on their types. It is also possible to get details of particular folder content. These filetypes are grouped as MATLAB code file, live code, SLX file, MLAPP file, MEX file, MAT file, P-file, classes, and packages. The syntax is as follows:

```
what    %displays the grouped list of the files of the current
            working folder
what mydir        %displays the grouped list of the files of
                      'mydir' folder
```

- **type**: This command displays the content of the specified file in the command window. We can specify the full path and extension too. It can display three types of files: **.m**, **.mlx**, and **.mlapp**. The command syntax is as follows:

  ```
  type filename          %displays the content of the file in the
                                  command window
  type diaryname         %example displays the content of the diary
                                  file
  ```

- **which**: This command returns the full path or the type of the specified item if the particular item is present in the MATLAB search path. In the case of functions, files, or Simulink models, it shows the full path. For variables or the new Simulink model, it shows the type of item. The command syntax and example are as follows:

  ```
  which myitem   %returns full path or type of the mentioned item,
                          for example:
  which which    %which is a built-in function, available in
                          toolbox directory
  built-in (full path) %shows full path of the MATLAB file for
                          which function
  which myvar            %where 'myvar' is a variable in the current
                                  folder
    myvar is a variable. %response message
  ```

Session commands

The following commands support the user to manage the ongoing session efficiently:

- **clc**: The command clears the command window. The command syntax is as follows:

  ```
  clc              %clears the text from the command window
  ```

- **clear**: The command clears the variables from the workspace. There are options to choose from to clear specific types. The command syntax and options are as follows:

  ```
  clear                  %clears all variables from the workspace
  clear name1...nameN    %clears all mentioned variables
  clear Itemtype         %clears specified type, where the following
                                  Itemtypes are:
  clear all or classes or functions or global or import or java or
  mex or variables
  ```

- **ans**: The command returns the latest value of the ans variable. ans variable holds the answer to the operation when no variable has been assigned a return value. ans value is specific to the Workspace. The command and example are:

  ans   %displays the answer to the latest command where no
               variable was assigned to return value 1+1
  ans= 2   %by default, the result of the operation is assigned
               to the ans variable

- **diary**: This command toggles the availability of the command window to the text file logging facility. All commands, user inputs as well as command window outputs are logged into the text file. If the file name or path has not been specified, then by default, an ASCII file named diary is created in the current working folder. The command syntaxes with options and examples are as follows:

  diary   %toggles logging operation on or off
  diary on   %enables the logging to diary file
  diary off   %disables the logging to diary file
  diary diaryname   %creates the text file with a given name at a
                     given path
  get(0,'Diary')   %function suggests if logging is 'off' or
                     'on'

- **home**: This command brings the cursor to the top-left corner of the command window. It gives an illusion of having a clear window without actually clearing it. The command syntax is as follows:

  home   %brings the cursor to the top-left corner in the
               command window

- **more**: This command enables the paging of the content displayed in the command window so that the content is displayed one page at a time. At the end of the current page, --more-- is displayed. At that time, press *space* key to go to the next page. To go to the next line, press *Return*. By default, paging is disabled. The command syntax with options is as follows:

  more on   %enables the paging of the output in the
               command window
  more off   %disables the paging of the output in the
               command window

- **exist**: This command is used to confirm if a variable, function, class, script, or folder with the given name exists. The command syntax with return value is as follows:

```
exist name    %returns a code value for the mentioned 'name' item,
                  for example
```
```
exist myitem %returns a value between 0-8 depending on the myitem
type, where
```
```
0- does not exist, 1- variable, 2- matlab file(code, live code,
app), 3- MEX file, 4- Simulink file, 5- built-in function, 6-P-Code
file, 7-folder , 8- Class
```

- **echo:** This command toggles the availability of the echoing feature during the execution of the functions. The echoing feature displays the function statements during execution. By default, the echo function is disabled. The command options are as follows:

    ```
    echo                  %toggles echoing operation on or off
    echo on               %enables the echo function
    echo off              %disables the echo function
    echo fcnname          %toggles echo function for the specified
                              function name
    get(0,'echo')         %function suggests if echoing is 'off' or
                              'on'
    ```

- **who:** This command displays the list of all available variables in the workspace.

    ```
    who               %displays the list of variables from the
                          current workspace
    who –file filename %displays the list of variables from the
                          specified file
    who global        %displays the list of variables from the
                          global workspace
    ```

- **whos**: This command displays the list of all available variables in the workspace, including their names, sizes, and types. The command syntax and options are as follows:

    ```
    whos                    %displays the list of variables in the
              workspace with names, sizes, Bytes, classes, attributes
    whos –file filename     %displays the names, sizes, Bytes, classes,
              attributes of variables from  the specified file
    whos global             %displays the names, sizes, Bytes,
              classes, attributesof variables from the global workspace
    ```

- **format**: The **format** command adjusts the format of the command window display, as already explained in this chapter. Two types of formatting are possible, numeric format and line spacing. By default, the numeric format type is short, which is a fixed-decimal format with four digits after the decimal point, whereas the default line spacing is loose. The command syntax with options and examples is as follows:

```
format      %sets the formatting to the default type: short, loose
            line spacing
```

```
format style       %sets the format style to the specified type,
                   for example
```

```
a=1.234567890123456789;
```

```
format short                    %sets display numeric
                                format to short

  a = 1.2346                    %4-digits after decimal
                                point

format long                     %sets the display format to
                                long

  a = 1.234567890123457         %all other format options
                                are:
Numeric format: short(4dig), long(16dig), shortE(5dig+exp),
longE(16dig+exp),shortG(total 5dig), long(total 15dig),
shortEng(4dig+exp),longEng(15dig+exp),+(pos, neg, 0), bank(2dig),
hex(hexadecimal), rat(rational)
Line spacing format: loose(normal), compact(suppress blank line)
get(0,'Format') and get(0,'Formatspacing')       %return the
                                                  current format
```

Help commands

The following commands are used to seek MATLAB help or documentation:

- **help**: The **help** command provides another way to access MATLAB help through the command window. The help text in the command window is an abbreviated version of the help documentation. The command syntax is as follows:

```
help             %displays the help text for the previously
                 executed command
help name        %displays help text for the name, which could be
                 a function, variable, class, method, toolbox, etc.
```

- **doc**: The **doc** command launches the Help browser and searches for the name if provided, then displays the detailed documentation reference page for the name. The command syntax is as follows:

```
doc       %launches the Help browser
```

```
doc name    %displays the documentation for the name, which could be
            a function, block or app
```

- **demo**: The **demo** command launches the Help browser and searches for the examples if the type or name is specified. The command syntax and options are as follows:

```
demo                    %opens the Examples tab in the Help browser
demo type               %opens the Examples list for the specified type
                            'matlab' or 'simulink'
demo type name          %opens the Examples for the specific name of
                            the specified type, the possible types are 'matlab',
                            'simulink', 'toolbox' , 'blockset'
echodemo filename       %runs the specified example script stepwise in
the command window
```

- **lookfor**: It is difficult to remember the exact names of the commands. **lookfor** command helps to find the exact command based on the description keywords. The command syntax and options are as follows:

```
lookfor keyword             %looks for the mentioned keyword in the
            first comment line in the help text of program files of a
            search path
lookfor keyword -all        %looks for the mentioned keyword in the
            first comment block in the help text of all files
```

Vectors, matrices, and arrays functions

The functions help perform the following groups of several array operations.

Create array functions

The following functions support creation of the arrays:

- **zeros**: This function creates an array of zeros based on the arguments. The function syntax with variations and their examples are as follows:

```
zeros                   %creates a scalar with value 0
zeros(n) %creates an n-by-n matrix with value 0 for all elements,
            for example
zeros(3)                %creates an 3-by-3 matrix with value 0
zeros(sz1, sz2,..szn)   %creates an array of 0 with sz1-by-sz2-
                            by...szn elements
```

```
zeros([sz1 sz2 .. szn])  %creates an array of 0 with sz1-by-sz2-
                                      by...szn elements,
for example
a=zeros(3,4)             %creates a matrix of 0 with 3-by-4 elements
b=zeros([4 7])           %creates a matrix of 0 with 4-by-7 elements
size(a) = 3 4            %size(a) command displays the dimensions of
                                      the matrix a
size(b) = 4 7            %as per the given size command, b is a
                                      matrix of 4-by-7
zeros(n, typename)       %creates an n-by-n matrix with value 0 of
                                      specified type, for example
zeros(2, 'int8')         %creates an 2-by-2 matrix with value 0 of
                                      type int8
```

Figure 3.7 shows examples of arrays created using **zeros** function:

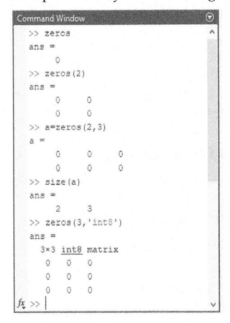

Figure 3.7: zeros command examples

- **ones**: Similar to **zeros** function, this function creates an array of ones based on the arguments. The function syntax with variations and their examples are as follows:

```
ones                     %creates a scalar with value 1
ones(n)    %creates an n-by-n matrix with value 1 for all elements,
```

```
    for example
    zeros(5)              %creates a 5-by-5 matrix with value 1
    ones(sz1, sz2,..szn)  %creates an array of 1 with sz1-by-sz2-by…
                                szn elements
    ones([sz1 sz2 .. szn]) %creates an array of 1 with sz1-by-sz2-by…
                                szn elements,
    for example
    a= ones(2,6)          %creates a matrix of 1 with 2-by-6 elements
    b= ones([4 7])        %creates a matrix of 1 with 4-by-7 elements
    size(a) = 2 6         %size(a) command displays the dimensions of
                                the matrix a
    size(b) = 4 7         %as per the given size command, b is a
                                matrix of 4-by-7
    ones(n, typename)     %creates an n-by-n matrix with value 1 of
                                the specified type, e.g.

    ones(3, 'int8')       %creates an 3-by-3 matrix with value 1 of
                                type int8
```

- **true**: Similar to **ones** function, this function creates an array of logical ones based on the arguments. The function syntax and examples are as follows:

```
    true              %creates a scalar of logical one
    true(n)           %creates an n-by-n matrix with logical ones for all
                            elements,
    for example
    true(4)           %creates a 4-by-4 matrix with logical value one
    true(sz_1,sz_2,..sz_n)  %creates an array of logical one with sz1-
                            by-sz2-by…sz_n dimensions, e.g.
    true(2,3)         %creates an array of 2-by-3 containing all logical
                            one elements
     ans =
         2×3 logical array
         1   1   1
         1   1   1
```

- **false**: Similar to the **true** function, this function creates an array of logical zeros based on the arguments. The function syntax and examples are as follows:

```
false       %creates a scalar with logical zero
false(n)    %creates an n-by-n matrix with logical zero elements,
                for example
false(7)    %creates a 7-by-7 matrix with logical value zero
false(sz_1,sz_2,..sz_n)    %creates an array of logical one with
                                sz1-by-sz2-by...sz_n dimensions
false([sz_1 sz_2 .. sz_n])    %where the argument command is a size
                                 vector of [sz_1,sz_2 .. sz_n]
```

- **rand**: This function creates an array of random numbers uniformly distributed within the interval of (0,1). The function syntax and examples are as follows:

```
rand                    %creates a single random number within the
                            interval(0,1)
rand(n)                 %creates an n-by-n matrix with random numbers,
                            for example
rand(3)                 %creates a 3-by-3 matrix with random number
                            elements
rand(sz_1,sz_2,..sz_n)    %creates random numbers array with
                             sz1-by-sz2-by...sz_n dimensions
rand([sz_1 sz_2 .. sz_n])    %where the argument command is a size
                                vector of [sz_1,sz_2 .. sz_n]
rand(3,4,5)             %creates a 3x4x5 random numbers
                            array
```

- **randn**: This function creates an array of normally distributed random numbers. The distribution has a mean value of 0 and a standard deviation of 1. The function syntax and examples are as follows:

```
randn        %creates a single random number from a normal
                distribution
randn(n)     %creates an n-by-n matrix with normally distributed
                random numbers
randn(sz_1,sz_2,..sz_n)    %creates random numbers array with sz1-
                               by-sz2-by...szn  dimensions
randn([sz_1 sz_2 .. sz_n])    %where the argument command is a
                                  size vector of[sz_1,sz2 .. sz_n]
randn(7,10,4)    %creates a 7x10x4 normally distributed random
                     numbers' array
```

- **randi**: Similar to **rand**, this function creates an array of pseudorandom integer numbers uniformly distributed within the specified interval.

    ```
    randi(max)   %creates a pseudorandom integer within the interval
                       [1, max]
    ```
    ```
    randi(max,n) %creates an n-by-n random integer matrix of value
                       within [1,max]
    ```
    ```
    randi(3,2)   %creates a 2x2 pseudorandom integer matrix of values
                       within [1,3]
    ```
    ```
    randi(max,sz1,sz2,..szn) %creates random int array with sz1-
    by…szn dimensions of values uniformly distributed in [1,max]
    interval, for example
    ```
    ```
    randi(2,3,4,5)  %creates a 3x4x5 random integer numbers' array of
    values[1,2]
    ```
    randi([min,max],sz_1,..sz_n) %creates an sz1-by-szn random integer matrix of values distributed within [min,max] interval

- **rng**: The preceding three **rand**, **randn**, and **randi** functions use a random number generator to generate the random array elements. They generate different results every time these functions are executed. The function **rng** returns the type of the generator. Suppose this return value is stored in a variable **x**. In that case, it is possible to restore the generator properties using **rng(x)** function so that the results of the functions are the same as the previous **rand**, **randi**, or **randn** execution, as shown in *figure 3.8*:

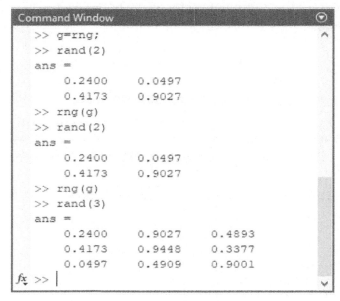

Figure 3.8: rand and rng function examples

- **eye**: This function performs the creation of the identity matrix, which has ones as the main diagonal elements and zero as the rest of the elements. The function syntax and examples are:

  ```
  eye                %creates a scalar with value one
  eye(n)     %creates an n-by-n matrix with value 1 on its main
                     diagonal, for example
  eye(3)             %creates a 3-by-3 matrix with diagonal value one and
                     others as 0
   ans =
       1     0     0
       0     1     0
       0     0     1
  eye(m,n) %creates an m-by-n matrix with value 1 on its main
                     diagonal, for example
  eye(2,3)           %creates a 2-by-3 matrix with diagonal value one and
                     others as 0
   ans =
       1     0     0
       0     1     0
  ```

- **diag**: This function performs the creation of the diagonal matrix, which has the elements of the argument vector as the main diagonal elements and zero as the rest of the elements. The syntax options are as follows:

  ```
  diag(a)            %creates an nxn matrix with values of n-element
                     vector a on the main diagonal
  diag(a)            %returns a column vector of n elements with values of
                     n-by-n diagonal matrix a
  diag(a,m)   %creates a square matrix with values of vector a, on
  the diagonalspecified by m, where main diagonal if m=0, m>0 then
  diagonal above main diagonal, m<0 then diagonal below the main
  diagonal
  ```

  Figure 3.9 contains some examples of **diag** function:

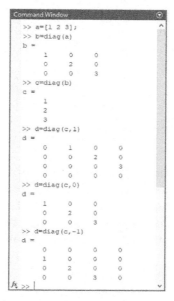

Figure 3.9: *diag function examples*

Combine array functions

The following functions support in combining the arrays:

- **cat**: The function **cat** concatenates the elements specified as arguments in the defined dimension. For concatenation of arrays, the length of arrays should match except in the dimension where the concatenation is required. For example, while concatenating two 2×2 matrices, if the dimension value is 1, the cat function converts the result into a 4×2 matrix. When the dimension is 2, it turns the result into a 2×4 matrix. The concatenation can also be performed using **[ ]** brackets. The function syntax and variations are as follows:

    cat(d,A,B)   %concatenates the arrays A and B in the dimension d.
                    For example

    cat(1,A,B)   %concatenates A with B into the first dimension, where d
                    is integer scalar

    [A,B] or [A B] %concatenates A with B horizontally

    [A;B]   %concatenates A with B vertically

    cat(d,A,B,C…)   %concatenates the multiple arrays A, B,C.. in the
                    dimension d

- **horzcat**: Similar to **cat**, the function **horzcat** concatenates the elements specified as arguments horizontally. For concatenation of the arrays, the length of the arrays must match except in the second dimension. The concatenation can be performed using elements separated by space or comma in square `[ ]` brackets. The function syntax and variations are:

```
horzcat(A,B)           %concatenates the arrays A and B
                           horizontally
[A,B] or [A B]         %concatenates A with B horizontally
horzcat(A,B,C…) %concatenates multiple arrays A,B,C.. in the
second dimension
```

- **vertcat**: Similar to **horzcat**, the function **vertcat** concatenates the elements specified as arguments vertically. For concatenation of the arrays, the length of the arrays must match except in the first dimension. The concatenation can be performed using elements separated by a semicolon (;) in square `[ ]` brackets. The function syntax and variation are as follows:

```
vertcat(A,B)           %concatenates the arrays A and B
                           vertically
[A;B]                  %concatenates A with B vertically
vertcat(A,B,C…)        %concatenates the multiple arrays A,B,C.. in
                           the first dimension
```

- **repmat**: This function creates a repeated array of the source array based on the specified repetition number. For example, suppose an array A has dimensions of 2×2, and the repetition number is 3. In that case, the resultant array will have dimensions of 6×6, with three times the repetition of elements of array A horizontally as well as vertically. The function syntax is as follows:

```
repmat(A,n)   %creates an array by creating n copies of array A by
multiplying the dimensions of A by n
```

Figure 3.10 shows some examples of the previous functions:

```
Command Window
>> A=[1 2;3 4];B=[5 6;7 8];
>> cat(1,A,B)
ans =
     1     2
     3     4
     5     6
     7     8
>> cat(2,A,B)
ans =
     1     2     5     6
     3     4     7     8
>> horzcat(A,B)
ans =
     1     2     5     6
     3     4     7     8
>> vertcat(A,B)
ans =
     1     2
     3     4
     5     6
     7     8
>> repmat(A,2)
ans =
     1     2     1     2
     3     4     3     4
     1     2     1     2
     3     4     3     4
fx >>
```

Figure 3.10: *cat function examples*

Grid functions

The following functions support the creation of vectors and grids:

- **linspace**: The function **linspace** creates linearly spaced vectors within a specified range, including boundary points. By default, the spaced elements are 100 unless specified. The output of the linspace function is similar to the colon (:) operator. The following are the function syntax and examples:

    linspace(x,y)   %creates a row vector of linearly spaced
                            100 elements between x and y, e.g.

    linspace(-10,10) %creates a row vector of linearly spaced 100
                            elements between -10 and 10

    linspace(x,y,n)   %creates a row vector of linearly spaced
                            n elements between x and y, e.g.

    linspace(0,5,5)   %creates a row vector of linearly spaced
                            5 elements between 0 and 5

- **meshgrid**: The function **[X,Y]=meshgrid(x,y)** creates 2D grids X and Y of dimension y-by-x of repetitive elements of row vectors x and y with the respective lengths **x** and **y**. X has repetitive elements of x in a row, and Y has repetitive elements of y in columns. **[X, Y, Z] =meshgrid(x,y,z)** is similar but with 3D grids X, Y, and Z having dimensions y-by-x-by-z for x,y, and z row vectors. The function syntax and variation are as follows:

```
meshgrid(x,y)       %creates a y-by-x grid with elements of x
                        repeated in y rows

[X,Y]=meshgrid(x,y)     %returns 2-D grids of y-by x dimensions,
where X has elements of x repeated in all rows, Y has elements of
y repeated in all columns

[X,Y,Z]=meshgrid(x,y,z)  %returns 3-D grids of y-by-x-by-z
                          dimensions, where

X has elements of x repeated in all rows, Y has elements of y
repeated in

all columns, Z has elements of z repeated in all elements
```

Array size, shape, order functions

The following functions determine the size, shape, and order of the vectors, matrix, and arrays:

- **size**: The function **size** is used to find the size of the array. It returns a row vector with the elements the same as the dimensions of the input array. The function syntax and example are:

  ```
  size(x) %returns a row vector with the dimension lengths of x as
              its elements
    ans =   %here the answer is a row vector for X, which is a 5-by-
              3-by-7 array
        5   3   7
  ```

- **length**: The function **length** returns the length of the largest dimension of the input array as an integer. The function syntax and example are as follows:

  ```
  length(x)       %returns an integer with the maximum value of
                      the dimension length of x
  ans =           %the answer is a 7 for x, which is a 5-by-3-
                      by-7 array
      7
  max(size(x))    %provides the results 7, which is same as
                      length function
  ```

- **numel**: The function **numel** returns the number of elements in the input array. The function syntax and example are as follows:

    ```
    numel(x)     %returns an integer with the total number of
                            elements of array x
     ans = 4     %the answer is a 4 for x, which is a 2-by-2 array
    ```

- **is***: The **is*** functions return a logical value of one or zero depending on the type of the input. The type could be scalar, vector, matrix, row, column, and empty. The return value shall be logical 1 if the function type matches with the input type; else, the return value shall be logical 0.

Table 3.3 explains the functions used to confirm the type of input:

Function	Use
isscalar(A)	True if the input A is a scalar with a 1×1 dimension
isvector(B)	True if the input B is a vector with n×1 or 1×n dimensions, $n >= 0$
ismatrix(C)	True if input C is a matrix with n×m dimensions, where $n, m >= 0$
issorted(D)	True if input D has the elements in ascending or descending order
isrow(E)	True if input E is a 1×n row vector, that is, the number of rows=1
Iscolumn(F)	True if input F is an n×1 column vector, that is, the number of columns=1
isempty(G)	True if the array is empty

Table 3.3: Array is functions*

Array reshape, resize functions

The following functions modify the size and shape of the arrays:

- **sort**: The function **sort** returns the sorted array of elements specified as the input. We can also specify the direction and dimension for the sort operation. The function syntax and example are as follows:

    ```
    sort(x)              %returns the array of sorted elements of x,
                            by default the order is ascending, where
    x=[9 3 6; 4 -2 5];
    ```

```
ans = 4    -2     5     %the array elements are sorted in
                              ascending order

        9     3     6
```

- **flip**: As the name suggests, the function **flip** flips the order of the array elements but retains the size of the array. The function syntax and example are as follows:

```
flip(A)         %returns the array of flipped elements of array A,
                    for example

A=[1 2;3 4];    %A is a 2x2 matrix

 ans =          %flip(A) function changes the order of the elements

    3    4
    1    2
```

- **transpose**: The **transpose** function interchanges the elements of rows and columns for the input array. Transpose can also be performed using the (.') operator. The function syntax and example are as follows:

```
transpose(A)    %returns the array of flipped elements of array A,
                    for example

A=[1 2;3 4];    %A is a 2x2 matrix.

transpose(A)    %The transpose interchanges the rows and columns
                    of the array

A.'             %Same as transpose(A)

 ans =
    1    3
    2    4
```

- **reshape**: This function **reshape** the input array by rearranging the elements into the specified arguments. The function syntax and example are as follows:

```
reshape(A,r,c) or   %returns the array A reshaped into rxc
dimensions

reshape(A,[r c])    %size vector of the desired dimensions can be
                        provided to the function

A= [1 2;3 4;5 6];   %A is a 3x2 matrix.

reshape(A,[2 3])    %Reshape rearranges the elements into 2x3
                        array

 ans =
    1    5    4
    3    2    6
```

Linear algebra matrix functions

The following functions support Matrix operations to solve linear algebra problems:

- **inv**: The inverse function returns the inverse of the specified square matrix. The function is equivalent to **x^(-1)** operation. A matrix, when multiplied by the inverse matrix, results in an identity matrix. These are the function syntax and examples:

  ```
  inv(x)              %returns the inverse matrix of x , for example
  x=[2 -6 8;-2 4 7;9 1 -5];   %where x is 3x3 square matrix
    ans =
        0.0399    0.0325    0.1095
       -0.0784    0.1213    0.0444
        0.0562    0.0828    0.0059
  ```

- **mtimes**: The **mtimes** function multiplies two matrices. It is equivalent to matrix product operator *****. For matrix multiplication, the column number of the first matrix is the same as row number of the second matrix, and the result shall have the number of rows of the first matrix and the number of columns of the second matrix. Each resultant matrix element is the summation of the products of elements in that row of the first matrix with elements in that column of the second matrix. The function syntax is as follows:

  ```
  mtimes(A,B) or A*B    %returns the matrix multiplication of A and B
  ```

- **mpower**: The **mpower** function returns A to the power B. It is equivalent to power operator **^**. For the operation, matrix A should be square, and power B should be a scalar. The function syntax is as follows:

  ```
  mpower(A,B) or A^B    %returns the matrix A to the power B
  ```

- **sqrtm**: This function returns the principle square root of the matrix. If matrix A has eigenvalues with negative real parts, the resultant matrix has complex numbers. A warning is displayed for the singular matrix. The function syntax is as follows:

  ```
  sqrtm(A)          %returns the principle square root of the matrix A
  ```

- **dot**: This function returns the scalar dot product for the given arrays. They must be of the same size. It treats the arrays as a collection of vectors. If the inputs to the function are vectors, the dot product produces a scalar result. In the case of a matrix, for example, of size 3, it shall produce a vector of three elements. The function syntax and example are as follows:

  ```
  dot(A,B)          %returns the dot products of A and B, for example
  ```

```
A=[1 2 3]; B=[4 5 6];
ans=32                    %ans=A1B1+A2B2+A3B3
```

- **cross**: This function returns the cross product for the given arrays. They must be of the same size. It treats the arrays as a collection of vectors. Whether the inputs to the function are vectors or multidimensional arrays, the cross product produces the result of the same size. In the case of vectors, the resultant vector is perpendicular to the input vectors. The function syntax and example are as follows:

```
cross(A,B)                %returns the cross products of A and B,
                           for example

A=[1 2 3];B=[4 5 6];
ans=  -3    6    3        %ans=A2B3-A3B2   A3B1-A1B3   A1B2-A2B1
```

- **det**: This function returns the determinant of the matrix. The matrix must be a square numeric matrix. The function syntax and example are as follows:

```
det(A)                    %returns the determinant of matrix A,
                           for example

A=[1 3 5;2 4 6;7 9 1];
ans=  20                  %ans=A1(B2C3-B3C2)+ B1(C2A3-
                           C3A2)+C1(A2B3-A3B2)
```

- **rank**: This function returns the rank of the matrix. The number of linearly independent columns determines the rank of the matrix. The rank of a matrix is the same as the size of the matrix; then, the matrix is full rank; else, it is rank deficient. The function syntax and example are as follows:

```
rank(A)                   %returns the rank of the matrix A,
                           where

A = [1 3 5;2 4 6;7 9 1];  %row 1 and 2 are linearly dependent
ans = 2                   %ans=2, as the row 2 elements are twice
                           those of row 1
```

- **trace**: This function returns the sum of the diagonal elements of the matrix. It must be a square matrix. The function syntax and example are as follows:

```
trace(A)                  %returns the sum of diagonal elements
                           of A, where

A=[1 3 5;2 4 6;7 9 1];
ans=  6                   %ans= A1 +B1 + C1
```

- **eig**: This function returns a column vector of eigenvalues of the matrix. It must be a square matrix. The function syntax is as follows:

    ```
    eig(A)              %returns the eigenvalue of the matrix A as a
                           column vector
    ```

String and character array functions

String array and character array functions support various operations on the text data. Character vector holds character sequences as a row of characters stored in a separate element, specified with single quotation marks. In contrast, a string array holds a text string as a single element, specified with double quotation marks. These array functions perform specific types of following operations.

Create, modify, and combine functions

The following functions support the creation, editing, and concatenation of character and string arrays.

- **Create character array**: We can specify the character string with single quotation marks and assign it to a variable. This way, a character array can be created. The example character array and the result of whose command for the character array are:

    ```
    chA='I love MATLAB'     %creates a character array of 1x13
                               which holds the assigned text
    whos ChA                %displays the character array
                               information
        Name       Size         Bytes    Class     Attributes
        ChA        1x13         26       char
    ```

- **Create a string array**: We can specify the character string with double quotation marks and assign it to a variable. This way, a string array can be created, as shown in the following example:

    ```
    StrA="I love MATLAB"   %creates a string array of 1x1 which holds
                              assigned text
    whos StrA              %displays the character array information
        Name       Size         Bytes    Class     Attributes
        StrA       1x1          166      string
    ```

- **char**: This function converts the specified array into a character array. The function syntax and example are as follows:

```
char(A)            %converts array A into a character array, for
                     example
StrA="MATLAB"; ChA=char(StrA);
ChA='MATLAB'       %converts string array StrA to character array
                     ChA
```

- **string**: This function converts the specified array into a string array. The function syntax and example are as follows:

```
string(A)          %converts array A into a string array, for
                     example
ChA='MATLAB'; StrA=string(ChA);
StrA="MATLAB"      %converts char array ChA to string array StrA
```

- **join**: This function joins the consecutive elements in the string array with space or specified delimiter. The function syntax and example are as follows:

```
join(str)                        %joins elements of the string str,
                                   for example
AuthorName=["Priyanka", "Patankar";    %creates a 2x2 string array
           "Swapnil", " Kulkarni";];
join(AuthorName)
 ans =   2×1 string array         %the respective row
                                    elements are joined
       "Priyanka Patankar"
       "Swapnil Kulkarni"
```

- **strcat**: This function horizontally concatenates character, string or cell arrays. The resulting datatype shall be same as input datatype. In case of a character array, the function shall remove white spaces while concatenating. The function syntax and example are as follows:

```
strcat(str1, str2,..strN) %horizontally concatenates strings
                            1..N, for example
str1="BPB";str2="Publications";
strcat(str1,Str2)          %concatenates given strings without
                            space
 ans = "BPBPublications"
```

- **append**: This function combines the character, string, or cell arrays in the given order. The resulting datatype shall be the same as the input datatype. Unlike "**strcat**" function, "**append**" preserves the white spaces in character arrays. It is equivalent to **+** operator. The function syntax and example are as follows:

```
append(str1, str2,..strN)    %combines  string 1..N, for example
                                 str1='BPB '; str2='Publications';
append(str1,Str2)            %combines given character vectors
 ans = 'BPB Publication      %white space from the first vector is
                                 preserved
```

- **reverse**: As the name suggests, the function reverses the character order of the specified string. The function syntax and example are as follows:

```
reverse(str)                 %reverses the characters in the string,
                                 for example
str=["BPB", "Publications"]
 ans = "BPB" "snoitacilbuP"            %reversed the characters of
                                           the string
```

- **upper, lower**: These functions convert the string to uppercase or lowercase. The function syntaxes are as follows:

```
upper(str)                   %converts the string str characters to the
                                 uppercase
lower(str)                   %converts the string str characters to the
                                 lowercase
```

- **split**: The function splits the string into substrings after the white space or specified delimiter. The result array type is the same as an input array type. The white space or delimiter shall be removed from the resultant string. The function syntax and example are as follows:

```
split(str)                   %converts the string str to the substrings,
                                 for example
str="Happy Birthday"; %The input is a 1x1 string array.
 ans=  "Happy"
       "Birthday"    %The output is a 2x1 string array.
```

Type and properties functions

The following functions suggest the type and properties of the arrays:

- **is***: The **is*** functions return a logical value of one or zero depending on the nature of the input. The type could be character array, cell array of characters, string array, and scalar string array. The return value shall be logical 1 if the function type matches with the input type; else, the return value shall be logical 0.

Table 3.4 explains the functions used to confirm the type of input:

Function	Use
ischar(A)	True if the input A is a character array
iscellstr(B)	True if the input B is a cell array of a character vector
isstring(C)	True if input C is a string array
isStringScalar(D)	True if input D is a string array containing a single element

Table 3.4: character array is* functions

- **strlength**: The function returns the total number of characters for a character or string array. In case of a string array, it returns an array, where each element provides the number of characters in the respective string. The function syntax and example are as follows:

```
strlength(str)      %provides the number of characters in str,
                        for example
str='The world is beautiful';
 ans= 22            %str is a character vector with 22 elements
str2=["The","world";"is","beautiful";]; strlength(str2);
 ans= 3    5       %str2 is a string array with 4 elements of
                        given lengths
        2    9
```

Find, replace and remove functions

The following functions perform string find, replace, and remove operations:

- **Find**: The following set of functions from *table 3.5* perform the find operation by returning the logical value 1 (true) if the pattern matches with the text data:

Function	Use
contains(str, pattern)	True if the string contains the pattern
matches(str, pattern)	True if the string matches the pattern
endsWith(str, pattern)	True if the string ends with the pattern
startsWith(str, pattern)	True if the string starts with the pattern

Table 3.5: String find functions

- **strfind, count**: These functions suggest the occurrences if the pattern matches with the string text. Count returns the total number of pattern occurrences in a string, whereas **strfind** searches for strings within strings and returns an array of all the character number of the occurrences. The function syntaxes are as follows:

    ```
    strfind(str,pattern)    %provides the array of all pattern
                                        occurrences in the string
    count(str,pattern)      %provides the number of all pattern
                                        occurrences in the string
    ```

- **strrep**: The function replaces from a string the occurrences of the old substring with the new substring. The function syntax is as follows:

    ```
    strrep(str,old,new)   %replaces all the old occurrences with the
                                     new substring
    ```

- **erase**: The function erases from a string all the occurrences of the pattern. The function syntax is as follows:

    ```
    erase(str,match)         %erases all the pattern occurrences
                                        from string str
    ```

- **strcmp**: The following functions return the logical value 1 (true) if the input strings match. In the case of a character vector or scalar string, the output is a logical value, whereas, in the case of a string array or cell array of character vector, the result is a logical array.

Function	Use
strcmp(str1,str2)	True if str1 and str2 are identical, case sensitive
strcmpi(str1,str2)	True if str1 and str2 are identical, case insensitive
strncmp(str1,str2,n)	True if the first n characters of the strings are identical, case sensitive
strncmpi(str1,str2,n)	True if the first n characters of the strings are identical, case insensitive

Table 3.6: String compare functions

Operators

In MATLAB, there are three types of operators: arithmetic operators, relational operators, and logical operators.

Arithmetic operations

The following operators and their functions support arithmetic operations on scalars and arrays, provided their sizes are compatible:

Operation	Function	Use	Inputs	Output
A+B	plus(A,B)	Addition of A with B	A=[1 4; 7 9]; B=[2 6; 5 4];	3 10 12 13
A-B	minus(A,B)	Subtraction of B from A	A=[15 23; 75 -116]; B=[70 100; 67 42];	-55 -77 8 -158
A.*B	times(A,B)	Multiplication of A and B	A=[2 4]; B=[3;5];	6 12 10 20
A.^B	power(A,B)	A raised to the power of B	A=[2 4]; B=3;	8 64
+A	Uplus	Unary plus operation on A	A=[5 -3; 4 -7]	5 -3 4 -7
-A	uminus	Unary minus operation on A	A=[5 -3; 4 -7]	-5 3 -4 7

Table 3.7: Arithmetic operations

Rounding and division operations

The following arithmetic functions support the division and rounding operations:

Function	Use
idivide(A,B)	Performs integer division of elements of A by B with an option of rounding
Mod	Result is the remainder after division; the result has sign of B
Rem(A,B)	Result is the remainder after division; the result has sign of A
ceil(A)	Each element of A is rounded to the nearest integer greater, which is greater than or equal to the element
fix(A)	Each element of A is rounded to the nearest integer toward zero; the output is same as floor (A) for positive integers, and ceil (A) for negative integers

floor(A)	Each element of A is rounded to the nearest integer, which is less than or equal to the element
round(A)	Each element of A is rounded to the nearest integer

Table 3.8: Rounding operations

Relational operations

The following functions return the logical value 1 (true) if the relation is fulfilled; else, they return logical value 0 (false). Depending on the type of the operands, the output type changes. In the case of scalars, the output shall be the logical value, whereas, for the vectors and arrays, the output shall be a logical array. The size of inputs in the case of vectors and arrays must be the same or compatible.

Operation	Function	Use
A==B	eq(A,B)	True if the input A is equal to input B
A~=B	ne(A,B)	True if input A is not equal to input B
A>B	gt(A,B)	True if input A is greater than input B
A>=B	ge(A,B)	True if the input A is greater than or equal to input B
A<B	lt(A,B)	True if the input A is less than input B
A<=B	le(A,B)	True if the input A is less than or equal to input B

Table 3.9: Relational operations

Logical operations

MATLAB provides the following logical functions to perform logical operations. Depending on the type of the operands, the output type changes. In the case of scalars, the output shall be a scalar, whereas, for the arrays, the output shall be an array. The size of inputs in the case of vectors and arrays must be the same or compatible.

Operation	Function	Use
A & B	and(A,B)	Logical AND operation of A and B
A | B	or(A,B)	Logical OR operation of A and B
A && B		Logical AND of A and B with short circuit behavior

A || B		Logical OR of A and B with short circuit behavior
~A	not(A)	Logical NOT operation of A
	xor(A,B)	Logical XOR operation of A and B

Table 3.10: Logical operations

Operator precedence

During the evaluation of various combination expressions, operator precedence decides the order of evaluation. *Table 3.11* suggests the operator precedence for different arithmetic, logical, and relational operations:

Precedence	Operator	Operation
1	( )	Parentheses
2	.' , '	Transpose, Complex Conjugate Transpose
	.^ , ^	Power, Matrix Power
3	+ , -	Unary plus, Unary minus
	~	Logical negation
4	.* , *	Multiplication, Matrix multiplication
	./ , .\	Right division, Left division
	/ , \	Matrix right division, Matrix left division
5	+ , -	Addition, Subtraction
6	:	Colon operator
7	< , <=	Less than, Less than, or equal to
	> , >=	Greater than, Greater than or equal to,
	==, ~=	Equal to, Not equal to
8	&	Element-wise AND
9	|	Element-wise OR
10	&&	Short-circuit AND
11	||	Short-circuit OR

Table 3.11: Operator precedence

> Here we have explained the most commonly used operators. For the extensive list of all functions supported by MATLAB, please visit https://www.mathworks.com/help/matlab/referencelist.html.

Important links

These are the important links specified in this chapter:

- For detailed categorization and explanation of data types supported by MATLAB:

    https://www.mathworks.com/help/matlab/data-types.html

- For an overall list and description of MATLAB functions with examples:

    https://www.mathworks.com/help/matlab/referencelist.html

Conclusion

We have discussed in detail the MATLAB Desktop interface in the previous chapter. The command window shortcuts make life easier for the readers, which will be helpful in executing commands. Variables and data types are the basic building blocks of MATLAB, and this chapter lays the foundation of MATLAB for novice readers. On this foundation, this chapter builds a strong platform with the help of functions and commands offered by MATLAB. Different syntaxes and examples reinforce these learnings to make the reader prepared for MATLAB programming. Based on this chapter, the upcoming chapter will throw insight into several programming aspects such as programming flow control, scripts, live scripts, as well as user-defined functions. The upcoming chapter also describes various visualization tools, for example, plots, graphs, and images.

Points to remember

- MATLAB provides various handy ways to work with command windows, such as execution of multiple commands in a single command line, use of arrow keys to access commands from command history, and so on.
- Variables names must follow the naming conventions.
- Variables are classified based on their classes (datatypes) and sizes.
- MATLAB offers several techniques to access elements from the vectors.
- Arithmetic operations on matrices are classified primarily into arithmetic array operations and matrix arithmetic operations.
- MATLAB offers a huge set of built-in functions and commands, which makes the programming more efficient.

- In this chapter, the function categories such as environment commands, vectors, matrices and arrays functions, string and character array functions, and operators are explained.

- Operator precedence decides the execution order while dealing with the combination of arithmetic, logical, and relational operations.

Multiple choice questions

1. Which of the following keys are used to navigate through the previously executed commands?

    a. Up and down keys

    b. Right and left keys

    c. Shift

    d. Ctrl+CapsLock

2. Which of the following options is a valid variable name?

    a. _abc

    b. 123_abc

    c. abc$123

    d. abc_123

3. Which of the following is not a valid numeric type?

    a. double

    b. single

    c. triple

    d. uint8

4. Which of the following is a valid declaration of a string variable?

    a. newvar='Hello World';

    b. newvar="Hello World";

    c. newvar='Hello World";

    d. newvar="Hello World';

5. Which of the following operators is not used to perform matrix operation?
    a. *
    b. +
    c. -
    d. &

6. Which of the following command is not described as a system command?
    a. clc
    b. matlbroot
    c. startup
    d. finish

7. Which of the following options do not result into an array of 5 1s?
    a. [1 1 1 1 1]
    b. newvar=ones(5)
    c. ones(1,5)
    d. newvar(1:5)=1

8. Which of the following options are used to concatenate horizontally?
    a. [A;B]
    b. [A,B]
    c. horzcat(A,B)
    d. B and C

9. What is the result of the command strfind("Today is a holiday", "Day");?
    a. 3 16
    b. []
    c. 1
       4
    d. None of the above

10. What is the output of the following operation?
    P=5; Q=15; R=-10; S=1; P*R*(Q/P-2*R+S);
    a. -6450
    b. 90
    c. -1200
    d. None of the above

Questions

1. What are the differences between the syntax of MATLAB commands and functions?
2. Explain the naming conventions for the variable.
3. What is the difference between a cell array and a structure?
4. Explain the difference between strings and character arrays.
5. How are the variables classified based on their sizes?
6. What are the ways to retrieve the elements of the arrays?
7. How to verify whether the variable name is in use as an existing built-in function?
8. Which command displays the content of .m file?
9. Which command retrieves the name of the command based on the description?
10. What is the difference between dot and cross-product operation? Explain with an example of 3×1 and 1×3 vectors.
11. Explain all matrix arithmetic operation functions with at least two examples each.
12. How can we generate similar outputs for the rand function?
13. Explain three built-in functions to combine the strings.
14. Explain the rounding operations with examples.

Answers

1. a
2. d
3. c
4. b
5. d
6. a
7. b
8. d
9. b
10. c

CHAPTER 4
Programming Basics, Control Flow and Visualization

Introduction

In the previous chapter, the reader has learnt the built-in functions and commands, variables, and built-in classes (types); and they have been introduced to the concept of scalars, vectors, matrices, and arrays. With this knowledge as a base, this chapter continues toward building the basic concepts of programming. With the help of examples, this chapter explains the creation of scripts, user-defined functions, and live scripts. The reader shall also learn to debug a MATLAB program. Then the focus of this chapter shifts to the second part, which is control flow. In this section, the reader shall learn to control the program flow using loops and conditional statements such as if-else, switch-case, while, and for.

A picture speaks more than a thousand words, and to realize it, MATLAB offers a powerful infrastructure in terms of visualization. MATLAB provides a wide range of graphics functions for 2-D and 3-D plots, graphs, charts, images, and so on. For the ease of the users, MATLAB also offers an interactive tool for effortless plotting. With the help of both functions and the tool, a user can create, modify, save and export the plots and images. Topics of plots and images are enormous, but in this chapter, we have tried to provide a basic idea of the working of plots and images with the help of some examples. The user can follow our directions and later gain more knowledge by self-practice.

Structure

In this chapter, we shall discuss the following topics:

- Scripts and functions
    - Scripts
    - Functions
    - Debug MATLAB program
    - Live scripts
- Control programming flow
- Visualization
    - Plots
        - Functions method
        - Interactive method
    - Images

Objectives

After studying this chapter, the reader will be able to:

- Learn the basics of programming using scripts, functions, and live scripts
- Learn how to debug a program
- Understand the control of programming flow
- Know the concepts of 2-D and 3-D plots
- Get introduced to the different types of images and image operations using functions

Scripts and functions

Until now, we have been able to comprehend how we can execute a sequence of commands or chunk of code in the command window. However, there may be a situation where we need to save the command sequence into a file and execute it as and when required.

Scripts

Scripts are simple MATLAB program files. These files are stored with .m file extension. .m files are text files that are executable in the MATLAB environment. Scripts contain a sequence of commands that can be executed in the command window. Variables created in scripts are stored in the base Workspace; similarly, variables available in the base workspace can be directly used in scripts. All variables, which are created using a command window or scripts, are stored in the base workspace. In *Chapter 2: MATLAB Desktop Interface*, the section editor can be referred to get more information on how to start with scripts. Let us write a script to display the area and perimeter of a circle. The mathematical formula to find out the area of the circle is πr^2, and the formula to find out the perimeter of the circle is $2\pi r$, where **r** is the radius of the circle. *Figure 4.1* shows the file **circleOperations.m** containing the code of the script that finds out the area and perimeter of the circle. We shall represent π with the in-built constant **pi**:

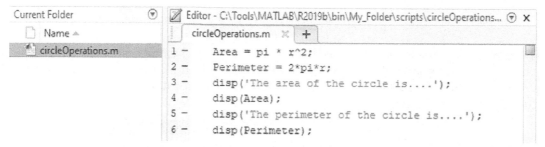

Figure 4.1: Script to do circle operations

To run the script, we can either simply type the name of the script in the command window followed by entering the key or drag and drop the script from the current folder browser to the command window. When we drag and drop .m file to the command window, then MATLAB executes **run** with the full path of the m-file. In script **circleOperation.m** we have not created variable **r**; hence, it is a must-have variable **r** already created in base Workspace. If variable **r** is not present in the workspace, then script execution stops with an error. *Figure 4.2* shows how to execute script and error when required variables are not available already in the base Workspace. In *Chapter 2: MATLAB Desktop Interface* section *Editor* also explains how to start with functions:

```
Command Window
>> circleOperations
Unrecognized function or variable 'r'.

Error in circleOperations (line 1)
Area = pi * r^2;

>> run('C:\Tools\MATLAB\R2019b\bin\My_Folder\scripts\circleOperations.m')
Unrecognized function or variable 'r'.

Error in circleOperations (line 1)
Area = pi * r^2;

Error in run (line 91)
evalin('caller', strcat(script, ';'));
```

Figure 4.2: *Execute script in the command window, and an error when required variables are not created*

Therefore, it is must to create a variable **r** with the desired value before executing the script. *Figure 4.3* shows the sequence of variable creation and then execution of the script. It also shows that after running the script, variables `Area` and `Perimeter` are stored in base Workspace:

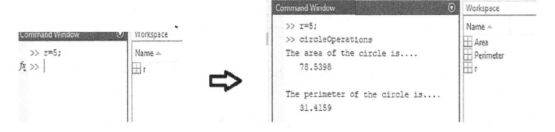

Figure 4.3: *Execute the script in the command window after creating the variable "r."*

Constants available in MATLAB

These are some of the generally used constants in MATLAB explained in *table 4.1*:

Constants	Usage
Pi	Equivalent of π
Inf	Infinity
Eps	Floating-point relative accuracy
NaN	Not a number

Constants	Usage
`Intmin`	Integer type smallest value
`Intmax`	Integer type largest value

Table 4.1: *Commonly used MATLAB constants*

Functions

Functions are also MATLAB program files, and these files are also stored with **.m** file extension. The Functions are different from scripts. They do not use variables from base Workspace; in fact, they do have their own workspace. This workspace is called a function Workspace. Function Workspace is active only until the time function is being executed. Once function execution is finished, all variables created inside the function will be destroyed from memory. The function does have a provision to pass arguments during function calls.

Furthermore, these arguments are used as internal variables of the called function. Let us write a function for the same operations to find out the area and perimeter of a circle. However, here we will pass radius **r** as an argument of the function. Required results will be returned by the functions. Therefore, the variable **r** is not required to be already created in base Workspace. **Area** and **Perimeter** will be returned by the function. *Figure 4.4* explains how to write a function to find out the area and perimeter of a circle and how to execute the same using the command window:

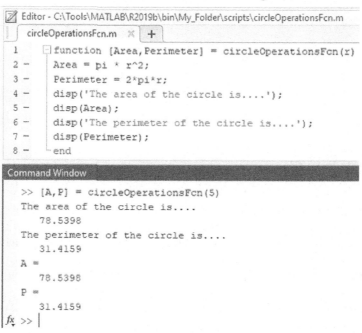

Figure 4.4: *Function execution*

The way functions are called in the command window, in the same manner, it is possible to call functions from other scripts or other functions. MATLAB functions support the recurrence phenomenon, meaning function can be called within itself.

Debug MATLAB program

MATLAB provides a graphical program to debug the code. The debugging of the code could be done using Editor. We can set a breakpoint at the specific line, and as and when execution hits that line, then execution is paused at that line. After this line, we do a step-by-step execution and see the results. To set the breakpoint, either we can hit the *F12* key or click the left key of the mouse on the dash (-), which is near the row number. Once the execution is paused, then, by using **Step**, **Step In**, and **Step out** button on the Editor toolbar, we can continue the step-by-step execution. After execution is paused, **Run** button changes to the **Continue** button, continue button carries on the execution until the next breakpoint is hit. *Figure 4.5* shows how a debugger looks like when execution is paused at a breakpoint.

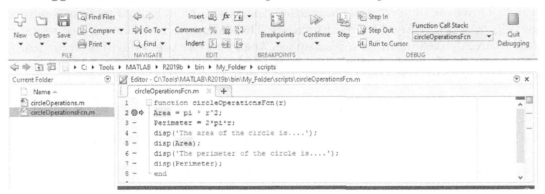

Figure 4.5: Debugging of the code

Add comments in m files

It is always advised to add some description of the code in the code program file to make any program better readable and maintainable. It eases others to understand the code. Character **%** is used to add comments or description lines in the program. During program development and testing, commenting can be used to comment out those commands which are not required to run. Text added after **%** is considered as commented text. MATLAB editor also provides the option to comment or uncomment multiple lines. Keyboard key combination *Ctrl + R* comments selected lines, and Keyboard key combination *Ctrl + T* uncomments the selected lines. Let us have a look at *figure 4.6*, where we can see that with the help of comments, the same program used to find out **Area** and **Perimeter** of the circle becomes much more readable and maintainable:

```
Editor - C:\Tools\MATLAB\R2019b\bin\My_Folder\scripts\circleOperations.m
  circleOperations.m   +
 1      %* NAME:          *******************************************
 2      %* DESCRIPTION:   *******************************************
 3      %* INPUTS:        *******************************************
 4      %
 5      %* OUTPUTS:       *******************************************
 6      %
 7      %* EXAMPLES:      *******************************************
 8      %
 9      %***********************************************************
10      %* HISTORY:       *******************************************
11      %*    Date           Version       Author       Comment           ***************
12      %*   (dd.mm.yy)      (x.y)                      changement)       ***************
13      %*-----------------------------------------------------------------------------
14
15 -    Area = pi * r^2;        % Calculate area of a circle
16 -    Perimeter = 2*pi*r;     % Calculate perimeter of a circle
17 -    disp('The area of the circle is....');
18 -    disp(Area);             % Print area in command window
19 -    disp('The perimeter of the circle is....');
20 -    disp(Perimeter);        % Print perimeter in command window
```

Figure 4.6: Comments in the program file

Live scripts

We have seen that m-scripts and functions are the MATLAB programs, which are used for Automation. Comments are used to describe the code written in m files. Imagine if we can add images, charts, formatted text, equations, and additional documentation to the program file, then program files will become much more interactive and very easy to maintain. MATLAB introduced Live Scripts in MATLAB R2016a. Live Scripts and Live functions are used to have formatted text with information and executable code together. The live script can have different sections such as **Text**, **Code**, **Image**, **Table of Contents**, **Hyperlinks**, and **Equations**. *Figure 4.7* explains various Insert options for Live Editor:

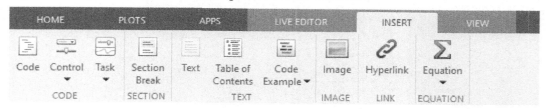

Figure 4.7: Various insert options.

Live Editor gives options to control variables such as slider, edit field, button, and so on, as shown in *figure 4.8*:

Figure 4.8: Various control options.

Now, let us observe the same program for **Circle** operations using a live script. *Figure 4.9* enlightens different usage of live script properties:

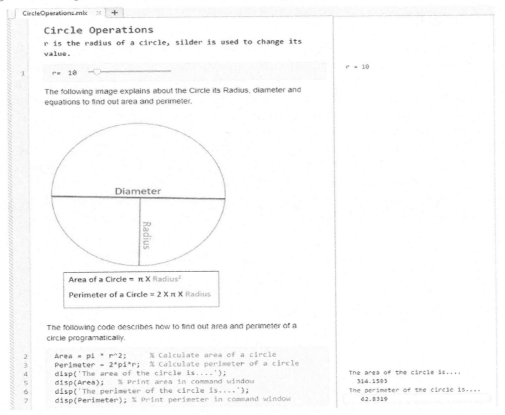

Figure 4.9: Live script for circle operations

The code mentioned in about image is as follows:

```
r=10;
Perimeter = 2*pi*r;  % Calculate perimeter of a circle
disp('The area of the circle is....');
disp(Area);   % Print area in the command window
disp('The perimeter of the circle is....');
disp(Perimeter); % Print perimeter in the command window
```

Control programming flow

We have perceived how to write the MATLAB program using m-scripts, custom functions, and live scripts. To write an effective and optimized program, we need to have control of program flow. This control flow can be achieved using the following statements:

- if, else, and if-else statements
- switch, case, otherwise statements
- try-catch statements
- for loop
- while loop
- continue, break, and return statement

"if", "else", and "elseif" statements

While writing the program, there may be a situation where we need to check the condition. If the condition is true, then a certain chunk of code should be executed; if the condition is not true, then a certain chunk of code should be executed. Suppose we want to write a program to find whether the given number is a prime number or not. If the given number is not a prime number, then we need to find out whether the given number is an even number or an odd number. So, to write a MATLAB program for this, we need to use these **if**, **elseif**, and **else** conditional statements. MATLAB provides a built-in function **isprime(num)** to find out if the given number is a prime number. If the given number is fully divisible by two, then that number is called as an even number; else, it is an odd number. We say any number is divisible by any other number when the remainder is zero. MATLAB provides built-in function **rem(a,b)** returns a reminder when a is divided by **b**. The following chunk of code shows how to use conditional statements:

```
function CheckNumPrimEvenOdd(num)
if isprime(num)
    disp('given number is prime');
elseif (rem(num,2) == 0)
    disp('given number is even');
else
    disp('given number is odd');
end
end
```

The following code shows command window output when **CheckNumPrimEvenOdd** function is called from the command window:

```
CheckNumPrimEvenOdd(5)
  the given number is prime
CheckNumPrimEvenOdd(9)
  the given number is odd
CheckNumPrimEvenOdd(16)
  the given number is even
```

"switch", "case", and "otherwise" statements

The switch, case, and otherwise statements are similar to the **if**, **else**, and **elseif** statements. They are also used to check conditions and control the flow. The execution of **switch**, **case**, and **otherwise** statements are based on the case of a "variable" that is used in the switch statement. *Otherwise* statement is optional and should be specified at the end, as it will be executed only when none of the cases is true. Let us take the same example where we want to display a message whether the given variable is a prime, an even, or an odd number. The following chunk of the code explains how to use switch case and otherwise statements:

```
function CheckNumPrimEvenOdd_SwitchCase(num)
if isprime(num)
    Switch = 1;
elseif (rem(num,2) == 0)
    Switch = 2;
else
    Switch = 3;
end
```

```
switch(Switch)
    case 1
        disp('given number is prime');
    case 2
        disp('given number is even');
    otherwise
        disp('given number is odd');
end
```

The following code shows command window output when **CheckNumPrimEvenOdd_SwitchCase** function is called from command window:

CheckNumPrimEvenOdd_SwitchCase(29)

 the given number is prime

CheckNumPrimEvenOdd_SwitchCase(35)

 the given number is odd

CheckNumPrimEvenOdd_SwitchCase(48)

 the given number is even

"try" and "catch" statements

Exceptions may occur during the execution of the program. If the program does not handle exceptions, then MATLAB stops program execution and throws the error on the command window. The most common example of the exception is **Index exceeds the number of array elements**. If we try to access an element of an array with an index, which is greater than the maximum index then this exception occurs. The **try** and **catch** statements are used for exception handling in MATLAB. Let us see the following code where **try-catch** statements are not used, and let us observe the exception thrown on the command window:

```
function displayArrayElements(index)
Array = [1,2,3,8,9,10,15];
disp(Array(index));
end
```

Let us observe the output on the command window when we try to access an element from an Array with an index of more than 7:

displayArrayElements(25)

Index exceeds the number of array elements (7).

```
Error in displayArrayElements (line 3)
disp(Array(index));
```

To handle this situation, we need to use, **try** and **catch** statements. The following code explains how we can use **try-catch** to handle `Index exceeds the number of array elements` exception:

```
function displayArrayElements(index)
Array = [1,2,3,8,9,10,15];
try
    disp(Array(index));
catch e
    if strfind(e.message,'Index exceeds the number of array elements')
        disp('Please use index between 1 to 7');
    end
end
end
```

The following is the output, where we can observe that the message, what is written in the **catch** loop, is displayed on the command window. So, this is how **try-catch** statements are used to have an uninterrupted flow of execution, and we can display custom messages based on the errors reported during the execution of the program:

```
displayArrayElements(25)
 Please use index between 1 to 7
```

"for" loop

There may be a situation where we need to execute the same statement repeatedly. For example, if we want to find out the factorial of any number. The mathematical formula to find the factorial is given as follows:

```
Factorial(n) = 1*2*3*……..*(n-2)*(n-1)*n
```

To find out the factorial of the number **n**, we need to form a loop in which we need to do multiplication sequentially. The following is the MATLAB code to find out the factorial of a given number using **for** loop:

```
function result = fact(n)
result = 1;
for i=1:n
    result = result*i;
```

```
end
disp(result);
end
```

The **for** loop iterates the loop for every element. In the preceding code, the **1:n** forms an array of **n** elements from 1 to n. Similarly, we can have any kind of Array for which **for** loop executes for the length of array iterations. The index used in **for** loop expression will carry the value of an element from the Array for each iteration. We can form nested **for** loop, meaning **for** loop inside other **for** loop. Nested **for** loop iterates for multiplication of length of arrays mentioned in each **for** loop expression. The following explains the output results on the command window when the function **fact** is called:

```
Factorial = fact(10)
     3628800
 Factorial =
     3628800
```

while loop

The **for** loop iterates the loop until index **i** takes the value of all elements, whereas the **while** loop iterates the loop until the condition mentioned in the while expression becomes false. Let us consider the same example to find out the factorial of the given number. Now, we will find out factorial using **while** loop. The following code explains how to find out the factorial of a given number using **while** loop:

```
function result = factWhileLoop(n)
result = 1;
i=1;
while i<=n
    result = result*i;
    i=i+1;
end
disp(result);
end
```

In the case of **while** loop, it is vital to make the loop condition in the while expression to false; else **while** loop may go into the infinite loop. In the preceding code, we are incrementing the value of **i** in each iteration. The loop executes until the value of **i** is less than or equal to **n**. When the value of **i** becomes more than **n,** then the loop breaks. The following code shows output results on the command window when function **factWhileLoop** is called:

factWhileLoop(10)

     3628800

ans =

     3628800

"break", "continue" and "return" statements

The **break**, **continue**, and **return** statements are used to have better control over the execution of the loop.

"break"

The **break** statement is used to break the **for** loop or **while** loop. The **break** statements moves program flow control to the end of the loop. The following code explains how to use the **break** statement in the loop:

```
function result = factWhileLoopBreak(n)
result = 1;
i=1;
while 1
    result = result*i;
    i=i+1;
    if i>n
        break;
    end
end
```

In the previous code, we can realize that the expression used in the while condition is **1**, which means that using **while** condition, it is not possible to come out of the **while** loop. So, it is required to **break** the loop explicitly. When the value of **i** becomes more than **n**, then we **break** the loop. The following code shows the output on the command window when function **factWhileLoopBreak** is called:

factWhileLoopBreak(10)

     3628800

ans =

     3628800

'continue'

The **continue** statement is used to skip execution of code from **continue** statement till **end** of **for** loop or **while** loop. After **continue** statement, control flow goes to the next iteration immediately. The following code explains how to use **continue** statement in the **while** loop:

```
function result = factWhileLoopContinue(n)
result = 1;
i=1;
while i<n
    i=i+1;
    if i == 9
        continue;
    end
    disp(i);
    result = result*i;
end
disp(result);
end
```

In the previous code, we can see that the continue statement is executed when the value of **i** becomes **9**. When the value of **i** becomes **9** then further statements **disp(i)** and **result = result*i** will be skipped from the execution. The following is the output displayed on the command window when **factWhileLoopContinue** is called:

```
factWhileLoopContinue(10)
     2
     3
     4
     5
     6
     7
     8
    10
      403200
ans =
      403200
```

"return"

The **return** statement returns the control to the invoking program before it executes the end of the script or function. If a function or script is called from the command window, then it returns the control to the command window after executing the **return** statement. All statements after **return** statements will be skipped. The following code explains how to use return in the function:

```
function result = factWhileLoopReturn(n)
result = 1;
i=1;
while i<n
    i=i+1;
    if i == 9
        return;
    end
    disp(i);
    result = result*i;
end
disp(result);
end
```

In the previous code, we can comprehend that the return statement gets executed when the value of **i** becomes **9**. When the value of **i** becomes nine, then further statements **disp(i)** and **result = result*i** will be skipped from the execution. It breaks the **while** loop and executes the end of the function. The following is the output displayed on the command window when **factWhileLoopReturn** is called:

```
factWhileLoopReturn(10)
     2
     3
     4
     5
     6
     7
     8
ans =
     40320
```

Visualization

Visualization is an integral part of MATLAB. MATLAB facilitates graphical illustration of the data in the form of plots, graphs, charts, images, and so on. It is possible to create various types of multidimensional plots, graphs, and charts with the help of built-in graphics functions. There are built-in functions that support different types of operations on images too. In this section, we shall learn about the creation, customization, import, and export of plots as well as images.

Plots

MATLAB offers various types of 2-D and 3-D plots to visualize the data effectively. There are two basic methods to implement plots: Functions method and Interactive method. In this section, we shall learn these methods.

Functions method

This method uses various graphics functions to create and perform several additional operations with the plots. The following are some of these operations.

Create a 2-D line plot

The plot function creates a 2-D line plot for the input argument versus the index. The plot is displayed in a pop-up **Figure** window. A blank figure window can be launched by executing figure command; execution of the new function overwrites the existing plot otherwise. Depending on the type as well as the number of inputs, the output of the plot varies. The function syntax and examples of plots are as follows:

```
plot(x1,y1,linespec1,…,xn,yn,linespecn)   %function syntax, where x and
y are scalar, matrix or vector with matching sizes and linespec specifies
line style, marker type and color plot(x,y)

%displays a 2D line plot of values of y to corresponding values of x,
where x and y are vectors of the same length, or matrices of same size,
or having either matching number of rows or columns if x is a vector,
for example
x=[10 20 30 40 50]; y=[2 4 6 8 10];   %x and y are vectors of length 5
plot(x,y);  %Figure 1 displays a 2D line plot of elements of y versus x
plot(y);    %Figure 2 displays a 2D line plot of elements of y versus
            its index
```

Figure 4.10 displays the outputs of the previous code:

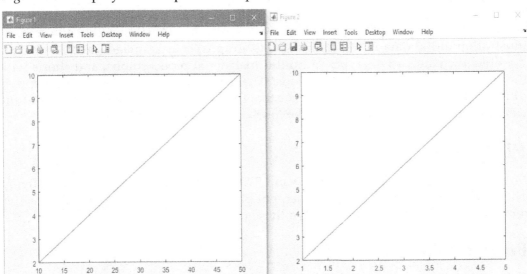

Figure 4.10: *plot(x,y) and plot(y) examples*

Create a 2-D line function plot

We can also use the function to plot **y**, which is a function of **x**. For example,

```
t=-pi:0.1:pi;        %value of vector t ranges from -π to +π
y=sin(t);            %vector y elements are sine of vector t
plot(t,y);           %displays a sine curve, where x-axis values range
                             from -π to +π and y-axis values range from -1
                             to +1, as per the following Figure 1
z=cos(t);            %vector z elements are cosine of vector t
plot(t,z);           %displays a cosine curve, where x-axis values range
                             from -π to +π and y-axis values range from -1
                             to +1, according to Figure 2
```

Figure 4.11 shows the outputs of the previous code:

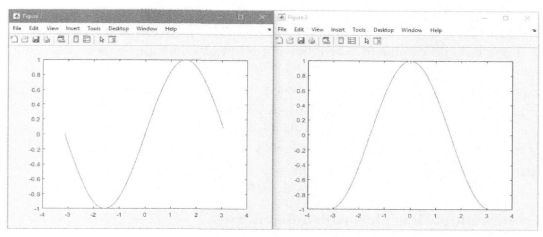

Figure 4.11: sine and cos function plot examples

Create multiple line plots with the same axes

It is also possible to plot multiple pairs of x- and y-axis in the same figure with the plot function. The function syntax and example are as follows:

```
plot(x_1,y_1,…,x_n,y_n); %plots n number of y vector pairs in a figure, for
                         example
plot(t,y,t,z); %displays plots of vectors y and z vs t in the same figure
               with different line colors.
```

Figure 4.12 is the output of the previous code:

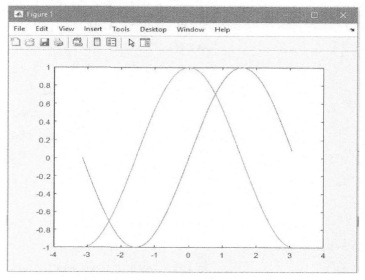

Figure 4.12: Multiple line plots with the same axes

Similarly, using the hold command, we can plot multiple lines using the same axes. Plot function results after the hold on command are displayed in the same figure until the hold off command. The following set of functions can achieve the result from *figure 4.12*:

```
plot(t,y);          %plots y versus t line plot in figure
hold on             %enables the use of the same figure for the
                        following plots
plot(t,z);          %displays z versus t line plot in the same figure
hold off            %disables the use of the same figure for the
                        following plots
```

Create multiple line plots with different axes

MATLAB offers the possibility to display multiple axes in the same figure with the **tiledlayout** function. The user can pass the desired layout dimensions as arguments to the function, and the function creates an invisible grid of input rows and columns. Using **nexttile** function in conjunction with **tiledlayout** function, one can create and lay the subplots in the same figure. These functions are available from the R2019b version. For earlier versions, subplot function is used. The function syntax and ellipse example are as follows:

```
a1=5;a2=2;a3=5;             %a is the x-axis length
b1=5;b2=5;b3=2;             %b is the y-axis length
t=-pi:0.01:pi;
tiledlayout(2,2);           %creates a 2-by-2 tiled layout
nexttile                    %selects first tile for the subplot
x1=a1*cos(t);               %x=x0+a*cos(t), x0 is x-axis centre
y1=b1*sin(t);               %y=y0+a*sin(t), y0 is x-axis centre
plot(x1,y1);                %plots the circle, as a1=b1
axis equal                  %both the axes have the same range
nexttile                    %selects second tile for the subplot
x2=a2*cos(t); y2=b2*sin(t);
plot(x2,y2,'r');            %plots vertical ellipse in red color
axis equal
nexttile                    %selects third tile for the subplot
x3=a3*cos(t);y3=b3*sin(t);
plot(x3,y3,'y');            %plots horizontal ellipse with yellow
                                color
```

```
axis equal
nexttile                    %selects fourth tile for the subplot
plot(x1,y1,x2,y2,x3,y3);    %function plots all three previous
                             plots together axis equal
```

In the previous as well as latest releases, one can achieve a similar behavior by replacing the **tiledlayout** and **nexttile** functions with a subplot function and providing the number of desired rows and columns along with the tile number for the plot followed by the function. The syntax and results are as follows:

```
subplot(m,n,tilenum);   %creates subplot grid with m rows and n columns,
tilenum chooses the tile for the plot; for example
subplot(2,2,1);         %creates a 2-by-2 tiled layout and places the
plot function result followed by this function at the first tile
```

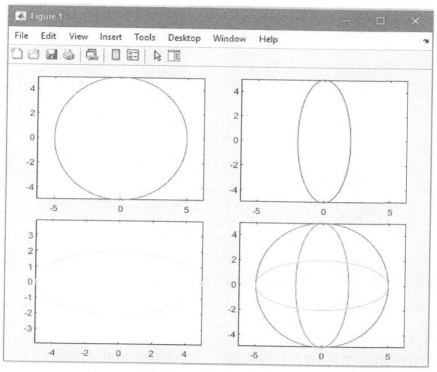

Figure 4.13: Multiple plots with different axes example

Create a matrix plot

In case of matrix, the plot function displays individual lines per column. Each line is displayed in a different color. For example,

```
n=[15 27 32  4 18;
   19 54 47 93 13;
   81 23 65 41 29;]   %n is 3-by-5 matrix
plot(n);              %displays 5 lines for columns vs index 5 in
                              different colors
```

Figure 4.14 is the output of previous code:

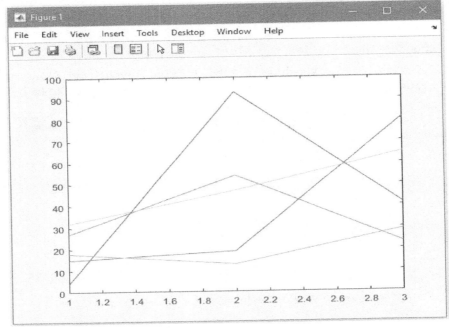

Figure 4.14: Matrix plot example

Create a 2-D plot with line specification

Line specification options such as line style, marker symbol, color are specified as arguments to change the line appearance after input variables while creating the plots. This feature helps to assess the data points and distinguish visually between multiple lines, mostly when multiple lines are plotted in the same figure. We can mention one or all of them as a character vector while specifying the arguments to the plot function. The following are the line specifiers:

- **Line style specification**: *Table 4.2* provides various line style options. By default, the line is solid. In case the marker type is specified without line style, then the line will not be shown:

Line style	Specifier	Syntax
Solid line	-	plot(x,y,'-')
Dotted line	:	plot(x,y,':')
Dashed line	--	plot(x,y,'--')
Dash-dot line	-.	plot(x,y,'-.')

Table 4.2: *Line style specifiers*

- **Marker symbol specification**: By default, there are no markers plotted. *Table 4.3* exhibits various marker symbols available for use:

Marker symbol	Specifier	Syntax
Circle	o	plot(x,y,'o')
Plus	+	plot(x,y,'+')
Point	.	plot(x,y,'.')
Cross	x	plot(x,y,'x')
Asterisk	*	plot(x,y,'*')
Diamond (◊)	d	plot(x,y,'d')
	diamond	plot(x,y,'diamond')
Square (□)	s	plot(x,y,'s')
	square	plot(x,y,'square')
Upward triangle (Δ)	^	plot(x,y,'^')
Downward triangle	v	plot(x,y,'v')
Left-pointing triangle	>	plot(x,y,'>')
Right-pointing triangle	<	plot(x,y,'<')
Pentagram (Five-point Star- ☆)	p	plot(x,y,'p')
	pentagram	plot(x,y,'pentagram')
Hexagram (Six-point star)	h	plot(x,y,'h')
	hexagram	plot(x,y,'hexagram')

Table 4.3: *Marker symbol specifiers*

- **Color specification**: It is possible to change the color of the lines by using color specifier. We can specify either the short specifier of the full-color name after the data input argument(s). The list of colors and their specifiers are explained in *table 4.4*.

Create and modify 2-D plot line properties

MATLAB offers several line property options to adapt the plot appearance as required. A user can apply these properties while creating the plot by specifying name-value pair arguments and also can retrieve and modify them later using dot notation. Few of these properties are available as line specifiers too. The syntax to set these properties for creation, storage, and modification are as follows:

```
p=plot(x,y,'name1','value1',...'namen',valuen');    %creates a y-versus-x
plot with specified n number of property name-value pairs

p.propertyName='value';           %the value can be assigned to a property
                                    of plot p

value1=p.name1;...valuen=p.namen; %The value of a property of p can be
                                    saved in a   variable
```

The following are some of the widely used line and marker-related properties:

- **Color**: This property specifies the line color. It accepts the value in the form of common color names, their short names, RGB triplets, or hexadecimal values. The color names or short names specified in the following table are accepted; else, the error "Invalid color value" is displayed. An RGB triplet is a three-element vector for a specific combination of Red, Green, and Blue color components. The values of these elements range between [0,1]. The hexadecimal color code is a specific hexadecimal value ranging between **#000000** and **#FFFFFF**. Variations of RGB values make numerous shades of colors. By default, the color of the first line is blue with RGB values **[0 0.4470 0.7410]**. Table 4.4 provides colors, their specifiers or short names, RGB triplets, and hexadecimal codes:

Color	Specifier/ short name	RGB triplet	Hexadecimal code
Blue	b	[0 0 1]	#0000FF
Red	r	[1 0 0]	#FF0000
Green	g	[0 1 0]	#00FF00
Yellow	y	[1 1 0]	#FFFF00
Magenta	m	[1 0 1]	#FF00FF
Cyan	c	[0 1 1]	#00FFFF
White	w	[1 1 1]	#FFFFFF
Black	k	[0 0 0]	#000000
None	NA	NA	NA

Table 4.4: Color specifiers with RGB triplets and hex codes

- **LineStyle**: This property specifies the line style. The possible options are the same as the line style specifiers mentioned in *table 4.1*. Additionally, it provides a chance to set line style as **none**, which means that no line shall be drawn.

- **LineWidth**: The property specifies the line width. By default, the line width is 0.5 points, where 1 point is equivalent to 1/72 inch. The property accepts any positive value as an argument.

- **Marker**: This property, same as the specifier, facilitates the plotting of marker symbols on the line. By default, there shall not be any marker. Apart from the markers listed under *table 4.2*, this property provides an additional option to specify **Marker** as **none**.

- **MarkerIndices**: This property specifies the data points where the markers shall be available. By default, the markers are shown at all data points. We can provide a vector of data points, or scalar value, where a marker is to be visible.

- **MarkerSize**: This property specifies the marker size. By default, the size of a marker is 6 points. We can select any positive value as an argument.

- **MarkerEdgeColor**: The property specifies the color of the outline of the markers. By default, the marker edge color is the same as line color, as the property value is **auto**. Similar to the **Color** property *table 4.3*, we can specify the marker outline color by using the full or short name, RGB triplet, or hexadecimal code.

- **MarkerFaceColor**: This property specifies the fill color of the markers. By default, the fill color is **none**. We can determine the marker face color similar to **Color** property with the help of color name, short name, RGB triplet, and hexadecimal code.

- **XData**: This property specifies the input values of the x-axis as a vector. The length of x- and y-axis inputs must be the same. If we do not establish **XData**, then by default index of the y-axis is taken as the x-axis.

- **YData**: The property specifies the input values of the y-axis as a vector.

- **ZData**: The property specifies the input values of the z-axis as a vector in the case of a 3-D plot.

The example of the preceding properties and the respective *figure 4.15* are as follows:

```
x=1:13;
y=[1 2 3 2 1 2 3 2 1 2 3 2 1];
p1=plot(x,y);      %creates a y-versus-x plot, as shown in Figure 1
```

p1.LineStyle='-.',p1.LineWidth=3,p1.Color='r',p1.Marker='s',

p1.MarkerIndices=2:2:length(y),p1.MarkerSize=15,p1.MarkerEdgeColor='g',

p1.MarkerFaceColor='y';   %updates the plot with the properties, as shown in Figure 2

figure,p2=plot(x,y,'LineStyle','-.','LineWidth',3,'Color','r','Marker','s',...

'MarkerIndices',2:2:length(y),'MarkerSize',15,'MarkerEdgeColor','g','MarkerFaceColor','y'); % creates a y-versus-x plot with the specified properties, as shown in Figure 2

Please note: the type of the variables p1 and p2 are returned as line, which have the above properties

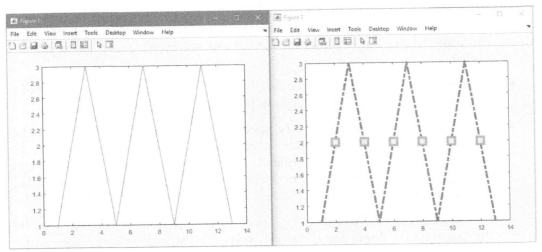

Figure 4.15: Line properties example

Add plot axes labels

An axis label provides a short description of the displayed information regarding the respective axis. Without any label of the axes, it is difficult to relate to the plot. In *figure 4.16*, the displayed example plot has three lines. As it does not have the axes labels, the plot does not convey the significance of these lines:

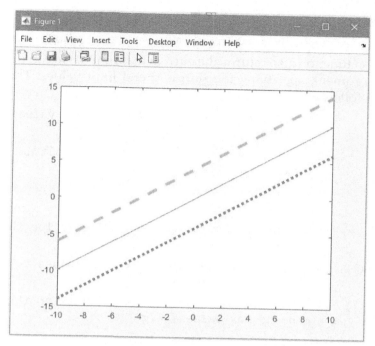

Figure 4.16: Line plot without additional properties

Using the following functions, we can apply labels to x-axis and y-axis:

```
xlabel('x-axis label');
      %displays text specified as x-axis label below x-axis tick points
ylabel('y-axis label');%displays text specified as y-axis label next to
                      y-axis tick points, for ex.
xlabel('x');
ylabel('y=mx+c');       %display plot x-axis label as x and y-axis label
                      as y=mx+c
```

Add plot title

With the help of the title function, we can display a title on the top side of the plot. The function syntax and example are as follows:

```
title('plot title');         %displays the text specified as
                             plot title on the plot, for example
title('Straight line equation plot');   %displays the text Straight line
                                       equation plot as the title
                                       of the plot
```

Add axis limits

To display the plot in a specific range of x- and y-axis values, **xlim** and **ylim** functions can be used. The function also returns the current axis limits. We can pass a numeric vector as an argument, specifying the start and end limit values. The syntax and example are as follows:

```
lim1=xlim          %returns the vector of start and end values of x-axis
                      limits
lim2=ylim          %returns the vector of start and end limit values of
                      y-axis, for example
lim1=-10 10        %returns the vector of x-axis limits for the example
                      from figure 4.16
lim2=-15 15        %returns the vector of y-axis limits for the example
                      from figure 4.16
xlim([min max])    %limits the display of   x-axis values to the
                      specified min and max values
ylim([min max])    %limits the display of y-axis values to the specified
                      min and max values, e.g.
xlim([-5 5])       %x-axis limits are set between -5 and 5
ylim([-5 5])       %y-axis limits are set between -5 and 5
axis([-5 5 -5 5])  %produces the same result as above
xlim([-inf inf])   %sets the x-axis limit as per automatic calculation
ylim([-inf inf])   %sets the y-axis limit as per automatic calculation
```

Add legend

The function **legend** adds a legend to the plot. Legend helps to identify the specific line among multiple lines available in the plot. It is possible to pass the string or character vector of legend labels as an argument to the function. The syntax with different properties and example is as follows:

```
legend('label')         %displays legend for the line in the plot

legend('label1'…'labeln','location', direction);   %displays labels
    1 to n in the legend, with the location of the legend as specified
    by direction, for example, 'northwest'; it is possible to show
    the legend outside of the plot with location property specified as
    'southeastoutside' for example

legend('y1=x','y2=x+4','y3=x-4')%displays the legend on the example from
                      figure 4.16

legend('off')                    %disables the legend
```

Add grid

Using **grid** command, one can add, remove or toggle the grid on the plot. By default, the grid is off. The syntax of the command is as follows:

```
grid              %toggles the availability of the grid
grid on           %shows the major grid on the plot
grid off          %hides the grid on the plot
grid minor        %appends the minor grid on the plot
```

Figure 4.17 plot applies the functions to add axes labels, limits, title, legend, grid, and so on, on the plot shown in *figure 4.16*:

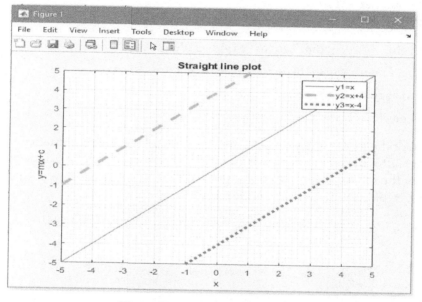

Figure 4.17: Line plot with properties

Add two y-axes to the plot

With **yyaxis** command, MATLAB provides an opportunity to have two y-axes for the same plot. Execution of **yyaxis** with the desired direction (left or right) as an argument opens the possibility of deciding the active side for the following **plot** function execution. The syntax of **yyaxis** command is as follows:

```
yyaxis direction    %defines the active direction, where direction=left or
                        right
```

The plot example of the **free-falling object motion without any air resistance** using **yyaxis** command is as follows:

```
t=0:0.1:10;            %here t is the time vector, in s
g=9.8;                 %g is gravitational acceleration in m/s2
v=g*t;                 %v=gt is the velocity of the free-falling object, in m/s
d=g*(t.^2)/2;          %d=gt2/2 is the distance of the object, in m
yyaxis left            %command activates left side y-axis
plot(t,v);             %plot of velocity versus time
xlabel('Time(sec)');
ylabel('Velocity(m/sec)');
yyaxis right           %activates right-side y-axis
plot(t,d);             %plot of distance versus time
ylabel('distance(m)');
title('Free falling object motion plot');
```

Execution of the preceding group of functions results in the plot image in *figure 4.18*, where the left side y-axis depicts velocity and the right side y-axis represents the distance of the falling object, as compared with the x-axis time. It can be seen that the value ranges of both the y-axes are different:

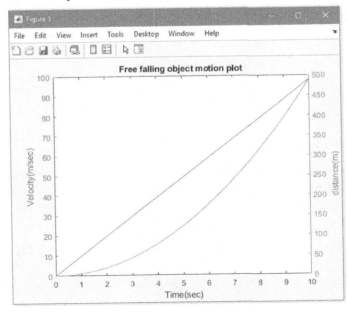

Figure 4.18: Two y-axes example

Create a Stairstep plot

Stairstep plot is similar to the line plot, but instead of a straight line connecting all data points, the stairstep graph connects the data points in steps. The stairs function is used to create these plots. The arguments and other customization and specifier options applicable to the line plot are available to the stairs plot too. The syntax and example of a stairstep graph are as follows:

```
stairs(x,y);    %function creates a y-versus-x staircase plot, for
                    example
x=0:0.2:4*pi;   %x varies from o to 4*pi
y=sin(x).^2;    %y is sin2(x)
```

Figure 4.19 shows the **stairs(x,y)** function results in comparison to the **plot(x,y)** function results.

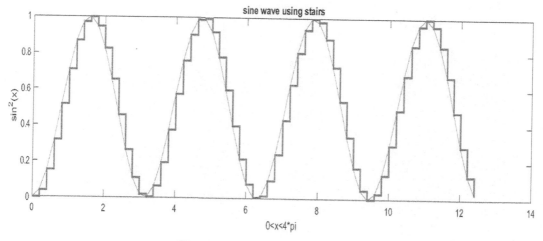

Figure 4.19: Stair step graph example

Create an area plot

The **area** function plots a graph similar to a line graph and fills the area beneath the lines. The input to the function is either a vector or a matrix. In the case of vectors, the area plot is plotted against the index. In the case of a matrix, the areas are plotted per column and are displayed in different colors. The values depict the area considering column-wise elements. The function syntax is as follows:

```
area(x,y);      %function plots y-versus-x area plot, where both are
vectors and x is a vector with increasing values and length same as y
area(y);        %plots area graph of matrix or vector y, x-axis are
automatically calculated according to the length of y
area(y,basevalue); %base value is a positive or negative integer value,
default value is 0 unless specified
```

The following example and *figure 4.20* show the area plots for **y**, where y is a 4×4 matrix:

```
y= [6 15 34 27;
    54 11 17 35;
    9 21 13 19;
    7 14 64 26];      %y is a 4x4 matrix
area(y);              %function plots the filled plot with four areas in
                         tile 1
area(y,5);            %function creates area plot with base value 5 in
                         tile 2
```

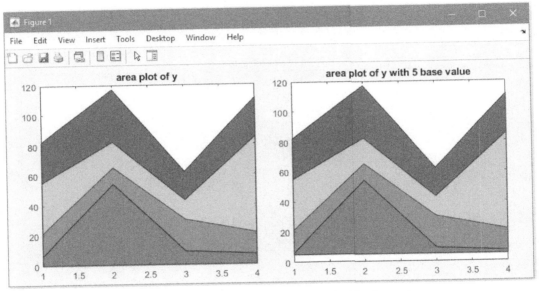

Figure 4.20: *Area plot example without and with a base value*

Create a function plot

MATLAB provides option to plot a function or an expression with **fplot** function. By default, the function displays the plot for the input argument function handle in the interval of **[-5 5]**, unless the interval is specified. The function syntax and variations as well as the resulting *figure 4.21* are as follows:

```
fplot(f);       %where f is a function of x for the interval [-5 5], for
                   example
fplot(@(x) x^3-x+1);         %function f(x)=x^3-x+1, where x varies
                                between [-5 5]
title('y=x^3-x+1');    %as shown in tile 1 of figure 4.21
```

```
fplot(f,xinteval);         %for f(x), xinterval is a vector [xmin xmax]
fplot(funcx,funcy) %funcx and funcy are function of t, the range of t=[-
                     5 5]
fplot(funcx,funcy,tinterval); %funcx and funcy are function of t, where
                               tinterval =[tmin tmax], for example
funcx=@(t) sin(t);         %x(t)=sin(t), for t=-2*pi to 2*pi
funcy=@(t) t*tan(10*t);    %y(t)=t*tan(10t), for t=-2*pi to 2*pi
tinterval=[-2*pi 2*pi];    %where tmin=-2*pi , tmax=2*pi
fplot(funcx,funcy,tinterval); %plot of funcx and funcy in the given
                               interval
title('x(t)=sin(t),y(t)=t*tan(10t)'); %as shown in tile 2 of figure 4.21
```

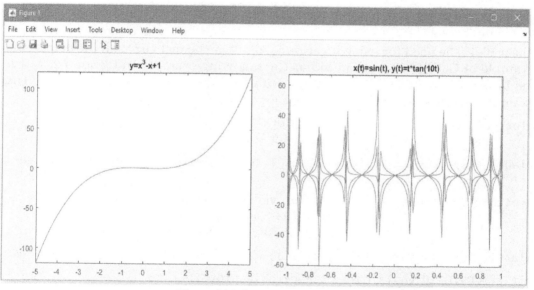

Figure 4.21: function plot examples

Create a logarithmic plot

Logarithmic plots are implemented in MATLAB by using any of the available functions: **loglog**, **semilogx**, and **semilogy**. The loglog function plots both the axes using a logarithmic scale. The function **semilogx** uses a logarithmic scale only on x-axis, and **semilogy** uses a logarithmic scale only on the y-axis. This plot has properties similar to the linear plot. Therefore, the specifiers and properties apply to this plot as well. The following is the syntax of the **log** functions:

```
loglog(y)                      %plots logarithmic chart based on the index of
                                  y
loglog(x_1,y_1,...x_n,y_n);    %plots the argument pairs of y-versus-x on a
                                  log scale
semilogx(y)                    %plots semi-logarithmic chart based on the
                                  index of y
semilogx(x_1,y_1,...x_n,y_n);  %plots the argument pairs of y-versus-x on a
                                  log scale for the x-axis and linear
                                  scale for the y-axis
semilogy(y)                    %plots semi-logarithmic chart based on the
                                  index of y
semilogy(x_1,y_1,...x_n,y_n);  %plots the argument pairs of y-versus-x on a
                                  linear scale for the x-axis and log
                                  scale for the y-axis
```

Logarithmic plots are very useful in analyzing the rate of change compared with the linear plot. The need for using logarithmic plots can be realized with the help of the example of COVID-19 cases in India. The following example and *figure 4.22* show the linear count versus day plot along with the logarithmic plot of the count. The example has considered the data for the first 221 days since the first case:

```
plot(Day, Count);      %linearly plots Total count per day as per the
                          first chart
xlabel('Day'); ylabel('Total cases');title('Covid-19 India cases linear
                          plot');
semilogy(Day,Count);   %plots Count-versus-Day chart on a linear scale
                          for x-axis and log scale for the y-axis, as
                          shown in the second chart of figure 4.22
xlabel('Day');ylabel('Total cases');
title('COVID-19 India cases logarithmic plot');
```

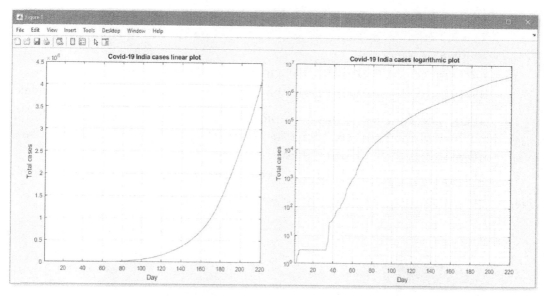

Figure 4.22: COVID-19 logarithmic plot example

From *figure 4.22*, we can conclude that the linear plot shows a very steep exponential line. So it becomes difficult to analyze the rate of growth. The logarithmic plot adjusts the rate of change in a way that the curve does not become too steep during rapid growth, so it gives an accurate indication of when the flattening of the curve becomes evident. Richter scale used to measure the magnitude of an earthquake is also based on the concept of a logarithmic scale.

Some common 2-D plots

MATLAB offers a wide variety of 2-D plots. These are some of the commonly used plots explained in brief:

- **pie**: Using the pie function, one can plot a pie chart. The input of the function is a vector or a matrix. The 3D version of the pie function is available as **pie3**. Along with the input argument, the property explodes, or a label vector can be provided. The function syntax is as follows:

    ```
    pie(x);              %plots pie chart for input vector or matrix x
    pie(x,explode,labels); %plots pie chart of x, with detached
    slices and vector of labels options
    ```

- **scatter**: As the name suggests, the function creates a scatter plot, where the circles(bubbles) are scattered based on the input vector values. There are also options to change the size, color, of filling of these points. The equivalent 3D plot function is **scatter3**. The function syntax is as follows:

    ```
    scatter(x,y);        %plots scatter plot for vectors y-versus-x
    ```

- **bar**: The function creates a bar graph for the input scalar, vector, or matrix. The 3D equivalent function is available as **bar3**. The function syntax is as follows:

  ```
  bar(x,y);      %plots bar chart for inputs y-versus-x
  bar(y);        %plots the bar chart for elements of y-vs-index
  ```

- **stem**: The function is used to plot the discrete sequential data. The 3D equivalent function is available as **stem3**. The function syntax is as follows:

  ```
  stem(x,y);     %plots stem chart for inputs y-versus-x
  stem(y);       %plots the stem chart for elements of y-vs-index
  ```

Figure 4.23 shows examples of the plots mentioned earlier:

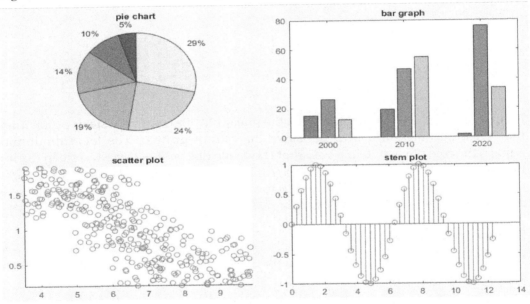

Figure 4.23: other 2D plot examples

Create a 3-D plot

Similar to the **plot(x,y)** function, **plot3(x,y,z)** function plots line or points in three-dimensional space, where **x**, **y**, and **z** are the coordinates. The function accepts any scalar, vector, or matrices as input arguments. In the case of scalars, the plot shows a point on XYZ coordinates when a marker is specified; else, it just updates the axes values. In the case of vectors, the length of all the coordinate arguments must match. In the case of the matrix, the sizes must be compatible. It is possible to plot multiple XYZ coordinate pairs in the same plot. The specifier and line property customizations are applicable for **plot3**, which are similar to the plot function. The function syntax and possible variations are as follows:

```
plot3(x,y,z);%plots the line or points in XYZ coordinates, where x, y, z
             could be a scalar, vector or matrix
plot3(x1,y1,z1,LineSpec1...xn,yn,zn, Linespecn) %plots the XYZ pairs of
coordinates  in figure with given line specifications
plot3(2,2,4,'o');             %plots a 'o' marker on 2,2,4
                              coordinates
```

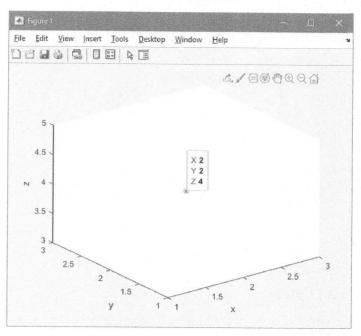

Figure 4.24: Scalar 3D plot example

The following example shows three 3D plots in the same *figure 4.25*:

```
t=0:0.01:2*pi; x=cos(t); y=sin(t);
t=x.*y;
plot3(x,y,t,'linewidth',4);           %plots x-y-t graph with line
                                         width 4
hold on;                              %plots the following plots
                                         in the sam
plot3(t,x,y, 'linewidth',4);          %plots t-x-y graph with line
                                         width 4
plot3(x,t,y, 'linewidth',4);          %plots x-t-y graph with line
                                         width 4
```

```
xlabel('x');ylabel('y');zlabel('z');        %labelling for axes
```

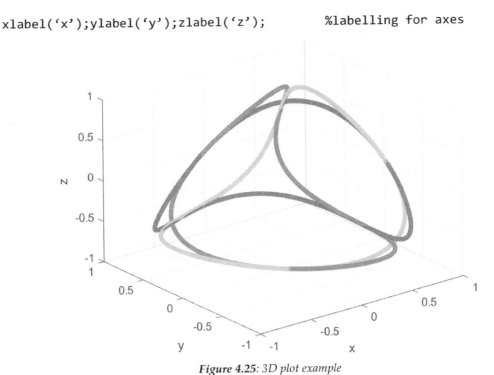

Figure 4.25: *3D plot example*

Some common 3-D plots

MATLAB offers a wide variety of 3-D plots. These are some of the commonly used plots explained in brief:

- **surface**: The function **surf** creates a surface plot, where the input arguments **x** and **y** can be vectors or matrix, and **z** must be a matrix. The function syntax is as follows:

    ```
    surf(x,y,z);         %plots the surface graph for x, y and z
                              arguments,  where z is a matrix
    surf(z);             %plots the surface graph for z as per
                              indices of x and y components
    ```

- **mesh**: The function **mesh** implements the mesh surface plot. Where the input arguments **x** and **y** can be vectors or matrix and **z** must be a matrix. The function syntax is as follows:

    ```
    mesh(x,y,z);         %plots the mesh graph for x, y and z
                              arguments, where z  is a matrix
    mesh(z);             %plots the surface graph for z as per
                              indices of x and y components
    ```

Figure 4.26 shows examples of the plots mentioned earlier:

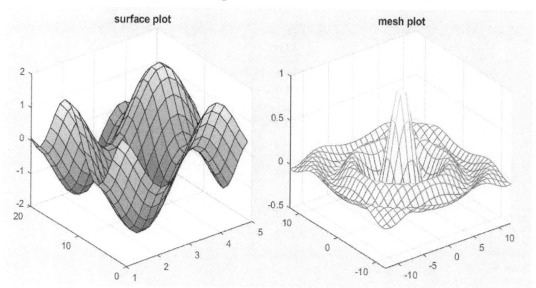

Figure 4.26: *Other 3D plot examples*

Interactive method

Besides the plotting functions, MATLAB offers the opportunity to create and edit the plots in an interactive manner using the plot tools interface. The interface provides simplified ways to create several types of plots, create plots by selecting the workspace variables, customize the graphic properties and display options, add annotations to the plot, and create subplots. This plotting interface is accessible by running **plottools** command in the command prompt. The plot interface consists of toolbars and panels. *Figure 4.27* shows the snapshot of the interactive plotting interface:

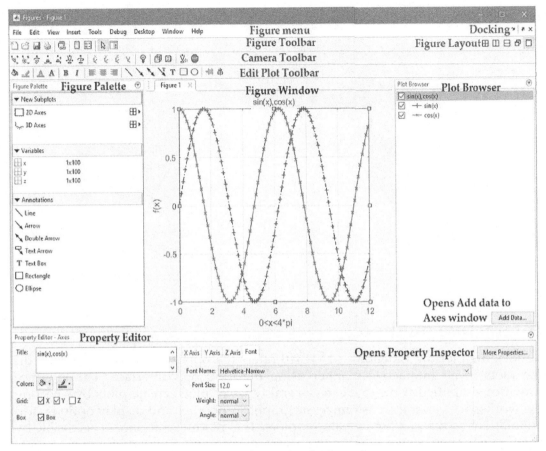

Figure 4.27: Interactive plotting tool

These panels are available as part of the interactive tool:

- **Figure palette**: This panel offers choices to add 2D and 3D subplots, add annotation, and plot the variables from the selection. The figure palette can be opened from the view menu or by executing **figurepalette** command in the command window. A right-click on the variable gives the option to plot the workspace variable. With the help of **plot** command, it is possible to search for relevant plots by providing the variable expression in the plotted variable window.

- **Plot browser**: The browser panel contains information on the axes, lines, legends, and other graphic objects available in the selected figure plot. When a plot is selected, it activates a button **Add data**, clicking which a window add **Data to Axes** pops up, where one can select the plot type, **x** and **y** data source variables, and **z** data source and colors in case of the 3D plot. The Plot Browser can be opened from the view menu or by executing `plotbrowser` command in the command window.

- **Property editor**: Based on the selection in the plot browser, the respective property editor pops up, which helps in customizing the plot properties. For example, for the selection of axes, the `Property Editor-Axes` opens, where the user can add or modify the title, axes labels, limits, fonts, colors, grids, and so on. If we click on the line, the options to select a data source, plot type, markers, colors, line width, and so on. options become available under `Property Editor-Line`. There is also a button **More properties**, which launches a `Property Inspector` window for the detailed customization of the plot. The `Plot Browser` can be opened from the view menu, or by executing `propertyeditor` command in the command window.

Save figure

To ease the users' efforts, the interactive tool prints all the customizations as functions on the command prompt. A user can save these functions in a script or function file to generate similar images later. To save the plot as a figure, the save option in the File menu of the figure window can be used. By default, the type of the plot figure is `.fig` (MATLAB figure file), but the figure can be saved in a different image format too. Similarly, the following functions are available to perform these operations:

```
print(file,format);     %prints or saves the file using a specified format
saveas(figure, file);   %saves the figure with the given name
savefig(file);          %saves the current figure as the figure file name
openfig(file);          %opens the given figure file
```

Images

MATLAB provides several functionalities that can be performed on images, for example, reading, writing, modification, and conversion. These operations discussed in the chapter do not need any additional toolbox, such as the Image Processing toolbox, to be installed. Similar to the other types, MATLAB stores and processes the images in an array format. Generally, the images are represented in a 2D or 3D array, where each element signifies a pixel. There are three basic types of images as follows:

- **RGB (truecolor) image**: MATLAB stores this image in an m-by-n-by-3 array, where each plane specifies the intensity of red, green and blue colors. These images are stored as 24-bit images, with each color component assigned 8 bits. Different 16 million color combinations are possible to achieve, therefore giving the name as **truecolor** image.

- **Grayscale image**: This type of image is also known as an intensity image, where each element of the single matrix represents the intensity of the pixel.
- **Indexed image**: This image contains two parts: data matrix and colormap matrix. colormap is an m×3 array with floating-point values in [0, 1] range. The colormap rows specify the red, green, and blue components. For the indexed image, the pixels are mapped directly to the `colormap` values. The integer element of the data matrix is an index to the `colormap` value.

MATLAB supports double (default) or uint8/uint16 datatype for the images. Some of the usable image formats are BMP, PNG, JPEG, GIF, HDF, TIFF, PCX, XWD, raw data, and so on. Various built-in functions are available to perform operations such as read, write, display, modify and convert the images. The following are some of the image functions:

- `image`: The function shows the input argument array into an image form on a figure window. By default, the direction of the y-axis is reverse. It is possible to specify the location of the image along with the input array. The syntax and example are as follows:

```
image(C);          %displays image for data of array C in a figure
                       window
image(x,y,C);      %displays image for data of array C at a
                       location specified
                   by vectors x and y
```

- `imagesc`: This function is similar to an image, but the function uses the whole color range by taking into account the minimum and maximum values present in **Array** to scale the range. The following examples and *figure 4.28* show the images created for matrix **C** using both **image** and **imagesc** functions.

```
x=[0 10];y=[10 20]; %x and y vectors specify the start and end
location for   the image
C=[100     44     320     240;
    260    78     39      21;
    47     200    64      27;]
image(x,y,C);      %displays a 3x4 color matrix, at given
                           locations
colorbar           %displays colorbar next to the image
imagesc(x,y,C);    %displays a 3x4 scaled color matrix, at given
                           locations
```

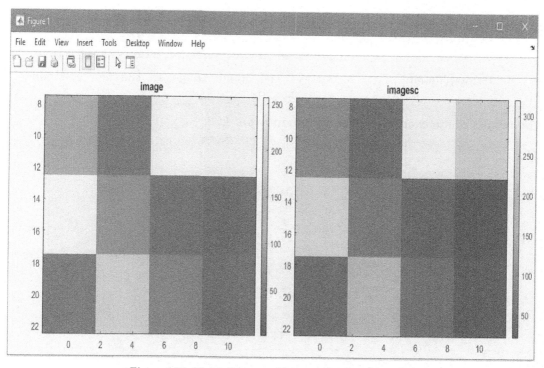

Figure 4.28: Matrix image and imagesc function examples

- **imread**: The function reads the specified image from the file name and returns a data array. This **Array** is created in the workspace. In the case of an indexed image, it returns a vector of data matrix and colormap. The function syntax and variations are as follows:

    ```
    ImageArray=imread(Filename);        %reads the Filename image and
                                                returns in ImageArray
    ImageArray=imread(Filename,Format); %reads the Filename image of
                                     given Format and returns in ImageArray
    [ImageArray,Map]=imread(Filename);  %reads the Filename indexed
    image and    returns Data matrix in ImageArray and colormap in
    Map
    ```

- **imshow**: The function displays an image in a figure window. The input argument to the function could be an RGB image, Grayscale image, Indexed image matrix with a colormap, or BW binary image. The name of the file is also a valid argument. The function syntax and example are as follows:

    ```
    imshow(x)      %where x could be RGB, Grayscale, BW image of
                             numeric  datatype
    imshow(x,colormap)   %displays indexed image
    ```

```
imshow(Filename)      %displays the file with the given name
flower=imread('flower.JPG'); %reads the RGB image 'flower.JPG' and
                 creates an array flower of 3159x4739x3 uint8
imshow(flower);       %displays the flower image in the figure window,
                 as shown in figure 4.29
```

The results of the example are as shown in *figure 4.29*:

Figure 4.29: imread and imshow function example

- **imwrite**: The function writes the image data to the given file name. The datatype and data format of the output file is similar to the input file unless the output file format is explicitly specified. In the case of an indexed image, both data matrix and colormap are provided.

    ```
    imwrite(ImageData,FileName);      %the image data from ImageData
                                 is written to the FileName
    ```

- **imresize**: As the name suggests, the function resizes the input image with the input scale. The scale value is a numeric scalar. For the original size, the image is scaled at 1. For scale >1, the output file is bigger, and for <1, it is smaller than the input file. In the case of an indexed image, the image data and colormap both are provided as inputs.

- **imfinfo**: The function returns a structure of information about the input graphics file.

The following functions are useful to convert the images from one type to another type:

- **im2double**: The function converts the image into a double-precision image. For the grayscale, binary or RGB images, the image name is specified as an argument to the function. For indexed images, the keyword **indexed** is specified along with the indexed image name.

- **ind2rgb**: The function converts the indexed image into **RGB(truecolor)** image. For the indexed images, the image data matrix and colormap array are specified as arguments to the function, and the resulting image is an RGB image.

- **rgb2ind**: The function converts the RGB image into an indexed image. The input to the function is the name of the RBG image and the number of quantized colors (65535 or lower) or uniform quantization tolerance. The output of the function is the data matrix and a colormap array. For example, for our previous flower example, the function **[IndM,ColMap]=rgb2ind(flower,65535);** creates **IndM** matrix of 3159×4739 and **ColMap** is created of 7133×3 size.

- **rgb2gray**: The function converts **RGB(truecolor)** image into grayscale images. The function returns the grayscale image. The function removes saturation and hue from the image, but it preserves the luminance data. The function also returns colormap adapted to grayscale. *Figure 4.30* shows the results of **grayflower=rgb2gray(flower); imshow(grayflower);** functions:

Figure 4.30: Grayscale flower image example

> This chapter contains information about widely used graphics functions. For detailed information about all the available functions, their syntaxes, and examples, kindly visit https://www.mathworks.com/help/matlab/graphics.html.

Conclusion

In this chapter, we have learnt the fundamentals of programming with the help of scripts, live scripts, and functions. We have also worked on the concepts of program control flow, with the introduction of `if-else`, `switch-case`, `try-catch`, and `for-while` loop. These learnings shall ultimately lead the reader towards Automation.

After programming, the chapter has introduced the reader to the concepts of 2-D and 3-D plotting using built-in functions and interactive plotting tools. The reader has also learnt to use the images in MATLAB effectively. Considering the plots and images, the reader has grasped the notions of visualization in MATLAB. In the upcoming chapter, we shall put the concepts we learnt until now to practice and provide some interesting examples.

Points to remember

- Variables used in the scripts are stored in base workspace, whereas functions have their independent workspace to store the variables.
- Variables must be cleared explicitly from base workspace; function variables are removed after the execution of the function.
- Live scripts/live functions are stored in .mlx files whereas functions and scripts are stored in .m file.
- Live scripts/Live functions use the output window to display the outputs, whereas scripts and functions use the command window to display the outputs.
- Program control flow using if-else, switch-case, try-catch, and for-while loops are essential in making the program optimized and readable in a better way.
- MATLAB offers a comprehensive set of built-in graphics functions to implement plots and images.
- The function syntaxes, variations, and examples are available for these functions in the MATLAB help documentation.
- Plotting is also possible with the help of an interactive plotting tool.

Multiple choice questions

1. Which of the following methods are not used to execute a script?
   a. Type the script name in the command window and press Enter key
   b. Drag the script file from the folder browser to the command window
   c. Open the script in the Editor window and click on the run button.
   d. None of the above

2. True or False: MATLAB script has its own workspace.
   a. True
   b. False

3. Which of the following is the valid declaration of a function?
   a. function C=add(A,B)
   b. C=function add(A,B)
   c. C=add(A,B)
   d. function C=add A,B

4. Which of the following has the documentation and MATLAB program in the same file?
   a. scripts
   b. functions
   c. plots
   d. live scripts

5. Which of the following is used to handle exceptions in MATLAB?
   a. if-else
   b. for loop
   c. try-catch
   d. break

6. Which statement is used to execute the case that has not been mentioned in the switch case?
   a. continue
   b. return

c. function

d. otherwise

7. Which of the following commands is used to implement multiple plots using the same axis?

   a. subplot

   b. hold on

   c. tiledlayout

   d. none of the above

8. Which of the following command is used to implement two y-axes in a single plot?

   a. imshow

   b. subplot

   c. yyaxis

   d. axis

9. What is the default range of the input variable for the function plot?

   a. [-5 5]

   b. [-100 100]

   c. [-10 10]

   d. None of the above

10. Which of the following functions can display an image?

    a. imshow

    b. image

    c. plot

    d. All of the above

Questions

1. What is the difference between a script and a function?

2. Explain the differences between a script and a live script.

3. Explain the different ways to execute the script.

4. Explain the difference between strings and character arrays.

5. Explain the user-defined functions with an example.
6. Explain the debugging of the .m file.
7. Explain how to control the programming flow using conditional statements and loops.
8. What are the different types of line specifiers available for a 2-D line plot?
9. Explain the subplot feature with an example.
10. What are the differences between 2-D and 3-D line plots?
11. How can we resize an image to its 75% size?
12. How to convert an indexed image to a grayscale image using only built-in image convert functions?

Answers

1. d
2. b
3. a
4. d
5. c
6. d
7. b
8. c
9. a
10. d

Section - II
Simulink

CHAPTER 5
Introduction to Simulink

Introduction

In the previous section, the reader has received a detailed overview of MATLAB. The reader has become familiar with the MATLAB interface, built-in functions, commands, classes, data input-output options, and so on. The reader also has been introduced to the concept of scalars, vectors, matrices, and arrays. The reader is comfortable with programming methods such as scripts, user-defined functions, live scripts, and debugging of programs. Additionally, the reader has been acquainted with various visualization techniques using 2-D and 3-D plots, charts, images, and so on. Based on these learnings, the reader can enhance the depth of knowledge by self-exploration and practice.

Simulink is an essential part of the MATLAB product group for multidomain modeling and simulation of complex dynamic systems. Many industries use the Simulink block diagram environment for their development activities, such as system and software analysis, design, implementation, simulation, code generation, verification, and validation. This chapter will introduce the reader to the essential features of Simulink and Model-based Design. Then the reader shall learn about different types of mathematical models that can be modeled with Simulink. The reader shall understand the basic system-design process flow. After that, the reader shall get hands-on knowledge on how to create a simple Simulink model; and shall be able to perform simulation too.

Structure

In this chapter, we shall discuss the following topics:

- Simulink overview
    - Highlights of Simulink
- Types of mathematical models
- Traditional system design vs. model-based design
    - Traditional design
    - Model-based design
    - Model-based design process steps
- Getting started with modeling
    - Create a simple Simulink model

Objectives

After studying this chapter, the reader will be able to:

- Learn the overview and capabilities of Simulink.
- Get to know about the fundamental differences between mathematical models
- Understand the primary differences between the traditional method and model-based design
- Learn the process steps of model-based design
- Learn to create and simulate a simple Simulink model

Simulink overview

Simulink is a MATLAB companion product for simulation and model-based design that offers an interactive block diagram-based graphical user environment. Simulink is widely used in various industries for system and software level design, analysis, simulation, code generation, and dynamic systems' verification. With the help of an interactive graphical editor, customizable block libraries, solvers, and programming APIs, Simulink enables users to model various linear and nonlinear systems in discrete time, continuous time, or combination. It supports the modeling and simulation of several real-world phenomena, such as friction, air resistance, thermodynamic, thermal, mechanical, electrical, electromagnetic, physical, hydraulic, and so on, behaviors, which quickly allows the users to create the prototype graphical models of the systems. The users can also predict the system behavior, and by adjusting a few parameters, they can fine-tune the design as per their requirements. All of this is possible without actually having to construct their physical prototypes, resulting in saving a significant amount of time, cost, and effort.

Simulink provides a highly interactive, easy-to-use Graphic environment and a vast set of prebuilt library blocks to make modeling fun and interesting. With some click-and-drag mouse operations, a user can implement the model at the speed of thought. The easy access to simulation and visualization induces the user's curiosity to try out different solutions and identify the most effective design. The design validation is also quite easy to achieve. Additionally, Simulink also provides an option to create, modify and simulate the MATLAB environment models programmatically. With the addition of application toolboxes, it is possible to expand the capabilities of Simulink in the area of application-specific design, rapid prototyping, validation and verification, code generation, and integration.

Highlights of Simulink

Simulink is preferred in many fields due to its key features in these three main areas.

Simulation and modeling

Simulink is used for modeling and simulation across multiple environments to simulate all parts of the system's functionalities. The Simulink vital features are as follows:

- Easy to use graphical user interface for adequate visualization and block diagram-based design and maintenance.
- A wide range of application-specific and predefined library blocks for multirate and multidomain modeling.
- Ability to develop large-scale models with the help of reusable system components, hierarchy, and libraries.
- One system-level simulation for the combination of models developed in multiple environments, including MATLAB functions, C, and C++ code.
- Possibility to package and share simulations using Web apps, Functional Mockup Units, or as executables.

Verification, validation, and testing

In many industries, Simulink is deployed for model-based design of complex embedded systems to generate production-quality code. Simulink offers verification and validation of these systems to identify errors during the initial stages, eliminating the need to develop expensive prototypes. It also provides the option to validate the design in various conditions with rapid prototyping and hardware-in-loop testing. The following are the key features of Simulink:

- Various options to instantly observe and analyze the simulation results
- Ensuring fulfillment of requirements with Requirement Traceability to design, architecture, code, and test cases
- Detect and resolve the critical errors at very early stages of development
- Conformance to regulations and quality guidelines to model and code
- Automatic test case generation to save manual efforts in increasing test coverage
- Report generation and adherence to standards

Automatic code generation

The provision to automatically generate mass production-ready code instead of manually writing thousands of code lines has made Simulink very popular in embedded system development. Simulink generates C or HDL code from a model for embedded processor or FPGA/ASIC to support different development stages with minimum effort. Simulink offers the following features:

- Generation of compact and more readable high-quality C, C++, CUDA, Verilog, VHDL, and Structured Text
- Availability of fixed as well floating-point design tools for practical analysis of quantization impact
- Software, Processor, and Hardware-in-the-loop verification testing of the generated code eliminates run-time errors.
- Generate popular safety and software standards-compliant code, for example, AUTOSAR, MISRA C, ISO-26262, DO-178, DO-254 for medical, railway, aerospace, and automotive embedded systems
- Simulink offers support package add-ons for code generation and prototyping on various embedded hardware platforms such as Raspberry Pi, Arduino, TI C2000, PLC, NVIDIA, Zynq, and so on.

Types of mathematical models

A mathematical model describes the system with the help of mathematical concepts and language. Mathematical models represent various physical as well as nonphysical real-world problems. The model represents the system, process, concept, and device, using interactions of variables such as system inputs, internal states, outputs, equations, and inequalities. Based on these models' results, the quantitative system responses are predicted and analyzed compared with experimental results. Additionally, mathematical models are used for optimizing system behavior and designing complex control systems. We can differentiate mathematical models into various categories:

Linear models

The model for which the response is directly proportional to the driving input is defined as a linear model. For linear models, the objective functions are described by linear equations. We can describe linear mathematical models with mathematical equations. For example, the slope-intercept form of the line equation $y=mx+b$ can be applied to many real-world linear systems, where m represents the slope of the line and b represents the y-intercept.

Nonlinear models

The model for which the system response is not linearly proportional to the driving input(s) is nonlinear. For these models, the objective functions and exceptions are represented with nonlinear equations. These models are difficult to describe as compared to linear models. For example, equation $y=x2$ describes a nonlinear mathematical model.

Static models

The static model describes the logical behavior of the system in an equilibrium state. These models are time-invariant, so the system response does not depend on any history of previous inputs, outputs, or internal states. Mathematical models that can be depicted using algebraic equations are considered static models. For example, system $y=f(x)$ that only relies on the current state of variables is represented by a static model.

Dynamic models

The models that describe the time-dependent behavior of the systems are known as dynamic models. Here, the system response is calculated based on the history of previous inputs, internal states, and outputs. Differential equations are used to represent dynamic models. For example, a mass-spring-damper dynamic system can be represented by a second-order differential equation.

Explicit models

The models for which all input parameters are well known and a finite calculation sequence derives output parameters are identified as explicit models.

Implicit models

The models for which all output parameters are well known and iterative procedures are used based on linearity to derive input parameters are recognized as implicit models.

Discrete models

Models, where the objects are discrete in time, are defined as discrete models. For example, a model with a finite number of states is considered a discrete model.

Continuous models

Models, where the objects are characterized in a time-continuous mode, are known as continuous models. One such example is the current flow in an electrical system.

Deterministic models

Deterministic models are the models that are exclusive of any randomness. Deterministic models have all variable states characterized by unique parameters and sets of previous states in the model. The outputs of these models are identical for a specific set of initial conditions. For example, truth tables, Celsius to Fahrenheit temperature conversion, simple interest calculation, and so on.

Stochastic (random) models

Stochastic models consider the element of randomness. These models are also known as probabilistic or statistical models, as some variables have the possibility of random values; therefore, the models consider probability distributions, and the results for the same initial conditions are different each time. For example, a transport system running with accuracy can be expressed using a deterministic model, whereas another transport system running with delays can be implemented as a stochastic model, where delay can be a random parameter.

Traditional system design vs. model-based design

The complexity and scope of embedded software systems have increased manifold over the years. The situation is challenging for organizations in almost every field where the lines of code have significantly grown. The permissible time to market has reduced, and there is an even higher demand for quality and a greater need to lower development costs. Therefore, various system design methods are being implemented in innovation-driven industries such as medical, automotive, aerospace, automation, communication, and so on to effectively balance among cost, time, and quality system requirements. The traditional system design and development methods have been proven less fruitful for highly complex systems. These processes are inadequate in successfully managing the trade-off of cost, time, and quality.

Traditional system design

Industries have followed the traditional design approach for several decades. In this method, the process steps such as analysis, design, implementation, testing, and production are performed sequentially using various tool setups. These design methods heavily rely on predefined processes and documentation; therefore, the methodology is known as the process-centric approach. As the overall process flow is sequential, the engineer must complete the earlier step first while moving to the next step.

Traditional design workflow

Based on the results of research and requirements, specifications are derived in a textual form during the analysis phase. As a result, the specifications are often misinterpreted, and any changes in requirements create troubles while maintaining consistency. According to the process, all requirements are to be made available for the initial analysis phase to avoid the impacts of changes introduced later. Using the specification, different designs, for example, electrical, mechanical, physical, or algorithm-based prototypes, are created. The creation of these prototypes is expensive as it is difficult to develop complete prototypes, and their system-level testing is possible only after the implementation stage. Therefore, the iterative steps become highly time-consuming. During the implementation phase, the developers manually convert these designs into codes. The hand-coding process is cumbersome and has the potential to introduce new errors. During the next stage, the testing is performed on integrated systems. At this point, the errors from earlier phases and integration issues are detected, causing repetitive iterations that ultimately result in high development costs and delayed timelines.

As explained in the process flow of *figure 5.1*, the traditional system design consists of several manual steps, introducing failures. Due to the lack of early system validation possibilities, the errors are identified at very late testing stages, costing significant delays, higher development costs, and efforts. The traditional approach would be a better choice for the smaller systems but managing the development with this approach would be challenging for more extensive and complex systems:

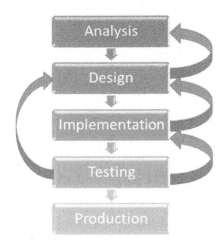

Figure 5.1: Traditional system design workflow

Model-based design

Model-based design enables faster and more cost-effective development of complex dynamic systems. In model-based design methodology, a system model is at the center of the overall development process during every phase-requirements analysis, design, implementation, and testing. Model-based design reduces development time and cost through early defect identification. The companies that adopt model-based design can deliver systems with high quality and lower costs within reduced time. According to Mathworks, a model-based design with Simulink can improve product quality and reduce development time by 50% or more.

A model describes a system in an abstract and simplified manner with mathematical equations and executable diagrams. Creating a virtual representation of a real-world scenario using block diagrams that one can simulate is referred to as modeling. Modeling and simulation help with testing, especially during early phases of development where hardware setup is unavailable. Early identification of the errors reduces the project time and cost and drastically improves software quality. Due to the possibility of generating code automatically once software and hardware requirements are considered, Testers can perform system testing early without waiting for the overall completion of the development stages. Automated code generation avoids errors, which are mainly introduced during manual coding, and it saves developers' time.

Advantages of model-based design

The model-based design offers the following advantages:

- Several project teams can share a common design environment
- Designs can be directly linked to the requirements
- It is possible to integrate testing with design to detect and rectify the failures continually
- Algorithms are refined through multidomain simulation
- Automatic generation of embedded software code
- Automatic generation of documentation
- Test suites can be developed and reused
- Hardware agnostic system design reuse

Model-based design workflow

Different project teams use the same design environment for all phases- requirement, analysis, design, implementation, and testing in a model-based design workflow. Models are enhanced and reused at every level, so the development time is reduced, and the interpretation errors are eliminated. Based on the research and requirements, system engineers define low-level requirements as executable specifications using models. Different physical behaviors are simulated using behavioral models, and then they are used to make decisions of design trade-offs, which makes the process more straightforward compared to the traditional approach. The models are used to clarify requirements and specifications. Software developers further enhance these models in detail. They can simulate these models to rectify any behavior or interface-related errors. After a few iterations of refining the models, the design is finally verified. From the models, production engineers automatically generate production-level HDL code. The system-level test cases are reused to test the generated code. The behavior is then also verified on the target hardware by reusing the test cases. Requirements can be imported into the model and linked to the design, thus establishing requirement-to-design traceability. In this way, the model-based design offers an excellent choice for a complex system that provides a shared development environment and reduces development costs, time, and efforts with simulation and auto code generation. Reuse of the model designs and test cases lowers the number of defects identified during later development stages and eliminates manual efforts. *Figure 5.2* explains the design workflow.

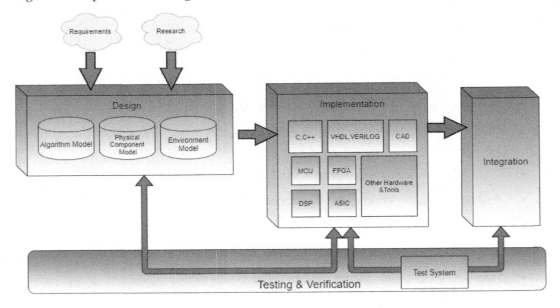

Figure 5.2: Model-based design workflow

Model-based design process steps

These steps are released during the model-based design:

- Derive the system requirements
- Define the system
- Design the system architecture
- Define the Simulink model behavior
- Simulate and verify model results
- Generate production code automatically
- Verification and validation

Figure 5.3 describe the V-cycle model-based design stages and their corresponding verification processes:

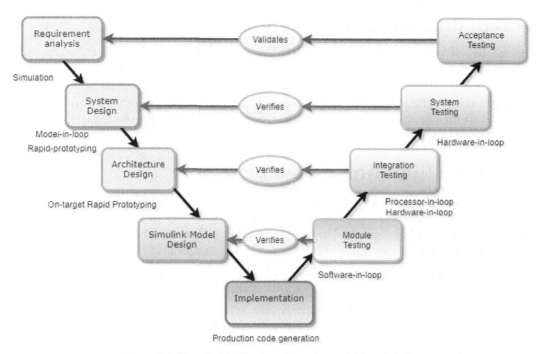

Figure 5.3: V cycle SDLC process flow for model-based design

Derive the system requirements

Based on customer goals and research, system engineers derive the system requirement specifications. The requirement specifications cover physical and functional aspects. Regulations and guidelines are also taken into account. The system engineers create executable system specification models, which can be reused and enhanced during further development phases. This process reduces the knowledge loss that could occur during the handover of the requirements to the engineers responsible for the subsequent stages and saves their efforts up to some extent.

Define the system

Once the system requirements have been fully defined, the next step is to create an exhaustive system definition. As per the size and complexity of the system, the respective system is modularized into different system components, which helps to effectively carry out the overall development cycle by enabling concurrent development and design reuse. In small iterations, the system definition is continually refined as per system specification. The uncomplicated layout of interfaces between the components is drawn. The components are to be modeled, simulated, and verified individually, and later they will again be integrated for verification of the complete system.

Design the system architecture

During the third step, the system architecture is described by elaborating the system components in detail. These components are broken into hierarchical model components or subsystems concerning their functional and physical behaviors for enhanced maintainability. This step is also called high-level design. For architecture design, different properties are further derived for each subsystem: inputs, outputs, internal signals, states (variables), and parameters (constants).

Define the Simulink model behavior

After all, the components previously mentioned are well defined, and their Simulink model behavior is described for their physical and functional properties using different mathematical models. This step is known as low-level design. Two types of models are developed during this phase: the plant model and the controller model.

- **Plant model**: Mimics the non-software behaviors of the real world, such as physical, thermal, pneumatic, hydraulic, electrical, mechanical, or environmental relationships with the system. They enable early validation of the control model logic in closed-loop simulations with near-real-world interactions. MATLAB offers various toolboxes based on applications to support physical and environmental plant modeling.

- **Controller model**: The controller models are designed for deployment on the hardware. The model algorithms can be explained with logical, algebraic, and linear/nonlinear differential or difference equations. These equations are further implemented using block diagrams in Simulink. The parameter values are also defined in the model. Model developers can share and reuse their models by creating libraries and files.

Simulate and verify model results

Once the Simulink model design is complete, the model is simulated to analyze the model's behavior with respect to the requirements. With simulation and debugging options, the expected behavior differences are quickly identified, and the model design is adjusted until all the failures are eliminated. The simulation is performed in a desktop environment.

Generate production code automatically

From the Simulink model block diagram, the production level code is generated automatically after the host hardware settings have been considered. For example, fixed-point properties are set for fixed-point systems. The code can be generated to be deployed on microcontroller, PLC, FPGA, ASIC, and so on. Auto code generation reduces errors due to manual code writing. The behavior results of generated software code simulation are then compared with the Model simulation results, and the model design and parameters are adjusted accordingly to get the desired performance.

Verification and validation

Model-based design with Simulink offers early and continuous verification of the components. For each design stage, the test cases are prepared or auto generated for verification in parallel with the development stage, saving testing time. Each module can be verified independently as a unit and later while integration and then on the target hardware. Different MATLAB toolboxes are available to validate the designed systems against their desired results.

Model-based simulation methods

The following simulation methods are used to verify, validate, and test the **system under test (SUT)** in the given order:

- **Model-in-Loop (MIL)**: MIL simulation is performed during the initial development stage to verify the development model's behavior in a desktop simulation environment. The developers can compare the behaviors with requirements and avoid defects at an early stage. In this method, the hardware components are not considered, so the timing-related and fixed-point properties are also not applicable.

- **Software-in-Loop (SIL)**: SIL is used to verify the generated production code in the host PC's modeling environment with non-real-time plant model simulation. After the fixed-point settings, the code is automatically generated (C and C++), and this code is verified compared with the MIL simulation results. It is possible to identify data type, time, and scaling-related issues during SIL.

- **Processor-in-Loop (PIL)**: PIL is a one-step further from SIL, where the generated code is verified on the actual processor hardware (microcontroller, DSP, FPGA, and so on). During PIL, the simulation of the plant model is performed in a non-real-time environment after the source code that cross-compiled on the host pc is converted to object code and then is downloaded and run on the target processor. When compared to SIL, PIL can indicate additional issues such as memory or fixed-point conversion.

- **Hardware-in-Loop (HIL)**: HIL is used to verify the integrated system with real system components and virtual plant model representation in real-time. HIL testing has been a proven practical and reliable method of testing. It includes all the system hardware/software components such as mechanical components, sensors, actuators, and so on. All the integration-related issues are identified during this stage.

Getting started with modeling

As described in the Simulink overview, Simulink is a block-diagram-based environment used for model-based design and multidomain simulation of systems. A model is a graphical block-diagram description of the dynamic system. With some click-and-drag mouse operations, the users can create and simulate models in Simulink. Simulink is integrated very closely with MATLAB; therefore, we can use any of the environments for creating, editing, simulating, or analyzing our continuous, discrete, or hybrid models. There are two basic methods of using Simulink for modeling and simulation: The interactive method and the Programmatic method.

- **Interactive method**: We can create, edit, configure, and simulate models using a block diagram with a Simulink interactive Model editing GUI environment.
- **Programmatic method**: We can programmatically create, edit, configure, and simulate models by executing functions in MATLAB command prompt or predefined scripts. This method helps in automation.

Create a simple Simulink model

In this section, we shall learn simple modeling techniques using the interactive method. The following is a stepwise procedure to create a simple Simulink model:

1. Start Simulink
2. Open Simulink Editor
3. Open Simulink Library browser
4. Add blocks to Model
5. Configure the block parameters
6. Connect the blocks
7. Define model configuration parameters
8. Run Simulation

In this section, the steps mentioned earlier are elaborated with examples.

Start Simulink

Starting Simulink is the first step toward model creation:

1. To start Simulink, open MATLAB first.

2. In MATLAB, there are three options to open Simulink:

    - In the MATLAB **HOME** tab under the **SIMULINK** section, click the **Simulink** button, as highlighted in *figure 5.4*.

    - In the MATLAB Home tab under the **FILE** section, select the **Simulink** model from "**New**" dropdown, as highlighted in *figure 5.4*.

    - In the MATLAB command prompt, execute the **simulink** command.

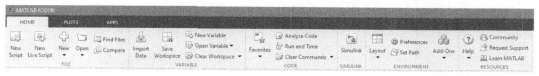

Figure 5.4: *Start Simulink from MATLAB Home tab*

3. After performing any of the three operations, the Simulink start page opens.

4. Under the **SIMULINK** section, click on the **Blank** model template.

5. A new blank model file is created.

6. Instead of a blank model template, you may also choose from already available or custom templates.

Open Simulink Editor

When we create a new model, it opens in the Simulink editor. Simulink editor is an intuitive graphical editing tool as part of a Simulink model editing environment.

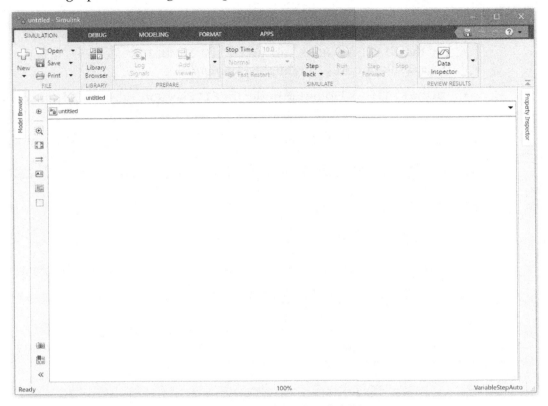

Figure 5.5: New model in Simulink Editor

As seen in *figure 5.5*, Simulink Editor can be divided into different parts:

- **Toolstrip**: On the top area of Simulink Editor, toolstrip can be found, which offers operations useful during modeling. It has different tabs: **Simulation**, **Debug**, **Modeling**, **Format**, and **Apps** provide functionality corresponding to each task. Based on the chosen operation, more contextual tabs become visible.

- **Canvas**: Where Simulink visual block diagrams are created using different types of blocks and lines.

- **Quick access toolbar**: For accessing frequently used operations.

- **Model browser**: For model hierarchical navigation.

- **Property inspector**: Simulink block properties can be visualized and modified.

- **Palette**: For model appearance and navigation, for example, zoom, or viewmark.

Open Simulink Library browser

Simulink blocks must be added to the Simulink editor's canvas for creating visual block diagrams. We can access these blocks from the Simulink Library Browser. A block is a fundamental element of a Simulink model that defines the mathematical relationship between input and output. There are two methods to open the Simulink library browser as follows:

1. Click the Library browser button present on the **SIMULATION** tab of the Simulink Editor toolstrip.

2. Execute **slLibraryBrowser** command in the MATLAB command prompt.

After performing any of the previous operations, the **Simulink Library Browser** window pops up. There are two sections of the **Library Browser**. On the left section, the library blocks are categorized based on their types. On the right window, the blocks of the selected library are available as follows:

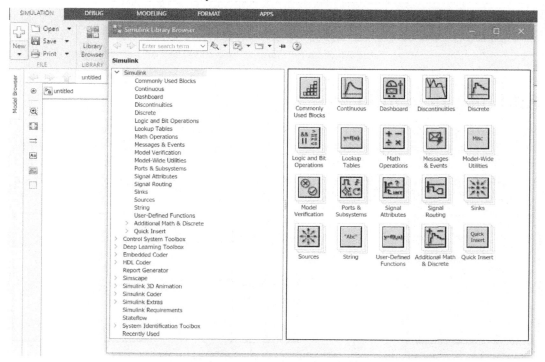

Figure 5.6: Simulink Library browser

As shown in *figure 5.6*, `Library Browser` has multiple categories of blocks, such as continuous, discrete, logic and bit operations, math operations, and so on. By hovering on the blocks, you may read the block description. *Table 5.1* describes the purpose of some of these libraries, along with example blocks:

Library	Description	Block examples
Continuous	Continuous state blocks	Derivative, Integrator
Discrete	Systems with discrete states	Delay, Memory
Logical and Bit Operations	Logical, relational, bitwise operation blocks	AND, OR, XOR
Lookup Tables	Interpolated search blocks	1-D Lookup Table, Prelookup
Math Operations	Mathematical operation blocks	Abs, Add, dot
Ports and Subsystems	In/Out ports, subsystem blocks	In1, Out1, Subsystem
Signal Routing	Signal grouping and navigation blocks	Demux, Bus selector
Sinks	Output visualization and storage blocks	Scope, Display
Sources	Model input simulation blocks	Pulse Generator, constant
User-Defined Functions	User-defined function blocks	Simulink Fcn, function caller

Table 5.1: Simulink Library Blocks overview

Add blocks to model

Before starting model building, it is necessary to identify the blocks required to build the model. Consider this continuous system as an example, where two different operations are performed on a continuous input signal: first-order Integration and Amplification. As a source of the signal, the Sinewave of amplitude 2 has been considered. The output signals are observed in scope.

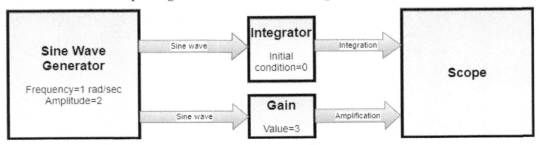

Figure 5.7: Example continuous state model block diagram

To build the system shown in *figure 5.7*, we need to bring these four different blocks to Simulink Editor from Simulink Block libraries:

- Sine wave generator: Sources
- Integrator: Continuous
- Gain: Math operations
- Scope: Sinks

There are several methods to add the identified library blocks to the model as follows:

1. In the **Library Browser**, navigate to the block in the right window

    a. Right-click on the block and select **Add block** to model the untitled option.

    b. Drag the block from the browser and drop it to the model in Simulink Editor.

2. Right-click the library name on the left section of the **Library Browser** and select the **Open library** option.

    a. Drag the desired block from the library and drop it to the model.

    b. Right-click the block in the library, select the **copy** option, and paste it to the model file.

3. On Simulink Editor canvas, double-click in an empty space and start typing the block name in the popped-up quick search window (applicable for release 2014b and newer). Select the relevant block from the list of all available blocks with a given name and press *Enter*.

4. On Simulink Editor canvas, press *Ctrl +*. (*Ctrl + Shift+* . for AZERTY keyboard) twice, and in the **Action** menu search window, type block name, press down arrow, choose desired block, and press *Enter* (applicable for release 2019b and newer).

Refer to *figure 5.8* to add the Integrator block as per the first method for our example model. It is available as part of the Continuous library:

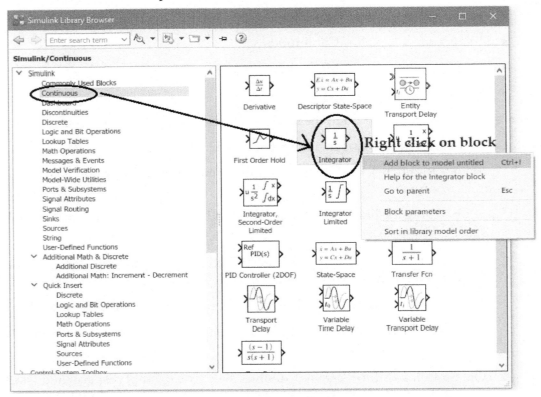

Figure 5.8: Add integrator block to model

Similarly, add all other blocks to the model file, as shown in *figure 5.9*:

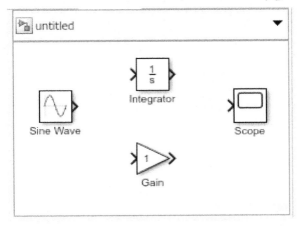

Figure 5.9: Add all blocks to model

Rearrange these blocks by drag and drop operation. To resize, click on the block and resize by holding it from its corners.

Configure the block parameters

We will adjust the parameters of the blocks according to our requirements. There are multiple methods to update the parameter values:

1. Select the block and adjust the block parameter values in **Property Inspector**.

2. Double-click on the block, and a window with parameter values pop-up. You can adjust the desired parameters; otherwise, they will have the default values.

3. Right-click on the block and select the **Block parameters** option.

4. Select the block and press *Enter* key.

5. Select the block and press *Alt + Enter* keys. There will be a pop-up to specify the value of the main parameter. In case you want to modify any other parameter, please refer to other methods.

For our example, we will edit the parameter value of all blocks from *figure 5.6*:

- **Sine wave Generator block**: Amplitude value to be changed from 1 to 2; refer to *figure 5.10*:

Figure 5.10: Sine-wave generator block parameters

- **Integrator block**: Initial value: 0, which is the same as the default value. Therefore, no change in block parameters
- **Gain block**: Gain value to be changed from 1 to 3, as per *figure 5.10*. You can also hover on value 1, and the option to edit the value will appear:

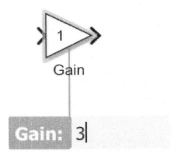

Figure 5.11: Gain block parameters

- **Scope block**: Three input ports are to be added, one for input signals, and two for output signals; refer to *figure 5.12*:

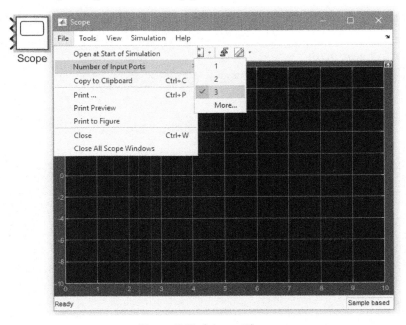

Figure 5.12: Scope settings

Connect the blocks

The output ports of blocks are connected to the block input ports through lines. Similar to blocks, lines are essential elements of Simulink Editor. Signal lines transfer the data from one block to another. Event lines are used for implementing control flow. For our example, we transfer the continuous waves using signal lines. Refer to any of these methods to create lines:

- To create a new line between blocks, click on the desired port of any of them, and all the corresponding unconnected ports of the model are highlighted. A red dashed line becomes visible as you drag the line until you drop it to the opposite port of the desired block. Thus, the solid line is created, and the line color changes to black.

- Select any one of the two blocks, press, and hold the *Ctrl* key and then select another block. The line is automatically created.

- Select both blocks, right-click and select connect blocks option. The line is automatically created between them.

- When the unconnected input and output ports are aligned in a straight line, Simulink Editor shows a blue suggestion line, and if you click on it, the line is automatically created.

- Press and hold the *Ctrl* key and drag and drop to create a line from the existing line.

It is a good practice to annotate the required signal with a signal label. It helps the reader to understand the data flow and debug issues if any. *Figure 5.13* shows the connected blocks. Now, the model implementation is complete. In the next step, we will simulate the model and observe the outputs:

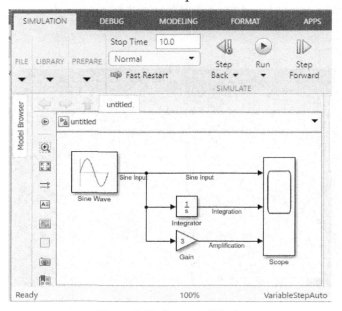

Figure 5.13: Connected blocks

Define model configuration parameters

Model configuration parameters are accessible from the model settings button available on the modeling tab. It includes settings, for example, simulation time, solver, step size, and so on. As visible in *figure 5.12*, the solver's default value is **VariableStepAuto**, and for our example, we will use default values only. We shall learn model configuration in *Chapter 8: Configuration Parameter Settings*.

Run Simulation

In Simulink Editor's Simulation tab, we can define simulation parameters such as Stop time and Simulation speed; we also have a **Run** button to start simulation and Data Inspector for observing scope data. The default stop time is 10 seconds, which is changed to 15 seconds, as shown in *figure 5.14*. Press the **Run** button for simulation. First, the model gets compiled, and if there are no errors, then the simulation starts:

Figure 5.14: Simulation settings

After the Simulation is complete, double-click on the scope block. The graph is available for visualization of Simulation results, as shown in *figure 5.15*. From the **View** menu, display-related options such as legend could be enabled. The model can be saved as in **.slx** format and modified/reused as required:

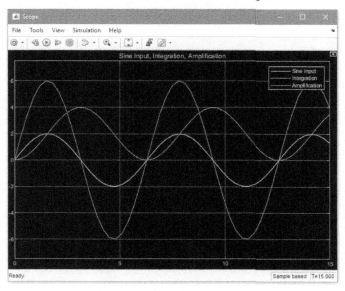

Figure 5.15: Example simulation results

By following similar steps, we shall implement another model, the Fibonacci sequence counter, where *x(n)=x(n-1)+x(n-2)* and so on. Desired simulation time is 2 seconds, and the sample rate is 0.2 seconds. We require these four blocks for Implementation:

1. **Unit delay 1: x(n-1)**: Discrete, Initial value=1 (first element of sequence)
2. **Unit delay 2: x(n-2)**: Discrete, Initial value=1 (second element of sequence)
3. **Sum block**: Math operations
4. **Scope**: Sinks

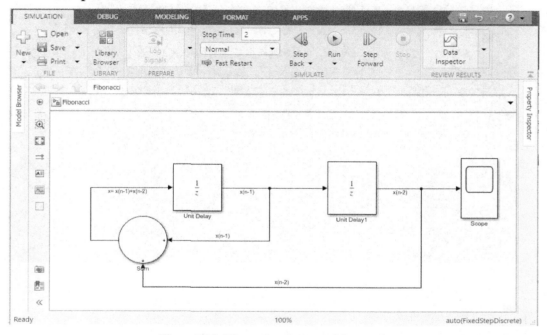

Figure 5.16: *Fibonacci sequence model example*

According to requirements, the sample time is 0.2 seconds, assigned in model settings | `Fixed-Step Solver` | `Step size`. The required simulation time is 2 seconds, which is updated in the toolstrip as stop time. After running the simulation, we get the graph as shown in *figure 5.17*:

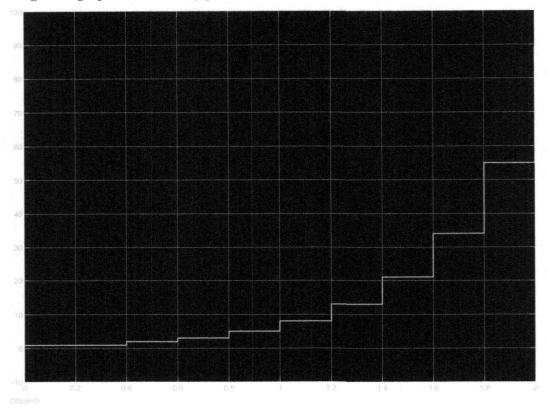

Figure 5.17: Fibonacci sequence model Simulation results

From the graph, we can observe that the values are updated at every 0.2 seconds in the sequence as shown in *table 5.2*:

0.2 sec	0.4 sec	0.6 sec	0.8 sec	1.0 sec	1.2 sec	1.4 sec	1.6 sec	1.8 sec	2.0 sec
1	1	2	3	5	8	13	22	55	89

Table 5.2: Fibonacci sequence model simulation results

MATLAB offers an exciting and wide variety of executable Simulink model examples: https://www.mathworks.com/help/examples.html.

Conclusion

In the previous section, we have learnt in detail MATLAB and the various possibilities offered by MATLAB. Being the first chapter of the Simulink section, this chapter has laid a strong foundation for Simulink. The readers have informed themselves of different types of mathematical models. They can compare **model-based design (MBD)** with traditional design and understand its benefits. The chapter has explained the process of Model-based design with the SDLC V cycle. The readers are now able to create and simulate simple Simulink models by themselves. In the upcoming chapter, the reader shall become familiar with the usage of Simulink Graphical Editor. The reader shall also learn to create a Simulation environment.

Points to remember

- Simulink is an essential part of system design and multidomain simulation for engineering and industrial services.
- Simulink is a visual block diagram-based environment used widely for research and product development purposes.
- Simulink enables automatic production code generation to reduce manual errors and efforts.
- Different mathematical models can be implemented and analyzed in Simulink.
- Simulink offers Verification and validation of systems during the early phases of development. Concurrent development in software development using the V-cycle process.
- Model-based design enables faster and more cost-effective development of complex dynamic systems vs. traditional system design.
- In the V-cycle Software development process, each development phase is linked with respective testing phases.
- Plant model and controller models are the types of models created during the design phase.
- **Model-in-loop (MIL)**, **Software-in-loop (SIL)**, **Processor-in-loop (PIL)**, and **Hardware-in-loop (HIL)** are the simulation methods used for verification, validation, and testing.
- Interactive and programmatic methods are used to create Simulink models.
- Simulink editor is an intuitive graphical editing tool as part of a Simulink model editing environment.
- A Simulink block is a fundamental element of a Simulink model that defines the mathematical relationship between input and output.

- The output ports of blocks are connected to the block input ports through lines. Signal lines transfer the data from one block to another.

Multiple choice questions

1. **Which of the following is the feature of Simulink?**
    a. Multidomain modeling and simulation
    b. Automatic code generation
    c. Early verification and validation
    d. All of the above

2. **Simulink allows only floating-point modeling.**
    a. True
    b. False

3. **Which of the following language does Simulink not support for code generation?**
    a. C++
    b. CUDA
    c. C#
    d. Verilog

4. **Which of the following model is not a mathematical model?**
    a. Linear model
    b. Dynamic model
    c. Discrete model
    d. None of the above

5. **What is the next phase after Implementation in traditional design workflow?**
    a. Analysis
    b. Testing
    c. Design
    d. Production

6. Which of the following models are designed during the design phase?
   a. Plant model
   b. Controller model
   c. A & B
   d. None of the above

7. Which of the following is not a simulation method used for verification and validation?
   a. Model-in-loop
   b. Software-in-loop
   c. Processor-in-loop
   d. System-in-loop

8. A block can be added to Simulink Editor from the library browser by drag-and-drop operation.
   a. True
   b. False

9. What is the default stop time for model simulation?
   a. 15
   b. 5
   c. 10
   d. 0

10. The signal line is used to transfer the control in the model.
    a. True
    b. False

Questions

1. Explain key Simulink features in the area of simulation modeling.
2. What is the difference between static and dynamic mathematical model?
3. What are the main differences between traditional and model-based design approach?
4. List advantages of model-based design.

5. Explain the procedure of model-based design with v cycle processes.
6. What is the different model-based simulation modes? Explain in brief.
7. List and explain the steps of model creation and simulation.
8. Create and simulate the model for Celsius to Fahrenheit unit conversion.

Answers

1. a
2. b
3. c
4. d
5. b
6. c
7. d
8. a
9. c
10. b

CHAPTER 6
Simulink Editor with Environment

Introduction

Simulink Editor is a vector graphics editor used for creating models in the form of block diagrams. It supports modeling by offering access to various data import and export tools, simulation, and model performance analysis. Simulink Editor makes modeling easy just with the help of mouse click, drag, and drop operations. This chapter familiarizes the user with Simulink Editor's graphical user interface layout. Simulink offers most of the process through toolstrip, on which this chapter throws some light. Using a simple PID controller example, the chapter explains basic model design methods. This chapter then moves towards environment creation techniques. This chapter covers different approaches to create an environment/wrapper for the developed model. The reader shall explore different signal loading options. The reader shall also learn visualization and logging methods. In the end, the chapter lists some of the popular Simulink modeling shortcuts that help the users with quick navigation and modeling. In this way, the reader shall learn everything necessary about Simulink Graphical Editor and its menus.

Structure

In this chapter, we shall discuss the following topics:

- Introduction to Simulink Editor

- Toolstrip
    - Simulation
    - Debug
    - Modeling
    - Format
- Model example: PID controller
- Signal loading, visualization, and logging techniques
    - Signal loading techniques
    - Signal visualization and logging techniques
- Simulink modeling shortcuts

Objective

After studying this chapter, the readers will be able to:
- Get familiarized with Simulink Editor interface layout
- Get a brief overview of the various operations offered by toolstrip
- Learn basic modeling process with the example of PID controller
- Understand how to create an input environment for the control logic
- Implement different techniques to visualize and log simulation data
- Familiarize themselves with a few Simulink keyboard and mouse shortcuts

Introducing Simulink Editor

Simulink Editor is a vector graphics editor used for creating models in the form of block diagrams. It supports modeling by offering access to various data import and export tools, simulation, and model performance analysis. Compared with traditional model design, Simulink editor makes it easier for system designers to build and edit models just with a few click and drag mouse operations to connect and add blocks, analyze, and refine them with the help of simulation.

Some of the features of Simulink Editor are listed as follows:
- Interactively build and edit models.
- Choose from available model templates or create your own model template.
- Select from the list of already available library model objects with drag-and-drop operations and place and connect added blocks on the editing canvas.

- We can click, shift-click to select multiple blocks and drag the selected objects.
- Model objects can be resized using handles and moved by dragging.
- Cut, paste and copy objects.
- Undo and Redo operations are possible up to 101 operations.
- We can perform zooming and scrolling the editing area.
- Simulink highlights model design issues with visual indication and simple issue descriptions.
- Simulink detects if the problem is known and shows a predefined fix, it will also give out a fix button to apply to the issue.
- Simulink Editor provides a Model Browser that helps showcase the model hierarchy using a tree structure, thus, displaying an overview of the model organization and helping in exploring systems within systems.
- Using Simulink Editor, we can set parameters and properties of different model elements affecting how the block should function, thus, having control of individual model blocks level.
- We can set properties of Stateflow charts, signal lines, visual elements such as annotations, and the model as a whole.

As we have observed in the previous chapter, Simulink Editor Interface consists of different components, as shown in *figure 6.1*:

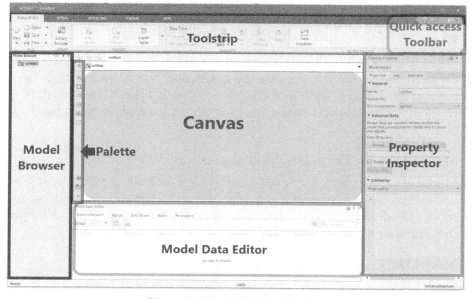

Figure 6.1: Simulink Editor interface

As per *figure 6.1*, these are the components of Simulink Editor:

- **Toolstrip: To explore Simulink capabilities**

    Toolstrip is located at the top of the Simulink Editor interface that supports everyday user workflow tasks. Toolstrip consists of the following tabs, which provide functionality corresponding to the tab's name:
    - **Simulation**: Creation of new model, saving, opening library browser, running simulation, and data control analysis.
    - **Debug**: Used for debugging the various steps in model execution, performance analysis, and diagnostics viewer.
    - **Modeling**: Supports modeling activity with different options, such as set environment preferences, model explorer and settings, model design and compilation, and simulation.
    - **Format**: Offers model formatting-related functions, such as font, color, style, auto-arrange blocks, and so on.
    - **Apps**: Provides access to applications from the Simulink family of products. Opens a new contextual tab, window, or configuration parameter.

Along with the preceding tabs, the toolstrip also has a quick access toolbar:

- **Quick access toolbar**: Contains frequently used operations, such as save, undo, and so on.
- **Canvas**: To create model block diagrams.

We can create a model design here using different blocks and signals.

- **Property Inspector: To edit model object parameters**

    Property Inspector is accessible by extending the Property Inspector pane located on the right side of the canvas. We can immediately update model element properties and parameters for the selected object with this dialogue box's help.

- **Model Browser: For hierarchical navigation**

    Model Browser can be extended on the left side of the canvas. In the case of multiple subsystems in the model, the whole hierarchy is visible for that model file. Just clicking the name of any subsystem, we can directly jump to that subsystem.

- **Model Data Editor: To edit model data**

    Model data editor pops up below canvas, where it is possible to update properties and parameters of multiple model elements.

- **Palette: To access navigation and modeling shortcuts**

    Palette is visible on the left side of the Simulink Editor canvas. It contains shortcut icons for model navigation and formatting, such as zoom, fit to image, annotations, and so on.

> Modeling operations with Simulink Editor are performed by various combinations of keyboard and mouse operations. Please go through the *Simulink Modeling shortcuts* section to learn frequently used shortcuts at the end of this chapter.

Now, we will have a detailed look at some of the essential operations offered by toolstrip.

Toolstrip

Toolstrip contains five fixed tabs: Simulation, Debug, Modeling, Format, and Apps.

Simulation

The simulation tab offers various operations required for the simulation as well as for accessing the files and libraries, as shown in *figure 6.2*:

Figure 6.2: Simulation tab

The simulation tab is further divided into these subsections: File, Library, Prepare, Simulate, and Review results:

- **File**: To create and save new or open existing model files, as well as printing. The following *table 6.1* describes the functions available in brief:

Operation	Symbol	Description
New model		Create a new model file as per the default settings
New	New	Select one of the options from the drop-down to create a new file: 1. Blank model 2. Blank subsystem Create from the template: 3. Model 4. Subsystem 5. Statechart 6. Library 7. Project
Open		• `Open`: Click on the Open button, and the browser window pops up • `Recent files`: Click on the arrow, and from the drop-down, select open or choose from recent files. • `Viewmarks`: Open from Viewmarks
Save		• `Save`: Click on the Save button for the new file browser window that pops up. By default, it saves in `.slx` format, which could be changed to `.mdl` format too. • `Save as`: Click on the arrow, and from the drop-down, select save as a browser window pops up. Here too, you have the option to choose the file format. • `Save as Viewmark`: The option enables saving the model as viewmark to be viewed later. • `Export to protected model`: For exporting as IP protected model copy • `Export as template`: To be reused as a template later • `Save as previous version`: You can save the model in `.slx` or `.mdl` format for older releases up to R2012b
Print		Print the model as per the requirements

Table 6.1: Simulation tab file menu

- **Library**: To launch the library browser, as shown in *table 6.2*:

Operation	Symbol	Description
Library Browser	Library Browser	The button opens the Simulink Library Browser, from where we can choose the library blocks for creating our model block diagram.

Table 6.2: Simulation tab Library menu

- **Prepare**: Supports operations for simulation, configuration, monitoring, and tuning, as specified in *table 6.3*:

Operation	Symbol	Description
		Signal monitoring
Log signals	Log Signals	Select a signal, and this button gets activated, clicking which the signal data is recorded upon running simulation. When enabled, a signal icon appears at the source of the logged signal. With this option, we can observe signal values in Simulink Data Inspector. We can compare them, and we can save and export the signal simulation data too. It is also possible to select multiple signals at once and apply logging.
Add Viewer	Add Viewer	Select a signal, then add viewer button gets activated, and if you click on that, the viewer gets added for the signal based on the chosen option: scope and XY graph. The viewer icon is visible at the source of the signal. Thus, the viewer can observe the signal values by opening them during or after running the simulation.
Signal Table	Signal Table	Opens Signals tab of Model Data Editor, where all the model signals are listed, and checkboxes for `Test Point` and `Log Data` can be enabled for multiple signals together.
Viewers Manager	Viewers Manager	Launches Viewers and Generators manager window, where all scopes and XY graphs are listed. In this window, we can add, configure and delete the viewers.
Configure Logging	Configure Logging	Data Import/Export page of the model configuration parameters pops up. We will discuss the configuration setting in the upcoming chapters.

	Inputs and Parameter tuning	
Connect Inputs	Connect Inputs	Opens the Root Inport Mapper Dialog box, where we can link the signals to the data from a spreadsheet, MAT file or workspace.
Signal Editor	Signal Editor	Launches Signal Editor dialog box, where we can create or edit the input signals or scenarios used with Root Inport Mapper.
Tune parameters	Tune Parameters	Opens the Parameter tab of the Model Data Editor, where all the blocks of the model are listed along with their parameter values. We can add/modify the parameter values for specific/multiple blocks.
	Configuration and Simulation	
Model Settings	Model Settings	Open Model Configuration Parameters dialog box.
Property Inspector	Property Inspector	Shows the property inspector dialog box on the right side of Simulink Editor. The values for the selected block can be viewed and updated.
Update Model	Update Model	Compiles the model and shows warnings or errors, if any

Table 6.3: Simulation tab Prepare menu

- **Simulate**: As the name suggests, provides simulation options such as simulation time, speed, steps, and so on, as described in *table 6.4*:

Operation	Symbol	Description
Stop time	Stop Time	Maximum time in seconds until which we want to run the simulation. The default stop time is 10.0 seconds. We can also give the value as inf if the simulation is required until it is manually stopped.
Speed	Normal / Normal / Accelerator / Rapid Accelerator	Determines the simulation speed that can be set to the normal accelerator or rapid accelerator. The default value is normal.

Operation	Symbol	Description
Fast Restart	Fast Restart	Model is compiled only once in the beginning and not later.
Step Back	Step Back ▼	1. **Step back**: To go to the previous simulation state as configured 2. **Configure Simulation stepping**: Enable stepping back, configure the number of past steps being saved, the interval between saved steps and the number of steps to go back/forward during each operation. By default, the stepping is disabled, the number of past steps saved, the interval is 10, and the number of steps for step/back and forward is 1, but we can edit these values.
Step Forward	Step Forward	Step forward by configured step number. By default, the simulation steps forward by 1 step (1 sample time).
Run/Pause	Run ▼	• **Run**: Start the simulation of the model • **Pause**: Pause the simulation • **Simulation pacing**: Enable the pacing to slow down or expedite simulation; the dialog box also has a slider to set the simulation time per wall clock second
Stop	Stop	Stop the ongoing simulation of the model

Table 6.4: Simulation tab Simulate menu

- **Review Results**: It opens Simulink Data Inspector, as described in *table 6.5*:

Operation	Symbol	Description
Data Inspector	Data Inspector	Launches Simulink Data Inspector, where we can see the simulation results of the logged signals. The data inspector offers the following functions: • Log Signals from Simulink Model • Import Data from MATLAB • Export Data to MATLAB • Write scripts

Table 6.5: Simulation tab review results menu

Modeling

The modeling tab offers various operations required during modeling for setting up preferences and configuration, design creation, and simulation, as shown in *figure 6.3*:

Figure 6.3: Modeling tab

Modeling tab is distributed into various sections: **EVALUATE & MANAGE**, **DESIGN**, **SETUP**, **COMPONENT**, **COMPILE**, and **SIMULATE**:

- **Evaluate & Manage**: It supports evaluation of the model as per guidelines and standards, find and compare, and setting preferences and environment, as explained in *table 6.6*:

Operation	Symbol	Description
Model Advisor	Model Advisor ▼	• **Model Advisor**: Launches Model Advisor dialog box and we can run modeling guidelines and standards compliance checks for the system we have selected. These checks are grouped by task and by-product, and we can choose these checks individually. Once we run the checks, a detailed report specifies the total number of fails, passes, warnings, and not run checks. • **Model Advisor Dashboard**: This shows a small status bar of modeling guidelines and standards checks. It gives Run checks, Open reports, Enable Highlighting, and switch to standard mode options. It also shows the checks of last run checks, with a hyperlink to generated report. • **Preferences**: Let the user set model advisor preferences.
Find	Find	To search a particular string in the model
Compare	Compare	To compare two files, browse and select the paths of these files. Comparison type can be set either to Simulink model or Binary.
Environment	Environment	• **Set environment settings for the model**: We can enable/disable Model Browser, Explorer bar, Zoom, Smart guides, toolstrip, and Status bar. • **Simulink Preferences**: Simulink Preferences window opens, where we can adjust General, Editor, and Model File category preferences.

Table 6.6: Modeling tab Evaluate and Manage menu

- **Design**: This menu supports evaluation of the model as per guidelines and standards, find and compare, and setting preferences and environment, as explained in *table 6.7*:

Operation	Symbol	Description
Data repositories		
Base Workspace	Base Workspace	The base workspace variables are visible to all Simulink models (global variables). Upon clicking the button, it shows base workspace variables under the Simulink Root section of Model Explorer.
Model Workspace	Model Workspace	Opens Model Workspace tab of Model Explorer browser and shows the Data object view of model local workspace variables, where we can create/edit variables.
Data Dictionary	Data Dictionary	Opens the data dictionary Design Data linked to the model in Model Explorer. If there is no data dictionary linked, it can be linked through the `Link to Data Dictionary` option. Here, we can either browse to the existing Data dictionary or create a new one in `.sldd` format.
Data management		
Property Inspector	Property Inspector	The Property Inspector dialog box pops up.
Model Data Editor	Model Data Editor	Inports/outports tab of Model Data Editor becomes visible at the bottom for multiple elements.
Model Explorer	Model Explorer	Launches Model Explorer, where it lists all model elements along with their information in different columns. There are multiple options to adjust the hierarchy and views.
System Design		
Schedule Editor	Schedule Editor	Launches Schedule Editor window, where the users can manage and arrange the partitions in the diagram and specify execution orders.

Model Interface	Model Interface	Enables the model Interface view
Model Dependencies	Model Dependencies	Launches Model Dependency Viewer, where one can analyze the dependency of referenced model subsystems on user-defined and built-in libraries and models.

Table 6.7: Modeling tab Design menu

- **Setup**: It provides access to Model configuration settings, as explained in *table 6.8*:

Operation	Symbol	Description
Model Settings	⚙	Opens Model configuration settings window, where the users can set different configuration settings distributed in different tabs. We shall learn in detail the configuration settings in upcoming chapters.
Model Properties	▤	Opens Model properties dialog box, which contains different tabs such as Main (contains model information: source file, created and modified timestamp, model version, and so on), callback, History, Description, and Data (similar to Link to Data Dictionary option).

Table 6.8: Modeling tab Setup menu

- **Component**: This menu provides various options to insert a component into the model, convert it or create a new component from the selected model elements:
    - **Insert component:**

    The following options are available under the `Insert` component:

    - **Subsystem**: A subsystem is a set of model blocks grouped into a single block to maintain the model hierarchy. There are two basic types of subsystems: virtual and non-virtual. A virtual subsystem is only for a more manageable model representation and does not create any other impact, whereas non-virtual subsystems are treated as a single unit during execution. `Insert Subsystem` option adds a blank virtual subsystem in the model with one input

and one output. Insert Atomic subsystem inserts non-virtual subsystem. Variant subsystem option adds variant subsystem template with two variants.

- **Chart**: A state chart is used to design an event-driven system that has finite states. This option inserts a blank chart, opening which a new interface opens that supports state chart design.

- **Area**: Area is used for annotation, where this block is placed over the model elements to be annotated. This option inserts an area block into the model.

- **Bus**: A bus is a name-based composite signal grouped as model signals for better readability in complex models. Insert Bus Creator option inserts a bus creator that creates a bus from the connected input signals. Insert Bus Selector adds the bus selector that provides an alternative to extract signals from the bus.

- **Library Browser**: Opens Simulink Library Browser, where all the available library blocks can be viewed and added to the model.

o **Create component from the selection:**

In addition to inserting a blank subsystem, another method adds a subsystem to the model. We can create subsystems from the already developed logic by selecting the desired blocks and selecting the appropriate subsystem type: non-virtual, atomic, Enabled, Trigger, Function-call, and so on.

o **Convert or expand selected subsystem:**

Provides an option to convert the existing subsystem to another type of subsystem.

Figure 6.4 shows the options available under the component menu:

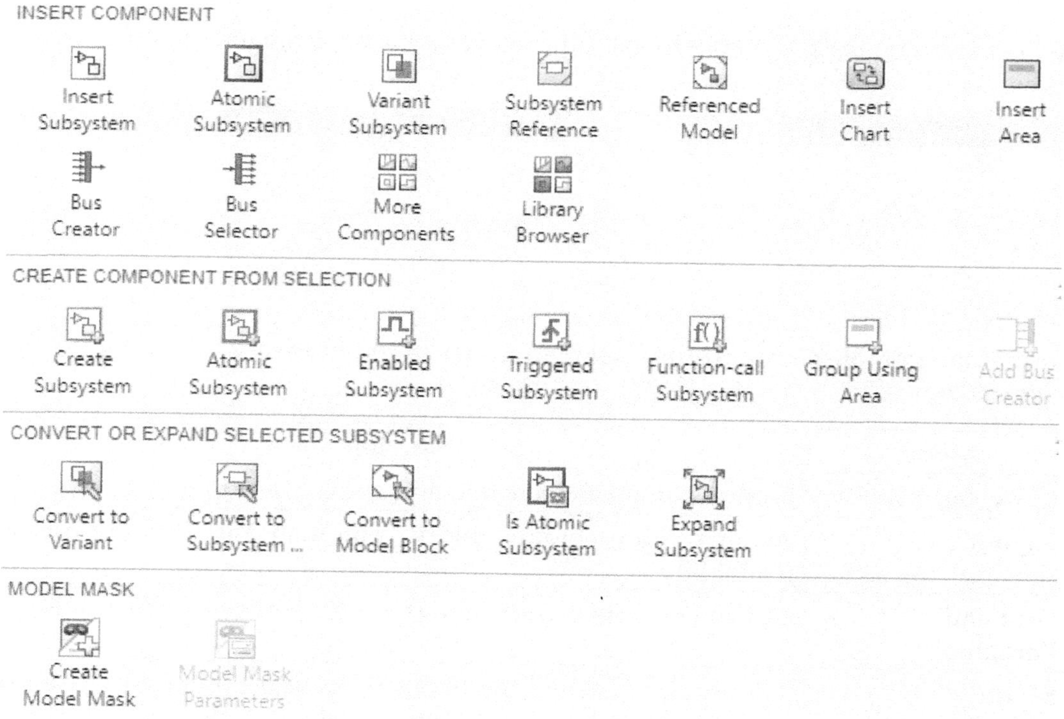

INSERT COMPONENT

- Insert Subsystem
- Atomic Subsystem
- Variant Subsystem
- Subsystem Reference
- Referenced Model
- Insert Chart
- Insert Area
- Bus Creator
- Bus Selector
- More Components
- Library Browser

CREATE COMPONENT FROM SELECTION

- Create Subsystem
- Atomic Subsystem
- Enabled Subsystem
- Triggered Subsystem
- Function-call Subsystem
- Group Using Area
- Add Bus Creator

CONVERT OR EXPAND SELECTED SUBSYSTEM

- Convert to Variant
- Convert to Subsystem...
- Convert to Model Block
- Is Atomic Subsystem
- Expand Subsystem

MODEL MASK

- Create Model Mask
- Model Mask Parameters

Figure 6.4: Modeling tab component menu

- **Compile**: It covers the option to compile as well as refresh the model, as explained in *table 6.9*:

Operation	Symbol	Description
Update Model	 ⬇	With this option, Simulink tries to compile the model and displays warnings or error messages in the Diagnostic viewer if any issues are detected.
Refresh Blocks	 ↻	If the model contains library blocks, model referencing, variants and so on, then this option reflects any change done in these blocks to the model.

Table 6.9: Modeling tab Compile menu

- **Simulate**: This menu is identical to `Simulate` menu of the `Simulation` tab.

Format

As its name suggests, the **FORMAT** tab offers several visual arrangement options, as shown in *figure 6.5*:

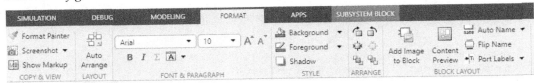

Figure 6.5: Format tab

Format tab operations are further grouped under different menus, as explained in *table 6.10*:

Menu	Operation
Copy and View	Format painter, Screenshot, and Show Markup
Layout	Arranges the model block automatically to improve readability
Font and Paragraph	Adjust Font, Size, Color, and so on properties for the model
Style	Allows us to change the Background and Foreground color of the selected blocks and offers to display shadows for the block
Arrange	Rotate or flip the blocks as required, bring them to the front or send them to the back
Block Layout	Add Image or preview the insides of the subsystem, make the name display on/off, select the parameter for indicating port name, flip name
Align **Distribute** **Match**	These menus get enabled when multiple blocks or subsystems are selected. Align options align the model blocks to the left, right, center, middle, top, and bottom. Distribute distributes the blocks horizontally, vertically, or with even gaps. Match matches the size, height, width, and so on, of the selected blocks.

Table 6.10: Format tab menus

Debug

This tab offers significant operations for visualizing and debugging models during simulation, as shown in *figure 6.6*:

Figure 6.6: Debug tab

Debug tab operations are grouped under several menus: Performance, Diagnostics, Tools, Breakpoints, Compile, and Simulate. *Table 6.11* explains the functions in brief:

Operation	Symbol	Description
Performance	Performance advisor	Performance Advisor is used to analyze the model to identify ineffective conditions to improve simulation speed automatically. Clicking the icon launches the Performance Advisor dialog box, where we can run the checks on the model after creating a baseline. The .html report is generated, and the list of the pass, fail, warning, and not run checks.
	Solver Profiler	This option launches the Solver Profiler window used to examine solver and model patterns to identify issues leading to reduced simulation performance. The profiler logs all significant events that can affect solver performance.
Diagnostics	Diagnostic Viewer	Launches Diagnostic Viewer window, where we can observe the errors and warnings generated during compilation or simulation
	Simulink Diagnostics	Opens the Diagnostics tab of model configuration settings, where users can set diagnostic parameters, which we will discuss in detail in *Chapter 8: Configuration Parameter Settings*.
		Shows the following additional model information for better analysis of model behavior (refer to *figure 6.7*): 1. **Sample Time:** • **Color**: Highlights the different model sample times as signal colors • **Legend**: Shows the Timing legend according to the sample time

contd...

Operation	Symbol	Description
Diagnostics	Information overlays	**Text**: Displays short name for the Sample time at the output port of the signals, for example, cont for continuous, D1, D2, D3,…, and so on for different discrete sample time. 2. **Library Links** • **Show all links**: Shows all library links as link symbols on the bottom left corner of the block. • **Show user-defined links**: Shows links for user-defined blocks • **Disabled links**: Shows disabled links too as a broken link symbol • **Hide all links**: Hides all library links 3. **Blocks** • **Execution Order**: Displays the execution order of the blocks and ports using a task-based sorting method. • **Variant Conditions**: Shows Variant conditions legend window that shows Annotation, Simulation, and Code generation information of the variants. • **Hide automatic block names**: Shows/hides model block names 4. **Signals** • Signal dimensions • Signal Data ranges • Propagated Signal labels • Storage class • Nonscalar signals 5. **Ports** • Units • Base Data types • Alias Data types • Execution contexts 6. **Signal Badges** • Logging and viewers • Test Points

Operation	Symbol	Description
Tools	Trace signal	1. **Trace to Source**: Highlights to the originator of the selected signal 2. **Trace to Destination**: Highlights to the endpoint of the selected signal 3. **Remove Trace**: Removes the previously enabled highlighting
	Comment Out	1. **Comment Out**: Opts the block entirely out of the simulation 2. **Comment Through**: Passes the signal value through the block 3. **Uncomment**: Re-enables the commented block
	Output Value	1. **Show output value**: Displays the selected signal value during simulation 2. **Remove Value Displays**: Removes the value display of the selected signal 3. **Toggle Value Displays**: Enables/Disables the value display when clicking the signal 4. **Value label display options**: Offers the possibility to adjust Font, Refresh rate, the number of elements, Display format, display while hovering/always-on/toggle, and so on.
Breakpoints	Pause time	Specify the pause time in seconds
	Add Breakpoint	1. **Add Breakpoint**: Add a conditional breakpoint to the selected signal, specify relational condition, and value receiving which simulation is to be paused. A red breakpoint symbol appears on the source of the signal. 2. **Enable/Disable breakpoints** 3. **Clear breakpoints**
	Breakpoints List	1. **Breakpoints List**: Shows a list of all model breakpoints along with the signal name, condition, enable tick box, number of Hits, delete, and so on. 2. **Debug Model**: Launches model debugger, which has enhanced debugging options for observing values during breakpoints or errors.

Operation	Symbol	Description
Compile	Update Model	Compiles the model and displays warnings or errors in the diagnostics viewer if any
Simulate	Simulate	Same as Simulation and Modeling Simulate menu

Table 6.11: Debug tab menus

The *figure 6.7* displays the visual indicators offered by Simulink to analyze the model data flow in an enhanced way:

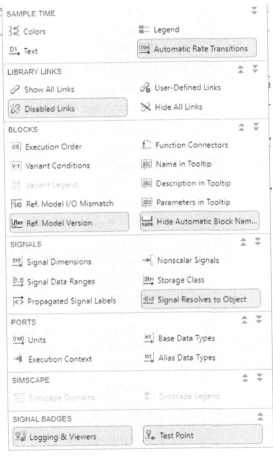

Figure 6.7: Information overlays menu

Model example: PID controller

Proportional-Integral-Derivative (PID) Controller is a control-loop feedback compensator system widely used in industries to control process variables such as flow, current, temperature, pressure, speed, simplicity, and effectiveness. In the PID control system, the actuating signal u(t) consists of a proportional error signal added with derivative and integral error signal e(t). Thus, three control variables manipulate the process variable, as shown in *figure 6.8*:

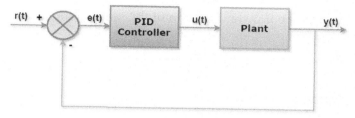

Figure 6.8: PID feedback compensator system

Figure 6.9 shows a block diagram of the PID controller explaining its basic structure:

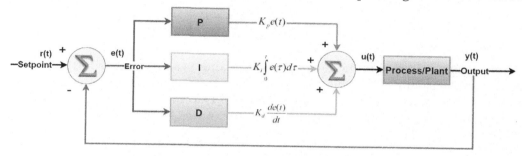

Figure 6.9: PID block diagram

As we can notice in the block diagram from *figure 6.9*, three different error terms: proportional (P) term multiplied by constant gain K_p, Integral (I) term multiplied by constant gain K_i, and Derivative(D) term multiplied by constant gain K_d. They are added together to generate actuating output that controls the process or plant to the setpoint.

From the image, controller output u(t) can be calculated as follows:

$$u(t) = K_p\, e(t) + K_i \int_0^t e(\tau)\, d\tau + K_d \frac{de(t)}{dt}$$

where τ=Integral time constant, and t = derivative time constant

Using Laplace transform, control output can be converted to the frequency domain:

$$U(S) = \left(K_p + \frac{K_i}{s} + sK_d\right) E(S) C(S) = \frac{U(S)}{E(S)} = \frac{K_d s^2 + K_p s + K_i}{s}$$

The closed-loop transfer function for the system is as follows:

$$\frac{Y(S)}{R(S)} = \frac{C(S)P(S)}{1 + C(S)P(S)}$$

Now, let us assume that the transfer function of the plant model is as follows

$$P(S) = \frac{1}{s^2 + 10s + 20}$$

So, the closed-loop transfer function for the system shall be

$$\frac{Y(S)}{R(S)} = \frac{\frac{K_p + K_d s + K_i/s}{s^2 + 10s + 20}}{1 + \frac{K_p + K_d s + K_i/s}{s^2 + 10s + 20}}$$

$$= \frac{K_d s^2 + K_p s + K_i}{s^3 + (10 + K_d)s^2 + (20 + K_p)s + K_i}$$

We can design a Simulink model for the preceding system, and with the help of simulation, we can fine-tune the values of K_p, K_i, and K_d so that the system provides an output that matches the input value. The goal is to tune K_p for fast rise time, K_d for the minimum overshoot, and K_i to eliminate the steady-state error.

Based on *figure 6.8*, we understand that we need a PID controller and Plant components. Additionally, we also need to provide simulation input and output. So, after creating a new model file, as explained in the previous chapter, we identify and bring all required blocks on the canvas located in Simulink Editor. We can get the blocks either from the library browser, as shown in *figure 6.10*, or click and type the block's name on canvas and select the suitable one from the drop-down:

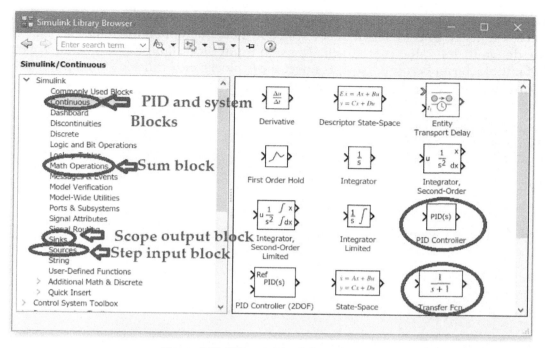

Figure 6.10: PID example—Library browser

The desired library blocks: Sum block as an accumulator, PID controller as control block, and transport function block for the system to be added to the canvas and step block as input source and scope as output visualizer, as shown in *figure 6.11*. The control logic model elements create the desired logic, and the source and sink blocks provide support for simulation and verification of the logic. For ease of understanding only, three areas blocks: **Source**, **Control logic**, and **Sink** are added from the Palette:

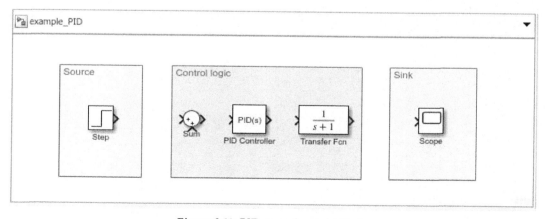

Figure 6.11: PID example: model blocks

First, let us observe the open-loop response of the system. We need to configure the default transfer function block to our system, where the numerator value is [1], and the denominator value is [1 10 20]. The step input block (amplitude 1) and scope default block can be used. Now, connect these blocks and run the simulation; the open-loop step response can be observed in *figure 6.12*:

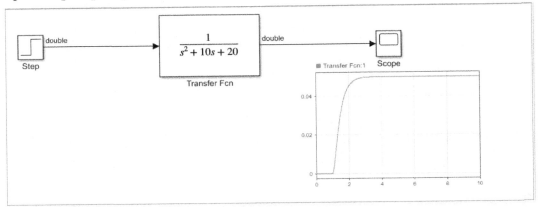

Figure 6.12: PID system open-loop response

As can be observed from the results in *figure 6.12*, the output value is 0.05 for the unity step input value. The steady-state error is 95%, the rise time is 1 second, and the settling time is approximately 1.5 seconds. Now we add to model the model blocks: sum and PID controller and configure them in Sum block; the list of signs setting to be configured to +- from ++. The PID controller block can be configured to the values shown in *figure 6.13*:

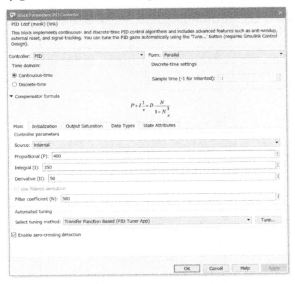

Figure 6.13: PID controller block configuration

Figure 6.14 shows the closed-loop PID control model, where values of K_p=400, K_i= 350, and K_d=50 have been considered, but you can try adjusting these parameters to get the best results. If Simulink Control Design License is available, you can use the PID tuner app GUI that helps you automate the overall tuning process without multiple trials. The app provides the exact gain values for maximum results. We have also used the desktop scope block to observe the simulation results at the same level and the scope block. We can see in the graph that the system output shows significant improvement during closed-loop simulation with PID controller. You can open the scope block for a detailed analysis of the results compared with a unity step input:

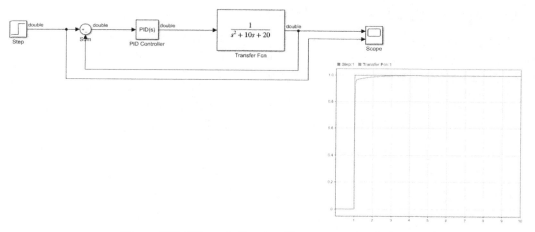

Figure 6.14: *PID controller closed-loop system simulation*

Signal loading, visualization, and logging techniques

During model-based design, modeling only the system logic is sometimes not enough. It is also essential to know whether the system behaves in the desired manner. Simulink offers multiple options to provide inputs during the simulation and observe the system outputs. In the previous example, we simulated the system model with a sine wave input source and visualized the results on scopes. To successfully simulate the model logic, we need to define internal or external interfaces for input data and control signals. In addition, we need to define output signals for analyzing and exporting simulation results. There are multiple methods of signal loading and logging, which we shall discuss in the following section.

Signal loading techniques

Signal loading with the help of Library blocks is a valuable option for testing reusable system models. In the Sources section of the Simulink Library Browser, various types of blocks are available that enable simulation of inputs, for example, Input port, constant, Sine wave, step, ramp, clock, Pulse generator, Waveform generator, Signal generator, Counter, Ground, Signal builder, Signal Editor and many more, as well as blocks that allow the users to fetch signals From Workspace, File, and Spreadsheet, as follows.

Using Simple Source blocks

Multiple source blocks are available in the Simulink Library, such as constant, step, ramp, sine wave, and so on, which generate input signals for system models. These blocks provide input to the model based on the variable values specified in the block dialog, for example, amplitude, frequency, and so on. They do not record any data. Hence, we can use these blocks to perform simple model behavioral checks. For example, *figure 6.15* shows an implementation of the following differential equation.

$$\frac{d^2y}{dx^2} + 3\frac{dy}{dx} + 2y = 4 \implies \frac{d^2y}{dx^2} = 4 - 3\frac{dy}{dx} - 2y$$

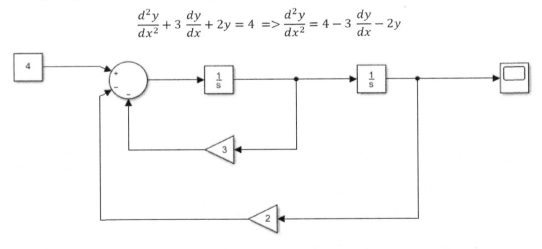

Figure 6.15: Example signal loading using Source blocks

As shown in *figure 6.15*, the blocks constant, sum, integrator, gain, and scope blocks are used in the example. The parameter values of Constant and Gain blocks are provided manually for the differential equation. However, there is another more accessible way to make these values configurable to reuse the same model to resolve similar differential equations. We can create variables in the base, model, or function workspace for the parameters: **y0**, **G1**, and **G2** and mention these names in the model block settings. Then, before running the simulation, either we provide the values at the MATLAB command prompt or Simulink Model Explorer, or we can also create and run a MATLAB script that contains desired values of **y0**, **G1**, and **G2**, as shown in *figure 6.16*:

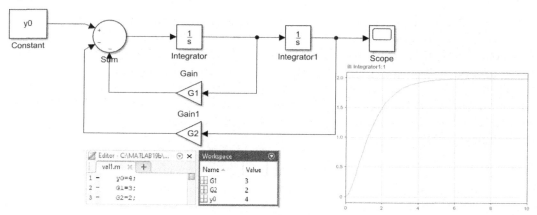

Figure 6.16: *Signal-loading using simple script and workspace variables*

There are various other blocks available in the Sources section that help input signal generation. For example, the Signal Generator block generates signals using sine, square, sawtooth, or random function according to the block amplitude and frequency input settings. Similarly, Waveform Generator supports different waveforms such as sine, square, Gaussian, step, sawtooth, and so on, based on the input arguments. Pulse generator generates the input pulse based on these parameters: amplitude, period, pulse width, and phase delay. Signal Builder has been popular in generating desired input signals, as it provides the option to create the signals and export/import the combinations manually. Now, Signal Editor is preferred to perform these tasks.

Using Dashboard blocks

In the Dashboard section of the library browser, we can find various input generators that can be used for simulation with user interaction. Some of these blocks are slider, checkbox, edit, knob, push and radio button, rocker, slider, and toggle switch. Detailed information on all library blocks is available in the help section. The *figure 6.26* under Signal Visualization shows some of these library blocks.

Using From Workspace block

The **From Workspace** block is available in the Sources section of the Simulink Library Browser. As the name suggests, it allows the users to read signal data from MATLAB base/function/model/mask workspace. The signal data is to be stored in workspace variable in a timeseries, matrix, or structure format. The first column is designated to the time stamp in the matrix format, and the second column(s) indicates signal data value. The structured format contains time values, data values, and dimensions.

Consider the following example of Saturation logic implementation. For testing, we have used the **From Workspace** library block. The Data field contains the Workspace variable name. Here, **simin** is a 101×2 sized variable array in MATLAB base workspace. Its first column specifies the time interval from 0 to 2 seconds with increments of 0.02 seconds, and the second column has corresponding amplitude values ranging from −2 to 2. The Saturation block has an upper limit as one and a lower limit of −1. The *figure 6.17* shows the implementation, the block settings, and simulation results:

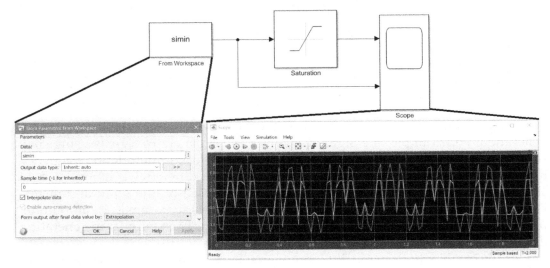

Figure 6.17: From workspace block example

Using From File block

The **From File** block can be used from the **Sources** section of Simulink Library Browser. This block allows the users to access the signal data from the .mat file and use it as input to the system. The following example explains the usage of the block. The data present in the MAT file **myfile.mat** can be seen in the image, where the first-row values determine the timestamps and the rest of the rows define signal data values, and the same can be observed from the scope results, as shown in *figure 6.18*:

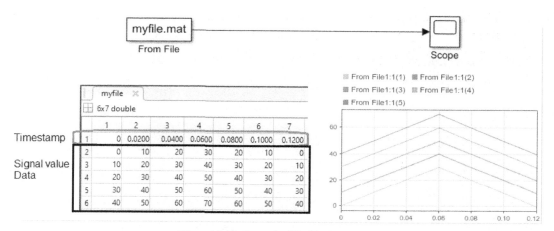

Figure 6.18: From the File block example

Using From Spreadsheet block

The block enables users to access signal values from Excel or CSV spreadsheets. The block setting provides the option to navigate to the desired file, import signal data from a specific sheet, and specify the range. To read data from the file, the Excel file should contain timestamp data in the first column, and the rest column shall contain signal values.

Using Signal Editor

Signal Editor Block can be accessed from the **Sources** section in Library Browser. The block allows us to create, modify, and display interchangeable scenarios; therefore, it is preferred against the Signal Builder block as it functions similarly yet with greater flexibility. The dialog box of Simulink Editor Block has the option to choose MAT-file containing the data set. From the drop-down, we can select **Active Scenario** out of all available scenarios. In the Signal properties section, there is an option to launch the Signal Editor user interface to create, modify, or observe the scenarios and signals present in the dataset. Based on that, we can choose **Active Signal**. The *figure 6.19* shows the Signal Editor Interface example, where the signal **MySigIn** has been created manually using **Draw signal** option. We can also use the **create**

blank signal option and input values in a tabular form. The scenario is specified as **mysignal**, but we can add multiple scenarios in the data set:

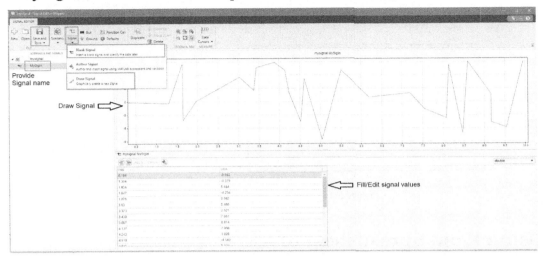

Figure 6.19: Signal Editor interface example

Using Root Inport mapper

Root level Inport mapping allows us to create, import, and map the signal data to root level Inports, which can be Inport, Enable or Trigger block. Root Inport Mapper tool is accessible from **Model settings** (Configuration Parameters) | **Data Import/Export** pane, where one has to click **Connect Input**. The root Inport mapper tool dialog box pops up, where we can link the existing scenario dataset from a spreadsheet, MAT-file, or workspace. If there is no current data, the tool also provides an option to create a new MAT-file using Signal Editor. Once the signal is created, as shown in *figure 6.19*, we can create a new MAT-file **mysignal.mat**; link the newly created signal [**MySigIn** using the **From MAT-file** scenario link option. A window will pop up to browse to the desired MAT file and select the data set. After import, we need to link the signal to Inport to select any of the five mapping modes: block name, block path, signal name, port order, or custom mapping. Select the dataset, then click the **Map to Model** button. If the mapping is successful, the status changes will simulate; else, shows an error or warning. For our example model, the Inport block name is **MySigIn**, and the signal name present in the MAT-file **mysignal.mat** matches with it, so the status can be seen as green in *figure 6.20* mapper tool interface snapshot:

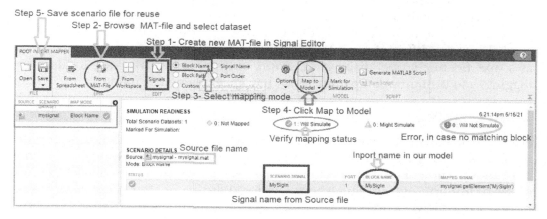

Figure 6.20: Root Input Mapper tool interface

After mapping is done, the mapped signal command **mysignal.getElement('MySigIn')** becomes visible in the configuration parameter Input dialog box. The signal values are now accessible at model Inport **MySigIn**. *Figure 6.21* shows the configuration parameter dialog box, model, and simulation results:

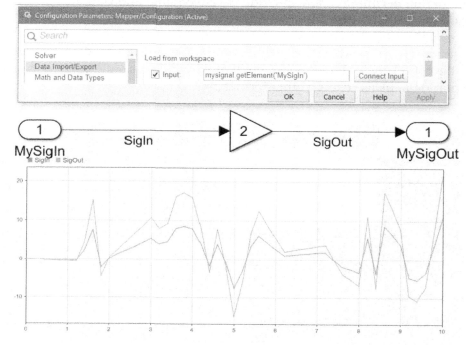

Figure 6.21: Root Input Mapper model example

Signal visualization and logging techniques

Simulink facilitates signal visualization and logging for better visualization, analysis, and debugging of the model behavior. The user can observe the signals, time, output, state, and data store values interactively or after simulation, based on the technique used. There are different ways to do so, some of which are using sink blocks such as scope, floating scope, display, XY graph, outport, and workspace, to file, signal logging, and configuration parameters. They are explained as follows.

Using scope

Scope block displays the signal waveforms as a function of time. The scope is widely used in observing and logging simulation signal data. The scope is located under the **Sinks** section of the Simulink Library Browser. The users can connect to it with single or multiple output signals to be observed during or after simulation. We also have a scope viewer and floating scopes with similar functions. It provides various options to show the plot of the connected signals on the common or multiple y-axes. There are also possibilities to configure the style and visualization tools. Simulation can be controlled using the **Run**, **Pause**, **Stop**, and **Step** forward-backward buttons. The triggers could be introduced in the scopes, and the availability of cursers helps see the exact values and differences between multiple values. In addition, for better analysis post-simulation, we also have the Logging option, where we can limit data points, define decimation, and provide variable name and data format options to choose from data set, structure, structure with time, and array. The *figure 6.22* shows a plot example and logging option in configuration properties. The variable **myData** shall store data in Array format, which can be found as part of simulation output in the base workspace. Please note here that Array allows only single port data. For multiport data, please choose other formats:

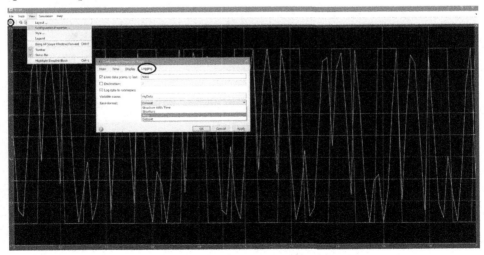

Figure 6.22: Scope signal logging example

Using To Workspace block

Input signal data is written to the workspace using the To Workspace block. The data is transferred to the workspace during simulation pause or stop. By default, the data is written to the base workspace. To workspace, a block is also available under sinks in Simulink Library Browser. By opening the block, we can define various parameters, such as variable name to be stored, data points limit, decimation, sample time, and format of the saved data that could be Timeseries, structure, structure with time, and time Array. The example in *figure 6.23* shows that the Timeseries format output of multiplication result will be stored in workspace under simulation output with **simoutmul** name:

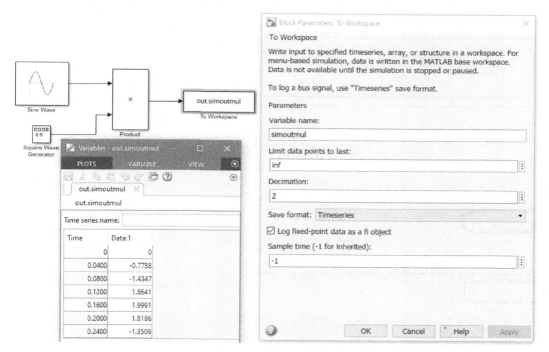

Figure 6.23: To workspace block example

Using To File block

The **To File** block, available under **Sinks**, stores the logging data into MAT-file in **TimeSeries** or Array format. The file is written during simulation pause or stop. By default, the file name is **untitled.mat**, the variable name is **ans**, and the default data format is Timeseries. The user can also adjust the sample time, which could be longer than the base sample time. The file is overwritten before each simulation.

Using Signal logging

Signal logging enables the logging of the selected signal(s) without adding any additional block. There are various ways to enable logging, such as the **Simulation** tab | **Log Signals**. Another method is to select the signal and right-click; there is an option in the menu to **Log Signals**. In addition, from the **Properties** menu, where the **Signal properties** window pops up, and in the logging and accessibility tab, there is a tick box to enable logging of the signal. In addition, by clicking on signals, three dots appear clicking which the option to Log signal data appears. The *figure 6.24* shows where to find these options:

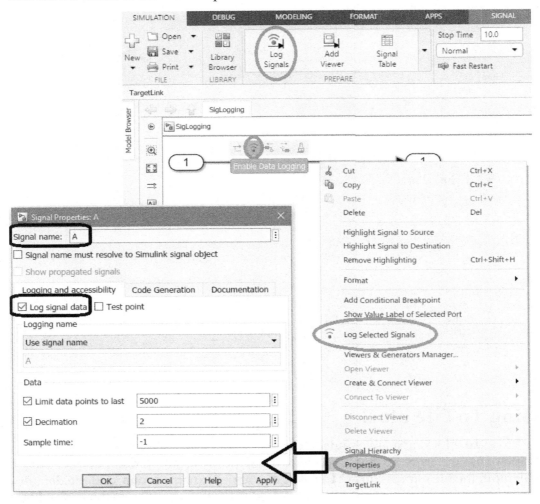

Figure 6.24: *Signal logging options*

Using Simulation Data Inspector

Simulation Data Inspector is used to inspect, compare, and export the simulation data to validate the model. Users can also import previously exported simulation data. Simulation Data Inspector allows the users to observe and compare data from multiple simulations runs so that it becomes easier to adjust the desired model behavior. The zooming and cursor features allow straightforwardly monitoring of the signals. Moreover, one can also replay the simulation data. During the comparison, we can define the acceptable tolerance values and compare the results from multiple runs.

Simulation Data Inspector is accessible from **Simulation** tab | **Review Results** | **Data Inspector**. The steps to inspect the signal data are as follows: select the signals and enable logging using any of the methods shown in *figure 6.24*, simulate the model, and then tick desired signals in the inspect area to plot. The *figure 6.25* shows simulation results in Simulation Data Inspector for PID controller from *figure 6.14*. The output of the transfer function is plotted for the four different PID parameter-tuning combinations. We can select the signals to be plotted from the left side window and adjust the plot style and color. On the left side above the plot, we have different options to replay, hide/show cursor, select layout; create subplot, zoom, pan and select, snapshot, customization, and so on. on the leftmost side, there are buttons to create, open, or save simulation session; import, export the simulation data; generate a report and set simulation preferences:

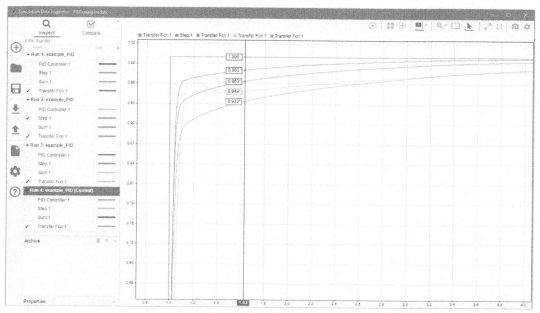

Figure 6.25: Simulation Data Inspector—PID tuning

Using Dashboard blocks

Dashboard blocks help create interactive displays in your model. Simulink offers exciting options to create visual displays such as dashboard scope, gauge, display, lamp, and so on, where users provide inputs and can simultaneously see the results. For example, after adding Dashboard scope to Simulink editor, it shows **Connect** button on top; clicking **Connect** followed by the signal to be connected adds to the scope, and the real-time plot can be observed in the block. *Figure 6.26* shows the Dashboard section as part of Simulink Library:

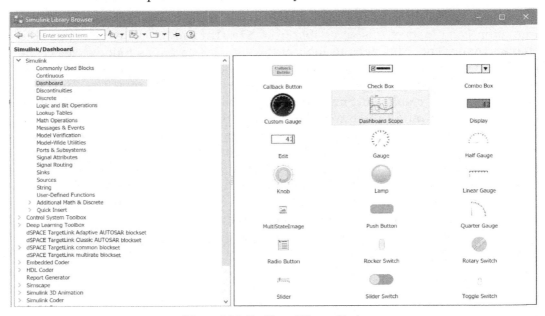

Figure 6.26: Dashboard library blocks

Using Outport

Simulink Outport block saves simulation output data to MATLAB base workspace under name **yout**. From **Data Import/Export configuration** parameter settings, one can enable logging to workspace or file. By default, time tout, output **yout**, signal logging **logsout**, data stores **dsmout**, and signal simulation output **out** are enabled. The users can change the variable names as per their choice. There is also a **tickbox** to enable logging to **.MAT** file **out.mat**, states **xout,** and storage of final states **xFinal**. The storage format can be chosen from dataset, array, structure, and structure with time. Clicking **Configure Signals** to **Log** option launches the Simulink Signal logging selector window, where the list of logging enabled signals and settings are available. The *figure 6.27* shows the configuration settings. We shall discuss these settings in *Chapter 8: Configuration Parameter Settings*:

Figure 6.27: Logging configuration settings

Simulink modeling shortcuts

As Simulink is a visual tool where we need to perform tasks using a mouse and keyboard, various shortcuts are defined to make users' modeling activities faster. *Table 6.12* provides some of these useful shortcuts:

Operations	Shortcuts	Operations	Shortcuts
Select object	Mouse click	Disconnect block	*Shift* + drag
Select multiple objects	*Shift + click*	Add port to block with multiple inputs	Drag to the edge of the block
Select all object	*Ctrl + A*	Create subsystem from the selection	*Ctrl + G*
Copy objects	*Ctrl+ drag*	Open selected block	*Enter*
Move objects	drag	Find block	*Ctrl + F*
Delete	*Delete / Backspace*	Mask block	*Ctrl + M*
Cut- paste	*Ctrl + X, Ctrl + V*	Look under mask block	*Ctrl + U*
Copy-paste	*Ctrl + C, Ctrl + V*	Comment out block	*Ctrl + Shift + X*
New model	*Ctrl + N*	Comment through block	*Ctrl +Shift + Y*
Open model	*Ctrl + O*	Go to parent	*Esc*
Save model	*Ctrl + S*	Refresh blocks	*Ctrl + K*
Close model	*Ctrl + W*	Go to library	*Ctrl + L*
Set block parameter	*Ctrl + Enter*	Open model explorer	*Ctrl + H*

Operations	Shortcuts	Operations	Shortcuts
Copy blocks from one window to another	Drag from one window and drop to another	Name the line	Double-click line + Type
Add block	Double click + Type + Select from the list	Delete the label	Right-click + *Delete*
Move block	arrow keys	Copy signal label	*Ctrl* + drag label
Resize block, keeping ratio	*Shift* + drag	Open configuration parameters	*Ctrl* + E
Resize block from center	*Ctrl* + drag	Update Diagram	*Ctrl* + D
Rotate block clockwise	*Ctrl* + R	Build model	*Ctrl* + B
Rotate block counter clockwise	*Ctrl* + *Shift* + R	Start simulation	*Ctrl* + T
Flip block	*Ctrl* + I	Stop simulation	*Ctrl* + *Shift* + T
Connect blocks	Click first and then second port Select first block + *Ctrl* + Click second block Drag from first to second port	Copy block formatting	Select source block + select paintbrush from ellipsis menu + select the destination block
Connect branch line	*Ctrl* + drag Right-click + drag	Fit diagram to screen	spacebar
Zoom in	*Ctrl* + + / forward mouse wheel	Zoom out	*Ctrl* + - / backward mouse wheel
Refresh library pane	F5	Open Library browser	*Ctrl* + *Shift* + L
Print model	*Ctrl* + P	Show/Hide block name	Right-click + Format
Add annotation	Double-click + Type	Edit block name	Click on name + Edit

Table 6.12: Simulink modeling shortcuts

Conclusion

The previous chapter gave us a concise introduction to model-based design and the overall software development life cycle process. We also learnt how to create a simple Simulink model. That knowledge has been extended to this chapter. Simulink Editor is a critical component of Simulink modeling, so getting to know the tool's capabilities has allowed us to think about the possibilities without boundaries. With the classic example of the PID controller, the chapter has made the users understand how they can adapt Simulink to their own design needs. In addition, the signal loading and logging techniques offer excellent options to simulate, analyze, and validate the logic under various circumstances. Finally, the Simulink shortcuts come in handy when the reader wants to navigate quickly around the interface. In the upcoming chapter, the readers shall learn different Simulink library blocks and how to use them.

Points to remember

- Simulink Editor is a vector graphics editor used for creating models in the form of block diagrams.
- Simulink Editor supports data import and export, simulation, and model performance analysis.
- Simulink Editor Interface consists of Toolstrip, quick access toolbar, canvas, model browser, palette, model data editor, and property inspector.
- Toolstrip is located at the top of the Simulink Editor interface that supports everyday user workflow tasks.
- Toolstrip consists of five tabs: Simulation, Debug, Modeling, Format, and Apps.
- Canvas is a model diagram editing area of Simulink Editor.
- An easy way to do signal loading is using simple Simulink sources library blocks.
- It is also possible to load signal data from the workspace, spreadsheet, File, and so on.
- Signal Editor is recommended for use instead of the signal builder.
- Using the scope, File, workspace, and so on, options are available for signal visualization, logging, and further analysis.
- Modeling turns out more convenient and quicker with the help of mouse and keyboard shortcuts.

Multiple choice questions

1. Which Simulink Editor section provides an option to navigate through model hierarchies?
   a. Property Inspector
   b. Model Browser
   c. Quick access toolbar
   d. Canvas

2. How many undo and redo operations are allowed by Simulink Editor?
   a. 500
   b. 2,000
   c. 101
   d. Infinite

3. Which of the following tabs allows the model font and color change operations?
   a. Format
   b. Debug
   c. Modeling
   d. Simulation

4. Which source block allows sawtooth generation?
   a. Signal Generator
   b. Waveform Generator
   c. Both A and B
   d. None of the above

5. What is the shortcut to rotate the block?
   a. Ctrl + K
   b. Ctrl + Enter
   c. Shift + Ctrl + T
   d. Ctrl + R

Questions

1. Explain the user interface essential components of Simulink Editor.
2. What are the operations available under Debug tab?
3. Implement PID controller using P, I, and D manual adjustments.
4. Describe various signal logging techniques with some examples.
5. How can we visualize signal simulation data using Simulation Data Inspector?
6. Please explain different block and line operations using shortcuts.

Answers

1. b
2. c
3. a
4. c
5. d

Chapter 7
Library Browser Overview

Introduction

Simulink Library Browser is the built-in user interface enabling access to the Simulink blocks for model-based design and simulation. Simulink blocks are the foundation blocks of any model, where the users can add various instances of the suitable Simulink blocks from Simulink libraries to perform specific operations. The library blocks are generally parametrized to adapt to model requirements. Users have to drag and drop these blocks to Simulink Editor and start connecting them. With extensive Simulink Help documentation and a wide range of examples, the users can quickly identify the desired blocks and understand their usage. This chapter provides a short overview of the library browser interface and then introduces the users to the widely used libraries and some of the available popular blocks. By looking at the number of Simulink blocks, it is not feasible to describe each block, so this chapter emphasizes making the readers familiar with the concept of library blocks and the parametrization of the popular blocks. This chapter also explains some of these blocks with simple examples. The users are suggested to practice different implementations using library blocks by providing inputs and observing the outputs. With regular self-practice, the modeling skills can be polished.

Structure

In this chapter, we shall discuss the following topics:

- Simulink Library Browser
    - Sources
    - Sinks
    - Math operations
    - Logic & bit operations
    - Continuous
    - Discrete
    - Signal routing
    - Lookup tables

Objectives

After studying this chapter, the reader will be able to:

- Familiarize with Simulink Library Browser user interface
- Get a brief overview of the built-in block libraries offered by Simulink
- Learn about the widely used library blocks and their parametrization
- Practice model implementation with simple examples

Simulink Library Browser

The **Library Browser** provides access to the Simulink Block libraries during model-based design. The library blocks and annotations are categorized and displayed in a tree view. They are added to the canvas of Simulink Editor to create visual block diagram models. The **Library Browser** has two sections: in the left section, the library blocks are listed in a tree view. In the right window, the blocks of the selected library become visible. The desired block can then be added to the model by drag-and-drop or **right-click + Add block to model** operation.

There are three different methods to open the Simulink library browser as follows:

1. Click the **Library Browser** button present on the **Simulation** tab of Simulink Editor toolstrip.
2. Execute the **slLibraryBrowser** command in the MATLAB command prompt.
3. Press *Ctrl + Shift + L* keys in Simulink Editor.

After performing any of the preceding operations, the Simulink Library Browser window pops up. *Figure 7.1* shows the Library Browser window:

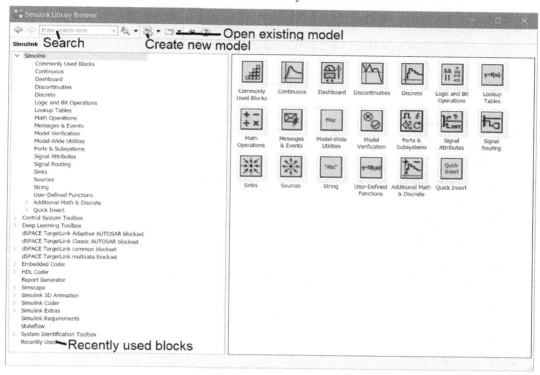

Figure 7.1: Simulink Library Browser

As observed in *figure 7.1*, the Simulink Browser window has a toolstrip at the top, a Library tree view on the left with toolbox-wise libraries and sub-libraries, and on the right side, the blocks and annotations for the selected toolbox library or sub-libraries. From here, users can get more information on the block or add the block to the model. It is also possible to add custom library blocks as part of the Simulink Library Browser. A **Recently used blocks** section enables quick access to the last used blocks.

There are three methods to add the identified library blocks to the model as follows:

1. In the Library browser, navigate to the block in the right window

    a. Right-click on the block and select **Add block to model untitled (or model file name)** option.

    b. Drag the block from the browser and drop it to the model in Simulink Editor.

    c. Select the block and press the "*Ctrl + I*" keys.

2. Right-click the library name on the left section of the Library Browser and select the open library option.

    a. Drag the desired block from the library and drop it into the model.

    b. Right-click the block in the library, select the copy option, and paste it to the model file.

3. In Simulink Editor Canvas of MATLAB 2014b or newer release versions, double-click in an empty space and start typing the block name in the popped-up quick search window. Select the relevant block from the list of all available blocks with a given name.

As mentioned previously, each toolbox has a separate library, which has further sub-libraries. From *figure 7.1*, we can see that Simulink has a library divided further into sub-libraries, and these sub-libraries comprise library blocks and annotations.

The Simulink library has the following sub-libraries; out of these, we shall discuss some of the popular ones:

- Sources
- Continuous
- Discrete
- Discontinuities
- Logic and Bit operations
- Math operations
- Lookup tables
- Sinks
- Dashboard
- Ports and Subsystems
- String
- Signal Attribute
- Signal Routing
- Additional Math and Discrete
- Messages and Events

Sources

Simulink/Sources library contains library blocks used in a model to generate or Import signal data. *Figure 7.2* shows the blocks available under the sources library.

The Sources library is divided into two categories: Model and subsystem Inputs and Signal Generators. Usage of some of these blocks is already explained in *Chapter 6: Simulink Editor with Environment*.

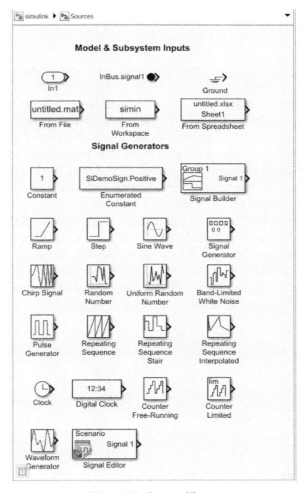

Figure 7.2: Sources library

Model and subsystem inputs

This section contains library blocks, which help connect or import the input signal data to the model. It contains the following six different blocks:

1. Inport
2. In bus element
3. Ground

4. From File
5. From Workspace
6. From Spreadsheet

Inport

Inport block links signal from outside a system into the top-level system. The block is also used to forward input to a subsystem from the outport of another subsystem. The default name of the block is **In1**, the port number is 1, and later the number is increased for subsequently added blocks. The port number signifies the sequence number of the input port for the parent block. When a signal connection is created to the open port visible outside the subsystem, the respective Inport block passes on signal properties such as scaler/vector value, signal label, color, and so on. By clicking the Inport name, the block can be renamed with a meaningful name. To add multiple Inports to the model, right-click the first block and drag and drop in the model or use the select, copy, and paste operation. Based on the selected option, duplicate, or paste, the block will either be duplicated with the same port number with a different name or added as a new block with a different port number and name. The block parameter window can be accessed either by double-clicking the library block or by performing right-click and selecting **Block parameters** (**Inport**) option. *Figure 7.3* shows Inport block parameter settings:

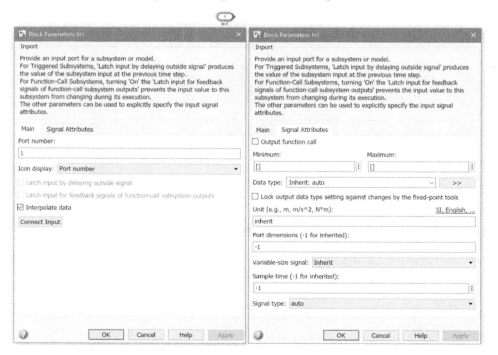

Figure 7.3: Inport block parameters

As observed in *figure 7.3*, the block parameter window has different sections, and the general pattern stays the same for other library blocks. The top-most section provides a short description of the block. In the following description, we can see two tabs: **Main** and **Signal Attributes**.

Main offers the parameters as follows:

- **Port number**: Specifies the position of the port in the parent block
- **Icon display**: Could be Port number, Signal name or both
- Latch input options for Triggered and Function-call subsystems
- **Interpolate data**: Only for Top-most Inport
- **Connect input**: Visible only for Top-most Inport, launches root Inport mapper tool, the input signal can either be created or imported from the tool, as explained in *Chapter 6: Simulink Editor with Environment*.

Signal attributes tab offers many different options, as follows:

- **Output Function call**: Available for top-level ports
- Minimum and maximum value range
- **Data types**: For Inport datatype, different options such as Inherit, int, uint, fixed, single, double, Boolean, enum, bus, expression, and so on, are available in the drop-down; by default, inherit option is available.
- **Unit:** Inport value unit can be specified in this setting. The default value is inherited.
- **Port dimensions**: Define port dimension; -1 is the default value for inherit.
- **Variable-size signal**: Specify whether the signal is variable-size or not.
- **Sample time**: Specify the sample time for the input signal; –1 is for inherit.
- **Signal type**: Define the signal time- real, complex, or auto.

At the bottom of the window are available buttons: **Ok**, **Cancel**, **Help**, and **Apply**. Help launches the documentation for the block.

The other library blocks commonly have a similar structure, where the block parameters offer options for customization of the library block based on user needs.

In bus element

The In Bus element block works as a combination of **Inport block** and **Bus Selector** block. A bus is a structure that can group signals of various data types. The block is used to select a bus and a non-bus input signal into the subsystem. For bus signal, users can choose either a complete bus by removing the signal name from a port or a single element from the bus by specifying the signal name or signal hierarchy in the block label. If multiple elements from the same bus are read, the user can create various ports for each signal. For non-bus input, the signal can be chosen by deleting the signal name in the block label. In the dialog box, one can also rename the bus input name and select the bus element name. When the element name matches the input bus element name, the new signal can be used.

Figure 7.4 shows an example usage of in bus element port:

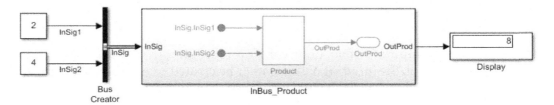

Figure 7.4: *In bus element example*

The subsystem in *figure 7.4* shows identical bus In Bus elements **InSig.InSig1** and **InSig.InSig2**. It indicates that the input to the subsystem shall be a bus input, and the port name is **InSig**. The elements of the received bus signal are **InSig1** and **InSig2**. From the previous example, we can understand that the in-bus element eliminates the need to use a bus selector and allows to specify bus name and signal name in a single port.

Ground

The Ground block connects to the open blocks or ports where input ports do not connect further to any other blocks. Usually, Simulink issues a warning on unconnected ports during simulation. To avoid the warning, the Ground block is connected to the open port or block. When connected, Ground provides the value 0 to the signal where connected.

From File, From Workspace, From Spreadsheet

The usage of these blocks has been discussed in *Chapter 6: Simulink Editor with Environment*. These blocks allow the possibility to read signal input values from a file, a workspace, or a spreadsheet.

Signal generators

As suggested by its name, the library contains model input generator blocks, as shown in *table 7.1*:

Library Browser Overview — 255

Operation	Symbol	Description	Key Attributes
Constant		Generates constant input value for the model	Value, Sample time, Min-Max, Data type
Clock		Outputs the current simulation time for each simulation step	Display time, decimation
Sine Wave		Generates sinusoidal waveform, can be used time or sample-based mode. The time can be Simulation time or external input	Amplitude, bias, frequency, phase, sample time
Step		Generates step function between two values	The step time, initial value, final value, sample time
Ramp		Outputs a ramp signal starting at the specified time	Slope. Start time, the initial output
Pulse Generator		Generates square wave pulses at given intervals. It can be used in time or sample-based mode. The time can be Simulation time or external input	Amplitude, period, pulse width, phase delay
Waveform Generator		Outputs one signal at a time out of the defined signal. Supported waveforms: step, pulse, square, Gaussian noise, and so on.	Waveform definition: Wave type (amplitude, frequency, phase), Min-max, datatype, sample time
Repeating sequence		Outputs periodic signal with repeating sequence from time-value input vectors	Time vector, Value vector
Chirp Signal		Outputs chirp sine wave with linear frequency increase	Initial frequency, target frequency, frequency at the target time
Counter free running		Output sets to zero after reaching maximum value based on selected data	Number of bits, sample time

Operation	Symbol	Description	Key Attributes
Signal Editor	Scenario Signal 1	Displays and allows to create or edit interchangeable scenarios of signal sources	File name, active scenario, active signal, unit, sample time
Signal Generator	▭▭▭▭ 0 0	Generates signal of selected type: sine, sawtooth, square, and random	Amplitude, Frequency, unit

Table 7.1: Signal generators library blocks

Sinks

With the help of library blocks available in the Simulink/Sinks library, the users can display or export the simulation signal data. The library has three subcomponents: **Model & Subsystem Outputs**, **Data Viewers**, and **Simulation Control**. *Figure 7.5* depicts the library blocks.

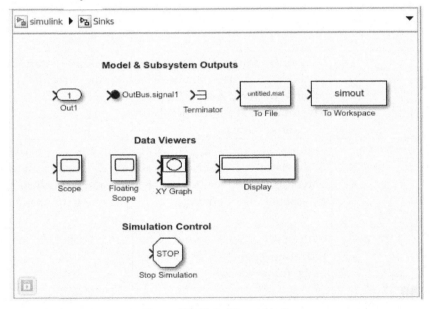

Figure 7.5: Sinks library blocks

Model and subsystem outputs

In this section, we can find the library blocks that help display and export model and subsystem output data. The blocks are as follows:

1. Outport

2. Out bus element
3. Terminator
4. To File
5. To Workspace

Outport

Outport blocks are used to connect the signals from one subsystem to another or outside the model. The outports are automatically numbered. If the outport is part of a subsystem, then based on the assigned outport number, an open port is created on the output side of the subsystem, which can be connected to other blocks or subsystems. On the root level, outport can connect and export the output signal values external to the model. The default name of the block shall be **Out1**, and the number shall be 1; after clicking the block, they can be changed. Furthermore, depending on the location of the outport block—whether it is located at the root level, inside the normal subsystem, or conditional subsystem; **simulink** provides various options to customize the output signal, as indicated in *figure 7.6*:

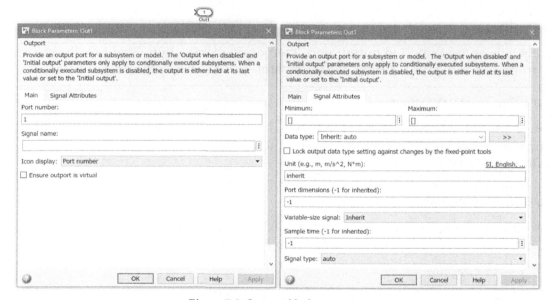

Figure 7.6: Outport block parameters

- **Port number**: Can be changed maximum up to a total number of outports present at that level.
- **Icon display**: Could be Port number, Signal name, or both.

- **Signal name, ensure output is virtual**: These settings are available only at the root level. One can provide a signal name manually.

- **Output when disabled, Initial output**: The settings are available only for conditionally executed subsystems.

- **Signal attributes tab**: Parameters are similar to Inport parameters.

Out bus element

The block is used to combine the functionality of the **Outport** and **Bus Creator** block (a block that combines signals with different data types). In the dialog box of the output bus element, we can add or remove signals or sub-buses. For each signal, a separate block shall be created. Using the dialog box, one can rename or edit the properties of the output signal. The dialog box has various parameters: Out bus element port name and number, color, add signal, add sub bus, refresh, and remove the signal. We can also see the hierarchy of created signals under the bus element port. These signals or sub buses can be renamed, and the relevant attributes can be adjusted as well. These attributes are similar to outport—Data types, Dimension, dimension mode, Unit, sample time, complexity, and min-max values.

Terminator

If there is an unconnected output port, then during simulation, Simulink throws a warning. To avoid the warning, the terminator is connected to the output port.

To File, To Workspace

These blocks help export the output signal data to a specified file or workspace variable. We have discussed the usage of these blocks in *Chapter 6: Simulink Editor with Environment*.

Data viewers

As the name suggests, the viewers help visualize and export data during simulation. The blocks available for viewing data are as follows:

1. XY Graph
2. Scope
3. Floating scope
4. Display

XY Graph

XY Graph block displays Y (second scalar input) versus X (first scalar input) plot for each time step using MATLAB figure window after the simulation is stopped. The XY Graph block has parameters to limit the min and max values for X and Y, and the values outside these ranges are ignored. *Figure 7.7* shows the XY graph for equation $y=2x2$, where x is a ramp input, ranging from −1 to 1, and y is the square of input x multiplied by the constant value 2. Here the *x* value limits are -1 and 1, and *y* value limits are 0 and 2. The X Y plot image shows that the result is a parabola:

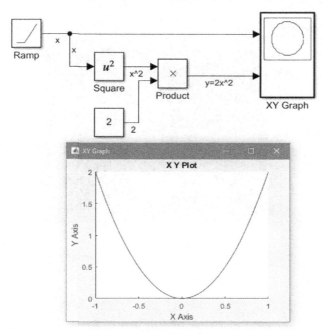

Figure 7.7: XY Graph example

Scope and floating scope

The function of these blocks is to display the signals in the time domain during and after simulation. The difference between these blocks is that the scope block has input ports, whereas the floating scope does not have input ports, and users can connect to it virtually any desired signals in the model. The block display has different buttons, such as Simulation control with stepping/running options, signal selector, zoom, scaling, and so on. To enable scope for signals, click on the signal selector, click on the desired signal, and click on the link icon, so it shows a tick box to enable/disable display for the signal.

Additionally, the scope has the triggers option to set triggers to synchronize the repeating signals and pause the display when events occur. Cursor measurements help measure signal values with the help of vertical and horizontal cursors. *Figure 7.8* shows the plotted values of signals x, x^2, and $y=2x2$ in the time domain. It is possible to have multiple Y-axes for the given X-axis:

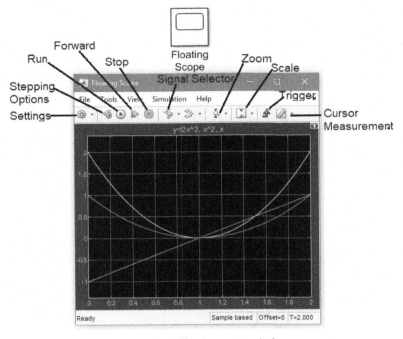

Figure 7.8: *Floating scope window*

Display

The Display block shows the value of the input data. In case the output is scalar, it will show the value of the connected signal. In the case of an array, it will show multiple windows, one for each array element. In the dialog box of the display block, these are a few parameters:

- Numeric display format: choose from one of the formats—**hex**, **binary**, **decimal**, **octal**, **short**, **long**, **short_e**, **long_e**, **bank**, and so on.
- Decimation: default is 1
- Floating scope: makes the scope floating, by default disabled

Simulation control

The section has one block, stop simulation. The block stops simulation whenever the input value turns to non-zero.

Math operations

The library blocks from Simulink/Math operations library enable the users to perform various scalar and vector mathematical operations. It supports complex number handling too. The library is divided into three sub-topics: math operations, vector/matrix operations, and complex vector conversions. *Figure 7.9* shows the library blocks:

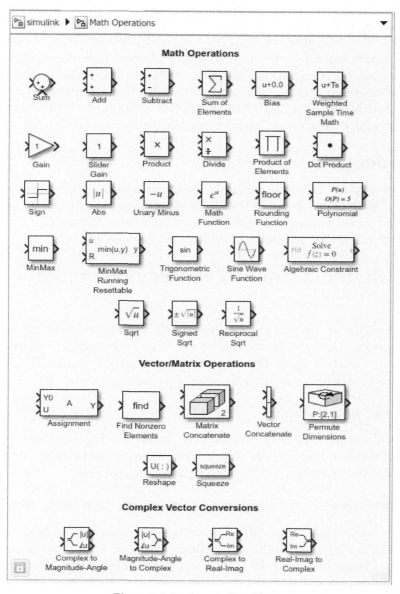

Figure 7.9: *Math operations library*

True to its name, the math operations library provides access to library blocks that support different mathematical operations. These are the library blocks, some of which are widely used, whereas a few others are used for specific purposes based on the requirements:

Sum, add, subtract, and the sum of elements

These blocks are variants of the Sum block. Sum block is used to add or subtract multiple scalar or vector inputs. Based on the specified list of signs, the operations are performed. The default list of signs is ++ for addition and +− for subtraction. | is used as a separator among ports. For example, ++|−|+− shall create ports +, +, then −, and then + and −. Users can set the shape of the block to either round or square. The sum of elements block has one more parameter that specifies the sum over all or specified dimensions. The signal attributes tab is similar to Inport, Outport, and many other blocks, except for an additional parameter to set accumulator data type.

Gain, slider gain

Using these blocks, the users can multiply the input signal with a constant gain. The input signal can be of any type. In the slider gain, users can choose any gain value between specified minimum and maximum value limits. We have seen an example of a Gain block in *Chapter 6: Simulink Editor with Environment*.

Product, divide, a product of elements, and dot product

The block provides an option to perform multiplication or division elementwise or matrix product. The operations can be defined in the number of ports with a combination of * and / signs. The dimension can also be chosen from the dropdown. Dot product helps perform dot (inner) product operation.

Sign, Abs, and unary minus

The output of the sign block is +1 for positive, −1 for negative, and 0 for 0 input. Abs provides an absolute number for the input. Zero crossing can be enabled for both the blocks, whereas unary minus provides unary minus output for the respective input.

Math function, rounding function, trigonometric function, minmax

The blocks, as mentioned earlier, offer various functions to choose from. For example, one can select from mathematical functions such as logarithmic, exponential, power, and modulus functions. We can select output signal type and auto, real, or complex. Rounding functions provide the option to perform floor, ceil, round, and fix. Trigonometric function block allows functions such as sin, cos, tan, and so on, minmax block offers an option to select min or max function. The **Sqrt** function allows square root, signed square root, or reciprocal square root.

Assignment

The assignment block is used to assign values to the specified signal elements. We need to select the indices of the elements. The input signal U provides values to output Y. When the number of output dimensions parameter value is specified, and rows are created for each dimension. It has the option to choose from Index options: Assign all, Index vector (dialog), Index vector (port), Starting index (dialog), and Starting index (port). In case the port option is selected, then additional **Indx** input ports are created for the index. For indexing, there are two modes, one-based and zero-based.

Matrix oncatenate, vector concatenate

Both blocks are variants of concatenate block. The Concatenate block supports concatenation of the input signals of the same data type. The number of input signals needs to be provided. The mode could be either vector or multidimensional matrix. In the case of a multidimensional matrix, an additional parameter-concatenate dimensions 1 (vertical) or 2 (horizontal) is to be specified. *Figure 7.10* shows an example of the usage of **Reshape** and Matrix Concatenate blocks. Input 1 is a column vector [11; 22; 33; 44] and Input 2 is row vector [55, 66, 77, 88]. Using **Reshape** block, the vectors are converted into a 2×2 array with mentioned settings. Then horizontal and vertical matrix concatenation is performed on them. Therefore, we get concatenated 2×4 and 4×2 matrix.

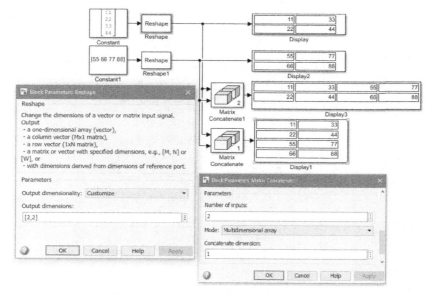

Figure 7.10: *Matrix Concatenation example*

Complex vector conversions

This category contains four conversion blocks—complex to magnitude angle, magnitude angle to complex, complex to real imaginary, and real imaginary to complex. As the name suggests, these blocks perform conversion based on the parameter settings and inputs. For example, if real value input is 3 and imaginary value input is 4, then the output of block real imaginary to complex shall be complex number output 3+4i.

Logic and bit operations

This library is essential in the development of logic-driven models. *Figure 7.11* shows the library blocks:

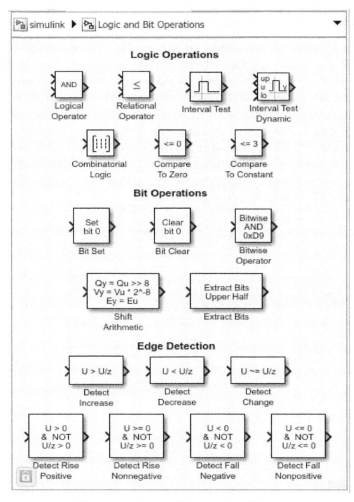

Figure 7.11: Logic & bit operations library

As explained in *figure 7.11*, the library has three sub-sections: Logic operations, Bit operations, and Edge detection. These blocks are described in *table 7.2*:

Operation	Symbol	Description	Key Attributes
Logic Operations			
Logical Operator	AND / Or	Performs chosen logical operation on Boolean input and provides Boolean output accordingly. The output is TRUE when • **AND**—all inputs are TRUE • **OR**—at least one input is TRUE • **NAND**—at least one input is FALSE • **NOR**—no inputs are TRUE • **XOR**—odd number of inputs are TRUE • **NXOR**—even number of inputs is TRUE • **NOT**—the input is FALSE	Operator, number of input ports, Icon shape—Rectangular or distinctive
Relational Operator	$\leq$	Performs chosen relational operation on input signals and generates Boolean output. The output is TRUE (1) when • ==: equal inputs • ~=: unequal inputs • <: less than • <=: less than or equal to • >=: greater than or equal to • >: greater than • isInf—infinite • isNaN—Not a number • isFinite—Finite	Relational operator enables zero crossing and requires all inputs to have the same data type.

Operation	Symbol	Description	Key Attributes
Interval test		Output becomes TRUE(1) when the input is between lower and upper limits	Interval closed on Right, Left, output datatype, Upper limit, the lower limit
Bit Operations			
Bit set	Set bit 0	Sets the specified bit of the input signal to 1, where 0 is the least significant bit.	Index of bit
Bit clear	Clear bit 0	Clears the specified bit of the input signal to 1, where 0 is the least significant bit.	Index of bit
Bitwise operator	Bitwise AND 0xD9	Performs the specified bitwise operation on the input. For a single input, a bit mask can be defined and used. If bit mask use is disabled, then specify the number of input ports.	Operator: AND, OR, NAND, NOR, XOR, NOT, number of input ports (if not bit mask), use bit mask, bit mask
Extract bits	Extract Bits Upper Half	Extracts bits based on the selection- Upper half, Lower half, Range starting with the most significant bit, Range ending with least significant big, and Range of bits	Bits to extract, Output scaling mode
Shift Arithmetic	Qy = Qu >> 8 Vy = Vu * 2^-8 Ey = Eu	arithmetically shift specified bits in a given direction and/or specified binary point	Bits to shift: source, direction, number; Binary points to shift: number

Operation	Symbol	Description	Key Attributes
Edge Detection			
Detect Increase / Decrease / change	U > U/z U < U/z U ~= U/z	The block detects increase, decrease or change in the input value concerning previous conditions. Input processing can be done sample-based or frame-based.	Initial condition, Input processing, output data type-Boolean, uint8

Table 7.2: Logic and Bit operations library blocks

The example in *figure 7.12* shows a simple full adder implemented using logical operator blocks. The users can provide the inputs and observe the outputs *S* and *Cout*, where and

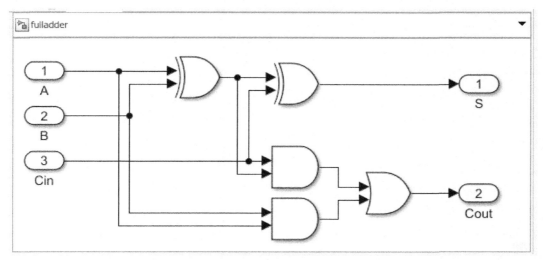

Figure 7.12: Full adder example

Continuous

The blocks, which perform continuous functions such as derivation, integration, and so on, are part of the **imulink/Continuous** library. *Figure 7.13* shows the blocks available in the library. These blocks are categorized into six categories as integrators, transfer functions, PID controllers, delays, derivatives, and conversion.

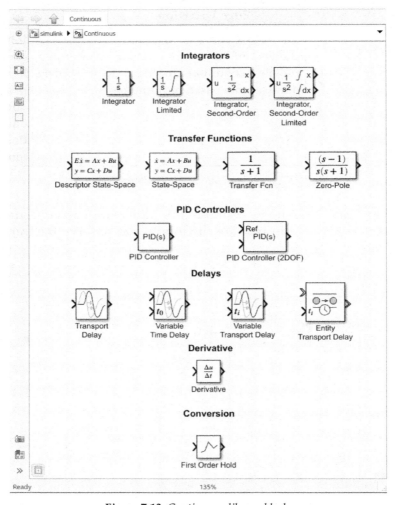

Figure 7.13: *Continuous library blocks*

Integrators

This section contains library blocks, which are used for integration operations. It contains the following four different blocks:

1. Integrator
2. Integrator Limited
3. Integrator, Second-Order
4. Integrator, Second-Order Limited

Integrator

Integrator block is used to integrate the input function. For example, if you give the sine wave as an input to the integrator block, it converts it to a wave similar to the cosine wave. *Figure 7.14* shows the input and output of the integrator block. The upper graph is the output of the integrator block, whereas the lower graph is the input sine wave:

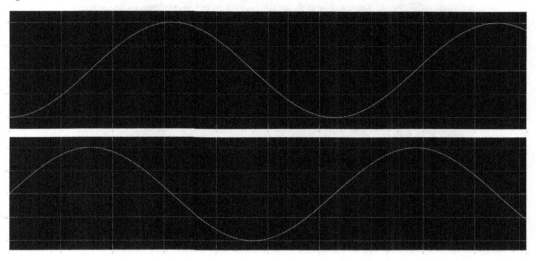

Figure 7.14: Integrator block output wave vs. input wave

Integration operation is used to find the area under the curve. Here, the output wave gives the area under the curve for the input wave. Let us try to realize this with mathematical equations. First, we integrate *sin(x)* with fixed limits:

$$\int_0^\pi \sin(x)\,dx$$

Integration of *sin(x)* is *–cos(x)*, when we put *–cos(x)* under fixed limit then the equation becomes:

$$[-\cos(x)]_0^\pi$$

It gives

$$(-\cos \pi) - (-\cos 0)$$

The operation results into

$$\{-(-1)-(-1) = 1 + 1 = 2\}$$

So, an area under the curve for sine wave between x=0 to x = π is 2 square units. Let us realize this in detail in the following image. In *figure 7.15*, we can see that in the encircled area, the time is 3.14, and the value is 2; time represents x, whereas the value represents the area under the curve:

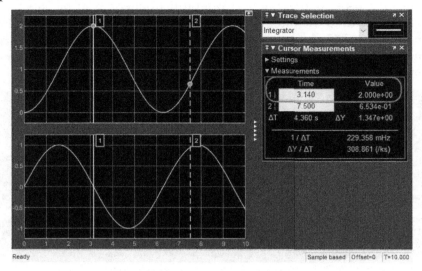

Figure 7.15: *Area under the curve for sine wave*

Integrator block can be configured for some parameters such as initial condition, output limits, and so on. *Figure 7.16* shows some properties of the integrator block:

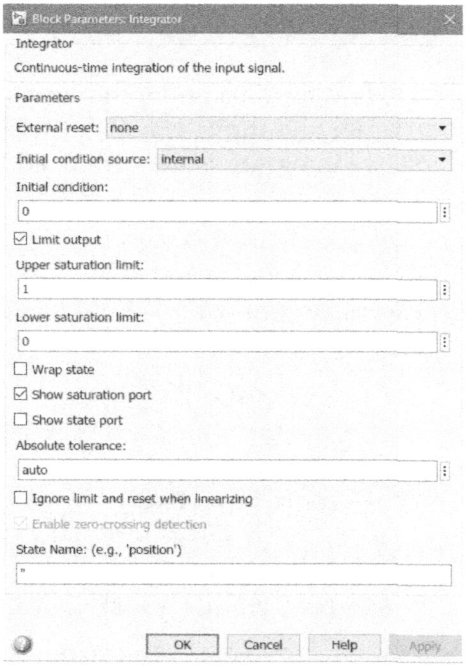

Figure 7.16: *Properties of the integrator block*

Table 7.3 describes the usage of different parameters of the Integrator block:

Parameter	Block display when option enabled	Description
External Reset		External rest is used to reset the initial condition of the integrator block. By default, it is set to none. It can be configured to rising, falling, or either level and level hold values.
Initial condition source	When external selected	Initial condition source can be configured to either internal or external. When configured to internal, its initial condition is taken based on the initial condition parameter; by default, its value is zero. External provides an option to give initial condition externally. By default, its value is internal.
Initial condition	No change in the block display	The initial condition parameter is enabled when the Initial condition source is configured as Internal. By default, its value is zero.
Limit output		Limit Output checkbox allows providing upper limit and the lower limit cutoff values.
Upper saturation limit	No change in the block display	The upper saturation limit gives an upper cutoff value when output crosses the upper saturation limit.
Lower saturation limit	No change in the block display	A lower saturation limit provides a lower cutoff value when output goes below the lower saturation limit.
Wrap state		The rate of change of the cyclic or periodic signals to obtain the state of movement is done by the Simulink to model the cyclic, periodic, or rotary objects in nature. Over an extended period, this may result in integrating large values, and having large values for integration results longer time for computation. By resetting the angular state to 0 when it reaches 2π, we can overcome this issue, improving accuracy, and reducing computation time. The wrap state option enables a user to provide the values for the upper wrap state and lower wrap state

Parameter	Block display when option enabled	Description
Upper wrap state	No change in the block display	When an angurate state reaches the upper wrap state, then it resets it to 0.
Lower wrap state	No change in the block display	When the angurate state reaches the lower wrap state, then it resets it to 0.
Show saturation port	$\frac{1}{s}$	This checkbox adds an output port, which indicates whenever output reaches the saturation values.
Show state port	$\frac{1}{s}$	This checkbox adds an output port to show the state of the output signal; This signal indicates the same value as the output except for the condition when the integrator block resets. When the integrator block resets, the output value appears on the state port first and then on the output port in the current timestamp. That is why state port could be used to avoid algebraic loops.
Absolute tolerance	No change in the block display	Absolute tolerance provides an option to specify the most appropriate value to provide the error control while computing the output value of the integrator block. By default, its value is auto. In that case, the absolute tolerance value given in the "error tolerance for variable step solvers" configuration setting dialog box is used.
Ignore limit and reset when linearizing	No change in the block display	When this checkbox is checked, the block is treated as unresettabe, and the output is unlimited.

Table 7.3: *Integrator blocks*

Integrator limited

Integrator limited block is an integrator block with enabled limit output check, upper saturation, and lower saturation limit.

Integrator, second-order

A second-order integrator is also called a **double integrator**. This block integrates twice the input function. *Figure 7.17* shows the second-order integral of sine wave with respect to sine wave.

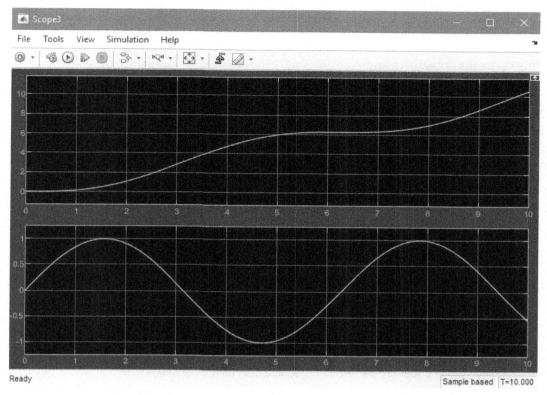

Figure 7.17: Integrator, second-order block output wave vs input wave

Let us try to realize the output of a second-order integrator with mathematical equations. First, we integrate *sin(x)*.

$$\int \sin(x) \, dx$$

which results into

$$-\cos(x) + C$$

We need to find the value of . We know that for $x = \pi$ value of = 2. This gives the value of = 1, so the first-order integrator of the sine wave function becomes:

$$-\cos(x) + 1$$

When we integrate this then,

$$\int -\cos(x) + 1 \, dx$$

When we integrate this between 0 to π, then it becomes:

$$[-\sin(x) + x\,]_0^\pi$$

This gives

$$(-\sin(\pi) + \pi) -$$

This operation results into

$$\pi$$

Now, we shall consider the output waveform value when time is π. *Figure 7.18* shows in the encircled area the value when time is π.

Figure 7.18: *Integrator, second-order result when time is π*

Similar to the Integrator block, the Second-order integrator block also has configuration parameters in three different tabs. *Figure 7.19* displays other parameters available for input function x:

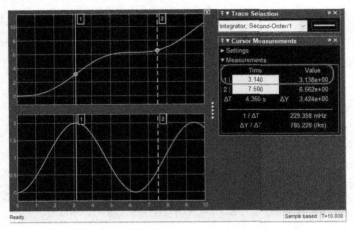

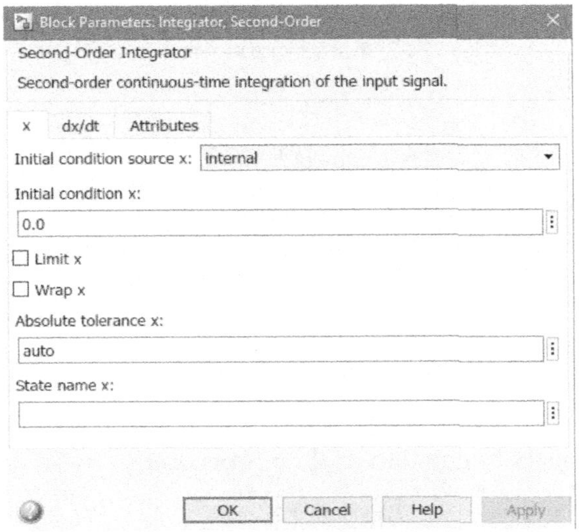

Figure 7.19: *Parameters for the input function*

Since the Second-order integrator does double integration, it provides some parameters for the first-order integrator result. *Figure 7.20* depicts the different parameters available for it in the tab :

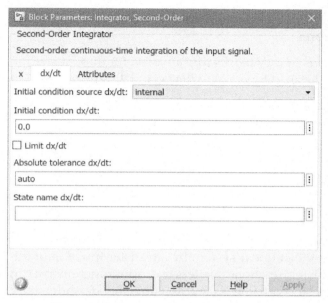

Figure 7.20*: Parameters for first-order integral*

We have seen parameters available for . The attribute tab has some generic parameters. *Figure 7.21* shows the parameters available under the **Attributes** tab:

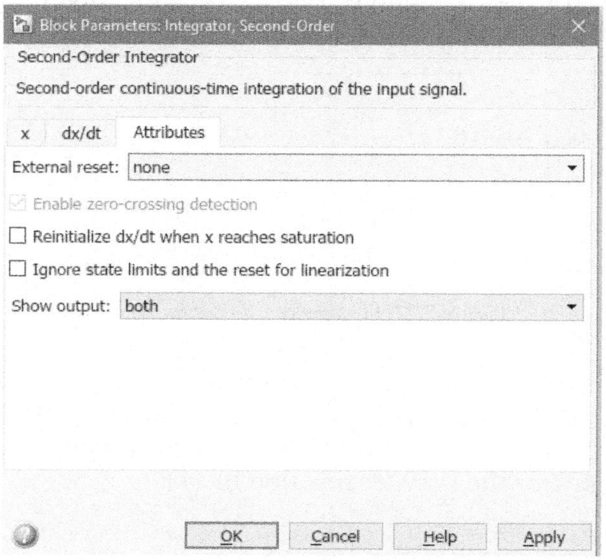

Figure 7.21*: Parameters under attribute tab*

Integrator, second-order limited

Integrator, second-order limited block is an integrator, second-order block with enabled limits check for .

Transfer functions

This section contains library blocks that are used for the transfer function. It includes four different blocks as follows. We will check the transfer function in detail.

1. Descriptor State-Space
2. State-Space
3. Transfer Fcn
4. Zero-Pole

Transfer Fcn

Transfer Fcn is the most used library block among transfer function blocks. This block is used to model a linear system by a transfer function of the Laplace-domain variable s. The transfer function transfers the input function in a different form. Most of the time, the transfer function is used as a filter. Let us understand how the transfer function can be used in automotive applications. Suppose we are developing the system for the power window of a car. User requests to open or close the window. Or maybe the user gives a request to set the target position of the window. In that case, we cannot change the window position abruptly. Window movement should be done smoothly. The transfer function is used to reach the target position effortlessly. *Figure 7.22* explains how to implement the transfer function as a filter:

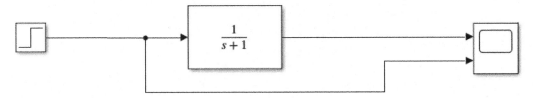

Figure 7.22: First-order transfer function

The step function is used to set the target position. The transfer function block has dialog parameters for setting numerator and denominator coefficients. Users can provide vectors according to the order of the transfer function. *Figure 7.23* depicts the dialog parameters for the transfer function block:

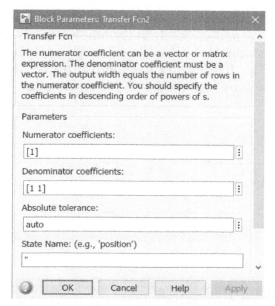

Figure 7.23: *Transfer function dialog parameters*

The numerator and denominator coefficient are kept as 1. *Figure 7.24* shows the graph of the output of the transfer function. The upper graph is the output of the **transfer** function, whereas the lower graph is the input:

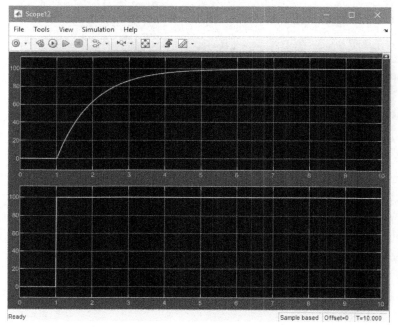

Figure 7.24: *Output vs. input graph for a transfer function*

The graph in *figure 7.24* shows that target position 100 is received at the 1st second, but it is achieved slowly and smoothly at the 6th second. By varying the coefficient of numerator and denominator, we can slow down or rapid up the flow of achieving the target. In *figure 7.25*, the transfer has ramped up because the numerator and denominator coefficient are increased to 5. Now, the target is achieved in the 2nd second:

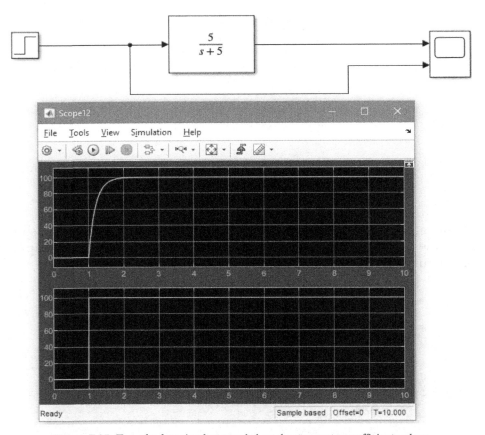

Figure 7.25: Transfer function has speeded up due to greater coefficient values

In the same way, we can slow down the transfer flow by reducing the coefficient values. In *figure 7.26*, we can check how a reduction in the coefficient values changes the output graph. By changing the coefficients to 0.5, the transfer function takes 10 seconds to achieve the target position:

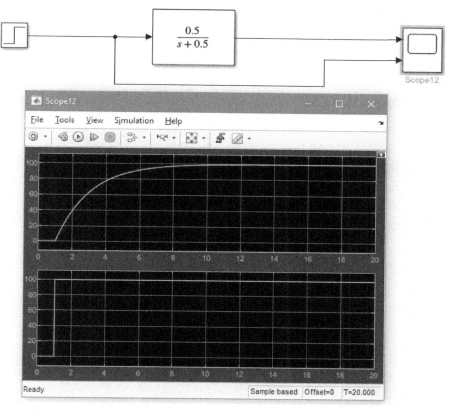

Figure 7.26: Transfer function has slowed down due to lesser coefficient values

PID controllers

PID controllers are already explained in *Chapter 6: Simulink Editor with Environment* in the section Model example: PID controller.

Delays

This section contains library blocks that are used to provide delay for continuous waveforms. It includes four different blocks as follows. We will learn about transport delays in detail:

1. Transport delay
2. Variable time delay
3. Variable transport delay
4. Entity transport delay

Transport delays

Transport delay is used to delay the input waveform. Transport delay has dialog parameters available to provide time for delay and initial value during the initial delay time. *Figure 7.27* explains the usage of transport delay with its dialog parameters. The delay time is kept as 1 second, whereas the initial value during the first second is 0:

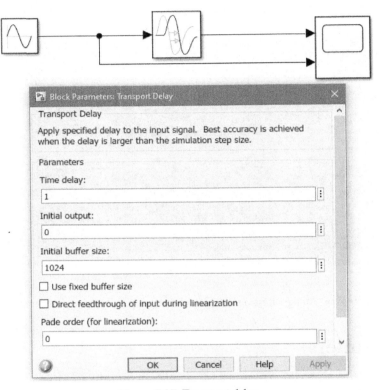

Figure 7.27: Transport delay

We have used a transport delay block to delay the sine wave by 1 second. In *figure 7.28*, we can see the output graph vs. the input graph. The upper graph is a delayed sine wave, whereas the lower graph is an input sine wave:

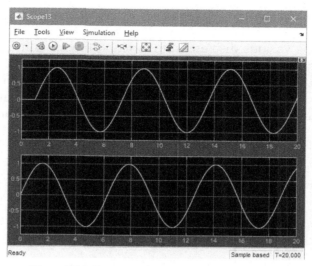

Figure 7.28: Transport delay output vs. input graph

Derivative

A derivative block differentiates the input wave for time *t*. *Figure 7.29* shows the usage of the derivative block. The derivative of sine is cosine. We can see the output cosine wave vs. input sine wave as well in *figure 7.29*:

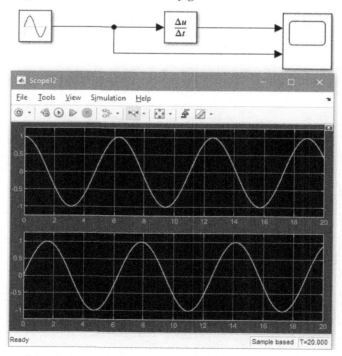

Figure 7.29: Derivative block implementation with output vs. input graphs

Discrete

The library contains various discrete-time function blocks, some of which are the equivalents of continuous-time function blocks. The library offers possibilities to implement discrete-time systems using block diagrams, difference equations, or transfer functions. The discrete library blocks can be divided into discrete-time linear systems and sample & hold delays. *Figure 7.30* shows the library blocks:

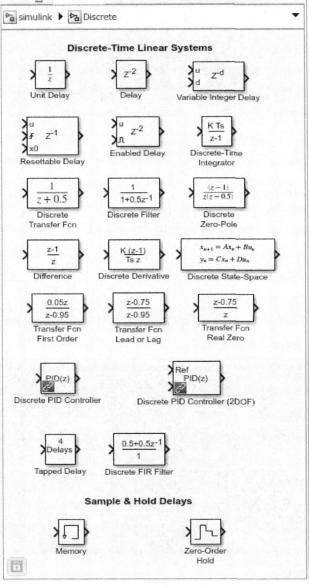

Figure 7.30: Discrete library blocks

Table 7.4 gives a brief overview of some of the widely used blocks:

Operation	Symbol	Description	Key Attributes
Delay	z^{-2}	Delay the input signal based on the samples specified in the dialog box or received through the input signal	Delay length: through a dialog box or input port, Initial condition, algorithm, external reset
Difference	$\frac{z-1}{z}$	Provides the difference between the current input value and the previous sample value	The initial condition for the previous input
Discrete FIR Filter	$\frac{0.5+0.5z^{-1}}{1}$	Implements FIR filter for each channel. Coefficients can be specified through a dialog box or input signal.	Coefficients, coefficient source, filter structure, Initial condition, external reset
Discrete Filter	$\frac{1}{1+0.5z^{-1}}$	Implements **Infinite Impulse Response (IIR)** filter. The coefficients for numerator and denominator are specified in ascending order of $1/z$.	Filter structure, numerator coefficients (scalar/vector, matrix), the denominator (scalar, vector), Initial states, external reset
Discrete PID Controller	PID(z)	The block is the same as the continuous library PID controller block.	Controller, Form, Integrator, and filter method, P, I, D, N
Discrete State-Space	$x_{n+1} = Ax_n + Bu_n$ $y_n = Cx_n + Du_n$	Implements following discrete state-space model: $x(n+1) = Ax(n) + Bu(n)$ $y(n) = Cx(n) + Du(n)$	Coefficients A, B, C, D, Initial conditions, sample time
Discrete Transfer Fcn	$\frac{1}{z+0.5}$	Implements z-transform discrete transfer function	Numerator, denominator, Initial states
Discrete Zero-Pole	$\frac{(z-1)}{z(z-0.5)}$	Implements the system using poles and zeros of discrete transfer function	Zeros (vector-matrix), Poles (vector), Gain, sample time

Operation	Symbol	Description	Key Attributes
Discrete-Time Integrator	K Ts / z-1	Performs discrete-time integration or accumulation of the input signal using forward/backward Euler or trapezoidal method	Integrator method, Gain, External reset, input state, limit, saturation
Memory		The block introduces one major integration step delay; the output shall be the same as the input	Initial condition, inherit sample time (specifying time is not possible)
Unit Delay	1/z	Implements delay by one discrete sample time as specified; state logging is possible.	Initial condition, Input processing, sample time
Zero-Order Hold		Implements zero-order hold. Converts input signal with a continuous sample time to output signal with discrete sample time.	Sample time

Table 7.4: Discrete library blocks

Discrete-time integrator example

The example in *figure 7.31* shows the difference between continuous vs. discrete-time integrator blocks. In this model, the upper part shows continuous sample time logic, which produces a smooth sine wave due to integration, when a sine wave with amplitude 1, frequency 2, and sample time 0 is provided as an input signal.

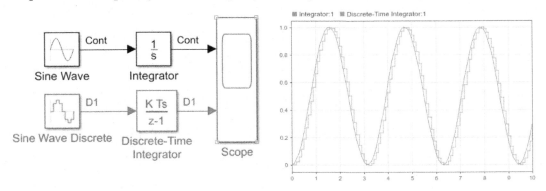

Figure 7.31: Discrete-time integrator example

The lower part of the preceding image shows discrete sample time, where the sine wave sample time is 0.1 second. The input of the discrete-time integrator is a sine wave with small steps of 0.1 second width, and the output of the block is a discrete sine wave signal with 0.1 second wide small steps, as can be observed in the scope.

Delay block example

The model in *figure 7.32* shows implementation to find factorial of a number using delay blocks supported by add, product, switch, and so on, blocks. The input number from the constant is provided to the subsystem factorial, where it is processed to decrement the number by one and multiply with the previously stored multiplied value.

As seen in *figure 7.32*, factorial of $5 = 5! = 5 \times 4 \times 3 \times 2 \times 1 = 120$

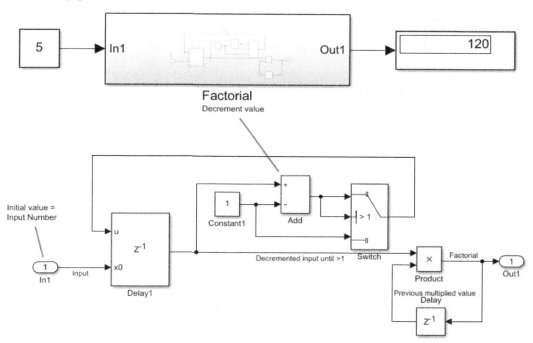

Figure 7.32: *Delay block—factorial example*

Signal routing

This library offers multiple types of blocks for signal routing as well as for signal storage and access. These blocks are widely used in the model, as it is not always possible to route all the signals throughout the model. Some of the popular blocks are as follows:

- bus selector and bus creator
- mux and demux
- merge
- switch and multiport switch
- from and go to
- Data store read, write, and memory

Figure 7.33 shows the blocks that are part of the Simulink library—signal routing:

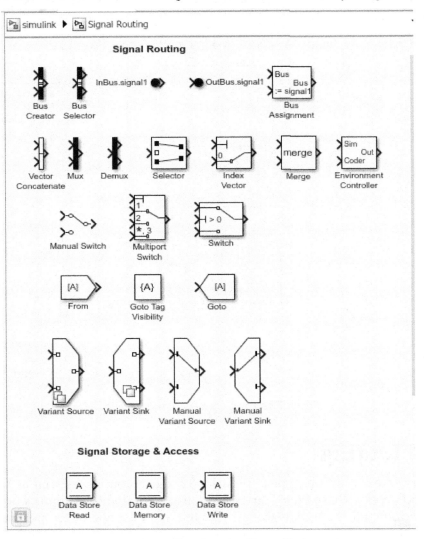

***Figure 7.33**: Signal routing library blocks*

Bus selector and Bus creator

The Bus creator block is used to virtually combine a group of input signals of different data types into a single bus. A bus can be considered equivalent to a Structure in C. Bus selector block is used to extract one or more input signals from the signal bus. Combining these two blocks reduces the visual complexity and efforts of the modeler to navigate the signal from one subsystem to another. For example, 100 inputs are received in the model, and we need to share this information from subsystem 1 to subsystem 2. Therefore, instead of creating 100 individual outports at subsystem 1 and 100 inputs at subsystem 2, we shall use bus creator with an input number specified as 100—that results in the creation of 100 open ports at the input and one open port at the output of bus creator block. We connect these 100 signals to the block and create only one outport connected to the inport of subsystem 2. As the second subsystem, we shall use a bus selector block, where a window pops up that shows all input signals located under the bus in the left window. With the select option, we can select the required signals and move them to the right side of the window. Based on the number of these signals on the right side, open ports shall be created at the output of the bus selector block. Usage of the bus creator block can be observed in *figure 7.4*.

Mux and demux

These blocks virtually combine and derive input signals of the same data type. Mux creates signal vector output out of scalar or vector input signals, whereas demux helps decompose the vector. The input cannot be a bus signal. The order of the decomposed signals shall be considered from top to bottom input signals.

Merge

The block combines signals from conditionally executed subsystems into a single signal. It outputs the value of the last received input signal. All the input signals must be updated at an identical sample rate.

Switch and multiport switch

Switch block combines two scalar or vector input signals into a single signal. Based on the second control input threshold, it decides whether to propagate the data input signal 1 or 3. It is equivalent to the `if` condition in `C`. The threshold of the control block can be set to `>` or `>=` to a specified threshold or `~=0`. The output data type can be either inherited or specified explicitly. The multiport switch has the first input as a control input, the other inputs shall be data inputs, and based on the control input value, the output signal shall be chosen out of input data signals. It is also possible to make the last data input as default input or have separate default input. The default port shall be indicated with an asterisk. The multiport switch works similarly to the switch case in `C`.

From and Goto

From and Goto blocks allow us to pass a signal from one block to another without actually connecting them. They are linked with the tags on the Goto block. One Goto block can become a source of multiple From blocks, but one From block can have only one corresponding Goto block. It helps the users avoid crossing lines, especially in the case of many signals or multiple connections.

Data Store Read, Write, Memory

The Data Store Memory block shall define the data store based on the input name and the location where it has been used. The data store read and write can read and write respectively using the same name at the same level, either as a memory block or inside these subsystems. It works similarly to the global variables.

Ports and subsystems

These topics shall be discussed in *Chapter 10: Advance modeling techniques-II*.

Lookup tables

This section contains library blocks, which are used to find values from lookup tables. It includes nine different blocks as follows. We will learn the 1-D Lookup Table and 2-D Lookup Table in detail:

1. 1-D Lookup Table
2. 2-D Lookup Table
3. n-D Lookup Table
4. Prelookup
5. Interpolation Using Prelookup
6. Direct Lookup Table (n-D)
7. Cosine
8. Sine
9. Lookup Table Dynamic

Figure 7.34 shows different blocks available under the lookup tables section:

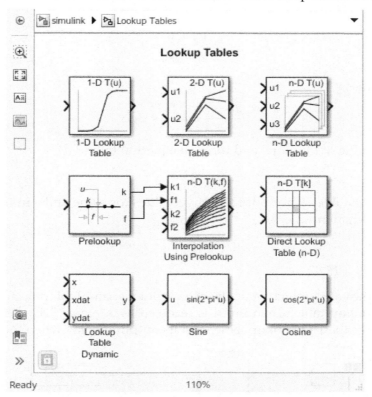

Figure 7.34: *Blocks under lookup table section*

1-D Lookup Table

Lookup tables determine output values based on existing data. We can either form mathematical equations to find the output values or have lookup tables based on existing trials. Most of the time, lookup tables are implemented when it is difficult to form a mathematical equation. As the name suggests, a 1-D lookup table is a one-dimensional lookup table that contains one single-dimensional array for table data and one single-dimensional array for breakpoints. The output value is determined based on table data, whereas input values are compared with breakpoints. To understand the 1-D lookup table operation in detail, we assume we have table data as [10 20 30 40 50] and Breakpoints as [1 4 6 8 10]. That means input value 1 is associated with output value 10, 4 with 20, 6 with 30, and so on. Let us consider we need to find the output value for input 3. Since value 3 falls between 1 and 4, we can form a linear equation between points (1, 10) and (4, 20). The equation of the straight line is $y = mx + c$. Where m is the slope of the line and c is constant. The slope of the line could be calculated as follows:

$$\frac{y_2 - y_1}{x_2 - x_2}$$

Which becomes,

$$\frac{20 - 10}{4 - 1} = \frac{10}{3} = 3.33$$

If we put a value of the slope and form an equation to find c,

$$20 = 3.33 \times 4 + c$$

Which gives $c = 6.68$. If we put respective values for slope and c in the equation to find output when input is 3,

$$y = 3.33 \times 3 + 6.68$$

Which gives $y = 16.67$.

We observe the value, which we shall get if we put the same table data and breakpoints in the 1-D lookup table when input is received as 3. *Figure 7.35* shows the dialog parameters for the 1-D Lookup table with its output display when the input is 3:

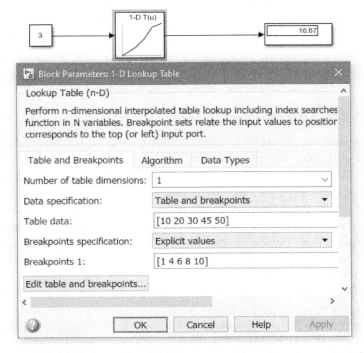

Figure 7.35: 1-D lookup table with dialog parameters and input vs. output data

2-D lookup table

Similar to the 1-D Lookup table, Simulink provides a 2-D Lookup table. Here we have table data in the form of a two-dimensional array with provision for two breakpoints for two inputs. The output value is decided based on the input values and their associated breakpoints with 2-D table data. For a 2-D lookup table, manually finding the output value is a very tedious task because there are several aspects we need to consider while forming the equations. *Figure 7.36* illustrates the input, output, and dialog parameters for a 2-D lookup table.

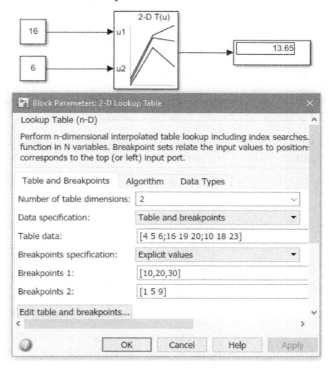

Figure 7.36*: 2-D lookup table with dialog parameters and input vs. output data*

Conclusion

In *Chapter 6: Simulink Editor with Environment*, we have accustomed ourselves to the Simulink Editor interface. The help of an example has helped readers understand the procedure to design and simulate a Simulink model using Simulink Editor. Therefore, after providing an understanding of how to use the tool, this chapter has laid a robust foundation for model-based design by introducing the readers to the building blocks of Simulink. With the help of some examples, the readers can gain practical experience in experimenting with library blocks. The reader has also learnt options to adapt the library blocks based on the need. In the upcoming chapter, the readers shall get to know the options available under different sub-panes of configuration settings—such as Solver settings, Data Import/Export, Math and Datatypes Pane, and Diagnostics Pane.

Points to remember

- The Library Browser provides access to the Simulink Block libraries during model-based design.
- The Library browser has two sections: in the left section, the library blocks are listed in a tree view. In the right window, the blocks of the selected library become visible.
- The Simulink library has many sub-libraries. Sources, Sinks, Discrete, Logic and Bit operations, Math operations, Ports and Subsystems, and Signal Routing are the most commonly used libraries.
- The Port number of the Inport block specifies the position of the port in the parent block.
- "Output when disabled, Initial output" setting of outport block is available only for conditionally executed subsystems.
- Scopes display the signals in the time domain during and after simulation.
- The library blocks from Simulink/Math Operations library enable the users to perform various scalar and vector mathematical operations.
- Logic and bit Operations library is essential in the development of logic-driven models.
- The integrator block finds the area under the curve.
- Many times, the transfer function is used as a filter.
- The library discrete contains various discrete-time function blocks, which are the equivalents of continuous-time function blocks.
- Buses contain the data of different data types, whereas Mux includes the data of the same data type.

Multiple choice questions

1. Which of the following sub-library is not part of the default Simulink Library browser?
    a. Sources
    b. Continuous
    c. Discrete
    d. Enums

2. Terminator block is a part of the Sources sub-library.
    a. True
    b. False

3. Which of the following is not the block parameter of the Inport block?
    a. Port Number
    b. Port Size
    c. Data Type
    d. Port dimension

4. Can product block be used to multiply more than two inputs?
    a. Yes
    b. No

5. Pulse Generator generates the sine wave.
    a. False
    b. True

6. Which of the following blocks is used to export the signal data outside of the Simulink model?
    a. To Workspace
    b. To File
    c. Both
    d. None of the above

7. Display block shows the waveform of the connected signal through the time domain.
    a. False
    b. True

8. Which of the following blocks perform matrix operations?
    a. Add
    b. Product
    c. Matrix concatenate
    d. All of the above

9. What would be the output of set bit 2 for input "010"?
    a. 5
    b. 6

c. 7

d. 8

10. Which of the following parameter does not change the display of the integrator block?

    a. External reset
    b. Initial condition
    c. Initial condition source
    d. Limit output

Questions

1. What are the different libraries available in Simulink? Give a short overview of each of the libraries.
2. Explain various methods to read data and write data from and outside the model.
3. Explain the use of bus element block.
4. Describe various types of data viewers.
5. Explain matrix and vector concatenation with the help of an example?
6. Create the logic for half adder using logical blocks.
7. Explain how the integrator block could be used to find the area under the curve.
8. Explain the use of the Transfer function as a filter.
9. Describe the behavior of the 1-D lookup table.
10. Implement the Fibonacci series using different basic blocks and plot the output for the first 10 numbers.

Answers

1. D   2. B
3. B   4. A
5. A   6. C
7. A   8. D
9. B   10. B

CHAPTER 8
Configuration Parameter Settings

Introduction

Simulink provides a wide range of building blocks for model-based design and simulation of complex dynamic systems. In this chapter, the reader shall get familiar with model configuration parameters and know the options available under different sub-panes of configuration settings, such as solver settings, data import/export, math and datatypes pane, and diagnostics pane. It is crucial for the readers to understand model configuration settings correctly to realize the full potential of Simulink software.

Structure

In this chapter, we shall discuss the following topics:

- Introducing model configuration parameters
- Solver settings
- Data Import/Export
- Math and data types pane
- Diagnostics pane
- Hardware implementation

- Model referencing
- Simulation target

Objectives

After studying this chapter, the reader will be able to:

- Work with different model configuration parameter settings.
- Understand in detail options available under solver settings, data import/export, math and data types, and diagnostics pane.
- Learn about hardware implementation, model referencing, and simulation target.

Introducing model configuration parameters

Every program needs some mechanism to monitor the program execution. For example, when overflow occurs for internal local variables, there should be some technique to inform the user about these errors. Simulink offers several configuration parameters where users can define their configurations based on their system needs. In this section, we will look into all these parameters. It is an excellent practice to be informed of these settings beforehand while developing a Simulink model. Model configuration settings decide the execution flow of the model.

The following list shows the brief categorization of the configuration parameters:

- Solver
- Data Import/Export
- Math and data types
- Diagnostics
- Hardware implementation
- Model referencing
- Simulation target

The Model Configuration Parameters are available in **Model Settings** in **Modelling Context** menu. The *figure 8.1* shows how to access configuration parameters in Simulink Editor:

Figure 8.1: Model setting button on toolbar

The *figure 8.2* shows how the configuration settings parameters panel looks in the Simulink editor:

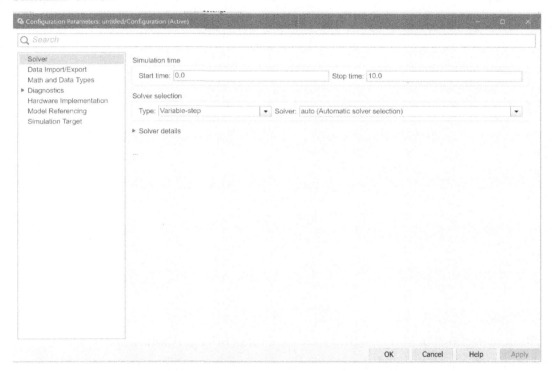

Figure 8.2: Model configuration parameters

Solver settings

Solver settings help configure Solver for a Simulink Model. A solver calculates a dynamic system's states at consecutive time steps during a specified period. The solver pane offers many parameters such as time, type, detailed settings, and so on. These parameters specify one of the most significant settings for model configuration.

The *figure 8.3* shows parameters available under Solver Pane:

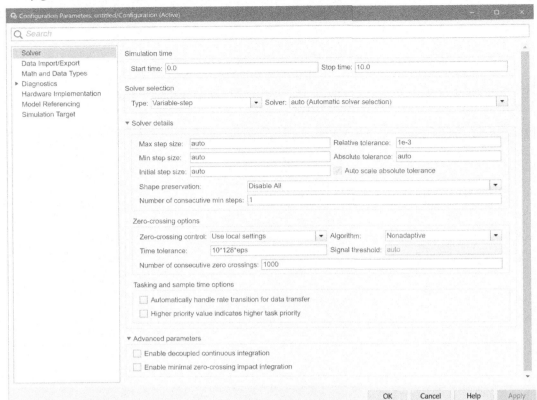

Figure 8.3: Solver pane

Different sections of Solver settings are explained briefly as follows:

Simulation time

The simulation time section contains two parameters: Start time and Stop time:

- **Start Time**: User can specify the start time of the simulation in seconds. The default start value is 0 seconds.
- **Stop Time**: The user can specify the stop time of the simulation in seconds. The default stop value is 10 seconds.

Solver selection

This section allows the users to select the solver type and respective Solver:

Type

Users can specify the type of Solver. There are two types of Solvers: variable-step and fixed-step. The default solver is variable-step. The parameter set for variable-step and fixed-step is different. There are some common parameters between fixed-step type and variable-step type.

Fixed-step type and its parameter set

The fixed-step type solver maintains the step size constant throughout the simulation. All fixed-step solvers other than ode 14× determine the next step as shown here:

$$x(n+1) = x(n) + h\, dx(n)$$

In the preceding equation, X represents the state, h represents the step size, and dX is the state derivative. $dX(n)$ is calculated by a particular algorithm using one or more derivative evaluations depending on the method's order. The *figure 8.4* shows parameters available for fixed-step type:

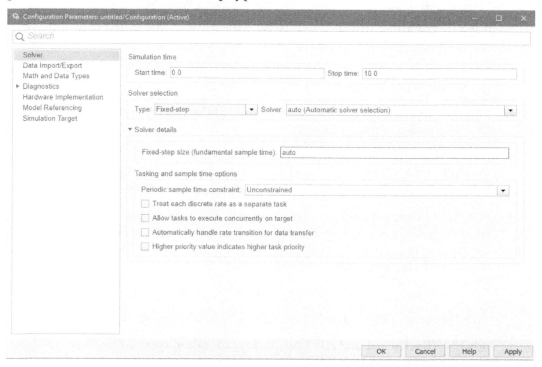

Figure 8.4: *Solver pane fixed-step parameters*

Fixed-step Solver

The Solver determines the states of the model during simulation. The solvers are used to find the next time step. Simulink Fixed step type supports several solvers. The following list shows supported solvers:

- **Auto (Automatic Solver detection)**: It calculates the state of the model using the Fixed-step type of Solver. It detects the required Solver based on model behavior.

- **Discrete (no continuous states)**: It determines the time of the next step by adding a step size. The discrete Solver should be used for those models that have no continuous states.

- **ode3 (Bogacki-Shampine)**: It uses the Bogacki-Shampine Formula integration technique for the next step calculation.

- **ode8 (Dormand-Prince RK8(7))**: It computes the model state at the next cycle using the eighth order Dormand-Prince formula.

- **ode5 (Dormand-Prince)**: It determines the model state at the next time step using the fifth order Dormand-Prince formula.

- **ode4 (Runge-Kutta)**: It computes the model state at the next cycle time using the fourth order Runge-Kutta (RK4) formula.

- **ode2 (Heun)**: It calculates the model state at the next sample time step using the Heun integration technique.

- **ode1 (Euler)**: The model state at the next sample time-step is calculated using the Euler integration method. This Solver is faster than other Fixed-step type solvers, but it is less accurate than other higher-order solvers.

- **ode14x (extrapolation)**: Newton's method and extrapolation from the current value are used to determine next, the model state. The following expression is used to find out the next cycle time where X is the state, dX is the state derivative, and h is the step size:

$$x(n + 1) - x(n) - h\, dx(n + 1) = 0$$

This Solver is comparatively slower but highly accurate.

- **ode1be (Backward Euler)**: The Backward Euler type solver uses a fixed number of Newton iterations.

Solver details

Based on the solver selection, the users have the following options to parametrize the Solver in detail:

- **Fixed-step size (fundamental sample time)**: This parameter is used to specify a time step that could be taken to execute the next cycle. By default, its value is Auto. The value auto uses 0.2 seconds as the step size.
- **Periodic sample time constraint**: This parameter is used to specify constraints to sample times. The model should adhere to the specified constraint; else, it results in an error. By default, the value of this parameter is Unconstrained. The following is the list of different values supported by this parameter:
  - **Unconstrained**: This option allows the user to specify an explicit sample time value. It does not provide any constraints on Periodic sample time.
  - **Ensure sample time-independent**: This setting does not allow to specify explicit sample time value. The sample time is calculated based on the context of Model Blocks.
  - **Specified**: It enables the `Sample time properties` parameter. The sample time properties parameter is used to specify and assign priorities to model sample times. They allow a user to assign different sample times with priorities.
- **Treat each discrete rate as a separate task**: This property decides whether model blocks should get executed in a group or individually.
- **Allow tasks to execute concurrently on target**: This parameter permits simultaneous tasking behavior for the model.
- **Automatically handle rate transition for data transfer**: Suppose model blocks have different task rates, and Rate transition blocks are used to transfer data. In that case, this parameter enables automatic handling of rate transition for data transfer.
- **Higher priority value indicates higher task priority**: If asynchronous transfers are implemented in the model, then using this parameter, a higher priority is executed as a higher tasking rate.

Variable type and its parameter set

The variable-step type solver varies the step size according to the model states throughout the simulation. It increases or decreases the step size to maintain accuracy. When model state changes quickly, it reduces step size; on the other hand, it increases the step size when the model state changes slowly. The *figure 8.5* shows the parameter set of variable-step type:

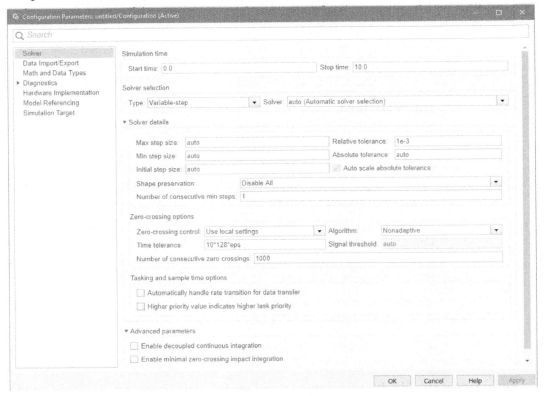

Figure 8.5: Solver pane variable-step parameters

Variable step Solver

The Solver determines the states of the model during simulation. The solvers are used to find the next time step. The variable step type supports several solvers. The following is the list of supported solvers:

- **auto**: It calculates the state of the model using a variable-step type of Solver. It detects the required Solver based on model behavior.

- **ode45 (Dormand-Prince)**: It determines the model's state at the next time step using an explicit Runge-Kutta (4,5) formula (the Dormand-Prince pair) for numerical integration.

- **Discrete (no continuous states)**: It calculates the next step's time by adding a step size that varies depending on the rate of change of the model's states. The discrete Solver should be used for those models with no continuous states.

- **ode23 (Bogacki-Shampine):** It computes the state of the model at the next time step using an explicit Runge-Kutta (2,3) formula (the Bogacki-Shampine pair) for numerical integration.

- **ode113 (Adams):** It determines the model's state at the next time step using a variable-order Adams-Bashforth-Moulton PECE numerical integration technique.

- **ode15s (stiff/NDF):** It computes the state of the model at the next time step using variable-order numerical differentiation formulas (NDFs).

- **ode23s (stiff/Mod. Rosenbrock):** It calculates the model's state at the next time step using a modified Rosenbrock formula of order 2.

- **ode23t (Mod. stiff/Trapezoidal):** It calculates the state of the model at the next time step using an implementation of the trapezoidal rule with a *free* interpolant.

- **ode23tb (stiff/TR-BDF2):** It computes the state of the model at the next time step using a multistep implementation of TR-BDF2, an implicit Runge-Kutta formula with a trapezoidal rule first stage, and a second stage consisting of a backward differentiation formula of order two. By construction, the same iteration matrix is used in evaluating both stages.

- **odeN (fixed step with zero crossings):** The model state is computed using an Nth order fixed-step integration formula as an explicit function of the current value of the state and the state derivatives approximated at intermediate points.

- **daessc (Solver for Simscape):** It determines the model's state at the next time step by solving systems of differential-algebraic equations resulting from Simscape models. daessc is only available with Simscape products.

Max step size

This parameter specifies the maximum step size. Variable-step solver increases the step size according to the model's state; it limits step size to this *Max Step size* upper limit. The discrete Solver used models shortest sample time. Start and stop times determine the max step size for continuous solvers when it is specified as Auto. When the stop time equals the start time or is inf, then 0.2 seconds is used as the maximum step size. Else, it sets the maximum step size using the formula $((t_{stop} - t_{start})/50)$. For Sine and Signal generator source blocks, Simulink computes the max step size by finding a minimum of $((t_{stop} - t_{start})/50)$ and $((1/3)(1/Freq_{max}))$, where $Freq_{max}$ is the maximum frequency in Hz used in the model blocks.

Min step size

This parameter describes the least step size. Variable-step Solver reduces the step size according to the model's state; it limits step size to this *Min Step size* lower limit. The default of this parameter is *auto*. The step size is calculated based on other parameters and Model dynamics in the *auto* min.

- **Initial Step size**: This parameter is used to set the first step size when the simulation starts. In this case, also, the default value of this parameter is *Auto*. Besides, it is determined based on other parameters and model dynamics.

- **Relative tolerance**: This parameter is used to set up the tolerance value, which is the maximum acceptable solver error. If solver error becomes more than the tolerance value, then solvers reduce the time step size. The default of this parameter is 1e–3.

- **Absolute tolerance**: This parameter specifies the maximum acceptable solver error when the state approaches zero. In this case, solver error becomes more than the tolerance value; then, solvers reduce the time step size. The default value for this parameter is Auto.

- **Auto scale absolute tolerance**: This parameter allows adjusting absolute tolerance at each model state. By default, its value is true.

- **Sharp preservation**: This parameter allows using derivative information at each sample time to increase the integration accuracy. By default, the value for this parameter is `Disable All`. The value `Enable All` increases the accuracy but may decrease the performance.

- **Number of Consecutive min steps**: This parameter sets a maximum number of min step size violations during the simulation. By default, its value is 1. Min step size violations occur when simulation takes a step size lesser than the specified Min step size.

- **Zero crossing control**: This parameter enables zero-crossing detection. Meaning, that for any block used in the model if the value of signals is changing from positive to negative or negative to positive, then at zero-crossing additional time step is taken by the Solver to achieve the most accurate results. `Use Local Setting` is the default value for this parameter. In this case, zero-crossing detection happens according to each block setting. `Enable All` enables zero crossing detection for all blocks, and `Disable all` disable the zero-crossing detection. Disabling zero-crossing detection may speed up the simulation but reduces accuracy.

- **Algorithm**: This parameter tells which algorithm should be used to detect zero crossings. By default, its value is non-adaptive. The non-adaptive algorithm has better accuracy but may result in a more extended simulation run time for those systems with strong chattering or Zeno behavior. The Adaptive algorithm activates or deactivates zero-crossing dynamically.

- **Time tolerance**: This parameter specifies a factor that defines how closely zero-crossing events should occur to call as consecutive events. By default, its value is 10*128*eps, where eps have a value 2^{-52}. It is the next larger double-precision after 1.0.

- **Signal Threshold**: The signal threshold is auto by default for the non-adaptive algorithm, whereas it could be specified when the Adaptive algorithm is selected. Even for the Adaptive algorithm, its value by default is "auto", and its value can be any real number greater than zero. The signal threshold specifies the deadband region used during zero-crossing detection. When signal values fall in a particular region, then Simulink considers it as zero crossing. This region is called as deadband.

- **Number of consecutive zero crossings**: This parameter is used to specify the number of consecutive zero crossings allowed during the simulation. By default, its value is 1,000. Once a maximum number of consecutive zero crossings are detected, then Simulink throws an error, or a warning based on configuration settings in the diagnostic pane.

- **Automatically handle rate transition for data transfer**: Suppose model blocks have different task rates, and Rate transition blocks are used to have data transfer among them. In that case, this parameter enables automatic handling of rate transition for data transfer.

- **Higher priority value indicates higher task priority**: If asynchronous transfers are implemented in the model, then using this parameter, a higher priority is executed as a higher tasking rate.

Advanced settings

The following advanced settings become visible when the variable-step Solver is selected:

- **Enable decoupled continuous integration**: This parameter is used to decouple the continuous and discrete rates. This coupling may result in slowing down the model.

- **Enable minimal zero-crossing impact integration**: This parameter minimizes the impact of zero-crossing during the integration of continuous states.

To get more information on Solver pane configuration parameters, visit Solver Pane MATLAB help https://www.mathworks.com/help/simulink/gui/solver-pane.html.

Example to realize the difference between Fixed step solver and Variable step Solver

Until now, we have learnt that a fixed step solver executes the simulation with a fixed sample time. Variable step solver opts for variable sample time according to min step and max step to execute the simulation based on model dynamics. Let us take an example. Suppose we have to implement as adder logic where we add numeric 1 in the received input. The *figure 8.6* shows the behavior of the input signal:

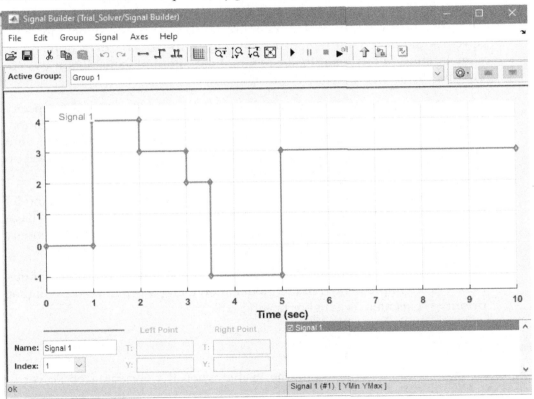

Figure 8.6: Input signal to adder

In *figure 8.6*, we can see that zero crossing is happening approximately at 3.5 seconds. *Figure 8.7* shows the adder logic:

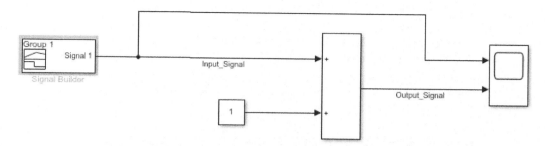

Figure 8.7: Adder logic to understand fixed step vs. variable step

Let us run the simulation with a fixed type solver having a sample time as 1 second and observe the output in *figure 8.8*:

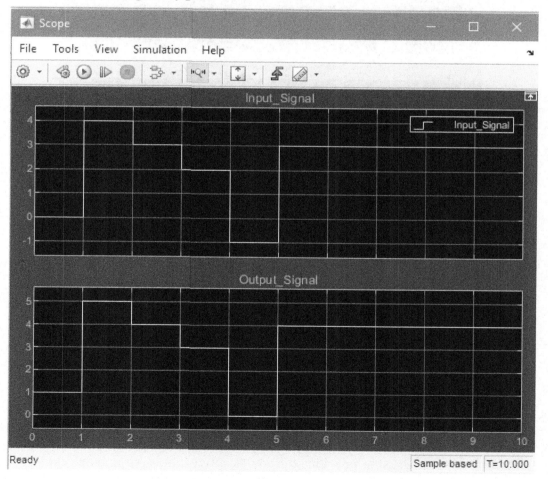

Figure 8.8: Input signal vs. output signal with fixed type solver

In *figure 8.8*, we can see that the zero-crossing is not captured in the output. Simulink computes the output at every fixed time step. So, the output value at time of 3 seconds is 3, whereas at 4 seconds it is 0. Now we run the same logic with a variable step Solver and observe the output in *figure 8.9*:

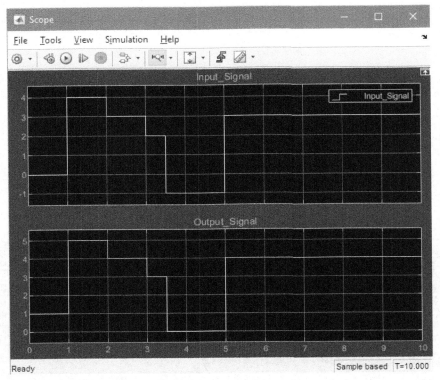

Figure 8.9: *Input signal vs. output signal with variable type solver*

In *figure 8.9*, we can see that the zero-crossing is captured in the output. We also realize that output is computed purely based on the dynamics of input. As per the change in the input, the output has also changed.

Fixed type solver is used for non-continuous real-time systems, whereas a variable type solver is used for continuous systems.

Data Import/Export

To run the simulation effectively and check the model behavior in all possible cases, it must feed different data to the model inputs and then fetch the model outputs. Data Import/Export pane provides different configuration parameters like input, initial states, signal logging, etc. These parameters are useful for simulations. The *figure 8.10* shows the parameters available in Data Import/Export pane.

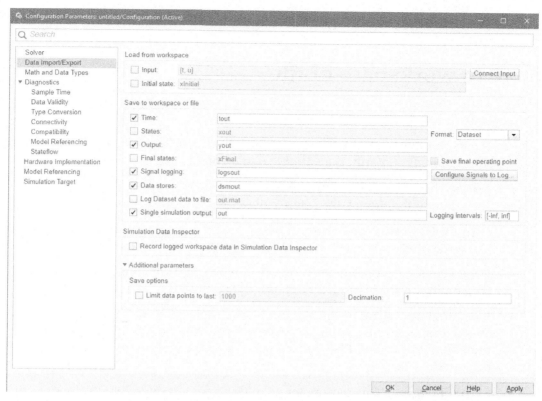

Figure 8.10: Data Import/Export pane

As shown in *figure 8.10*, there are different sub-sections to the Data Import/Export section as follows.

Load from workspace

The following Input options can be enabled under load from the workspace subsection:

- **Input**: This configuration parameter is used to load input data before the start of the simulation. The input data should be in the form of [t,u], whereas "t" contains the sample times when the respective data present in "u" must be loaded.

- **Connect Input**: Connect input button is used to select data from a spreadsheet or any MAT file.

- **Initial State**: This parameter specifies the workspace variable name that contains the values of the initial state. For example, this variable can have the past simulation states, so these states can be used as starting states for the next simulation. By default, the variable **xInitial** is used to load initial states.

Save to workspace or file

These are the output options that can be enabled under Save to workspace or file subsection:

- **Time**: This parameter specifies a variable that could store the time data of the simulation. By default, the variable name **tout** is used.
- **States**: This parameter is used to specify the variable name that could log the state data of the model. By default, the variable name is **xout**.
- **Output**: The model's root output data is saved in the variable that is specified using the output parameter. By default, **yout** variable is used.
- **Final states**: This parameter is used to save logged state data of the model at the end of the simulation. By default, data is stored in **xFinal** variable.
- **Save final operating point**: When the final states parameter is enabled, then "Save final operating point" parameter offers the possibility of storing only final operating states. Else, full snapshot data throughout the simulation will be stored.
- **Signal Logging**: This parameter enables signal logging globally. By default, signal data is logged into workspace variable **logsout**.
- **Data Stores**: This parameter enables the logging of data store memory bocks globally. By default, data store memory data is logged into workspace variable **dsmout**.
- **Log dataset data to file**: This option enables logging of the data into the MAT- file. By default, it saves data into the **out.mat** file.
- **Signal simulation output**: This parameter enables logging of all kinds of data, including outputs, signals, States, DSM logging, Scopes, and workspace block data into a single **Simulink.SimulationOutput** object variable. By default, a variable named **out** is created in the workspace.

Simulation data inspector

The following setting is applicable for the simulation data inspector:

- **Record logged workspace in Simulation data inspector**: By enabling this option, logged data other than **dataset** format and data logged using blocks shall be sent to the Simulation data inspector when a simulation is paused or completed.

Additional parameters

In addition to the previously mentioned settings, these parameters are available under the section:

- **Limit data points to last**: This parameter is used to limit data points. By default, the last 1,000 data points are logged.

- **Decimation**: This parameter specifies the decimation factor, after which Simulink outputs the data. By default, its value is 1, which means all data points are saved.

- **Output options**: This parameter is used only for variable-step type Solver. This parameter enables additional data logging options. The following are the values that could be set for this parameter:

    - **Refine outputs**: Refine outputs log data in-between as well as at time steps. Refine output enables one more parameter called a refine factor, which specifies the number of points generated during the simulation.

    - **Produce additional output**: It generates additional outputs at the specified time. The Output times are used to determine times when additional output is required to be generated.

    - **Produce specified outputs only**: It uses Output times at which Simulink generates output in addition to simulation start and stop times.

Advanced parameters

The following drop-down selection option is available under advanced parameters:

Dataset signal format

This parameter specifies the format of a data set. The data set can be saved in the following formats:

- **Time-series**: The time series format contains mainly time, time info, data, and data info fields. *Figure 8.11* shows the structure of time series:

```
>> yout{1}.Values
   timeseries

  Common Properties:
              Name: 'GainedValues'
              Time: [1x1 double]
          TimeInfo: [1x1 tsdata.timemetadata]
              Data: [1x1 double]
          DataInfo: [1x1 tsdata.datametadata]

  More properties, Methods
```

Figure 8.11: Time series structure

- **Timetable**: The time table format has several fields with respect to time series, such as start time, raw time, sample time, and so on. The *figure 8.12* shows the format of Time Table data:

```
Command Window
>> TimeTable_youts = yout{1}.Values;
>> TimeTable_youts.Properties
ans =
  TimetableProperties with properties:

               Description: ''
                  UserData: []
            DimensionNames: {'Time'  'Variables'}
             VariableNames: {'Data'}
      VariableDescriptions: {}
             VariableUnits: {}
        VariableContinuity: step
                  RowTimes: 0 sec
                 StartTime: 0 sec
                SampleRate: NaN
                  TimeStep: NaN
          CustomProperties: No custom properties are set.
         Use addprop and rmprop to modify CustomProperties.
fx >>
```

Figure 8.12: Time Table structure

Math and data types

Math and data types pane contain parameters that are used to specify data types and net slope calculations. *Figure 8.13* shows math and data types pane:

Configuration Parameter Settings ■ 313

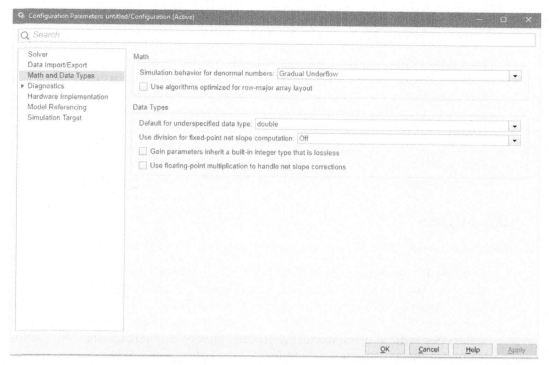

Figure 8.13: Math and Data Type pane

There are two subsections: math and data types:

Math

Math subsection offers two settings as follows:

- **Simulation behavior for denormal numbers**: The denormal numbers are any other numbers than zero which have their magnitude smaller than the smallest normalized floating-point number. The smallest normalized number for double precision and single precision is 2.225073858507201e–308 and 1.1754944e–38, respectively. This parameter is used to specify the required behavior for the denormal results of arithmetic operations. The following are the values possible for this parameter:

    o **Gradual underflow**: This is the default value. In this case, denormal results are used as it is in the arithmetic operations. All simulation mode supports Gradual Underflow behavior.

    o **Flush to Zero (FTZ)**: As the name suggests, this setting flushes denormal results to zero. Some hardware targets do have this feature to flush down the denormal results from arithmetic operations to zero. With the help of this setting, it is possible to simulate a similar behavior. The normal simulation model does not support this setting.

- **Use Algorithms optimized for row-major array layout**: This parameter enables algorithms for row-major format for simulation purposes as well as for code generation. There are two layouts to store the arrays, row-major, and column-major. The row-major layout stores the array row-wise, whereas the column stores the array columns-wise. By default, this setting is off. When an array layout of the block is selected as row-major, then turning on this setting helps to have an optimized layout. When the block's array layout is chosen as column-major, turning off this setting helps to have better results.

Data types

Data type subsection provides different configuration settings as follows:

- **Default for underspecified data type**: The Simulink has a property called data type propagation. We do not need to specify the data types at every block. Data types are either back propagated or inherited. There are two possible values for this parameter: *double* or *single*. The data type for underspecified datatypes will be used according to the value of this parameter. The default value for this parameter is double.

- **Use division for fixed-point net slope computation**: This property is explicitly used for fixed-point division operations. Before going into details of this property, we must understand net slope computation. During fixed-point computations, when a change of the slope is not in the power of two, the net slope calculation is required. Most of the time, net slope calculation is done using integer implementation shift operations. When division is more efficient than multiplication followed by shifts on the target hardware, it is possible to approximate net slope computation using fraction or reciprocal of integer. It is always more efficient to compute fixed point net slope using division operation. This parameter can have three values as per the following:

    o **Off**: In this case, net slope computation is done using integer multiplication followed by shifts.

    o **On**: In this case, net slope computation is performed using a rational approximation of the net slope. When simplicity and accuracy conditions do meet, then it may result in either multiplication or division.

    o **Use division for reciprocals of integers only**: In this case, net slope computation is achieved using division when the net slope is possible to represent by the reciprocal of an integer. Of course, it is required to meet simplicity and accuracy conditions here as well.

- **Gain parameters inherit a built-in integer type that is lossless**: This parameter decides whether the type of the gain parameter of a gain block should compile into a built-in integer or not. Whenever input datatype is a built-in integer type, and Gain parameter value is possible to represent in the built-in integer type without losing its precision, it is always more efficient that the type of gain parameter inherits a built-in lossless type. There are two more constraints for this, and the parameter datatype is set to `Inherit: Inherit via internal rule`, and the minimum and the maximum values in the Gain block parameters can be represented without losing any precision by a built-in integer. When the value of this parameter is set to off, and the parameter data type is set to `Inherit: Inherit via internal rule` then Simulink compiles the datatype of the gain parameter with maximum precision. By default, the value of this parameter is *off*.

- **Use floating-point multiplication to handle net slope correction**: Whenever type casing is implemented in the model from floating point to fixed point, and the value of this parameter is set to *on*, then floating-point multiplication is used to compute net slope correction. When the parameter value is set to *off*, then the division is used to perform net slope correction.

Advanced parameters

This subsection is usually hidden and can be expanded by clicking on .... It has the following parameters:

- **Application lifespan (days)**: This parameter with Simulink step-size determines the data type required to store time values. This parameter can have any positive scalar value until inf. When inf is used as application timespan, then 64 bits are allocated to store timer values. By default, its value is Auto. The underlying value for Auto may vary according to the selected target.

- **Implement logic signals as Boolean data (vs. double)**: This parameter decides whether Boolean data will be used for logical signals or double data for logical signals. Suppose datatypes are not explicitly mentioned in the model. Underspecified datatypes are used as *double* by default; in that case, they may give a compilation error if logical signals and double signals are operated together. In that case, this parameter's value should be set to *off* to resolve the error.

Diagnostics

The diagnostics pane contains configuration parameters, which play an essential role during compilation and simulation. The diagnostics pane also includes more panes classified based on sample time, data validity, type conversion, connectivity, compatibility, model referencing, and Stateflow. The *figure 8.14* shows the content of the diagnostic pane—the **Diagnostics** pane contains solver-related configuration parameters:

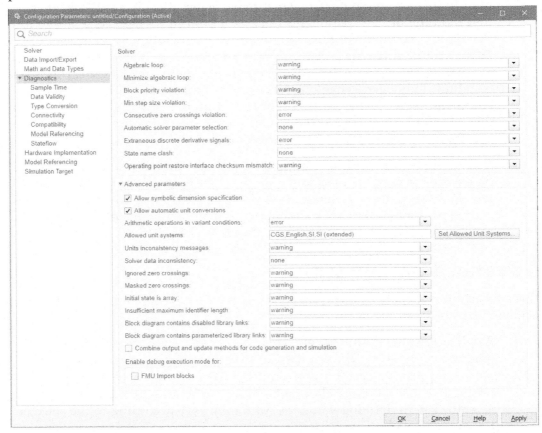

Figure 8.14: Diagnostics pane

Diagnostics pane consists of two subsections: Solver and Advanced parameters.

Solver

The settings available under Solver section are as follows.

Algebraic loop

This parameter allows selecting an action when Simulink detects an algebraic error. The algebraic error occurs when the input port of the block is connected to the output port of the same block. This connection may be a direct connection or a feedback path connection through other blocks. The *figure 8.15* shows two examples of the algebraic loop with direct connection and feedback path connection:

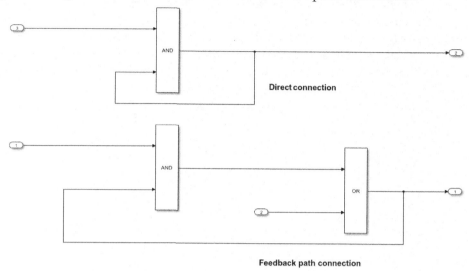

Figure 8.15: Algebraic loop

The algebraic loop occurs when the input value is not available to perform the operation, and this is possible in the two cases mentioned in the above figure. Let us consider the first case; the second input of AND operator is connected to its own output. At the time of the first sample time of the simulation to perform the AND operation, both inputs' values are required. Since the AND operation is not yet executed, the value of the second input of the AND operator is not available. This results in an algebraic loop. The behavior is similar in the second case. When an algebraic loop is detected, then the algebraic loop configuration parameter decides the action to be taken by diagnostics according to the values possible for this parameter: error, warning, and none. The default value is a warning.

Simulink tries to minimize the algebraic loop by calling a loop-solving at each sample time. This reduces the simulation performance and eventually increases simulation time.

Minimize algebraic loop

This parameter decides the action to be taken by diagnostic when the algebraic loop is not possible to minimize. The values could be set for this parameter are error, warning, and none. When an error is selected then, Simulink terminates the simulation and displays the error. When a warning is selected, then Simulink displays the warning. When none is selected, then no action is taken. The default value is a warning.

Block priority violation

This parameter decides the action to be taken when a priority violation occurs according to the value error, warning, or none. The default value is a warning. Let us see what a priority violation is. Simulink blocks have provision to assign priority to each block. For this, right-click on the block, then select properties. This will open a window where a priority order can be assigned, the lower value results in, the higher priority. The *figure 8.16* shows the property window:

Figure 8.16: Block properties

Let us have a look at *figure 8.17*. Here, we have two logical operators—AND operator and OR operator. From the logic implementation, it is visible that OR operation is dependent on AND operation since the output of AND is going to the input of OR. But the assigned priority of AND operator is 2, and the priority of the OR operator is 1. So, this should result in a priority violation:

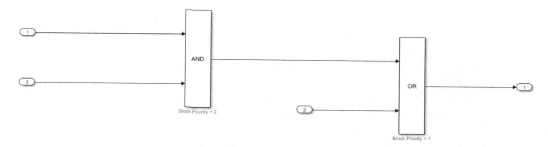

Figure 8.17: *Priority violation example*

The value of the block priority violation parameter in configuration settings is a *warning*. Therefore, after compilation, Simulink displays a warning. The *figure 8.18* shows the warning message when a priority violation occurs:

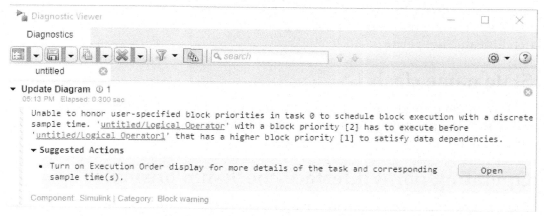

Figure 8.18: *Priority violation warning message*

Min step size violation

This parameter decides what kind of action shall be taken when a minimum step size violation occurs according to its set value, error, or warning. The default value is a warning. This violation can occur when the variable-step solver is selected. The specified error tolerance of the model requires a step size smaller than the Min step size specified in the solver pane.

Consecutive zero-crossing violation

This parameter decides the action to be taken when the Consecutive zero-crossing number exceeds the maximum number specified in the solver pane. The possible values for this parameter are error, warning, and none. The default value is an error. When an error or warning is selected and the violation is detected, then the message gets displayed by Simulink along with the count of consecutive occurrences of zero-crossing and block details (name and type of the block) where the error has occurred.

Automatic solver parameter selection

Sometimes Simulink changes the configuration parameter settings to make the model more stable considering other model settings. This parameter decides the action to be taken when Simulink changes the configuration settings. The possible values for this parameter are error, warning, and none. The default value is none.

Extraneous discrete derivative signals

When a discrete signal is passed to the model block, such as an integrator block with continuous states, Simulink cannot decide the minimum rate at which it needs to reset the solver. When this happens then, this parameter decides the action to be taken. The possible values for this parameter are error, warning, and none. The default value is an error.

State name clash

When a name is used multiple times for states in the model, this parameter decides the action. The possible values for this parameter are warning and none. The default value is none.

Operating point interface checksum mismatch

This parameter is used to ensure that the interface checksum is identical to the model checksum. The possible values for this parameter are error, warning, and none. The default value is a warning. When the value none is selected, then Simulink does not compare interface checksum with model checksum. When a value warning or error is selected, then Simulink compares the interface checksum with the model checksum. If the checksum in the operating point is different from the model checksum, then the warning message is displayed in the case of a warning. Simulink does not load the `ModelOperatingPoint` object, and an error is displayed in the case of error.

Advanced parameters

The settings available under the advanced parameters of the diagnostic pane are described as follows:

- **Allow symbolic dimension specification**: This parameter decides whether Simulink should propagate and preserve dimension symbols in the propagated signals or not. By default, its value is On. For example, variable `x` is defined in the workspace with a value 8. If a signal is defined in the workspace with the dimension mentioned as **x** then this is equivalent to 8. Using these configuration parameters, symbols like **x** could be used for dimension specification. The definition of signals in the workspace is explained in this chapter in the section signal sub-pane.

- **Allow automatic unit conversions**: When units have known mathematical relationships, then this parameter enables automatic unit conversions. By default, its value is On.

- **Arithmetic operations in variant conditions**: When arithmetic operations are performed in variant conditions mentioned in variant blocks, this setting decides the action taken by Simulink. The possible values for this parameter are error, warning, and none. When an error is selected, then Simulink stops the simulation and displays the error message. When a warning is selected, the Simulation continues, but a warning message will be displayed. When none is selected, then no action will be taken by Simulink, and simulation continues. The default value is an error.

- **Allowed unit systems**: This parameter is used to specify which unit systems are allowed. Click on the `Set Allowed Unit Systems` to set the allowed unit systems. By default, all Unit systems are allowed. The list of allowed unit systems is CGS, English, SI, and SI (extended). We can allow/disallow the unit systems using `Set Allowed Unit Systems` wizard. This wizard opens by clicking on `Set Allowed Unit Systems` button available in the diagnostic pane. The *figure 8.19* shows how the wizard looks like:

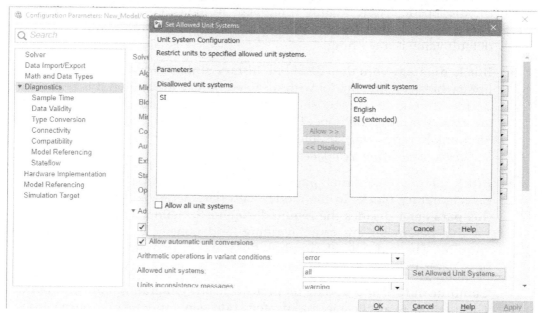

Figure 8.19: Priority violation warning message

- **Units inconsistency messages**: This parameter is used to specify whether unit inconsistencies should be displayed as a warning or not.

- **Solver data inconsistency**: The solver data inconsistency occurs when s-functions with continues sample times are used in the model, and it does not produce consistent results when executed multiple times. The possible values for this parameter are error, warning, and none. The default value is none.

- **Ignored zero-crossings**: This parameter decides the action to be taken when the Simulink ignores detected zero crossings. The possible values for this parameter are error, warning, and none. The default value is none.

- **Masked zero-crossings**: This parameter decides the action to be taken when the Simulink masks detect zero crossings. The possible values for this parameter are error, warning, and none. The default value is none.

- **Initial state is array**: This setting decides the action to be taken when the initial state is an array. The possible values for this parameter are error, warning, and none. The default value is a warning. When the order of elements in the array does not match the order in which the blocks initialize, Simulink may produce unexpected results.

- **Insufficient maximum identifier length**: This parameter is used for code generation. When the configuration parameter `Max Identifier length` is not enough to create global unique identifiers, then this parameter decides the diagnostic action. Mainly it happens in the case of referenced models. The possible values for this parameter are error, warning, and none. The default value is a warning.

- **Block diagram contains disabled library links**: When Simulink detects library blocks in the model with disabled library links, then this parameter decides the required diagnostic action. The possible values for this parameter are error, warning, and none. The default value is a warning. The concepts of Simulink libraries with disabled or broken links will be explained in *Chapter 9: Advanced modeling techniques-I*.

- **Block diagram contains parameterized library links**: When Simulink detects library blocks in the model with parameterized library links, then this parameter decides the required diagnostic action. The possible values for this parameter are error, warning, and none. The default value is a warning. The concepts of Simulink libraries with parameterized links will be explained in *Chapter 9: Advanced modeling techniques-I*.

- **Combine output and update methods for code generation and simulation**: This setting is applicable mainly for code generation. This setting forces Simulink to have identical execution order for simulation and code generation. When output and update code is in one function in the generated code, this parameter helps avoid a mismatch between potential simulation and code generation. By default, its value is Off.

- **FMU Import blocks**: Turning On this parameter creates a separate process to execute FMU binaries when debug execution mode is enabled and protects the MATLAB process from crashing. By default, its value is Off.

Sample Time pane

The sample time pane of Diagnostics settings contains the configuration parameters related to the sample time and sample time specifications. The *figure 8.20* shows how the Sample time pane looks like.

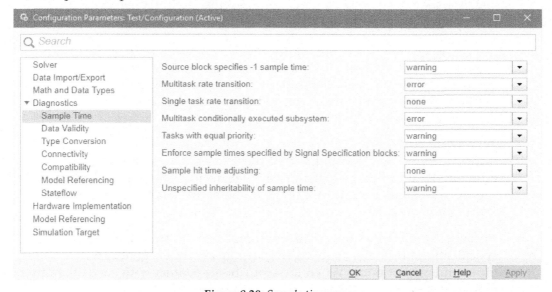

Figure 8.20: Sample time pane

The following settings are available under `Sample Time` pane of `Diagnostics`:

- **Source block specifies –1 sample time**: Some of the source bocks do have provision to mention sample time explicitly. This sample time should be in multiples of the model sample time. If sample time is mentioned as –1, then the block's sample time will be inherited from the model sample time. This parameter decides the action to be taken if source blocks such as sine wave specify sample time as –1. The possible values for this parameter are error, warning, and none. The default value is a warning.

- **Multitask rate transition**: Suppose two interdependent blocks are running in a multitasking mode with different sample times. If an invalid rate transition is detected between these two blocks, then this parameter determines the required diagnostics action. The possible values for this parameter are error and warning. The default value is an error. The use of rate transition blocks resolves these illegal rate transitions from the model.

- **Single task rate transition**: If two interdependent blocks are running in a single-tasking mode with different sample times, then this parameter determines the required diagnostics action. The possible values for this parameter are error, warning, and none. The default value is none. With the help of rate transition blocks, we can transition the sample rate to have the same sample time.

- **Multitask conditionally executed subsystem**: If the model contains an enabled subsystem that operates at multiple rates with the multitasking solver mode used by the model. Suppose the model contains a conditional subsystem, which can reset its states and has an asynchronous subsystem. In both cases, there is a possibility of data corruption or un-deterministic behavior. When Simulink detects data corruption or un-deterministic behavior, this parameter determines the required diagnostics action. The possible values for this parameter are error, warning, and none. The default value is an error.

- **Tasks with equal priority**: Suppose the model contains two tasks with equal priority. If there is a possibility that these tasks may stop each other in the target system. In this case, this parameter decides the required diagnostics action. The possible values for this parameter are error, warning, and none. The default value is a warning.

- **Enforce sample times specified by Signal Specification blocks**: The signal specification block allows to specify attributes of the signal connected to its input and output ports. When these attributes conflict with each other, then Simulink displays an error during compilation. This parameter is used to decide a diagnostic action when Simulink detects this conflict. The possible values for this parameter are error, warning, and none. The default value is a warning.

- **Sample hit time adjusting**: Sometimes, Simulink adjusts the sample hit time while running the model. The hit time is the instance when Simulink executes the block diagram logic. This adjustment is made most of the time to accelerate tasks to match the exact sample hit for the slower tasks. When Simulink makes this minor adjustment to a sample hit time, then this parameter decides a diagnostic action required to be taken. The possible values for this parameter are warning and none. The default value is none.

- **Unspecified inheritability of sample time**: When a model contains s-functions that do not specify the sample time rule, this results in preventing this model from inheriting sample times from the parent model. When Simulink detects this behavior, then this parameter decides a diagnostic action required to be taken. The possible values for this parameter are warning and none. The default value is a warning.

Data validity pane

The **Data Validity** pane contains the configuration parameters, which are related to the data validity. The *figure 8.21* shows how the Data validity pane looks like:

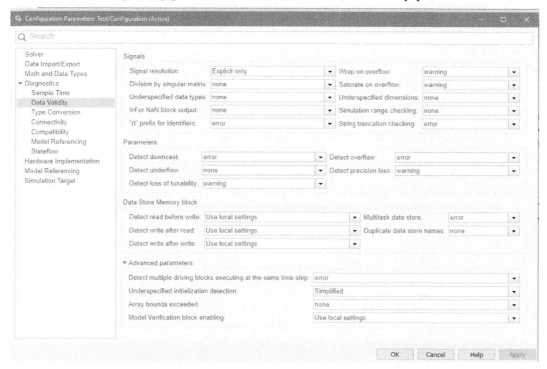

Figure 8.21: *Data validity pane*

The Data validity pane parameters are grouped under different sub-panes, such as signals, parameters, data store memory block, and advanced parameters.

Signals sub-pane

Before going into details of Signal related parameters, let us understand what is Signal. The Signals carry the data between two blocks. The data is nothing but an output of a block. We can define the behavior of signals in the workspace by creating a **Simulink.Signal** object. This object contains signal specifications such as data type, min value, max value, and so on. The following are the signal properties that are possible to specify for **Simulink.Signal** object.

- **CoderInfo**: Required for code generation of a signal.
- **Complexity**: Numeric complexity of a signal. Such as *real* or *complex*.
- **Datatype**: Data type of a signal.
- **Description**: The information about a signal.
- **Dimensions**: Dimension of a signal such as a row vector or character vector.
- **DimensionsMode**: Dimension mode of a signal such as fixed or variable.
- **Max**: The max value of a signal.
- **Min**: The min value of a signal.
- **InitialValue**: The initial value of the signal.
- **SampleTime**: The sample time of a signal.
- **Unit**: The physical unit of a signal value.

The *figure 8.22* explains how to define a signal in the MATLAB workspace:

```
>> Signal_On_Time = Simulink.Signal;
>> Signal_On_Time.DataType = 'double';
>> Signal_On_Time.Complexity = 'real';
>> Signal_On_Time.Description = 'The elapsed time for which state On is active';
>> Signal_On_Time.Dimensions = '1';
>> Signal_On_Time.DimensionsMode = 'fixed';
>> Signal_On_Time.Max = 10;
>> Signal_On_Time.Min = 0;
>> Signal_On_Time.InitialValue = '0';
>> Signal_On_Time.SampleTime = -1;
>> Signal_On_Time.Unit = 'minutes';
>> Signal_On_Time
Signal_On_Time =
  Signal with properties:

            CoderInfo: [1×1 Simulink.CoderInfo]
          Description: 'The elapsed time for which state On is active'
             DataType: 'double'
                  Min: 0
                  Max: 10
                 Unit: 'minutes'
           Dimensions: '1'
       DimensionsMode: 'Fixed'
           Complexity: 'real'
           SampleTime: -1
         InitialValue: '0'
```

Figure 8.22: Simulink signal definition

Different settings available under the signals sub-pane are described as follows:

- **Signal resolution**: This parameter describes how the model shall resolve the signals and the states to `Simulink.Signal` objects. When the option `Signal name must resolve to Simulink signal object` is used, it is defined as an explicit symbol resolution. The resolution that occurs only based on name match and without an explicit specification is considered implicit symbol resolution. This parameter has the following possible values:
    - **None**: The signal resolution is not performed by the model.
    - **Explicit only**: The signal resolution is performed only for explicitly specified signals. This is the default value of this parameter.
    - **Explicit and implicit**: The implicit and explicit both signal resolutions are performed. The implicit signal resolution is achieved wherever it is possible without displaying any warnings.
    - **Explicit and warn implicit**: The implicit and explicit both signal resolutions are performed. The implicit signal resolution is performed wherever it is possible to display the warnings.
- **Division by singular matrix**: When the product block detects a singular matrix during inverting one of its inputs in matrix multiplication mode, this parameter decides the required diagnostic action. The possible values for this parameter are error, warning, and none. The default value is none.
- **Underspecified data types**: This parameter defines the diagnostic action when Simulink could not infer the data type during data type propagation. The possible values for this parameter are error, warning, and none. The default value is none.
- **Simulation range checking**: When signals exceed their Min or Max values, then this parameter is used to decide the diagnostic action. The possible values for this parameter are error, warning, and none. The default value is none.
- **String truncation checking**: When the model contains string signals, and when Simulink detects truncation of string signals, then this parameter defines the diagnostic action. The possible values for this parameter are error, warning, and none. The default value is none.
- **Wrap on overflow**: Suppose a signal has datatype "unit8". Then min and max values for uint8 are 0 and 255, respectively. When we try to increment signal's value by 1 beyond 255, then the overflow occurs. At the same time, the next possible value is assigned to the signal, that is, 0. Therefore, for a uint8 signal, 255+1 results in 0. Similarly, when we try to decrement the value below 0 then, also overflow occurs. At the same time, the next possible

values are assigned to the signal, that is, 255. So for a unit8 signal, 0–1 results in 255. When this wrapping happens during overflow, then this parameter decides the diagnostic action. The possible values for this parameter are error, warning, and none. The default value is a warning. This warp on overflow happens only for integer and fixed-point datatypes. The division by zero operation is also reported by this diagnostic for all kinds of data, fixed and floating charges.

- **Underspecified dimensions**: This parameter specifies the diagnostic action when Simulink could not infer the dimension of a signal during compilation. The possible values for this parameter are error, warning, and none. The default value is none.

- **Saturate on overflow**: Similar to the Wrap on overflow, this parameter is also applicable for only integer and fixed-point datatypes. The arithmetic Simulink blocks have a dialog parameter called as **Saturate on integer overflow**. When **Saturate on integer overflow** parameter is checked, and Simulink detects overflow during the simulation, then **Saturate on overflow** decides the diagnostic action. The possible values for this parameter are error, warning, and none. The default value is a warning.

- **Inf or NaN block output**: MATLAB has some special numbers like Inf and NaN, where Inf stands for infinite number and NaN stands for **Not a Number**. When any of the blocks in the model generates the output of either inf or NaN, then this parameter is used to decide the diagnostic action. The possible values for this parameter are error, warning, and none. The default value is none.

- **"rt" prefix for identifiers**: This parameter is used for code generation. This parameter decides the diagnostic action when during code generation, any of the Simulink object names begins with **rt**. The possible values for this parameter are error, warning, and none. The default value is an error.

Parameters sub-pane

First, let us understand what a parameter is; then, we will see parameters related to configuration parameters. The parameters are workspace variables. Generally, the value of parameters remains constant throughout the simulation. The parameters are used in the block parameters, such as constant block, gain block, and so on. The parameters are used in the model to control the simulation behavior. By setting the parameter value, we can achieve the desired behavior without making any model changes. The Simulink parameters are defined in the base workspace by creating a **Simulink.Parameter** object. This object contains parameter specifications such as data type, value, min value, max value, and so on. The following are the properties of the parameter that are possible to specify for **Simulink.Parameter** object:

- **CoderInfo**: Required for code generation of a parameter.
- **Complexity**: This is a read-only property. Its value is always *real* for parameters.
- **Datatype**: Data type of a parameter.
- **Description**: The information about a parameter.
- **Dimensions**: Dimension of a parameter such as a row vector or character vector. Dimensions should be aligned with parameter values. If dimensions are not explicitly defined, then MATLAB computes them based on the parameter value.
- **Max**: The max value of a parameter.
- **Min**: The min value of a parameter.
- **Unit**: The physical unit of a parameter value.
- **Value**: The default value of the parameter used in block parameters.

The *figure 8.23* explains how to define a parameter in the MATLAB workspace:

```
>> On_Time = Simulink.Parameter;
>> On_Time.DataType = 'uint8';
>> On_Time.Description = 'The time for which state On is required to be active';
>> On_Time.Min = 0;
>> On_Time.Max = 10;
>> On_Time.Unit= 'minutes';
>> On_Time.Value = 10;
>> On_Time
On_Time =
  Parameter with properties:

         Value: 10
     CoderInfo: [1×1 Simulink.CoderInfo]
   Description: 'The time for which state On is required to be active'
      DataType: 'uint8'
           Min: 0
           Max: 10
          Unit: 'minutes'
    Complexity: 'real'
    Dimensions: [1 1]
```

Figure 8.23: Simulink parameter definition

The parameter settings are described as follows:

- **Detect downcast**: This configuration parameter is used during code generation. When it is required to convert the parameter's specified type to a type with the lower range of values, for example, from uint16 to uint8 for the computation of block output, then that is called as a parameter downcast. When parameter downcast occurs, then this configurable parameter decides the diagnostic action required to be taken. The possible values for this parameter are error, warning, and none. The default value is an error.

- **Detect overflow**: This configuration parameter decides the diagnostic action required to be taken when parameter overflow occurs during simulation. For example, a parameter has datatype uint8, which has value ranging from 0 to 255. If the value of the parameter is assigned as <0 or >255, then overflow is detected. The possible values for this parameter are error, warning, and none. The default value is none.

- **Detect underflow**: This configuration parameter decides the diagnostic action required to be taken when parameter underflow occurs during simulation. Parameter underflow occurs when the value assigned to the parameter is very small to be represented using the assigned datatype because the assigned datatype does not have enough precision. In this case, the value of the parameter is rounded to zero by the simulation. For example, a parameter has datatype uint8, which has a value ranging from 0 to 255 and resolution as 1. If the value of the parameter is assigned as 0.1, then underflow is detected. The possible values for this parameter are error, warning, and none. The default value is none.

- **Detect precision loss**: This configuration parameter decides the diagnostic action required to be taken when parameter precision loss occurs during simulation. Parameter precision loss occurs when the paramete's value cannot be represented using the assigned data because the assigned data type does not have enough precision. In this case, the parameter's value is rounded to the nearest value to the assigned value, which can be represented using the assigned. For example, a parameter has datatype uint8, which has a value ranging from 0 to 255 and resolution as 1. If the parameter's value is assigned as 10.7, then the precision loss is detected, and the simulation will use the value 11. Similarly, if the value of the parameter is set as 10.3, then the precision loss is detected, and the simulation will use the value 10. Since the values 11 and 10 are the nearest values in these two cases, respectively, which can be represented using datatype uint8. The possible values for this parameter are error, warning, and none. The default value is a warning.

- **Detect loss of tunability**: This configuration parameter is used during code generation. When an expression with tunable parameters is represented in its numerical equivalent, then the loss of tunability occurs. The configuration parameter decides the diagnostic action loss of tunability that occurs during code generation. The possible values for this parameter are error, warning, and none. The default value is a warning.

- **Data store memory block sub-pane**: The data stores carry signal data in the model. The data stores are used for signal routing. We will discuss in detail on data store blocks in *Chapter 7: Library Browser Overview*. There are three types of blocks used for data stores. These blocks are **Data store memory block** (Used to specify signal attributes), **Data store write block** (Used to write the output value of a signal), and **Data store read block** (Used to read the signal value). When a signal definition is already created in the workspace then **Data Store Memory block** is not required since **Simulink.Signal** object has all the required attributes.

- **Detect read before write**: When data store read operation occurs before data store write operation, this configuration parameter is used to decide the required diagnostic action. The following are the values possible for this parameter:
    - **Use local settings**: This is the default value. For the local data stores, which are defined by a Data Store Memory block or **Simulink.Signal** object in a model workspace, the block's setting is used. For the global data stores that are defined by a **Simulink.Signal** object in the base workspace; this diagnostic setting is disabled.
    - **Disable all**: For all data store blocks in the model, this setting is disabled.
    - **Enable all as warnings**: Warnings are displayed, but simulation continues.
    - **Enable all as errors**: Errors are displayed, and the simulation is terminated.

- **Detect write after read**: When data store writes operation occurs after data store read operation, this configuration parameter is used to decide the required diagnostic action. The following are the values possible for this parameter:
    - **Use local settings**: This is the default value. For the local data stores are defined by a Data Store Memory block or **Simulink.Signal** object in a model workspace, the setting specified by the block is used. For the global data stores, which are defined by **Simulink.Signal** object in the base workspace; this diagnostic setting is disabled.

- o **Disable all**: For all data store blocks in the model, this setting is disabled.
- o **Enable all as warnings**: Warnings are displayed, but simulation continues.
- o **Enable all as errors**: Errors are displayed, and the simulation is terminated.
- **Detect write after write**: When the data store write operation happens twice, then this configuration parameter is used to decide the required diagnostic action to be taken. The following are the values possible for this parameter:
  - o **Use local settings**: This is the default value. For the local data stores that are defined by a Data Store Memory block or `Simulink.Signal` object in a model workspace, the setting specified by the block is used. For the global data stores, which are defined by `Simulink.Signal` object in the base workspace; this diagnostic setting is disabled.
  - o **Disable all**: For all data store blocks in the model, this setting is disabled.
  - o **Enable all as warnings**: Warnings are displayed, but simulation continues.
  - o **Enable all as errors**: Errors are displayed, and the simulation is terminated.
- **Multitask data store**: When a data store read operation happens by one task that is written by another task, this configuration parameter is used to decide the required diagnostic action. The possible values for this parameter are error, warning, and none. The default value is an error.
- **Duplicate data store names**: When multiple data store memory blocks in the model are added for the same data store data, this configuration parameter is used to decide the required diagnostic action. The possible values for this parameter are error, warning, and none. The default value is none.

Advanced parameter sub-pane

This sub-pane contains an advanced parameter, which could be configured for Data validity.

- **Array bounds exceeded**: The Simulink detects array bounds exceeded when the s-function writes the allocated memory beyond its bounds when writing to the outputs, states, or work vectors. This parameter decides the diagnostic action when array bounds ate exceeded. The possible values for this parameter are error, warning, and none. The default value is none.

- **Model verification block enabling**: This setting is used to enable the model verification blocks in the model either globally or locally. We will discuss model verification blocks in *Chapter 7: Library Browser Overview*. The following are the values possible for this parameter:
    - **Use local settings**: This is the default value. Based on the value of enabling assertion parameter of each block, the model verification is enabled or disabled. When enabling assertion parameter is on, then the model verification block is enabled; else, it is disabled.
    - **Enable all**: Model verification blocks are enabled irrespective of enabling assertion parameter value.
    - **Disable all**: Model verification blocks are disabled irrespective of enabling assertion parameter value.
- **Detect multiple driving blocks executing at the same time step**: This configuration parameter is used to merge block execution. We will understand the details of *Merge* in *Chapter 7: Library Browser Overview*. When multiple blocks drive the outputs to the Merge block, this parameter is used to decide the respective diagnostic action. The possible values for this parameter are error, warning, and none. The default value is an error.
- **Underspecified initialization detection**: This parameter setting decides how to handle the initialization of initial conditions for a conditionally executed subsystem, Merge blocks, system elapsed time, and discrete-time integrator blocks. The possible values for this parameter are classic and simplified. When it is classic, then initialization happens in the same way as it was prior to MATLAB R2008b. When it is simplified, then initialization happens with enhanced behavior, which improves the consistency of simulation results.
- **Detect ambiguous custom storage class final values**: This configuration parameter is used to select the diagnostic action when the reusable custom storage class, which has more than one endpoint, is used in the model. The possible values for this parameter are error, warning, and none. The default value is a warning.
- **Detect non-reused custom storage classes**: This setting is used during code generation. This parameter is used to select the diagnostic action when the model contains a reusable custom storage class, which cannot be reused by the code with other uses of the same reusable custom storage class. The possible values for this parameter are error, warning, and none. The default value is a warning. When reusable custom storage classes are part of reference subsystems then for value *none* and *warning*, Simulink generates the error message to set the value as an *error*.

Type Conversion pane

The **Type Conversion** pane contains the configuration parameters that are related to the data type conversion. The *figure 8.24* shows the **Type Conversion** pane:

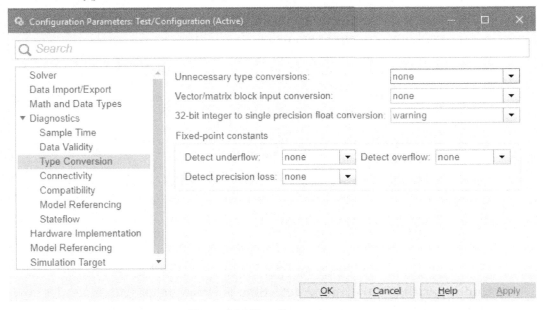

Figure 8.24: Type Conversion pane

- **Unnecessary type conversion**: This parameter decides the diagnostic action when Simulink detects that the Data Type conversion block is used in the model, but the type conversion is not required. The **Data Type Conversion** block converts the data type of a signal from one type to another, for example, from **int32** to **uint8**. The *Data Type Conversion* block we will discuss in *Chapter 7: Library Browser Overview*. The possible values for this parameter are warning and none. The default value is none.

- **Vector/matrix block input conversion**: When a vector signal is connected to an Inport of a block, which needs matrix input, then Simulink converts vectors to either a one-row matrix or one-column matrix. When a one-column matrix or one-row matrix is connected to an Inport of a block that needs vector input, then Simulink converts the matrix into the vector. When this conversion happens, then Vector/matrix block input, the conversion parameter decides the appropriate diagnostic action based on its value. The possible values for this parameter are error, warning, and none. The default value is none.

- **32-bit integer to single-precision float conversion**: When Simulink detects the conversation from 32-bit integer to then this parameter decides the appropriate diagnostic action based on its value. The possible values for this parameter are warning and none. The default value is none. When 32-bit integer value is converted into double then there is a possibility of precision loss.

- **Detect overflow for fixed-point constant**: This configuration parameter decides the diagnostic action required when fixed-point constant overflow occurs during simulation. The possible values for this parameter are error, warning, and none. The default value is none.

- **Detect underflow for fixed-point constant**: This configuration parameter decides the diagnostic action required when a 32-bit integer value is converted into a floating-point value during simulation. The fixed-point constant underflow occurs when the value assigned to the fixed-point constant is very small to be represented using its fixed-point datatype because the datatype does not have enough precision. In this case, the value of the parameter is rounded to zero by the simulation. The possible values for this parameter are error, warning, and none. The default value is none.

- **Detect precision loss for fixed-point constant**: This configuration parameter decides the diagnostic action required to be taken when a fixed-point constant precision loss occurs during the simulation. The fixed-point constant precision loss occurs when the value assigned to the parameter cannot be represented using its datatype because the assigned datatype does not have enough precision. The possible values for this parameter are error, warning, and none. The default value is none.

Connectivity pane

The connectivity pane contains the configuration parameters that are related to the signal line connections. The signal line is a line connecting two blocks to flow the data from one block to another. The *figure 8.25* displays the connectivity pane:

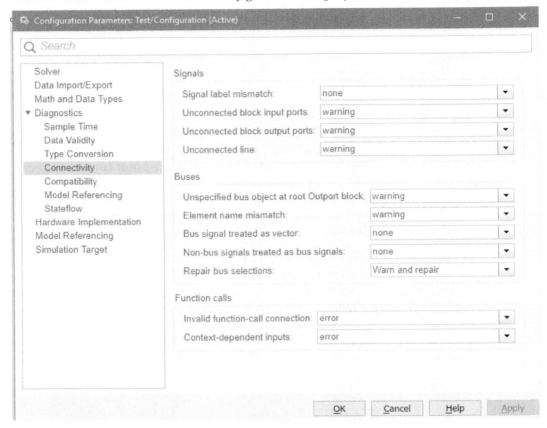

Figure 8.25: Connectivity pane

- **Signal label mismatch**: When the same signal propagates through the different subsystems and different blocks, but with different names, this parameter selects the diagnostic action according to its value. The possible values for this parameter are error, warning, and none. The default value is none. We will discuss signal naming and signal propagation in detail in the chapter *Create a Simple Simulink Model*.

- **Unconnected block input ports**: When the model contains the blocks with unconnected input ports, this parameter selects the diagnostic action according to its value. The possible values for this parameter are error, warning, and none. The default value is a warning.

- **Unconnected block output ports**: When the model contains the blocks with unconnected output ports, then this parameter selects the desired diagnostic action according to its value. The possible values for this parameter are error, warning, and none. The default value is a warning.

- **Unconnected line**: When the model contains an unconnected line or when the model contains the from- goto blocks where go-to tags are not matching, in that case, this parameter selects the diagnostic action to be taken according to its value. The possible values for this parameter are error, warning, and none. The default value is a warning. The *from and goto* blocks we will discuss in *Chapter 7: Library Browser Overview*.

- **Unspecified bus object at root Outport block**: If any model contains a root level outport that is connected to a bus without specifying the bus object. Moreover, this model is used as a referenced model to some other model. Then during the generation of simulation target, this parameter selects the diagnostic action according to its value. The possible values for this parameter are error, warning, and none. The default value is a warning. The concepts of *bus, bus object, and referenced model*, we shall discuss in *Chapter 10: Advanced Modelling Techniques-II*.

- **Element name mismatch**: When the element name of the bus in the model does not match the element name specified in the bus object, this parameter selects the diagnostic action according to its value. The possible values for this parameter are error, warning, and none. The default value is a warning.

- **Bus signal treated as a vector**: When all bus signals/elements contain the same attribute, and this bus is connected to a block in the model, which does not accept the virtual bus signal, then Simulink treats the virtual bus signal as a vector signal. When Simulink treats the virtual bus signal as a vector signal, this parameter selects the diagnostic action according to its value. The possible values for this parameter are error, warning, and none. The default value is none. We will discuss virtual buses in detail in *Chapter 10: Advanced Modelling Techniques-II*.

- **Non-bus signals treated as bus signals**: When the non-bus signals are connected to the bus assignment block or bus selector block then to support this connection, Simulink indirectly covers the non-bus signal to the bus signals. When this conversion happens then, this parameter selects the required diagnostic action according to its value. The possible values for this parameter are error, warning, and none. The default value is none. We will discuss the bus assignment block and bus selector block in detail in *Chapter 7: Library Browser Overview*.

- **Repair bus selections**: The bus creator block is used to create the bus from the individual signals, and the bus selector block and bus assignment block are used to select the individual bus element from the bus. When any element's name is updated in the bus creator block, and if the same element is already selected in the bus selector or bus assignment block, this issue is called the broken selection issue. When the broken selection happens, Simulink tries to repair it by selecting the newly updated signal in the bus selector or bus assignment block. This parameter decides what action Simulink shall take. The possible values for this parameter are as follows:

- o **Warn and repair**: In this case, as explained preceding, Simulink tries to repair the broken selection and displays the warning.

- o **Error without repair**: In this case, Simulink displays the error message and does not repair the broken selection.

- **Invalid function-call connection**: When Simulink detects the incorrect use of a function-call subsystem, then this parameter selects the desired diagnostic action according to its value. The possible values for this parameter are error and warning. The default value is an error. We will discuss the function-call subsystem in detail in *Chapter 7: Library Browser Overview*.

- **Context-dependent inputs**: When the output of a function-call subsystem is connected to the input of the same function-call subsystem via a feedback loop, then Simulink has to compute the function-call system's input during the execution of a call to a function-call subsystem. So, whenever Simulink has to compute the inputs of function-call subsystems directly or indirectly during the execution of a call to a function-call subsystem, this parameter selects the diagnostic action to be taken according to its value. The possible values for this parameter are error and warning. The default value is an error.

Compatibility pane

It is a very common occurrence that the models created in the earlier releases of the MATLAB versions are also used in the later releases of MATLAB versions. The compatibility pane contains the parameter that detects compatibility issues because of different versions of MATLAB. The *figure 8.26* shows the compatibility pane:

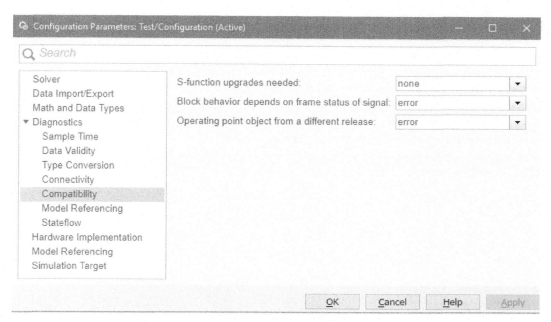

Figure 8.26: *Compatibility pane*

- **S-function upgrades needed**: If Simulink detects any block in the model, which was created in the previous release of MATLAB and requires an upgrade to use the current release features. Then this parameter is used to decide the required action. The possible values for this parameter are error, warning, and none. The default value is none.

- **Block behavior depends on frame status of signal**: The frame status is one of the attributes of the signal. The frame status of a signal is used to identify whether the blocks' inputs should be treated as frames of data or samples of data. In the future release, this frame status attribute of a signal shall not be supported. So, this parameter is used to identify all those blocks, which are dependent on the frame status of a signal. The possible values for this parameter are error, warning, and none. The default value is an error.

- **SimState object from earlier release**: If SimState was generated by the earlier releases of MATLAB, this parameter can be used to detect this behavior. The possible values for this parameter are error and warning. The default value is an error. When the value is selected as a warning, Simulink tries to restore SimState as possible and displays the warning. When the value is chosen as an error, then Simulink does not load the object and shows the error.

Diagnostic model referencing pane

The model referencing is one of the widely used functionalities of Simulink. When a model calls another model using the Model reference block, this phenomenon is called as model referencing. Model referencing helps to achieve better reusability and modularization. We shall discuss in detail on model referencing in *Chapter 10: Advanced Modelling Techniques-II*. The *figure 8.27* shows the configuration parameters available for the diagnostic model referencing pane:

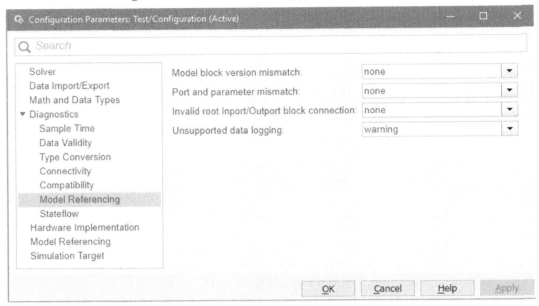

Figure 8.27: Diagnostic model referencing pane

- **Model block version mismatch**: When Simulink detects a mismatch between the version of the referenced block and the referenced model referred in the model block, this parameter selects the relevant diagnostic action. To solve this, Simulink needs to refresh the reference model block. The possible values for this parameter are error, warning, and none. The default value is none. When the value is selected as none, then Simulink refreshes the reference model block. When the value is chosen as a warning, then Simulink displays the warning and refreshes the model block. When the value is selected as an error, Simulink does not refresh the model block and shows it.

- **Port and parameter mismatch**: When Simulink detects a port or parameter mismatch between the referenced model block and referenced model, then this parameter is used to select the diagnostic action. The port mismatches occur when input and output ports of reference model blocks do not match the input and output ports at the root level of the reference model. When the parameter argument used by the model block does not match the declared parameter arguments of the referenced model, then parameter mismatch occurs. To solve this, Simulink needs to refresh the reference model block. The possible values for this parameter are error, warning, and none. The default value is none. When the value is selected as none then Simulink refreshes the reference model block. When the value is chosen as a warning then Simulink displays the warning and refreshes the model block. When the value is chosen as an error, Simulink does not refresh the model block and displays it.

- **Invalid root Inport/Outport block connection**: When Simulink detects invalid Inport and outport connections at the referenced model's root level, this parameter is used to decide the required diagnostic action. The possible values for this parameter are error, warning, and none. The default value is none. When the value is specified as none, then Simulink silently adds a hidden block to resolve the problem. When the value is selected as a warning, Simulink displays the warning and adds the hidden block to solve it. When the value is defined as an error, then Simulink does not add hidden blocks and displays the error.

- **Unsupported data logging**: Simulink does not use scope block with data logging enabled or to workspace block in the referenced model. When Simulink detects these blocks are used in the referenced model, then this parameter decides the diagnostic action. The possible values for this parameter are error, warning, and none. The default value is a warning.

- **No explicit final value for model arguments**: In the Model data editor, property inspector, or Model Explorer, the default value of the model argument is used as either *inherited* or *from below*. When the argument checkbox is selected, then "inherited" will be displayed. *Inherited* signifies that the parent provides model argument value. If the argument check box is cleared, then *from below* message will be displayed. *from below* specifies that the model argument value will be fetched from the last model in the model hierarchy. Therefore, when the topmost model in the model hierarchy uses the default value for model argument rather than providing an explicit value, then this parameter decides the diagnostic action. The possible values for this parameter are error, warning, and none. The default value is none. When the value is specified as none, then Simulink uses the last value specified in the model hierarchy below. When the value is selected as a warning, then Simulink displays the warning and uses the last value specified in the model hierarchy below. When the value is selected as an error, then Simulink does not use the last value specified in the model hierarchy below and displays the error.

Diagnostic Stateflow pane

We will discuss the diagnostic Stateflow pane in *Chapter 12: Getting started with Stateflow*.

Hardware implementation pane

The hardware implementation pane configures parameters that are required to configure a hardware board. The hardware implementation pane does not have to do anything with controlling the target hardware or compiler behavior. The parameters in this pane specify target hardware characteristics so that Simulink can detect the error conditions during model simulation that may occur during code execution on the target hardware board. To begin with Simulink, we do not really need to go into details about these configuration parameters. We will discuss these parameters in *Chapter 10: Advanced Modelling Techniques-II*.

Model referencing pane

When a model calls another model, it is known as model referencing. It is better to learn the model referencing configuration parameters once we go through model referencing concepts. Therefore, we shall discuss the Model referencing Pane in detail in *Chapter 10: Advanced Modeling Techniques-II*.

Simulation Target pane

The Simulation Target pane contains the configuration parameters to control MATLAB function blocks, Stateflow, or Truth table blocks. Using these parameters, we can include C code in the model simulation. To learn these configurable parameters, one must know function blocks, state flows, and Truth table block. Therefore, we shall discuss the Simulation target Pane in detail in *Chapter 10: Advanced Modeling Techniques-II*.

Conclusion

In this chapter, we have explored configuration parameter settings. With the help of Simulink's model configuration parameters, readers are now capable of fine-tuning configurations based on system needs. The reader understands the actions performed by essential parameters grouped under several sub-panes such as Solver, Data Import/Export, Math and Data Types pane, and Diagnostics pane. This knowledge will show the right direction to the readers while learning advanced Simulink model development by making the most of Simulink's capabilities. In the next chapter, the reader shall become familiar with some of the Advanced modeling techniques such as custom libraries, the usage of masking for library development, and a few other custom approaches toward efficient model development.

Points to remember

- Auto solver detects the required solver based on model behavior.
- Zero crossing related configuration parameters are available only in the case of variable-step type.
- To run the simulation effectively and check the model behavior in all possible cases, it must feed different data to the model inputs and then fetch the model outputs.
- The Simulink has a property called data type propagation. We do not need to specify the data types at each block. Data types are either back propagated or inherited.
- The diagnostic pane contains configuration parameters, which play an important role during compilation and simulation.
- The algebraic loop occurs when the input value is not available to perform the operation.
- Use of rate transition blocks resolves these illegal rate transitions from the model.
- The Signals are used to carry the data between two blocks.
- Data Store memory blocks are used to specify signal attributes.
- It is a very common occurrence that the models created using earlier releases of MATLAB versions are being used in the later releases of MATLAB versions.

Multiple choice questions

1. **Which of the following Solver type is the default solver type?**
    a. Variable-step type
    b. Fixed-step type

2. **When the configuration parameter "Periodic sample time constraint" is set to "Ensure sample time independent", a fixed-step size value is possible to configure.**
    a. True
    b. False

3. Max step size and Min step size configuration parameters are available for variable-step type solver.
    a. True
    b. False

4. When the model contains the continuous states, then which of the following solver should not be used?
    a. Discrete
    b. Ode113(Adams)
    c. Ode 45 (Dormand-Prince)

5. Which of the following variable is used for Signal logging?
    a. dsmout
    b. logsout
    c. xFinal
    d. yout

6. The denormal numbers are any other than zero, which have their magnitude greater than the smallest normalized floating-point number.
    a. True
    b. False

7. Which of the following is not the sub-pane of diagnostic?
    a. Data Validity
    b. Sample Time
    c. Hardware Implementation
    d. Connectivity

8. Minimizing algebraic loop results in better simulation performance.
    a. True
    b. False

9. What value for sample time is used to inherit the sample time from the model sample time?
    a. inf
    b. −1

c. 0
d. All of the above

10. **Simulink.Signal and Simulink. Parameters are the objects stored in the workspace, which can be referred to in the model.**
    a. True
    b. False

11. **Which of the following is not the data store blocks?**
    a. Data store memory
    b. Data store read
    c. Merge
    d. Data store write

12. **It is possible to detect all unconnected lines in the model.**
    a. True
    b. False

Questions

1. What is the difference between a Fixed-step and Variable-step solver?
2. Why do we need configuration parameter settings?
3. Explain the configuration parameters available in Data Import/Export pane.
4. Explain the denormal numbers.
5. What are row-major and column-major layout?
6. Explain the net slope correction phenomenon.
7. Describe the algebraic loop and explain when it occurs.
8. What does zero-crossing mean?
9. Explain the significance of −1 sample time.
10. Explain how to define Simulink. Signal and Simulink.Parameter variables.
11. What is the difference between wrap on overflow and saturate on overflow?
12. When does the loss of parameter tunability happen?

13. Explain the data store memory block.
14. When does the element name mismatch issue occur for the buses?
15. Explain the bus repair operation.
16. Explain the necessity of the Compatibility pane.

Answers

1. a
2. b
3. a
4. a
5. b
6. b
7. c
8. b
9. b
10. a
11. c
12. a

CHAPTER 9
Advanced Modeling Techniques-I

Introduction

Until now, readers have gone through the basic concepts of Simulink. The readers have learnt to create a simple Simulink model and have understood the process to Simulate and Debug the Simulink model. They have learnt the usage of the graphical editor, and they have become aware of the process of environment model creation. The readers have also been able to educate themselves about the library browser and model configuration settings. In this chapter, we shall be learning some advanced modeling techniques. The reader will get an overview of custom libraries and mask editors. The readers will go through mask callbacks as well as block callbacks. Overall, these techniques are realized in order to ease the model design process by offering a greater degree of customization and automation. The upcoming chapter is the continuation of the advanced modeling techniques.

Structure

In this chapter, we are going to cover the following topics:

- Basics of custom library creation
    - Creating Simulink logic
    - Creating Simulink library

- - o Library link
  - Creating custom libraries with mask options
    - o Creating library mask
    - o Mask Editor options
    - o Model callbacks
    - o Block callbacks

Objectives

After studying this chapter, the reader will be able to:

- Get familiarized with Simulink library concepts
- Learn library creation and Library link options
- Get a brief overview of mask block concepts
- Apply mask creation steps
- Understand mask editor options
- Shall be able to understand different model callback functions
- Get familiarized with block callback functions

Basics of custom library creation

Before getting into the basics of custom library creation, we need to understand its necessity. Consider an example where we need to perform an operation on several input signals. For each input signal, we need to find the quotient and remainder when divided by 10. We have total five input signals a, b, c, d, and e. For each signal, we can create the same logic, but it is always challenging to maintain. In the future, if there is a change in the requirement, the divisor becomes 20 rather than 10. In that case, if we do not use a library, then at all five places, we need to change the divisor from 10 to 20. That is a manual process, which is always error prone. If we have a custom library block for these operations, it is sufficient to change the divisor from 10 to 20 only in the library. It reflects all places automatically in the Simulink model where the active link to the library block is present. In this section, we shall also go through the linking concepts of library blocks. First, let us create logic to find out the quotient and remainder with Simple Simulink logic.

Creating Simulink logic

To create logic for calculating quotient and remainder, we would require a divide block with any signed or unsigned output datatype and **math** function block configured as **rem** to calculate quotient and remainder. The *figure 9.1* shows simple Simulink logic to calculate quotient and reminder:

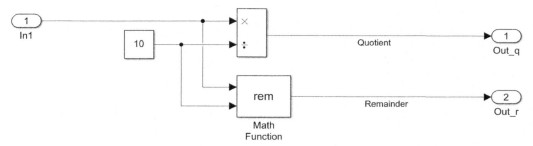

Figure 9.1: *Simulink logic to find quotient and remainder*

The *figure 9.2* shows the datatype setting of the **divide** block. This datatype is selected from the dropdown available for **Output data types**. In our logic, we need an integer data type, so we have chosen **unit16**:

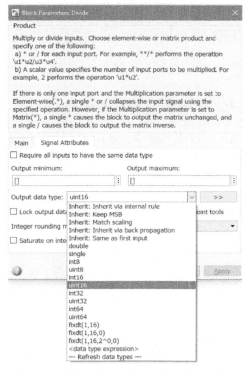

Figure 9.2: *Datatype selection for divide block*

The *figure 9.3* explains the remainder function selection from the **math** function block. In the library browser, we have a **math** block, which is used to implement different functions such as power, square, transpose, remainder, and so on. We shall use the remainder **rem** function from the dropdown menu for the function of our logic:

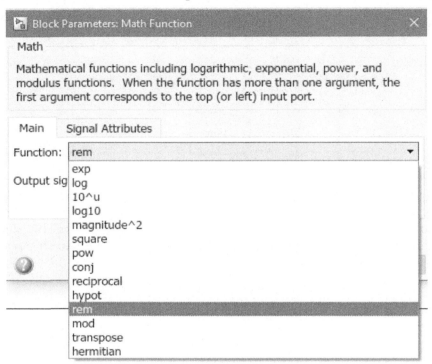

Figure 9.3: *Function selection from math function block*

There are five inputs, for which we want to find quotient and remainder when divided by 10. Therefore, we need to copy-paste the same logic five times. The *figure 9.4* shows how the model looks when we copy-paste the same logic five times. The subsystems **Find_q_r_a**, **Find_q_r_b**, **Find_q_r_c**, **Find_q_r_d**, and **Find_q_r_e** contain the identical logic as depicted in *figure 9.1*.

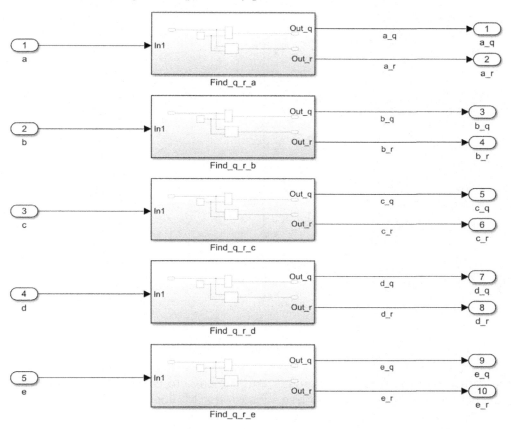

Figure 9.4: *Subsystems to find out quotients and remainders for input signals*

To simulate this logic, we need sources and sinks. To provide values for signals a, b, c, d, and e, we use Constant blocks to see the outputs, quotients, remainders, and display blocks. The *figure 9.5* shows the environment to simulate logic to find quotients and remainders. Here is the snapshot after the execution is completed:

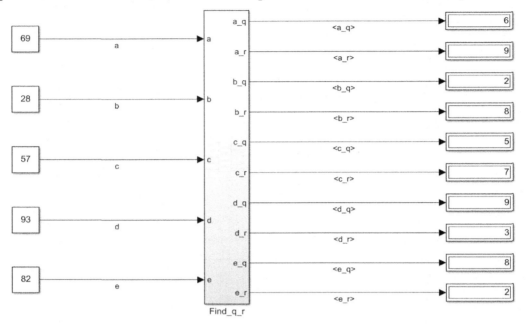

Figure 9.5: *Environment to simulate the logic*

If in future requirements are changed, and we have to change the divisor from 10 to 20, then we need to update all five subsystems. Maybe updating the logic in five subsystems is not a very difficult task. However, imagine if there are hundreds of input signals, and all require the same operation, then copying the same logic 100 times may not be a good solution concerning the maintenance efforts. To solve this problem, we require libraries. Therefore, let us learn how we can create a library.

Creating Simulink library

To create Simulink Library, perform the following steps. Please note that these steps are listed in reference to newer software versions, but the steps for older release versions would stay somewhat similar:

- Open any Simulink model.
- Go to the **SIMULATION** tab.
- Click on the dropdown arrow new button.
- Select the **Library** option from the dropdown menu, as shown in *figure 9.6*.

- The pop-up window for Simulink start page will appear.
- Select blank library. The untitled library will open.
- Save library by clicking the save button from the **Library** tab.

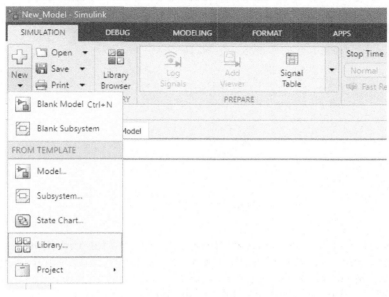

Figure 9.6: Drop-down menu for button "New"

The *figure 9.7* shows the pop-up window when the **Library** option is selected from a dropdown menu. It provides the blank library creation option:

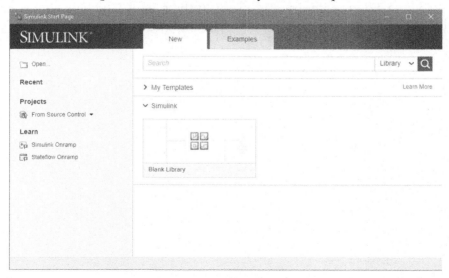

Figure 9.7: Pop window for library creation

The *figure 9.8* shows the process to save the library. Similar to saving a model, press the **Save** button or type *Ctrl + S* on the keyboard:

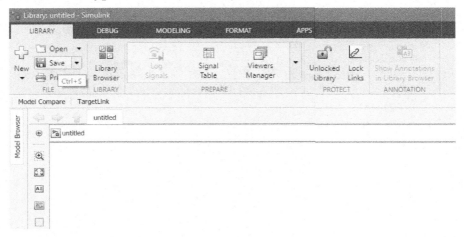

Figure 9.8: Save library

> **The significant difference between the Simulink model and Simulink Library is that we can simulate the Simulink model independently, whereas we cannot simulate the Simulink library on its own. We should instantiate the Simulink library block in the Simulink model to perform simulation.**

Now, let us create a library block to identify the quotient and remainder when divided by 10 to the input signal. We also try to demonstrate that usage of **Library** blocks for repetitive logic makes MATLAB modeling very easy. Therefore, we create the same logic inside the library and use it in the model. The *figure 9.9* shows the library block to find out the quotient and remainder:

Advanced Modeling Techniques-I   355

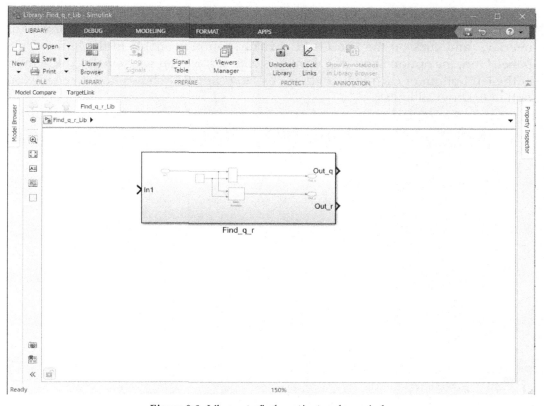

Figure 9.9: Library to find quotient and remainder

To add a library block to the model, open the library, copy it, and paste it into the model at the desired place. It could be copied and pasted at all desired places. The *figure 9.10* shows how it looks when libraries are used in the model:

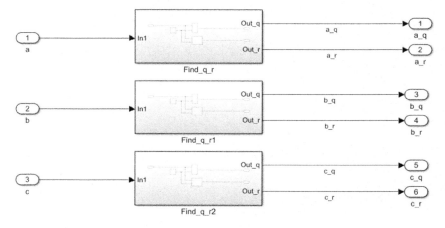

Figure 9.10: Library blocks added in the model

Library block and the non-library block look precisely identical here. To differentiate between them, go to the debug tab, click on the dropdown arrow at **Information** overlays, and click on the `Show all Links` option available in the library links panel. Once the option `Show all Links` is enabled, we can see a small **Link** symbol at the left bottom of each linked library block. *Figure 9.11* shows how to enable the option to show all links:

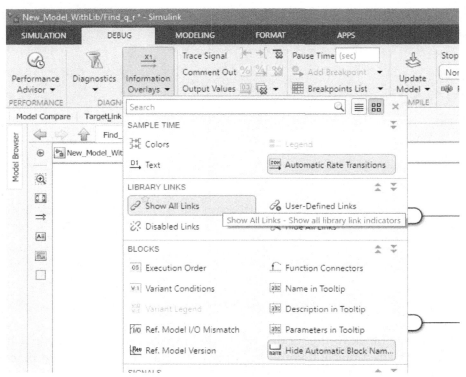

Figure 9.11: Enable the "show all links" option

We can rename the library blocks added to the model according to convenience and functionality. The model simulation does not differ concerning library blocks. For simulation, every library block is considered as a separate independent block. So, simulation results are mainly based on the block diagram. If we have the same block diagram in library and non-library blocks, they produce the same effect. The *figure 9.12* shows the library blocks after renaming and enabling the `Show All Links` option:

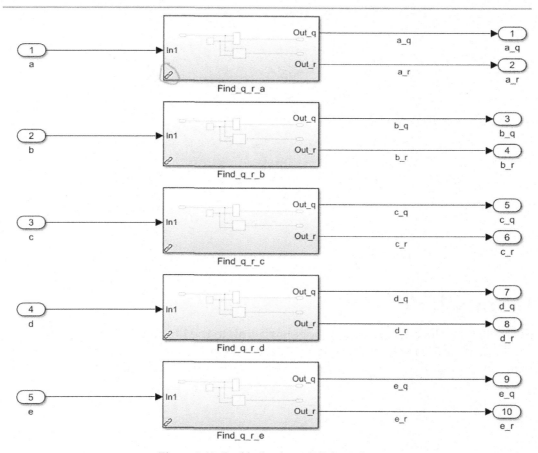

Figure 9.12: Enable the show all links option

When the logic in the library block is updated, then automatically same logic is updated in all those places where the library block is used. The *figure 9.13* explains how it changes the divisor from 10 to 20 in all library blocks used in the model when we update it in the library:

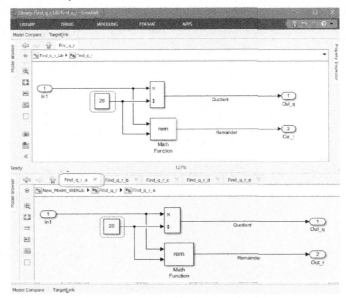

Figure 9.13: *Changes made in Library reflects in the model*

Library link

Every library block used in the model has a link to the library. To see the operations available on the library link, right-click on the library block and then click on the **Library,** as shown in *figure 9.14*. We can perform these operations to the library link:

Advanced Modeling Techniques-I 359

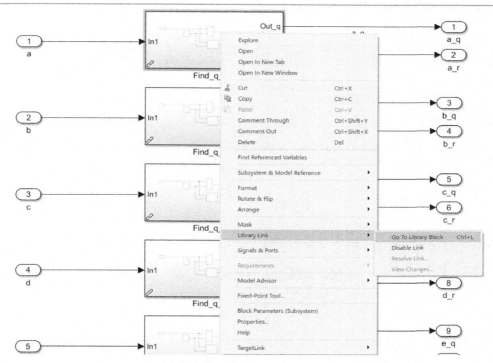

Figure 9.14: Option available for Library link

- **Go To Library Block**: We can highlight the library block using this option. After selecting **Go To Library Block**, Simulink opens the library file where **Library Block** is situated, highlighting the library block.

- **Disable Link**: This option is beneficial when we want to update the block logic without opening the actual library block. When the link with the library block is active, Simulink does not allow the change in the block logic from a model. However, when a link is disabled, then we can perform the changes in the block logic. We can highlight the library block using this option. After selecting **Go To Library Block**, Simulink opens the library file where **Library Block** is situated and highlights the library block.

- **Resolve Link**: Generally, the link to the library block is disabled when the logic implemented in the library block does not satisfy the requirements, or logic optimization is required. In that case, we need to update the block logic and test it. Once updated logic is validated successfully or updated logic is necessary to be discarded, the **Resolve Link** option must be used. The *figure 9.15* shows the wizard when **Resolved Link** option is selected:

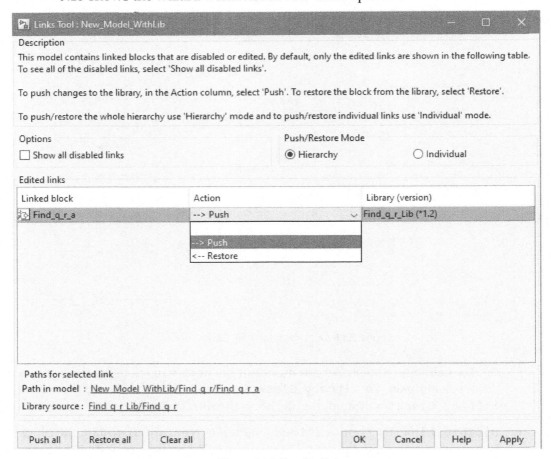

Figure 9.15: Resolve link

Push action is used to **Push** changes made in the library block from Model to Library. **Restore** action is used to discard the changes made in the block logic after disabling the link. After both actions, the **Library Link** status changes from **Disabled to Active**.

> **Resolve Link** option is enabled in the **Library Link** menu only when the **Link** to the library block is disabled.

- **Break Link**: The **Break Link** option is used when library block logic must be reused by modifying existing logic without keeping any relation with the library. The **Break Link** option is visible in the **Library Link** menu only for **Disabled Link** blocks. When the link is broken, the block acts as a normal model block and does not impact library changes after that. The *figure 9.16* shows the option of **Break Link** in the **Library Link** menu:

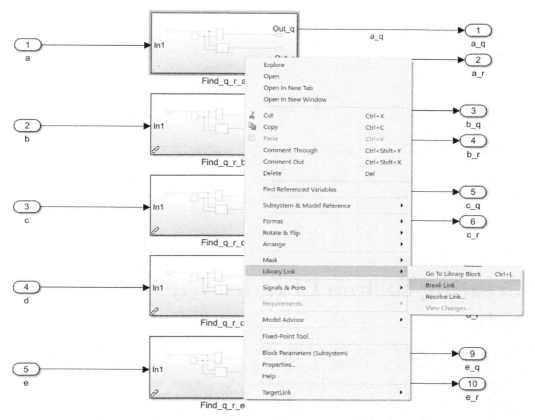

Figure 9.16: Break link

- **View Changes**: Let us consider that we want to make changes only in the dialog parameters inside the library block logic. In the example mentioned in *figure 9.13*, to find quotient and remainder, if we want to update the divisor to 30 for some of the blocks in the model by keeping the library link active, then that is possible. When dialog parameters of the blocks used in library logic are modified, that link is called **Parameterized Link**. In addition, when the library block link becomes parameterized, the **View Changes** option in the **Library Link** menu is enabled. At the end, when the library link is parameterized, a red star appears near the link icon. The *figure 9.17* displays the window, which pops up after right-clicking and selecting the view changes operation.

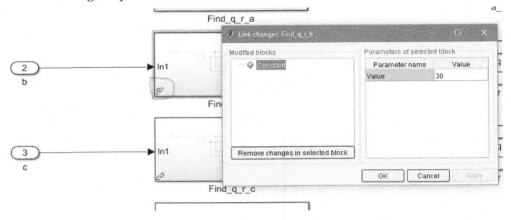

Figure 9.17: View changes

Creating custom libraries with mask options

Until now, we have learnt how to create libraries in Simulink and what are its advantages. Let us consider the same example of finding the quotient and remainder of input signals when divided by 10 or 20. The divisor was constant for all input signals. Now, imagine if the divisor is changing. It is different for different signals. Based on what we have learned until now, we might think that how can the libraries solve this problem? Just like we can pass different input arguments to the C-function, we have dialog parameters for custom libraries. Using this dialog parameter, we can pass on different values to the library block. In our example, we pass on the divisor as a dialog parameter. First, let us learn to mask and mask callbacks.

Creating library mask

First, we need to open the library, and then we need to unlock it. When a library is locked, we are not allowed to make any changes to the library. So, to make any changes in the library, it is required to unlock the library. It is straightforward to lock– unlock libraries. In the **Library** panel, a button states the current state of the library, whether it is locked or unlocked. If it says **Locked Library**, then it unlocks the library by clicking once. If it says **Unlocked Library**, then it locks the library by clicking once. The most common and followed method to unlock the library is to try to change anything. A pop-up message at the top appears, which has the link to unlock the library. Whatever the change we try to do in the library when it is locked, it will not occur by Simulink graphical editor. This procedure is just used to unlock the library. The change that we intend to do has to be done again when the library is unlocked. For example, we would like to change the position of any library block, and we attempt that when a library is locked. Then this attempt is just used to unlock the library, and we should make the same attempt again when a library is unlocked. The *figure 9.18* shows how to lock a library:

Figure 9.18: Lock unlock libraries using button in the Library panel.

Similarly, *figure 9.19* depicts how to unlock the library:

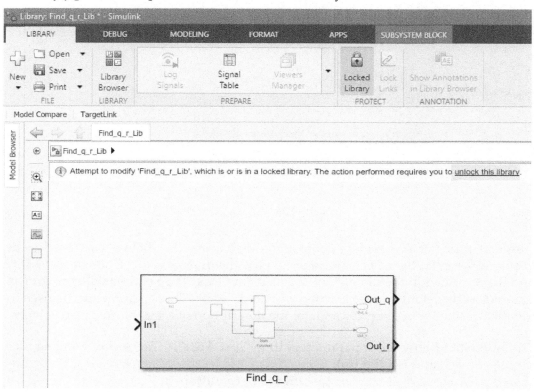

Figure 9.19: Unlock library by changing the position of the library block

To create a mask, first right-click on the library block in the library, select **Mask**, and then select **Create Mask**. If a mask is already available, it shows **Edit Mask** while trying to create the mask. A **Mask Editor** pops up after clicking on **Create Mask** or **Edit Mask**. This editor is used to create or edit **Mask**. To get more info on **Mask Editor**, we can click on the help option highlighted in the following image. The *figure 9.20* also shows the **Parameters & Dialog** pane from **Mask Editor**:

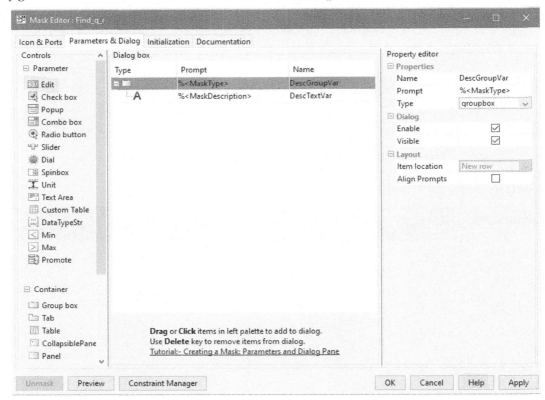

Figure 9.20: Create Mask

Different types of parameters could be added using the dialog. For the divisor example, we need the **Edit** parameter to pass the divisor value. Click on the **Edit**, and it gets added in the dialog box. We also have **MaskType** and **MaskDescription** parameters by default available when we edit the **Mask**. These parameters are used to identify mask blocks uniquely and get the description of mask blocks, respectively.

> **To understand how other parameters like "Text Area", "Check box", and so on, are used, we can visit the link** https://www.mathworks.com/help/simulink/gui/mask-editor-overview.html **or just hit the help button.**

Every parameter has different properties. Following are the properties of the edit parameter:

- **Name**: Name of the parameter. This name is a part of Mask workspace. We use this name in mask logic. In our case, this name will be used in the divisor constant block.

- **Value**: This is a default value; this value will be used if no other value is provided.

- **Prompt**: This is used as a parameter label to identify the parameter in the dialog box.

- **Type**: Type of the parameter.

- **Evaluate**: This option decides whether whatever we input in the **Edit** dialog parameter is required to be evaluated or not. We can use arithmetic operations or any base workspace variables in the dialog parameters. If **evaluate** is true, then evaluation of expression happens; else, the value mentioned in the edit dialog will be used as it is.

- **Tunable**: This parameter allows changing the value of the dialog parameter during simulation.

- **Read Only**: If we do not want users to write the value, the read-only option shall be selected.

- **Hidden**: To indicate that parameter should not be displayed in the dialog box.

- **Never Save**: To indicate parameter value will never be saved in the model file.

- **Constraint**: This option allows the selection of constraints. We can create the constraints. For example, if we want the user to enter a number within a specific range, we can add min-max constraints.

- **Enable**: To allow the user to set the value in the dialog.

- **Visible**: To show the parameter in the dialog box.

- **Callback**: We can add a MATLAB command to execute when the user enters the dialog's value.

- **Tooltip**: Text to be displayed when the user brings curser on the parameter dialog.

- **Layout**: This is used for positioning the dialog parameter in the dialog box.

The *figure 9.21* shows how the dialog box looks after adding the `Edit` parameter in the dialog box:

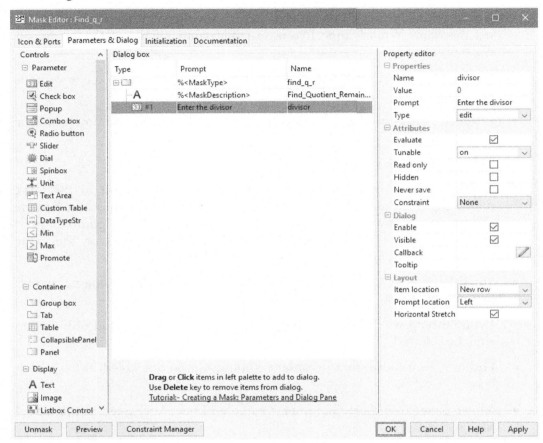

Figure 9.21: Create Mask

The *figure 9.22* shows the dialog box when we double-click on the library block:

Figure 9.22: Dialog box

As double click on the block opens the dialog box. Therefore, to see logic under the mask, either we can hit *Ctrl + U* or right-click on the block, select **Mask** and then select **Look Under mask**. The *figure 9.23* shows how to look under the mask:

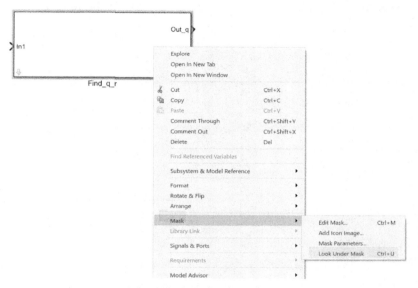

Figure 9.23: *Dialog box*

We shall need to put **divisor** as a constant block value to use the model logic's dialog parameter **divisor**. The *figure 9.24* shows how to assign a divisor in the constant block:

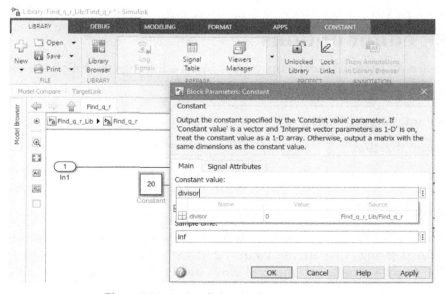

Figure 9.24: *Assign divisor in the constant block*

Now, whatever value we put in the dialog parameter will be used in the constant block. This mechanism allows us to have different behavior of the same logic using library blocks. The *figure 9.25* shows the result of simulation when the values of the divisor for inputs a, b, c, d, and e are given as 10, 20, 30, 40, and 50, respectively:

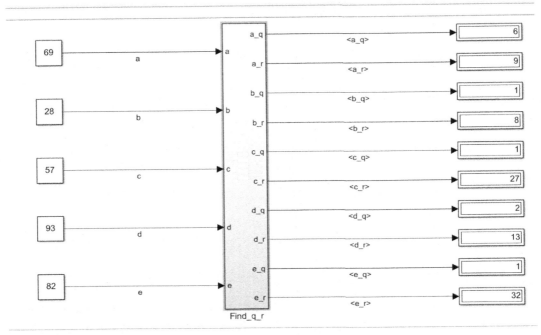

Figure 9.25: Simulation result when divisor value is provided through dialog parameter

Mask editor options

Let us learn more about the mask options. Mask editor has the following four panes:

- Icon & Ports
- Parameters & Dialog
- Initialization
- Documentation

Icon & Ports

This pane is used to shape the mask block, where we can write commands to display user-defined strings or variable values, and so on. The *figure 9.26* and *figure 9.27* show the **Icon & Ports** settings and block display before and after settings:

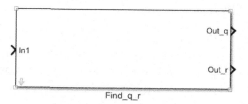

Figure 9.26: Library block display before applying Icon & Ports settings

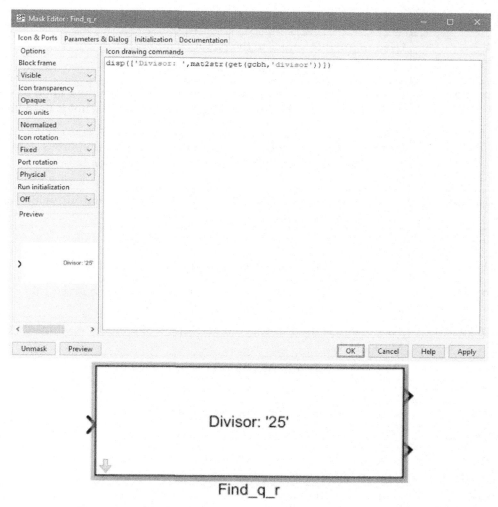

Figure 9.27: Library block display after applying Icon & Ports settings

We can see that, using MATLAB commands, we can display the divisor value on the block itself. Therefore, we do not need to look into the dialog parameters to check the divisor value.

Parameters & Dialog

As shown in the `Create library mask` section, this pane adds different dialog parameters. We can add the following types of **parameters**, **containers** to group parameters, display's to display texts and images, and **actions** to take actions.

Parameters

Table 9.1 explains various options available for parameters and their usage:

Menu	Description
`Edit`	Used to provide values to the parameters.
`Check Box`	Used to handle the Boolean type of parameter.
`Combo Box`	Used to select parameter values from the list. When the combo box is used to determine the value from the list, the variable holds the actual value.
`Pop up`	Used to select parameter values from the list. When Pop up is used to determine value from the list, then the variable holds the value of the index.
`Radio Button`	This dialog is used to select a value from a list, but all values are displayed in the dialog box.
`Slider`	This dialog is used to select a value from the given range.
`Dial`	It is similar to the slider but has a circular shape.
`Spin Box`	Using this dialog user can select the value within a given range by spinning through the values.
`DataTypeStr`	This dialog is used to provide datatype to the blocks used inside the Mask blocks.
`Min`	Used to provide min value for the selected datatype.
`Max`	Used to provide max value for the selected datatype.
`Unit`	Used to provide a unit for the selected datatype.
`Custom Table`	Used to provide the data in the form table to the mask block
`Promote Parameter`	Used to promote dialog parameter of an underlying block to the top level of Mask.
`Promote all`	Promotes all dialog parameters of underlying blocks to the top level of Mask.

Table 9.1: Parameters options

Containers

Table 9.2 shows different options available for containers. The containers are groups of different parameters:

Menu	Description
`Panel`	Used for logical grouping of parameters
`Group Box`	Used to group containers.
`Tab`	Used to create a separate tab.
`Table`	Used to group parameters such as `Edit`, `Check Box`, and `Pop up` parameters in the tabular form. Used to provide values to the parameters.
`Collapsible Panel`	It is similar to the panel, but it has expanded or collapsed options

Table 9.2: Containers options

Display

Table 9.3 shows different options available to display texts, images, tables, and so on:

Menu	Description
`Text`	Used to add text to be displayed in the dialog box.
`Group Box`	Used to display an image in the dialog box.
`Text Area`	Used to add custom text or MATLAB commands in the dialog box.
`Listbox control`	Used to select possible values from the Listbox. Multiple values are possible to choose by pressing *Ctrl + Click*.
`Tree control`	Used to select possible values from the hierarchical tree structure. Multiple values are possible to choose by pressing *Ctrl + Click*.

Table 9.3: Display options

Action

Table 9.4 shows different options available for actions:

Menu	Description
`Hyperlink`	Used to display a hyperlink in the dialog box
`Button`	Used to perform some actions after pressing the button

Table 9.4: Action options

Initialization

The initialization pane is used to initialize the mask blocks. The MATLAB commands or expressions are written in the Initialization command text area. These commands or expressions are executable during the update diagram, the start of a simulation, start of code generation, or click the apply button on the dialog box. The variables created due to these commands or expressions are stored in the **Mask** workspace. These variables are accessed only within the scope of the mask block. In the **Create mask** section mentioned earlier, we assign the **Divisor** value entered directly to the constant block. Rather than using the parameter **Divisor** in the constant block, we want to check for zero value to avoid the **divide by zero** exception. If it is zero, then use hard code value **10** as a divisor; else, the dialog parameter divisor should be used as a value of the constant block. But to do that, the check box **Allow library block to modify its content** should be checked. When we are changing the value parameter of the **Constant** block from **divisor** to **10**, we are changing the content of the mask block. Let us see how we can use initialization commands to do so. *Figure 9.28* shows initialization commands to check divisor value and assign value according to the user-entered value:

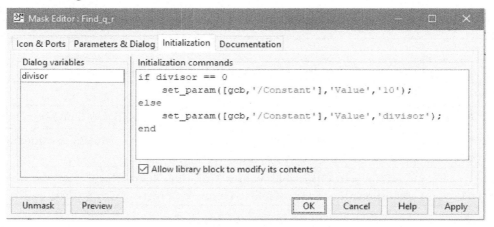

Figure 9:28: Initialization commands

Figure 9.29 shows the results of the initialization commands when the user enters the value **0**. We can see that the constant block in the library block has a hardcoded value of **10** due to initialization commands:

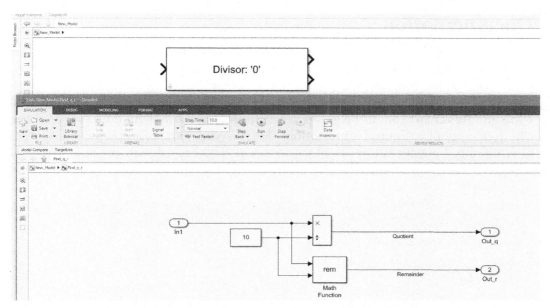

Figure 9:29: *When value zero is entered, then hard code "10" is used in the constant block*

Figure 9.30 explains the results of initialization commands when the user enters a nonzero (85) value. We can observe that the constant block in the library block has value as a variable **divisor**:

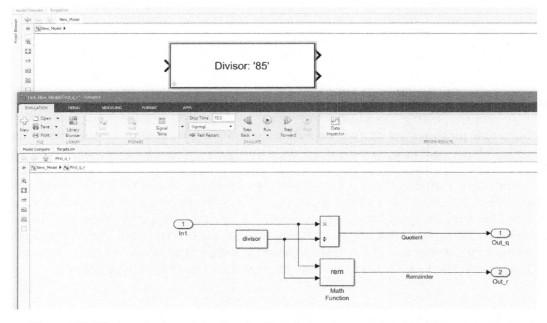

Figure 9:30: *When a value is non-zero then the direct divisor parameter is used in the constant block*

Documentation

As we have seen, we can mask a generic functionality using Mask editor. That is being used as a single block. Because this masked functionality is unique and different from the built-in block, it is always a good idea to describe this mask block. The mask editor provides a pane called the **documentation pane** to add the **Mask Type** and **Description**. If the given description is not sufficient, then we can create a help document with more descriptions. Maybe with some examples which explain functionality beneath the mask block in detail. The help document could be used using the **eval** command. The *figure 9.31* shows the documentation pane from the mask editor:

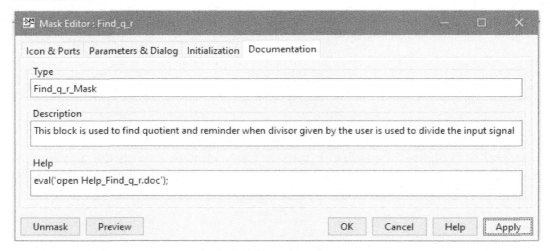

Figure 9:31: Documentation pane

Model callbacks

Simulink provides an option for automation during model load, simulation, and save. These callbacks are used to set some preconditions before or after these operations. Additionally, Model callbacks are also applicable for Libraries except for simulation-related callbacks. Let us see how to access model callbacks. The model callbacks are available in the property inspector. To open the model callbacks, we need to open the **Property** inspector first. To open the property inspector, click on the **Modelling** tab, click on the arrow present in the **Design** panel, and click on the **Property Inspector**. By default, **Property Inspector** loads on the right side of the screen. The *figure 9.32* shows how to open the **Property Inspector**:

Advanced Modeling Techniques-I   375

Figure 9:32: Property inspector

The *figure 9.33* explains how to access callbacks from the property inspector. We can see a dropdown menu available for the callbacks to select the desired callback function:

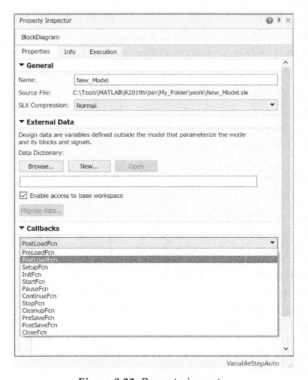

Figure 9:33: Property inspector

From the dropdown, we can select the **Callback** function for which we want to add **MATLAB** commands. The text area below the selection of the callback function is used to add **MATLAB** commands. Model callbacks are categorized as follows:

- **Model Load/close callbacks**: The following callbacks are used during model load and close operations:
    - **PreLoadFcn**: **PreLoadFcn** is executed before the model is loaded. Model parameters cannot be used in this callback since model parameters are loaded after model load. This function is used to set some variables, which are required for the model to load. For example, if a constant block in the model uses a variable name **Const_var**, this variable could be assigned to the required value in **PreLoadFcn** so that when the model is loaded, the variable **Const_var** would be available in the workspace. In this callback function, we cannot use **get_param** since model parameters are not available; we cannot access this function programmatically.
    - **PostLoadFcn**: **PostLoadFcn** is executed after the model is loaded. Unlike **PreLoadFcn**, the model parameters can be used in this callback. Structural changes are possible in this callback. Suppose we want to add certain interfaces in the model before opening the Simulink editor, then this could be done in this callback. Because this function always runs after model load, Simulink does not set the model dirty flag to indicate unsaved changes. We cannot make Simulink editor-related changes in this callback function, such as setting the zoom factor. Also, we cannot access this function programmatically.
    - **CloseFcn**: **CloseFcn** is executed before closing the model. Opposite to the **PreLoadFcn**, this function can be used to clear variables from a workspace.
- **Model save callbacks**: The following callbacks are used during model save operation:
    - **PreSaveFcn**: **PreSaveFcn** function is executed before saving the model. If some conditions are required to be set before saving the model, this could be done here.
    - **PostSaveFcn**: **PostSaveFcn** is executed after saving the model. Similar to the **PostLoadFcn**, Structural changes made in the model during **PostSaceFcn** do not make the set model dirty flag to indicate unsaved changes.
- **Model simulation callbacks**: The following callbacks are used during model simulation operations:

- o **InitFcn**: **InitFcn** is executed during the model update phase before the evaluation of block parameters. Similar to the **PreLoadFcn**, this function is used to create variables required during a model update.
- o **StartFcn**: **StartFcn** is executed at the start of the simulation. This call back is not called during a model update.
- o **PauseFcn**: **PauseFcn** is executed when a simulation is paused.
- o **ContinueFcn**: This function is executed before simulation continues from the pause state.
- o **StopFcn**: This function is executed after the simulation is stopped. Simulation writes the outputs to workspace variables before **StopFcn** executes. When simulation is triggered using command-line, then Simulation outputs are not available in the **StopFcn**.

Block callbacks

Similar to model callbacks, Simulink has a provision to have block callbacks. The model callbacks are associated with Model operations, whereas Block callbacks are associated with block operations. To access the block callbacks, first right-click on the block for which callbacks are required to be added, select **Properties**, and select the tab callbacks. *Figure 9.34* shows how to add or edit block callbacks:

Figure 9:34: Right-click on the selected block.

Figure 9.35 shows different types of callbacks available for a block. To add content to the callback function, we need to add **MATLAB** commands and then a test area next to the list of callback functions:

Figure 9:35: Callback functions available for block callbacks

These functions are executed during the opening, editing, compilation, simulation, saving, and closing operations mentioned as follows:

- **Block opening-related callbacks**: The following callbacks are used during block open or block load operations:
    - **OpenFcn**: This callback is executed when a block is opened. So, when **open_system** with block argument is executed or after double-clicking on the block. This callback function works as an override to the normal dialog box of the block.
    - **LoadFcn**: This callback is executed after the block diagram is loaded.

- **Block editing-related callbacks**: The following callbacks are used during block edit operations:
    - **MoveFcn**: This callback is executed when a block is moved or resized.
    - **NameChangeFcn**: This callback is executed when the block name or path is changed.
    - **PreCopyFcn**: This callback is executed before copying the block. This callback is also executed when **add_block** is used to copy a block or subsystem where the block resides.
    - **CopyFcn**: This callback is executed after pasting the copied block. Like **PreCopyFcn**, this callback is executed when **add_block** is used to copy a block or subsystem where the block resides has been copied.
    - **ClipboardFcn**: This callback is executed when a block is copied or cut to the clipboard.
    - **PreDeleteFcn**: This callback is executed the block is deleted. This callback is also executed when a **delete_block** is used to delete the block or subsystem where the block resides is deleted.
    - **DeleteFcn**: This callback is executed the block is deleted. This callback is also executed when **delete_block** is used to delete the block or subsystem where the block resides is deleted, or the model containing the block is closed. In this callback, we can still access the block parameters of the blocks using **get_param**.
    - **DstroyFcn**: This callback is executed when the block is destroyed from memory. In this callback, the block handle could not be accessed using **get_param**.
    - **UndoDeleteFcn**: This callback is executed when the block deletion is undone.
- **Block compilation and Simulation callbacks**: The following callbacks are used during the model simulation and compilation:
    - **InitFcn**: **InitFcn** is executed during the model update. It runs before block parameters are evaluated.
    - **StartFcn**: **StartFcn** is executed at the start of the simulation. This callback is not called during a model update.
    - **PauseFcn**: **PauseFcn** is executed when the simulation is paused.
    - **ContinueFcn**: This function is executed before simulation continues from the pause state.

- o **StopFcn**: This function is executed after the simulation is stopped.
- **Block save and close callbacks**: The following callbacks are used during the save and close operation of the block diagram:
  - o **PreSaveFcn**: This is executed before saving the block diagram.
  - o **PostSaveFcn**: This is executed after the block diagram is saved.
  - o **CloseFcn**: This is executed when a block is closed using **close_system**. This callback is not executed when the block dialog is closed interactively.
  - o **ModelCloseFcn**: This function is executed before the block diagram containing the block is closed.
- **Subsystem-related callbacks**: The following callbacks are used when some changes are done in child blocks or parent subsystem:
  - o **DeleteChildFcn**: This is executed after a block or line is deleted in the subsystem.
  - o **ErrorFcn**: This is executed when the error has occurred in the subsystem. For error display, the **errorHandler** command could be used in the callback.
  - o **ParentCloseFcn**: This is executed when the subsystem containing the block is closed or the block is moved to the new subsystem. This callback is not called for the blocks available at the root level when the model is closed.

Conclusion

In this chapter, we have learnt the fundamentals of Library creation, usage of Libraries, and how they make the modeling activities easy with library blocks. We have also worked on the concepts of block masking, with different mask editor options and Mask callbacks. After Mask editor options, this chapter has introduced the reader to the concepts of callbacks. The reader has learnt to use model callbacks and Block callbacks. So, using the concepts the reader can implement and maintain the complex logic in the model, automate the model, and block behavior using callbacks. This makes modeling easy. In the upcoming chapter that is in continuation of this topic, the reader shall be familiarized with further advanced modeling techniques such as virtual/non-virtual subsystems and buses model referencing/variant subsystem with configuration setting pane for reference subsystem and hardware implementation.

Points to remember

- Whenever identical logic is implemented at multiple places, it is always recommended to create libraries.
- Library blocks are easy to maintain. Change in the logic at one place reflects changes in all places where library block is used.
- Using mask editor options, one can use the same library block for multiple purposes.
- Parameters in the mask editor are used to receive inputs from users.
- For custom mask block documentation is possible to do separately. Documentation helps to understand the block usage in a better way.
- Initialization commands are used to initialize the mask block.
- Mask block is nothing but a subsystem containing a specific functionality with masked parameters.
- Model and block callbacks are used to automate model or block behavior at certain modeling phases, for example, model simulation, model/block diagram open/load, model save.

Multiple choice questions

1. **Simulink model maintenance becomes easy using library blocks.**
    a. True
    b. False

2. **Which of the following option from Information Overlays is one of the library options?**
    a. Signal dimensions
    b. Units
    c. Execution Order
    d. Show All Links

3. **After selecting a library block, *Ctrl + L* is used for what purpose?**
    a. Highlight a parent block
    b. Highlight the associated reference library block
    c. Highlight a child block
    d. None of the above.

4. How can we make the changes in the library block from the Simulink model?

   a. By using resolve link option

   b. By using restore option

   c. By using Disable link option

   d. By using push option

5. How can we modify the logic inside the library block from the Simulink model without relating to the library?

   a. By using disable link

   b. By using break link

   c. By using restore link

   d. None of the above

6. How to make Library link active after disabling it from Simulink model?

   a. By using restore operation

   b. By Using Push operation

   c. Both A and B

   d. None of the above

7. When we change some of the parameters inside the library block, a red star symbol appears on the left bottom. What is indicated using this red star.

   a. Disabled link

   b. Parameterized link

   c. Broken link

   d. Restored link

8. How to add Mask parameters?

   a. Using Mask Editor options

   b. Using workspace editor options

   c. Both A and B

   d. None of the above

9. How to see the logic inside the block?
   a. Create Mask
   b. Edit Mask
   c. Look under mask

10. Which parameter is used to handle Boolean type parameters from the Parameters dialog in Mask editor options?
    a. Edit
    b. Pop up
    c. Radio Button
    d. None of the above

11. Which of the following is not the part of containers in Mask editor options.
    a. Panel
    b. Table
    c. Custom Table
    d. Tab

12. Which of the following is part of the Block callback but not the Model callback?
    a. ClipboardFcn
    b. InitFcn
    c. LoadFcn
    d. PauseFcn

13. CloseFcn is executed in block callbacks when the block dialog is closed.
    a. True
    b. False

Questions

1. Explain the importance of Simulink Library.
2. Explain the process of Masking.
3. Explain the process to restore or push the logic in the disabled library blocks.
4. Why do we need Masking?

5. What is the purpose of the initialization tab in the Mask Editor options?

6. How to add help for the Mask blocks?

7. Explain different types of options available in the Parameters & Dialog tab in Mask editor.

8. Why do we need a model callback?

9. Explain different types of model callbacks and when they are executed.

10. Why do we need block callbacks?

11. How are block callbacks categorized?

12. Create a mask block to perform addition and multiplication based on selected parameters. Specification of the block is as follows.

13. Use a combo box to have two values 1 and 2.

14. Use slider to provide value for operand 1

15. Use the edit box to enter the value for operand 2

16. When 1 is selected in the combo box, then the mask block should output the addition of operand 1 and operand 2.

17. When 2 is selected in combo box, then the mask block should output the multiplication of operand 1 and operand 2

Answers

1. A
2. D
3. B
4. C
5. B
6. C
7. B
8. A
9. C
10. D
11. C
12. A
13. B

CHAPTER 10
Advanced Modeling Techniques-II

Introduction

Until now, the readers have gone through the basic concepts of Simulink with some advanced modeling techniques. We have learnt to create custom library blocks with different properties of libraries. The readers know where to use custom libraries and how these library blocks are fitted in different requirements based on reusability. We have educated ourselves about the different types of callbacks, such as model callbacks, block callbacks, and mask editor callbacks options. Let us learn some more advanced modeling techniques in this chapter. These techniques help us to understand Simulink execution flow in an enhanced manner.

Structure

In this chapter, we are going to cover the following topics.

- Subsystem
    - Execution order of the blocks
    - Virtual subsystems
    - Non-virtual subsystems
    - Conditionally executable subsystems

- Model referencing
- Variant subsystems
- Variant model
- Model referencing pane
- Signal bus
  - Virtual signal bus
  - Non-Virtual signal bus
  - Signal conversion block
- Hardware implementation pane

Objectives

After studying this chapter, the reader will be able to:

- Learn different subsystems
- Understand the execution flow of Simulink blocks
- Get a brief overview of virtual/non-virtual subsystems
- Learn model referencing concepts
- Understand different model referencing configuration parameters
- Know signal bus with virtual/non-virtual buses
- Familiarize with the hardware implementation pane

Subsystem

A subsystem is a grouping of Simulink blocks. These blocks are used to execute a function. The subsystems are either virtual or non-virtual. By default, they are virtual. Meaning, depending on the logic in the Simulink model, the blocks present in the same subsystem may not execute simultaneously. Simulink calculates the execution order of the blocks inside the model based on their inter-dependency. Let us see how we can check the execution order of the blocks.

The execution order of the blocks

Suppose we have two operations in our subsystem addition of Input 1 and Input 2, then multiplication of result of addition and Input 3. The output of multiplication goes out of the subsystem. To check the execution order, click on the information overlay dropdown array and click on the execution order. The *figure 10.1* shows the execution order option from the dropdown menu:

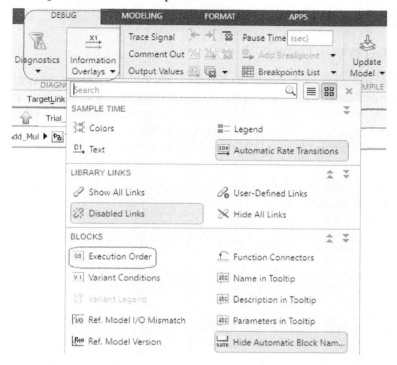

Figure 10.1: Execution order menu from information overlays

Once clicked on **Execution Order**, Simulink compiles the model and calculates the execution order. Then, it shows the calculated execution order as shown in *figure 10.2*:

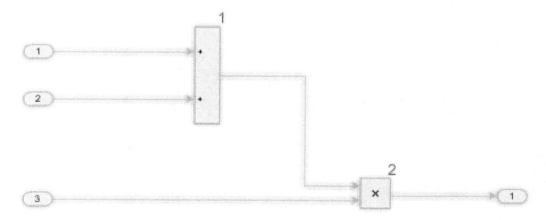

Figure 10.2: Execution order displayed for every operation

We can see the execution order of the addition and multiplication block. Lower the value higher the order. Therefore, addition operation executes first and then the multiplication operation.

Virtual subsystems

Virtual subsystems are used to group blocks only for the graphical representation. They do not have any impact on the execution order of the blocks located inside them. Let us realize this using an example. Suppose we have two subsystems, **Trial_Subsystem_1** and **Trial_Subsystem_2**. The *figure 10.3* depicts the logic inside these subsystems:

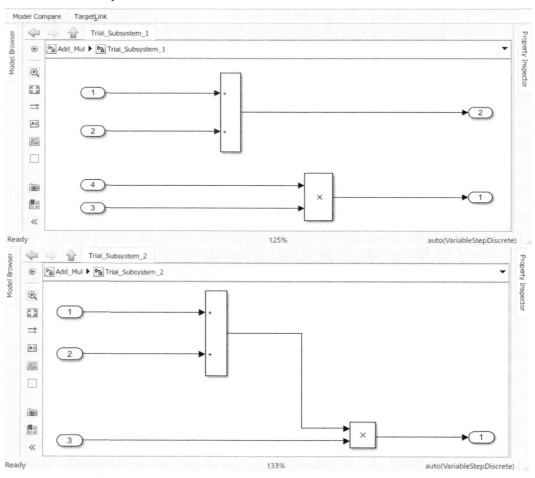

Figure 10.3: *Logic inside the "Trial_Subsystem_1" and "Trial_Subsystem_2"*

The connection between **Trial_Subsystem_1** and **Trial_Subsystem_2** is implemented according to *figure 10.4*:

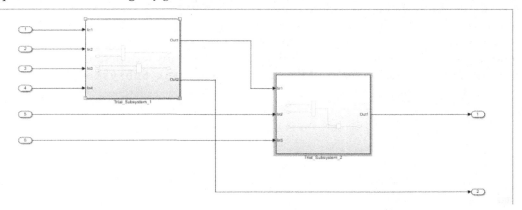

Figure 10.4: *Connection between the "Trial_Subsystem_1" and "Trial_Subsystem_2"*

Let us see the execution order of the blocks inside these two systems. The *figure 10.5* shows the execution order of the multiplication block and addition block from **Trial_Subsystem_1**:

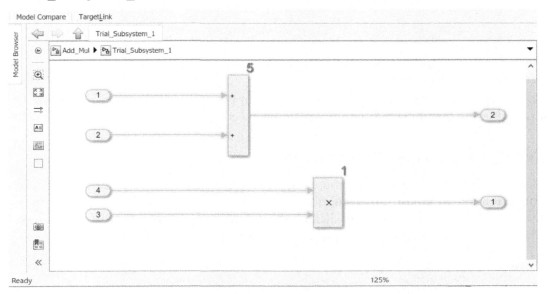

Figure 10.5: *Execution order of the blocks inside "Trial_Subsystem_1"*

We can observe that the multiplication block and addition block are part of the same subsystem, but they have different execution orders. Multiplication is executed first; then execution control goes to **Trial_Subsystem_2** since multiplication output is connected to the input of **Trial_Subsystem_2**. This input port is further connected to the input of the addition block in the **Trial_Subsystem_2**. Therefore, this addition block has an execution order as **2**. Additionally, the output of that addition block goes to the multiplication block in the **Trial_Subsystem_2**. So, the execution order of this multiplication block is **3**. The addition operation in the **Trial_Subsystem_1** is executed in the last since the output of this subsystem is not connected to any other block in the model. So, this addition operation runs independently. The *figure 10.6* shows the execution order of the blocks inside **Trial_Subsystem_2**:

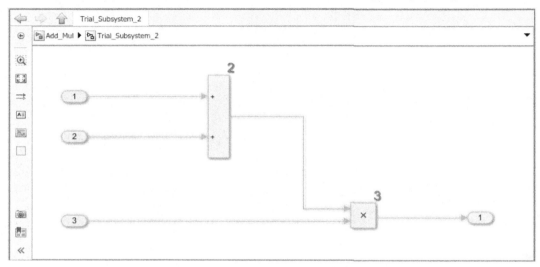

Figure 10.6: Execution order of the blocks inside "Trial_Subsystem_2"

So, we have seen that Subsystems does virtual grouping of the blocks. All blocks present in the virtual subsystem need not be executed simultaneously.

Non-virtual subsystems

Non-virtual subsystems are atomic subsystems. We can make any non-conditional subsystem as an atomic subsystem using block parameters. To make a subsystem into an atomic subsystem, right-click on the subsystem and select block parameters. The *figure 10.7* shows the procedure to open block parameters of the subsystems.

Figure 10.7: Open block parameters of the subsystem

Once we click the block parameters, we can see the dialog box from *figure 10.8*. We need to select the checkbox for the option of `Treat as atomic unit`:

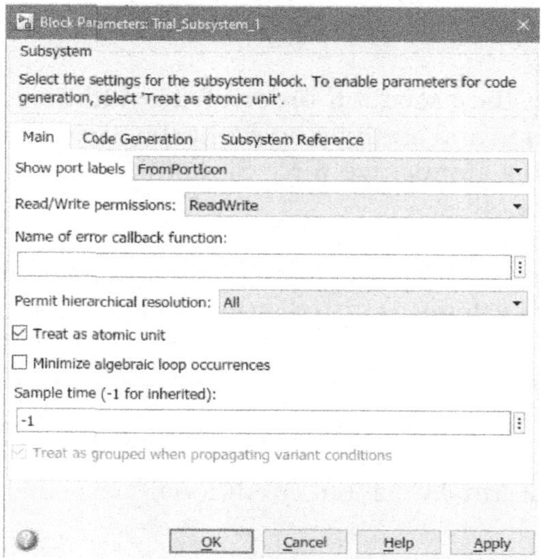

Figure 10.8: Dialog box for block parameters of subsystem

Once the **"Treat as atomic unit"** option is selected, Simulink changes the subsystems boundaries to bold. So that just by looking at subsystem block, we can understand that this subsystem is of atomic type. Let us use the same example we used to understand the virtual subsystems. Between **Trial_Subsystem_1** and **Trial_Subsystem_2**, we make **Trial_Subsystem_1** as an atomic unit. Let us check if there are any differences in the execution order after this change. The *figure 10.9* shows the execution order of the **Trial_Subsystem_1** after making it atomic:

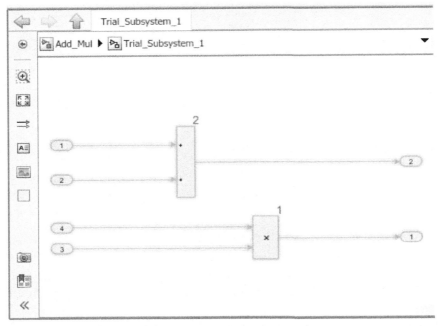

Figure 10.9: Execution order of the blocks inside "Trial_Subsystem_1" when made as an atomic unit

We can see that now the execution order of the addition block is 2. That means multiplication operation and addition operation happen together one after the other. By making subsystems atomic, we force Simulink to execute all blocks inside the subsystem one after another.

Unless and until there is a real need to make subsystem atomic, it is recommended to have as many subsystems as virtual subsystems to have better and optimized performance.

Conditionally executable subsystems

Table 10.1 gives the information about conditionally executable subsystems:

Subsystem	Display	Description
Enabled Subsystem	*Enabled Subsystem*	Enabled subsystem executes when the control input (input at top) is true.
Triggered Subsystem	*Triggered Subsystem*	Trigger subsystem executes when the control input has a configured trigger. Triggered subsystem can have the following triggers: • Rising • Falling • Either (rising or falling both)
Function-Call Subsystems	*Function-Call Subsystem*	The function call subsystem executes when a valid function call is received. This function call can be generated either using the "function call generator" block or Stateflow.
Enabled and Triggered Subsystem	*Enabled and Triggered Subsystem*	Enabled and triggered subsystem executes when control input for enable is true and configured trigger is received on trigger control.

Table 10.1: Conditionally executed subsystems

Since the blocks inside the "conditionally executed subsystems" execute when respective control is received, all conditionally executed subsystems are non-virtual subsystems.

Model referencing

Simulink gives an excellent provision to use the model inside another model. Means we can use already available model logic in another model. This approach is helpful for using the existing model in another model and has some additional advantages as the following:

- Modular development
- Accelerated simulation
- Incremental code generation

- Incremental loading

Any model can be referred to in any other model using model bock. *Figure 10.10* shows how the model block seems to be:

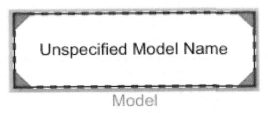

Figure 10.10: *Model block to call another model*

The **Block Parameter** dialog box appears by double-clicking on the model block. The model block dialog parameter can be seen in *figure 10.11*:

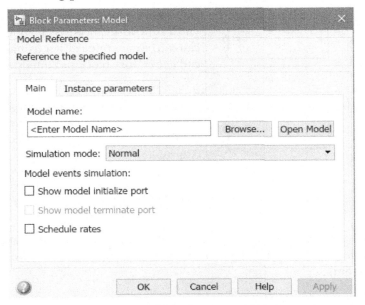

Figure 10.11: *Dialog box for model block*

Using the **Browse...** option, we can select the model required to be referred. The *figure 10.12* shows the display of the model block after choosing the model to be called:

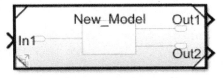

Figure 10.12: *Model block after selecting New_Model*

> `Instance parameters` tab provides values for New_Model's model workspace variables. Generally, variables used in the model are accessed from the base workspace. So, `Instance parameter` tab appears empty.

Variant subsystem

We may have some requirements where two functionalities would be mutually exclusive. Imagine different environments where a function has the same signature (that is, same inputs and outputs) but other behavior. So based on variant conditions, we can decide the functionality. Suppose in one environment, we need to add inputs, but in another environment, we need to multiply inputs, then we can use variant subsystems. The *figure 10.13* shows a variant subsystem:

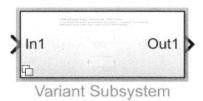

Figure 10.13: *Variant subsystem block*

To select variant subsystems, we need to define conditions. First, we rename the subsystem inside the variant subsystem to addition and multiplication. The *figure 10.14* shows the content of the variant subsystem before specifying the variant conditions and after renaming the subsystems:

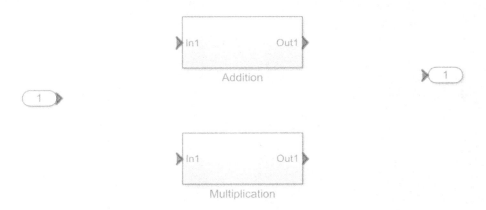

Figure 10.14: *Content of variant subsystem before specifying the conditions*

To specify the conditions, right-click on the variant subsystem, open block parameters, and add variant conditions. The *figure 10.15* shows variant conditions to select the addition subsystem of the multiplication subsystem. The *figure 10.15* also shows that the addition subsystem will be active when the **variant_par** parameter defined in the base workspace has the value **1**. Similarly, the subsystem multiplication will be active when **variant_par** has value **2**:

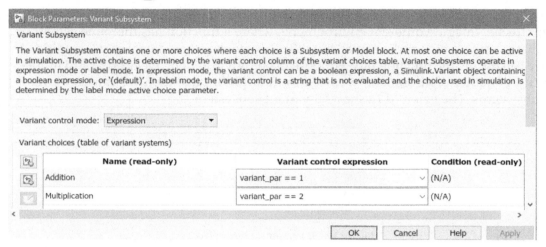

Figure 10.15: Variant conditions in control expression

The *figure 10.16* shows how the addition subsystem is active when the **variant_par** parameter in the base workspace has value 1:

1) Add Subsystem or Model blocks as valid variant choices.
2) You cannot connect blocks at this level. At simulation, connectivity is automatically determined, based on the active variant and port name matching.

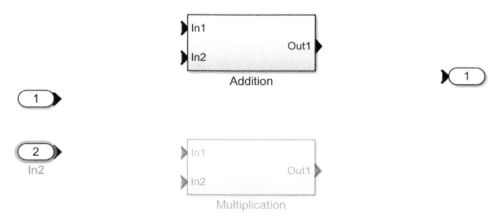

Figure 10.16: The addition subsystem is active in the variant subsystem

Variant model

The variant model block combines the model block and variant subsystem block. A variant model refers to multiple models based on the variant conditions. This block has a similar dialog box for block parameters as the variant subsystem block. The content of the variant model block when none of the models is referred, shown in *figure 10.17*. We can observe that the variant model block has multiple model blocks according to the variant conditions:

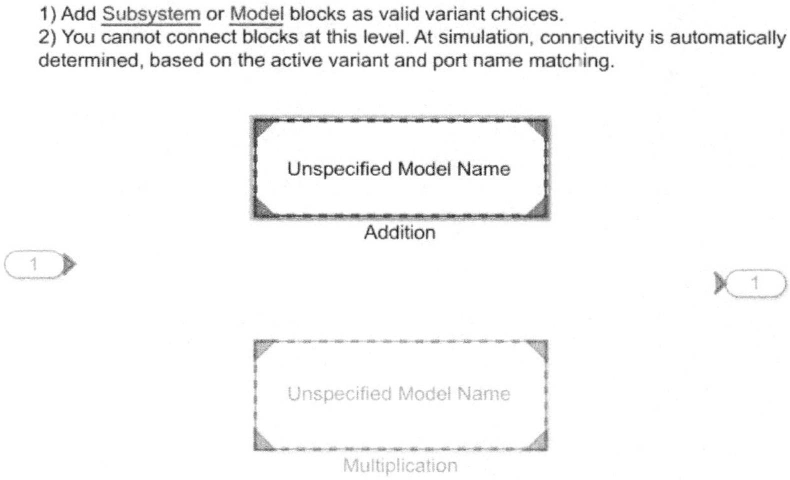
1) Add Subsystem or Model blocks as valid variant choices.
2) You cannot connect blocks at this level. At simulation, connectivity is automatically determined, based on the active variant and port name matching.
Unspecified Model Name
Addition
1
1
Unspecified Model Name
Multiplication

***Figure 10.17**: Content of variant model before specifying the conditions.*

Model referencing pane

In *Chapter 8: Configuration Parameter Settings,* we have learnt Simulink Model settings. We have some settings related to the model reference. A separate pane for these settings is called a model referencing pane. Let us learn model reference-related settings in this section. The *figure 10.18* shows the settings available in the model referencing pane:

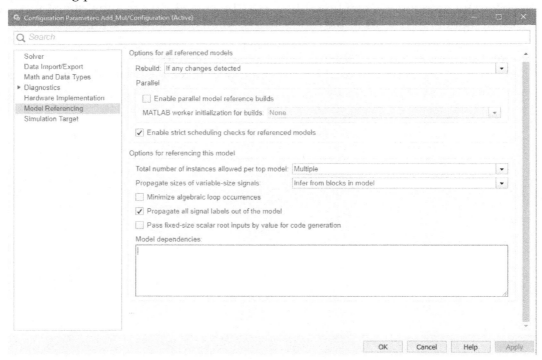

Figure 10.18: *Model referencing pane*

- **Rebuild:** This setting is used to determine how referenced models should be treated before updating, simulating, or even before code generation. This configuration parameter has the following values:
    o **Always**: This setting takes more time since Simulink always rebuilds the referenced models.
    o **If any changes detected**: Simulink checks if any changes are made in the referenced subsystem after the last build, then only rebuilding happens.
    o **If any changes in known dependencies detected**: For this setting, also Simulink rebuilds referenced models conditionally. Simulink checks if any changes are made from the last build and whether those changes will impact the results; then, only rebuilding of referenced models happens.
    o **Never**: Here, Simulink never rebuilds the referenced models. But if the referenced model is changed to the extent where the final results

are impacted, this setting may give wrong results. The user needs to build referenced models separately before the model update, simulation, or code generation.

- **Enable parallel model referencing builds**: This setting specifies whether the automatic parallel building of the model referencing hierarchy should be used or not. By default, its value is Off.

- **MATLAB worker initialization for builds**: When the **Enable parallel model referencing builds** setting is enabled, this setting is possible. Else this setting is disabled. This setting is used to specify how to initialize MATLAB workers for parallel builds. It has three values, **None**, **Copy base workspace,** and **Load top model**. **None** will indicate Simulink to take no action. It is also a default setting for this parameter. **Copy base workspace** will result in attempting the copying of the base workspace to each MATLAB worker. **Load top model** will load the top model at each worker. The vital thing to note is that these parallel build settings work only with MATLAB's parallel computing toolbox. The worker is each instance MATLAB creates for parallel computing.

- **Enable strict scheduling checks for referenced models**: This configuration parameter has a default value as "**On**". This parameter forces Simulink to perform the following checks for referenced models.
    - Scheduling the order consistency of function-call subsystems in referenced export function models.
    - Sample time consistency across the boundary of referenced export function models
    - Sample time consistency across the boundary of referenced rate-based models that are function-call adapted.

- **Total number of instances allowed per top model**: This parameter specifies how many instances of this model can be used in another model. By default, its value is **Multiple**, meaning; multiple instances of this model to be referred to in another model are possible. This parameter has values zero and one. The value **zero** indicates that this model cannot be referred to in other models, and one indicates at most once it could be referred.

- **Propagate sizes of the variable-size signals**: This setting determines how to propagate the variable-size signal to the reference model. By default, its value is **Infer from blocks in the model**. Simulink searches the blocks from the parent and reference models and determines the propagation strategy based on block categories. This parameter has two more values, **Only when enabling** and **During execution**. As the names suggest, the variable-size signal propagation will happen accordingly.

- **Minimize algebraic loop occurrences**: This parameter setting specifies whether Simulink shall eliminate the algebraic loop in the model to which the current model is referred. By default, its value is Off.

- **Propagate all signal labels out of the models**: This setting allows Simulink to propagate output signal names out of the model to the parent model. By default, its value is On.

Signal bus

Different types of signals can be grouped to form a bus. Signal buses are used to simplify signal wiring. Suppose we have two subsystems, **Master** and **Slave**, where outputs of **Master** are used as inputs in **Slave**. The **Master** subsystem has five outputs. The *figure 10.19* shows the connections between Master and Slave using non-bus outports and Inports:

Figure 10.19: Connections between Master and Slave

Since there are five outputs and five inputs, there are five lines to connect them. Using a bus, we can reduce this wiring. For that, we need to use two blocks, **Bus Creator** to create the bus and **Bus Selector** to select the bus elements. The *figure 10.20* shows how the bus creator is used to form a bus.

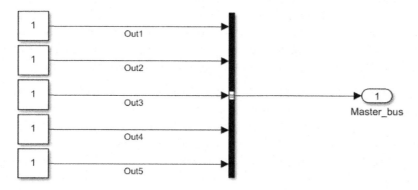

Figure 10.20: Bus creator

In our example, bus creator is used to create a bus of five signals. These signals are outputs of the **Master** subsystem. Similarly, let us see how the bus selector is used to select the signals from the bus. The *figure 10.21* shows the same:

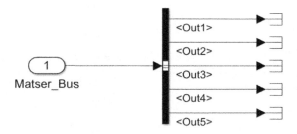

Figure 10.21: Bus selector

So, to use outputs of the **Master** subsystem, we need to use the bus selector block in the **Slave** subsystem. With buses, we can see how the signal wiring is simplified in *figure 10.22*:

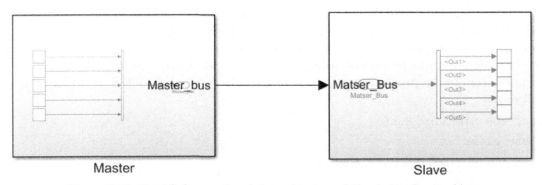

Figure 10.22: Simplified connections between Master and Slave using the signal bus

- **Both signal routings have no functional differences, either with separate outports/inports and buses.**
- **Depending on project readability guidelines, we may need to avoid using signal buses.**

Virtual signal bus

When we use buses in the Simulink model, by default, they are virtual. That means a grouping of signals is done only for the display purpose (that is, graphical representation). There is no impact on performance or memory, or simulation. The bus structure we saw in the previous example is a virtual bus. After the model update, we can identify the virtual bus with a different lining. The *figure 10.23* shows how the bus looks after the model update:

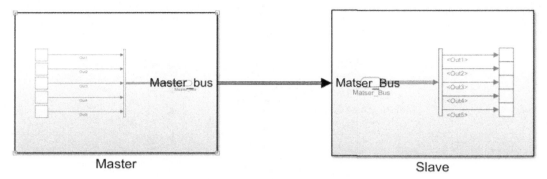

Figure 10.23: *Representation of bus lines after the model update for the virtual bus*

Non-virtual signal bus

We need to define a bus structure in the base workspace for non-virtual buses. We can create this bus structure using an m-file. This m-file must be loaded in the base workspace before opening the model. First, let us see how to create a bus object. We have created an m-function **Simulnk_Bus** in the file **Simulink_Bus.m**. This function can be called in the preload model call-back function. The content of the m-file is as follows:

```
function Simulink_Bus()
clear elems;
elems(1) = Simulink.BusElement;
elems(1).Name = 'Out1';
elems(1).DataType = 'double';

elems(2) = Simulink.BusElement;
elems(2).Name = 'Out2';
elems(2).DataType = 'double';

elems(3) = Simulink.BusElement;
elems(3).Name = 'Out3';
elems(3).DataType = 'double';

elems(4) = Simulink.BusElement;
elems(4).Name = 'Out4';
elems(4).DataType = 'double';
elems(5) = Simulink.BusElement;
```

```
elems(5).Name = 'Out5';
elems(5).DataType = 'double';

slBus1 = Simulink.Bus;
slBus1.HeaderFile = '';
slBus1.Description = '';
slBus1.DataScope = 'Auto';
slBus1.Alignment = -1;
slBus1.Elements = elems;
clear elems;
assignin('base','slBus1', slBus1);
```

Here, we have created a bus object **slBus1**, which contains the elements such as **Out1**, **Out2**, and so on. This bus object can be used as a datatype in the Simulink model. When we load/run this m-file in the command window, we see a variable named **slBus1** in the workspace window. This bus object can be used as a data type in the bus creator block, which makes this bus a non-virtual bus. The main difference between virtual and non-virtual buses is the bus object. Meaning, for a non-virtual bus, the bus structure is required to be already loaded in the base workspace. Non-virtual buses are often used when a definite data structure is essential to generate in the C code. Non-virtual buses are also used when buses are exchanged in-between the parent model and referenced model. Now, we will see how we use this bus object as a datatype in the bus creator block. The *figure 10.24* illustrates the same:

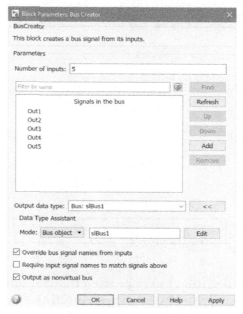

Figure 10.24: Bus objects are used as a datatype for bus creator block

The non-virtual bus can also be identified using a different lining like the virtual bus. The *figure 10.25* depicts the same:

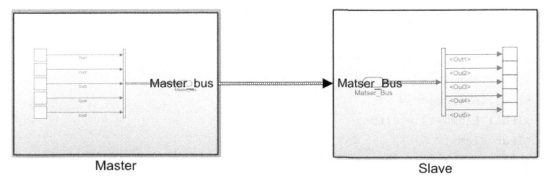

Figure 10.25: *Representation of bus lines after the model update for the non-virtual bus*

Signal conversion block

Signal conversion block is used to convert virtual buses into non-virtual buses and vice-versa. The *figure 10.26* shows different options available with their descriptions accordingly:

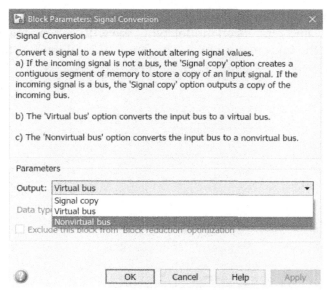

Figure 10.26: *Signal conversion block*

It is recommended that virtual buses be used in the model unless and until there is no real need for non-virtual buses since Simulink can do better optimization, which may give better performance.

Hardware implementation pane

The Simulink provides an option to simulate according to the target board. So, depending on the target board specification, we can select the **Hardware Board**, **Device Vendor,** and **Device type**. The hardware implementation pane contains many other configuration parameters for device details, test hardware, and so on. If we have not taken any particular hardware support packages, most of these settings are read-only. We do not need to consider the hardware implementation pane for basic implementation simulation explicitly. This pane is mainly required to be configured for code generation settings. Let us check some parameters in detail:

- **Hardware board**: This parameter is used to select the required hardware board. If we do not have any support hardware packages, we can default and keep them as none. The *figure 10.27* shows dropdown options for the hardware board.

Figure 10.27: Hardware board setting

- **Device vendor**: We can select the target device manufacturer using this parameter. The *figure 10.28* shows some of the options available in the dropdown menu.

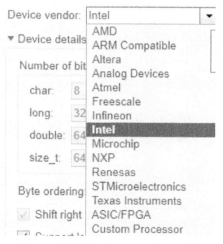

Figure 10.28: Hardware vendor menu

- **Device type**: Using this configuration parameter, we can select the type of hardware to be used to run the model logic. The dropdown options for this parameter are depicted in *figure 10.29*:

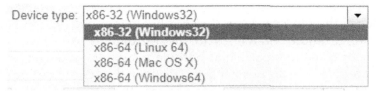

Figure 10.29: *Device type menu*

The typical settings with hardware board none, Intel as device vendor, and ×86–64 (Windows64) as device type (`All are default values`) can be seen in *figure 10.30*:

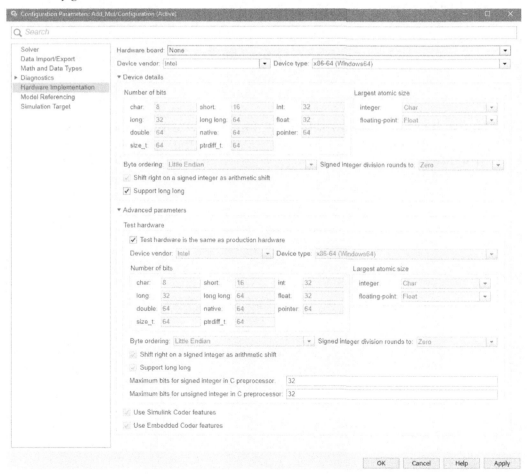

Figure 10.30: *Typical hardware implementation view*

Conclusion

In this chapter, we have learnt the fundamentals of Subsystems with different types of subsystems. We have also gone through the concepts of execution order and how it change depending on virtual/non-virtual subsystems. After virtual/non-virtual subsystems, the chapter takes the reader to different conditionally executed subsystems. The reader has learnt to use Model referencing and variant subsystems in combination as a variant model. The reader has been educated about the signal buses, including virtual/non-virtual buses. The chapter also shows a glimpse of some of the model configuration settings, such as model referencing pane and hardware implementation pane. So using these concepts reader can implement and maintain the complex logic in the model based on the requirements. This makes modeling more efficient. In the upcoming chapter, the reader shall be familiarized with one of the strongest MATLAB tools, Stateflow. The use cases when to use Stateflow, its advantages over Simulink, Stateflow diagram editor, data explorer, different menu bars, and so on.

Points to remember

- It depends upon the subsystem type, virtual or non-virtual, that the execution order of the blocks inside the subsystem changes.
- Atomics subsystems are the non-virtual subsystems. These subsystems should be used when explicitly required.
- More use of non-virtual subsystems may affect the efficiency and simulation performance.
- All conditionally executed subsystems are non-virtual subsystems.
- Model referencing subsystem is used to call another model from model.
- Variant subsystems are executed depending on the variant conditions.
- Variant model is the combination of Variant subsystem and Model referencing.
- Signal buses are used to combine different signals to have less connections and better signal routing.
- Simulink has two types of buses, virtual buses, and non-virtual buses.
- By default, all buses are virtual buses. The non-virtual bus is formed when a bus object is used as a type of bus creator block.
- Signal conversion block is used to convert virtual buses to non-virtual buses and vice-versa.

Multiple choice questions

1. Non-virtual subsystems have an impact on execution order.
    a. True
    b. False

2. How to make any subsystem as atomic?
    a. Using model parameters
    b. Using block parameters
    c. Using configurations parameters
    d. None of the above

3. Which of the following is not the conditionally executed subsystem?
    a. Triggered subsystem
    b. Enabled subsystem
    c. Function call subsystem
    d. Variant subsystem

4. Model block is used to call a model from another model ?
    a. False
    b. True

5. Which of the following can be achieved using model referencing.
    a. Modular development
    b. Accelerated Simulation
    c. Both A and B
    d. None of the above

6. Which of the following is the disadvantage of signal buses?
    a. Lesser connections
    b. Better readability
    c. Better signal routing
    d. None of the above

7. **Non-virtual buses are formed using bus objects.**
   a. True
   b. False

8. **How to convert non-virtual buses to virtual buses?**
   a. Using model block
   b. Using convert block
   c. Using signal convert block
   d. Using variant block

9. **Does Model referencing help in parallel computing?**
   a. True
   b. False

10. **Hardware implementation pane is used to have similar environment as target board.**
    a. False
    b. True

Questions

1. Explain how to calculate execution.
2. Explain the difference between virtual and non-virtual subsystems.
3. List the different conditionally executed subsystems.
4. What is model referencing?
5. What is the difference between variant subsystem and variant model?
6. Explain the importance of a signal bus.
7. What are the differences between virtual and non-virtual buses?
8. Explain the process of making of non-virtual buses.
9. Why do we need a signal convert block?
10. Explain some of the configuration parameters from the hardware implementation pane.
11. Develop a Simulink logic in a model **Trial_Math.slx** to perform mathematical operations among inputs a, b and c as . Call **Trial_Math.slx**

from `Test_Math.slx` using model block. Create a non-virtual bus at the top level of `Trial_Math.slx` to receive inputs from `Test_Math.slx`. Use the display block in `Test_Math.slx` to monitor the output of the mathematical operations, which come from `Trial_Math.slx`.

Answers

1. A
2. B
3. D
4. B
5. C
6. B
7. A
8. C
9. A
10. B

Section - III
Stateflow

CHAPTER 11
Getting Started with Stateflow

Introduction

In the previous chapters, we have learnt various aspects of MATLAB and Simulink-based development. This chapter takes the journey further with Stateflow and its applications in the area of model-based design and Simulation. Stateflow is a visual tool, which works either independently or in combination with Simulink, and offers the possibility of modeling complex systems using Statechart, flow graph, truth table, and so on. This chapter introduces the readers to the concepts of Stateflow and builds the foundation for coming chapters. After being aware of its key features, this chapter gives an overview of Stateflow Editor, a graphical interface of Stateflow. With this overview, the readers shall understand the capabilities and features accessible for development. The readers shall also get a glimpse of the usage of model explorer and diagnostics parameters. We request the readers to return to this chapter and reinforce their familiarity with Stateflow Editor.

Structure

In this chapter, we are going to cover the following topics:

- Introducing Stateflow
    - Key features of Stateflow

- Stateflow Editor
  - Title bar
  - Drawing area
  - Object palette
  - Model browser
  - Explorer bar
  - Status bar
  - Toolstrip
  - Symbols pane
  - Property inspector
- Model explorer
- Stateflow diagnostic parameters

Objectives

After studying this chapter, the reader will be able to:

- Get a brief overview of Stateflow
- Get familiarized with the features of Stateflow
- Learn in brief different components of Stateflow Editor
- Get introduced to functions available under toolstrip
- Become aware of Chart and Data properties
- Learn the application of symbols pane and property inspector
- Get an overview of the Model explorer window
- Become familiarized with Stateflow diagnostics parameters

Introducing Stateflow

Stateflow is a graphical design blockset that, in conjunction with Simulink, offers the possibility of design and development of control logic with the help of state transition diagrams, flow charts, state transition tables, and truth tables. Stateflow is available as part of the Simulink product and facilitates the design and develop supervisory control, task scheduling, fault management, communication protocols, user interfaces, and hybrid systems. Additionally, Stateflow describes complex system behavior using finite state machine theory in the same diagram. Stateflow allows modeling combinational and sequential decision logic together as a Simulink model block or as a MATLAB object. Simulating and debugging capabilities during runtime is beneficial to analyze and get the desired system behavior and performance.

Stateflow is chosen over Simulink to effectively implement State-based and conditional or timing-related logic. In case of continuous changes in a system, or when the system requires complex math operations, then Simulink is preferred over Stateflow. Stateflow is proven beneficial in various applications, especially in Embedded systems (Aviation, Automotive, Communication, Industrial, and Commercial), Graphical Interfacing, Hybrid systems, and so on. Stateflow runs on Microsoft Windows and UNIX systems. Before installing Stateflow, it is mandatory to get and activate the license as well as install MATLAB and Simulink. Additionally, a MATLAB-supported C/C++ compiler for generating code from a Stateflow model must be available. If you are using the Windows version on a laptop, please ensure that the Windows color palette is permitted to use more than 256 colors to avoid slow performance.

Key features of Stateflow

Stateflow has various applications in different areas as follows.

Designing control logic

Stateflow offers a simplified design tool to implement the complex logic design that can have defined operating modes with Statecharts, flow graphs, and truth tables, explained as follows. Stateflow can be implemented and simulated as part of a Simulink model using chart block:

- **Statecharts**: With the help of Stateflow, users can create graphical state diagrams by placing states, junctions, transitions, and so on in Stateflow Editor. It is also possible to create functions using flowchart notations, Simulink subsystems, MATLAB code, and truth tables. We shall discuss Statecharts in detail in *Chapter 13: Statecharts and Hierarchical State Model*.

- **Flowcharts**: Combinatorial logic can be implemented in Stateflow Editor using Flow charts, where the logic is implemented using junctions and transitions. Some commonly used pattern templates of decisive trees and iterative loops can be readily added with the help of Pattern Wizard. The flow chart logic can be implemented standalone or combined with state-based logic for transitions and internal logic. We shall discuss Flowcharts in detail in *Chapter 12: Flow Graph*.

- **Truth tables**: The combinatorial logic where output is dependent on input can be concisely implemented in tabular format using truth tables. Truth tables are generally used for decision-making during fault detection or mode switching. A Truth table can be used as a block in Simulink or a Stateflow function. The Truth table as a Simulink block required Stateflow. The Truth table as a function is executed only when the function is called. One needs to specify conditions, actions, and decisions for a truth table. We shall discuss Truth tables in detail in *Chapter 14: Event-Based Execution*.

Chart execution and debugging

An exciting feature of Stateflow allows users to visualize the system behavior during runtime so that they can ensure the behavior and performance with analysis and debugging:

- **Executing Stateflow charts**: The ability to run state diagram animations allows the user to visualize the system behavior effectively. Stateflow animation highlights the flow, currently active state, and transitions during runtime, observing which the system behavior can be visually analyzed.

- **Debugging Stateflow charts**: Along with the runtime animation options, Stateflow debugging options help debug the chart execution stepwise. The help of possibilities such as breakpoints with different settings, data value logging, and stepping options make debugging of Statecharts highly efficient.

Developing reusable logic with Stateflow

In order to save time and effort, Stateflow offers various options to implement and share reusable logic, explained as follows:

- **Implementing as a standalone chart**: With this option, the Statechart can be implemented as a standalone object without any Simulink model. The timing and state-based logic can be integrated directly with MATLAB as a chart object.

- **Implementing as functions**: With Stateflow, the State logic can be reused with Graphical functions, Atomic subcharts, and so on. Additionally, the functions developed in MATLAB can be integrated into Statechart as MATLAB functions. Similarly, Simulink logic can be reused in Statechart as Simulink functions. Furthermore, custom code can be reused as part of Stateflow too.

- **Sharing Stateflow chart logic**: When the Stateflow chart object is integrated with the MATLAB application, it can be later shared with users, including those who do not have Stateflow.

Validation and code generation

Stateflow facilitates design validation in combination with various Simulink products and supports code generation for the target hardware, explained as follows:

- **Design validation**: Stateflow can be used with different tools to achieve design validation. For example, there is a tool offered by Simulink named *Simulink requirements tool*, which supports linking requirements to Stateflow. Similarly, the coverage metrics are calculated with the Simulink Coverage tool. With the Simulink test tool, tests can be managed. Simulink checks and Simulink Design Verifier help validate the design against design errors, industry standards, and guidelines.
- **Code Generation**: Stateflow supports code generation for embedded systems with Simulink products. For example, C and C++ code generation is supported for the logic using Simulink Coder. Similarly, FPGA and ASIC-compliant VHDL and Verilog code can be generated with the help of HDL Coder. Structured text for PLCs and PACs can be generated with Simulink PLC Coder.

Stateflow Editor

Stateflow Editor offers an interactive user interface to manage the chart effectively. Stateflow Editor Interface looks somewhat similar to Simulink Editor Interface, with many options specially provided for chart operations. The interface allows its users to draw and manage graphical as well as non-graphical objects in a chart. The editor also offers options to simulate and debug the logic and is easy to access.

There are several ways to access the Stateflow Editor window, mentioned as follows:

1. Open a Simulink model and add a chart block to the model from the Stateflow library. Double-click the chart block, and the Stateflow Editor Window pops up.
2. Click **Simulink | Simulation | New** drop-down **| State Chart**. It adds a chart block as part of the Simulink model and opens it.
3. In the MATLAB command window, execute command **sfnew**, which opens a Simulink model with a chart block inside it.
4. In the MATLAB command window, execute the **Stateflow** command, and it will open a Simulink block containing a Chart block along with a Stateflow library file.
5. In the MATLAB menu, click **New** drop-down **| Stateflow Chart**. This option allows the user to create a standalone **.sfx** chart file.

Figure 11.1 shows the key elements of the Stateflow Editor Interface:

- Title bar
- Drawing area
- Object palette
- Model Browser
- Explorer bar
- Status bar
- Toolstrip
- Symbols pane
- Property inspector

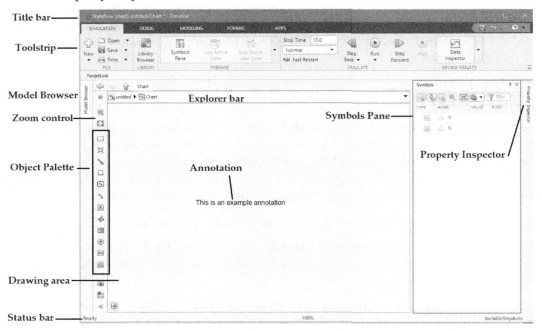

Figure 11.1: *Stateflow Editor Interface*

Title bar

The title bar is located at the top of the Editor window. For the chart placed in a Simulink model, the bar shows the Simulink model name/chart name. In the case of a standalone chart, the title bar indicates the chart name. The bar also shows with * next to the chart name if the file is unsaved.

Drawing area

The drawing area comprises the most significant area of Stateflow Editor. Users can see, add, and modify the chart with graphical and non-graphical objects such as states, junctions, transitions, annotations, images, and so on. In *figure 11.1*, we can see an example annotation located in the drawing area. More menu items are available for the chart from the right-click on the drawing area. Similarly, a menu specific to them shall appear from right-clicking the objects. These objects can be resized, moved, duplicated, renamed, formatted, and arranged with the help of such options. Zoom controls help navigate through the drawing area. For Simulink-based chart, on the bottom left side of the area, we can see a symbol indicating chart action language—MATLAB or C. For standalone charts, it is MATLAB by default.

Object palette

Object palette is located vertically on the left side of the drawing area, which makes adding regularly used objects, for example, state, connective junction, default transition, box, Simulink state, Simulink function, MATLAB function, graphical function, truth table, history junction, annotation, image, and so on, more convenient. For standalone charts, lesser icons are available in the Object palette. There are multiple ways to add an object from the Object palette to the drawing area as follows:

- Single-click the object icon, bring the cursor to the desired position in the drawing area and click again; the object shall be created at that location.
- Drag and drop the object icon from the Object palette to the drawing area, and a copy of the object shall be created.
- Double-click the object icon so that it is possible to click at different positions in the drawing area and add multiple objects at a time.

Model browser

Model browser is located on the left of the Object palette. The browser can be extended or hidden using the double arrow symbol at the bottom of the Object palette. The model browser displays a tree view of the chart, making navigation through different levels easier. It shows the name of the Simulink model and the charts and subcharts located within it; by clicking the chart name, a user can open any hierarchy level.

Explorer bar

The Explorer bar is located below the Toolstrip and above the drawing area. Explorer bar shows the complete hierarchy of the opened chart level, and by clicking the name of the specific chart level, one can jump directly to that hierarchy level. The Explorer bar can be hidden or displayed through an arrow symbol available at the top of the Object palette. There is a down arrow button at the right part of the Explorer bar, which shows the previous history of opened charts. Above the Explorer bar next to the chart name, three arrows- top, back, and forward arrows are available for navigating through the hierarchies of the Statechart and Simulink model.

Status bar

The Status bar is available at the bottom of the Stateflow Editor window. The bar shows different types of information, such as model processing state, diagnostic status, simulation time, current zoom level, solver name, and so on.

Toolstrip

Toolstrip is located below the Title bar. Toolstrip supports users by offering tools required regularly for development. In the case of a Chart as part of the Simulink model, the Toolstrip consists of five menu tabs containing various tools. These tabs are identical to Simulink models, with some operations specific to Stateflow. These tabs are—**SIMULATION**, **DEBUG**, **MODELING**, **FORMAT**, and **APPS**. In the case of a standalone Stateflow chart mode, a limited number of tools are available under three fixed tabs: state chart, debug, and format. As simulation and modeling-related tools are unavailable in standalone mode, we will focus on learning Simulink-based Toolstrip in this chapter.

Simulation

The **SIMULATION** tab provides tools for simulation, library, files, data, logging, and so on. Simulation tab is divided into five subsections: **FILE**, **LIBRARY**, **PREPARE**, **SIMULATE**, and **REVIEW RESULTS**. *Figure 11.2* shows the **SIMULATION** tab:

Figure 11.2: Simulation tab

- **FILE**: These tools are helpful to create and save new or open existing model files and print. *Table 11.1* briefly describes essential tools available in the File section, as mentioned earlier; some of the operations are the same as Simulink operations, explained in *Chapter 6: Simulink Editor with Environment*:

Operation	Symbol	Description
New model	✚	Creates a new model file as per the default settings
New	New ▼	Select one of the options from the drop-down to create a new file: • Blank model • Blank subsystem Create from the template: • Model • Subsystem • Statechart • Library • Project
Open	📁	• `Open`: Click on the Open button, and the browser window pops up • `Recent files`: Click on the arrow, and from the drop-down, select open or choose from recent files. • `Viewmarks`: Open from Viewmarks
Save	💾	• `Save`: Saves the changes made in chart and/or model. By default, the model file is saved in `.slx` format, which could be changed to `.mdl` format. Chart file is saved in `.sfx` format. • `Save as`: Click on the arrow, and from the drop-down, select save as; a browser window pops up. Here too, you have the option to choose the file format for Simulink. Available only for Simulink model integrated chart: • `Save as Viewmark`: The option enables saving the current chart and/or model as viewmark to be viewed later. • `Export to protected model`: For exporting as IP protected model copy • `Export as a template`: Chart can be reused as a template later • `Save as the previous version`: The user can save the model in `.slx` or `.mdl` format in any older release up to R2012b
Print	🖨	Prints the chart as per selected options

Table 11.1: Simulation tab file section

- **LIBRARY**: This option is used to launch the library browser, as shown in *table 11.2*:

Operation	Symbol	Description
Library Browser	Library Browser	This tool is available only for Simulink-based chart. It launches the Simulink library browser. Users can add any blocks from the library to the Simulink model file, but in the chart, the library blocks can be added only as part of the Simulink Function.

Table 11.2: Simulation tab Library Section

- **PREPARE**: These tools support operations concerning simulation, configuration, data, and logging, as specified in *table 11.3*:

Operation	Symbol	Description
Log Self Activity	Log Self Activity	Records logging data of the selected state and update the simulation results accordingly.
Log Child Activity	Log Child Activity	Records logging data of the selected state children and updates the simulation results accordingly.
Log Active State	Log Active State	Records the sequence of states becoming active.
Add Output Port	Add Output Port	Creates a Simulink output to monitor state during simulation
Configure Logging	Configure Logging	Opens Data Import/Export page of the model configuration parameters. For the description of the parameters, please refer to *Chapter 8: Configuration Parameter settings*.
Model Settings	Model Settings	This option also opens the Configuration Parameters dialog box.

Operation	Symbol	Description
Symbols Pane	Symbols Pane	Opens Symbols Pane of the right-side of the Drawing area. The symbols pane allows users to manage data. We shall discuss Symbols Pane in a further section.
Property Inspector	Property Inspector	Shows property inspector dialog box on the right side of the Drawing area. Property Inspector allows adjustment of Chart properties if no other object is selected. If another object, for example, state, is selected, it will enable editing state properties.
Update Model	Update Model	Compiles the model file and shows warnings or errors if any
Update Chart	Update Chart	Verifies Chart syntax and shows errors and warnings if any
Chart Properties	Chart Properties	Opens a dialog box with chart property settings similar to `Property Inspector` settings. It contains action language, State machine type, Update method, fixed point settings, and so on options.

Table 11.3: Simulation tab Prepare Section

- **SIMULATE**: As the name suggests, this section offers simulation options such as simulation time, speed, steps, and so on, as described in *table 11.4*:

Operation	Symbol	Description
Stop time	Stop Time	Maximum time in seconds until which we want to run a simulation. The default stop time is 10.0 seconds. We can also give the value as inf if the simulation is required until it is manually stopped.
Speed	Normal / Accelerator / Rapid Accelerator	Determines the simulation speed that can be set to the normal accelerator or rapid accelerator. The default value is normal.
Fast Restart	Fast Restart	Model is compiled only once in the beginning and not later.

Operation	Symbol	Description
Step Back	Step Back ▼	Step back: To go to the previous simulation state as configured
		Configure Simulation stepping: Enable stepping back, configure the number of past steps saved, the interval between saved steps, and the number of steps to go back/forward during each operation. By default, the stepping is disabled, the number of past steps saved, the interval is 10, and the number of steps for step/back and forward is 1, but we can edit these values.
Step Forward	Step Forward	Step forward by configuring step number. By default, the simulation steps forward by 1 step (1 sample time).
Run/Pause	Run ▼	• **Run**: Start the simulation of the Simulink model • **Pause**: Pause the simulation • **Simulation pacing**: Enables the simulation pacing to slow down or expedite; the dialog box also has a slider to set the simulation time per wall clock second (real-time)
Stop	Stop	Stops the ongoing simulation of the model

Table 11.4: Simulation tab Simulate Section

- **REVIEW RESULTS**: This option launches Simulink Data Inspector, as described in *table 11.5*:

Operation	Symbol	Description
Data Inspector	Data Inspector	Launches Simulink Data Inspector, where we can see the logged chart/state data simulation results. The data inspector offers the following functions: Log Chart/state-level data Import Data from MATLAB Export Data to MATLAB Write scripts

Table 11.5: Simulation tab review results section

Modeling

The modeling tab contains various options for modeling, such as setting up preferences, Design tools, objects, patterns, properties, simulation, and so on, as shown in *figure 11.3*:

Figure 11.3: Modeling tab

The modeling tab is distributed into various sections—**EVALUATE & MANAGE**, **DESIGN**, **SETUP**, **COMPONENT**, **COMPILE**, and **SIMULATE**, explained as follows:

- **EVALUATE & MANAGE**: This section is primarily similar to the section available in Simulink. We shall learn about some of the crucial functions in *table 11.6*:

Operation	Symbol	Description
Model Advisor	Model Advisor	• **Model Advisor**: Launches Model Advisor dialog box, and we can run modeling guidelines and standards compliance checks for the system we have selected. Same as Simulink. • **Model Advisor Dashboard** • **Preferences**: Lets the user set model advisor preferences
Find	Find	• **Find in Chart**: Search for a string in chart • **Find and replace in Chart**: Search the string and replace it with a new string
Compare	Compare	Compares model files, same as Simulink.
Environment	Environment	• **Set environment settings for the model**: Enable/disable Model Browser, Explorer bar, Zoom, Smart guides, Toolstrip, and Status bar. • **Stateflow Preferences**: Adjust style- color scheme and font for the Chart, and syntax highlighting- disable/enable or adjust highlighting color

Table 11.6: Modeling tab Evaluate & Manage Section

- **DESIGN DATA**: This section offers several different tools to manage the chart data effectively. Some of these tools are explained in brief in *table 11.7*:

Operation	Symbol	Description
\multicolumn{3}{c}{Data Repositories}		
Base Workspace	Base Workspace	The button shows base workspace variables under the Simulink Root section of Model Explorer, the same as Simulink
Model Workspace	Model Workspace	Opens Model Workspace tab of Model Explorer browser and shows the Data object view of model local workspace variables, where we can create/edit variables.
Data Dictionary	Data Dictionary	Opens the data dictionary Design Data linked to the model in Model Explorer. If there is no data dictionary linked, it can be linked through the `Link to Data Dictionary` option.
\multicolumn{3}{c}{Data Management}		
Symbols pane	Symbols Pane	Same as explained in `Prepare` tab. We shall discuss this pane later in this chapter.
Property Inspector	Property Inspector	Same as explained in `Prepare` tab. Shows the property inspector dialog box on the right side of the drawing area.
Model Explorer	Model Explorer	Launches Model Explorer, where it lists all model elements along with their information in different columns. It allows managing chart data and settings.
\multicolumn{3}{c}{System Design}		
Schedule Editor	Schedule Editor	Launches Schedule Editor window that allows users to manage and arrange the partitions in the diagram and specify execution orders.
Simulation custom code	C C++	Opens `Simulation Target` page in `Configuration` parameter
\multicolumn{3}{c}{Add Inputs from Simulink / Output to Simulink}		

Operation	Symbol	Description
Data Input Data Output		Data input option creates a new input port to the chart from the Simulink model. Data output option creates a chart output port to the Simulink model.
Message Input Message Output		Message input option creates a new input port for message to the chart from the Simulink model. Message output option creates a chart output port for message to the Simulink model.
Event Input Event Output		Event input option creates a new input port for the event to the chart from the Simulink model. Event output option creates a chart output port for an event to the Simulink model.
Add local variable to Chart		
Local Data		This option creates a local variable in chart
Parameter		This option creates a parameter in chart
Constant		This option creates a constant in chart
Datastore		This option creates data store variable in chart
Event		This option creates a new event in chart
Message		This option creates a message in chart

Table 11.7: Modeling tab design data section

- **SETUP**: This section provides access to chart and machine properties, as well as Model configuration settings, as explained in *table 11.8*:

Operation	Symbol	Description
Chart Properties		Launches Chart Property settings dialog box.
State Properties		The additional option becomes available when a state is selected. It opens the State properties dialog box that allows adjustment of the label, actions, and logging data output for the State.

Operation	Symbol	Description
Machine Properties		Launches machine property settings dialog box.
Model Settings		Opens Model configuration settings window.

Table 11.8: Modeling tab Setup section

- **COMPONENT**: This section provides options for inserting a chart element, component, or container into the drawing area or creating a new component from the selected model elements. *Table 11.9* gives an overview of such elements:

Operation	Symbol	Description
Insert State	Insert State	The State is an essential element of Stateflow. It represents the operating mode in the system. After clicking this button, click the desired location in the drawing area, and a new state shall be created. We shall learn more about states in *Chapter 13: Statechart and Hierarchical State Model*.
Insert Subchart	Insert Subchart	Inserts a new subchart block in the drawing area. Subchart represents a chart within a chart. It creates an additional level of hierarchy. We shall learn more about the Subchart in *Chapter 13: Statechart and Hierarchical State Model*.
Atomic Subchart	Atomic Subchart	An Atomic subchart is a type of subchart where the subchart behaves as a standalone chart within a chart. It helps create reusable components.
Insert Junction	Insert Junction	A connective junction shall be added to the chart with this option. A connective junction is a round-shaped graphical object that creates multiple variations in the decision path.
Default Transition	Default Transition	Default transition is connected in Flowgraph to a junction and to the state in Statechart to indicate the starting point of the simulation.
Graphical Function	Graphical Function	The Graphical function helps create reusable flow graph-based logic. It works as a normal function with arguments with a flow graph as its logic.

Operation	Symbol	Description
Simulink State	Simulink State	Simulink State block allows the users to implement a state containing Simulink-based logic in a Stateflow.
Simulink Function	Simulink Function	Enables the creation of a reusable Simulink logic-based function in a Stateflow.
MATLAB Function	MATLAB Function	Allows usage of MATLAB function into a Stateflow. Helps easy integration of MATLAB-based logic into Stateflow. We shall learn about these functions in *Chapter 14: Event-Based Execution*.
Truth Table	Truth Table	This block creates combinatorial logic in a table form. Like other functions, it has function arguments, conditions, and decisions. We shall learn about it in *Chapter 14: Event-Based Execution*.
Insert Box	Insert Box	Box creates a level of hierarchy in a chart. We can group states and functions under a box. To access box content from outside, for example calling a function located inside a box, the name of the box must be included as a prefix to the function name.
History Junction	History Junction	History junction is a graphical block that records the state data and restores it upon reactivation when placed inside a state.
Add Superstate	Add Superstate	For the selected state(s), this option places the selected objects into a Superstate. A superstate is a parent state containing one or more children states. Similarly, the other options place the selected objects into a subchart, a box, or a subcharted box.
Group Selection	Group Selection	This option changes the Group & Subchart setting of the selected state to Grouped, making the subcomponents located inside that state grouped, which helps in resizing or modifying.
Subchart Selection	Subchart Selection	The selected state converts into a subchart, and if there are any subcomponents, they become available as part of this new subchart, and the existing transitions change into super transitions.

Table 11.9: Modeling tab component section

- **EDIT**: This section comprises of two tools, pattern and decomposition, as explained in *table 11.10*:

Operation	Symbol	Description
Pattern		This tool is helpful, especially in the case of Flow graph-based logic. It offers the possibility to automatically create patterns in the chart such as If-else, For loop, While loop, Switch case, and so on. Moreover, it also has options to save and reload custom patterns. We shall understand the usage of this tool in *Chapter 12: Flow Graph*.
Decomposition		Chart decomposition specifies whether the substates of a state can be active, mutually exclusive, or in parallel. Exclusive (OR) composition is a default composition, and only the substates can be active at a time. Parallel (AND) decomposition makes the substates of a state simultaneously active. We shall learn more about decomposition in *Chapter 13: Statechart and Hierarchical State Model*.

Table 11.10: Modeling tab edit section

MODELING tab has two additional sections, **COMPILE** and **SIMULATE**. **COMPILE** tab offers **CHART** and **MODEL** options, same as explained in Debug tab. Similarly, **SIMULATE** section has options the same as the **SIMULATION** tab.

Debug

This tab offers tools for visualizing and debugging Statechart during simulation, as shown in *figure 11.4*:

Figure 11.4: Debug tab

Debug tab is divided into various subsections: **PERFORMANCE**, **DIAGNOSTICS & TOOLS**, **BREAKPOINTS**, **ANIMATION**, **COMPILE**, and **DEBUG**. *Table 11.11* explains some of the critical functions in brief:

Operation	Description
Performance	
Performance advisor	The behavior of Performance Advisor in Stateflow is the same as Simulink, where it is used to analyze the model for identification of ineffective conditions, which will, in turn, improve simulation speed automatically. This tool launches the Performance Advisor dialog box, where we can run the checks on the model after creating a baseline. The .html report is generated, and the list of the pass, fail, warn, and not run checks.
Solver Profiler	Like Simulink, this tool launches the Solver Profiler window that helps examine solver and model patterns to identify issues leading to reduced simulation performance. The profiler logs all significant events that can affect solver performance.
Diagnostics & Tools	
Diagnostic Viewer	Launches Diagnostic Viewer window, where we can observe the errors and warnings generated during chart and model compilation or simulation
Stateflow Diagnostics	Opens the Stateflow page in the Diagnostics tab of model configuration settings, where users can set diagnostic parameters.
Edit-time Errors and Warnings	This option is checked by default, enabling the display of possible errors and warnings during chart editing.
Information overlays	This tool offers four options for library links, mentioned as follows: • **Show all links**: Shows all library links as link symbols on the bottom left corner of the block. • **Show user-defined links**: Shows links for user-defined blocks • **Disabled links**: Shows disabled links too as a broken link symbol • **Hide all links**: Hides all library links
Comment Out	Any selected object can be commented out; in other words, it can be omitted from the simulation.

Operation	Description
Breakpoints	
Pause time	Specify the pause time in seconds; it pauses simulation precisely at a given time.
Add Breakpoint	• **Add Breakpoint**: Add a conditional breakpoint to the chart, selected state, or transition. A red breakpoint symbol appears on the object. For chart, breakpoint pauses simulation during Chart entry. In the case of State, simulation is paused on State entry, during, or exit. For transition, the simulation is paused, either when the transition is valid or when the transition is tested. • **Clear breakpoints**: Add breakpoints option changes into Clear breakpoints when a breakpoint is set to the selected object. It removes the breakpoint.
Breakpoints List	• **Breakpoints List**: Shows a list of all breakpoints along with a checkbox, delete button, path, type, condition, and hits.
Animation	
Animation speed	Animation speed can be adjusted to any of these options: Lightning Fast, Fast, Medium, Slow, and None. By default, the speed is fast.
Highlighting	There are two options: maintain highlighting after simulation stops and remove the highlighting. By default, the highlighting is maintained, which means that the active state boundary is highlighted, and transitions taken are highlighted in blue when the simulation is paused or stopped.
Compile	
Update Model	Compiles the model and displays warnings or errors in the diagnostics viewer, if any
Update Chart	Compiles chart and shows syntax errors or warnings in diagnostics viewer if any
Debug	
Stop time	Simulation stop time for Simulink model, same as mentioned in Simulation tab

Operation	Description
Run/ Continue	These are the available options for navigating through steps during debugging.
Step back/ forward	
Step Over/in/ Out	
Stop debugging	

Table 11.11: Debug tab

Format

Format tab contains some fixed and additional subsections that appear based on the selected object. Format tab has been shown in *figure 11.5* after selecting multiple objects:

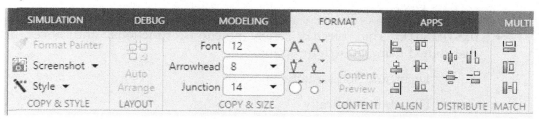

Figure 11.5: Format tab

Format tab has two fixed subsections: **COPY & STYLE** and **LAYOUT**. It has the following subsections: **COPY & SIZE**, **CONTENT**, **ALIGN**, **DISTRIBUTE**, and **MATCH**.

- **COPY & STYLE**: It has three functions: `Format painter`, `Screenshot`, and `Style`. Format painter is used to copying formatting. Screenshot offers two options: copy chart to clipboard—as bitmap image or as Windows metafile. Style offers two settings, Style, and Highlighting, as explained in the Environment setting as part of the `MODELING` tab.

- **LAYOUT**: Auto arrange option arranges the states and improves the chart layout. For example, it resizes the state if the text overlaps with transitions or state boundaries. Auto arrange option can also be accessed by keyboard shortcut *Ctrl + Shift + A*.

- **COPY & SIZE**: This subsection appears when a graphical object is selected. It has the possibility of three types of size adjustments—Font, Arrowhead, and Junction, based on the selected object. For example, for a State, Font and Arrowhead size can be adjusted, whereas Arrowhead and Junction sizes can be altered for a junction.

- **CONTENT**: This subsection appears when a Subchart is selected. It enables or disables the content preview, where the Subchart content can be seen from a higher hierarchy level. It helps the user to have a quick look at the content of Subchart without opening it.
- **ALIGN**: The selected objects such as states, junctions, functions, and boxes can be aligned to one another in six different ways:
    - Align left
    - Align center
    - Align Right
    - Align Top
    - Align Middle
    - Align Bottom
- **DISTRIBUTE**: The selected states, junctions, functions, and boxes are distributed using these four options:
    - Distribute horizontally
    - Distribute vertically
    - Even horizontal gaps
    - Even vertical gaps
- **MATCH**: For size matching of the selected states, junctions, functions, and boxes, Stateflow offers three options:
    - Match width
    - Match height
    - Match size

Symbols pane

Symbols pane is a tool that supports the management of chart data, events, and messages. Symbols pane can be accessed from **Modeling** → **Design Data** → **Symbols** Pane. After clicking this option, the Symbols pane window pops up on the right side of the drawing area. Symbols pane supports multiple data-related operations, for example, add, modify, or delete chart data variables. It also promotes updating the object name, port number, value, type, and so on, properties. The data can be added here manually or by clicking the Resolve undefined variables button. The hierarchy can be adjusted using the button. Moreover, the Symbols pane also can highlight the usage of data variables in the chart for all read or write operations. For advanced properties, **Property Inspector** is used in conjunction with **Symbols Pane**. *Figure 11.6* shows an example of **Symbols Pane** usage and the available functions.

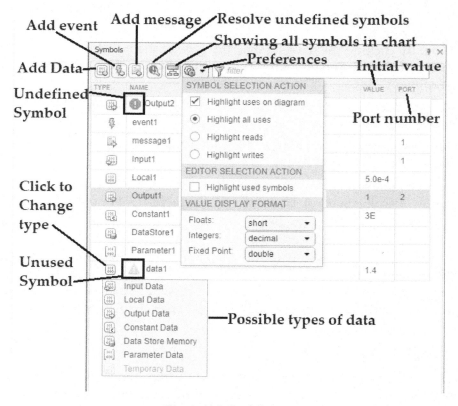

Figure 11.6: Symbols pane

As shown in *figure 11.6*, the Symbols pane supports the following operations:

- **Add data, event, and message**: Manually add data variable, event, and message.

- **Resolve undefined symbols**: The symbol pane shows all undefined variables in the chart with a red error symbol, for example, **Output2**. Based on the usage, it proposes the type of data for such variables used in the chart. Clicking the resolve undefined symbols option will automatically create variables for all such cases.

- **Showing all symbol in the chart**: Clicking this button toggles between showing all chart symbols and showing symbols on current and below levels of hierarchy.

- **Preferences**: This drop-down has tick boxes and a selection for highlighting the usage of selected variables in the chart. Based on the selection, it highlights all uses, read uses or write uses of that variable. This menu also has a drop-down for value display format in the case of **Floats**, **Integers**, and **Fixed point**.
- **Type**: By clicking the data symbol, the type of the variable can be modified to **Input**, **Local**, **Output**, **Constant**, **Data Store Memory**, **Parameter**, or **Temporary data**.
- **Value**: We can specify the initial value for the applicable variable types, such as constant, output, local variable, and so on.
- **Port**: Port numbers are assigned automatically but can be selected from the drop-down.
- **Delete unused data**: The pane shows the name of unused data with a yellow warning symbol. Users can choose to delete it or use it.
- **Update Advanced properties**: If any property other than the options mentioned earlier needs to be updated for the data, select the desired variable in the Symbols pane and open **Property Inspector**. In **Property Inspector**, the properties shall be adjusted. Alternatively, the **Data** properties can be updated with the help of **Model Explorer**, which can be accessed from **Modeling | Design Data | Model Explorer** button.

Property inspector

The Property Inspector window can be expanded from the right-most side of the Stateflow Editor. The window can also be opened from the **MODELING | Design Data | Property Inspector** button. Property Inspector is helpful in updating different types of properties: chart properties, data properties, object properties, and so on. In this section, we shall discuss chart properties and data properties.

Chart properties

Chart properties contain different settings as follows:

- **Update method**: When a model is part of a Simulink model, the **Update** method property indicates how the chart will be woken up during simulation. There are three settings available for this property: **Inherited**, **Discrete**, and **Continuous**. The default property value is Inherited. In the case of **Inherited**, the chart sample time is derived based on the fastest data input sample rate. If no data input or events are available, the chart sample time is derived from the Simulink parent subsystem. In the case of the **Discrete update** method, the chart is woken up cyclically based on the specified sample time. In the case of the **Continuous update** method, the sample time is derived based on the selected solver. The hit times are divided into major time steps and minor time steps for continuous sample time. The chart output is updated at every major sample time, and the calculations are performed at every minor sample time. To increase accuracy, `Enable zero-crossing detection` option is enabled for the `Continuous setting`, which can be disabled if required.

- `Sample time`: This setting is applicable only in the case of a `Discrete` setting. Any non-zero value can be given as sample time, which specifies the regular interval the chart is activated. In the case of `Inherited`, `Sample time` becomes -1.

- `Create output for monitoring`: This option is disabled by default but can be enabled for the chart using the tick box. When enabled, the output is created to monitor either the child state activity or the leaf state activity. Additionally, `Data` and `Enum` name options are enabled, which by default are `ChartMode` and `ChartModeType`, respectively. The enumerated type can be defined manually using another option, where the MATLAB template can be modified as per requirement.

Figure 11.7 shows the chart properties in property inspector.

Figure 11.7: Chart properties with property inspector

- **Execute (enter) chart at Initialization**: This setting is available under Advanced properties. By default, the tick box is unticked for this setting. As its name suggests, it determines whether to execute the chart during model initialization (time 0) or the first input event.
- **Saturate on integer overflow**: The setting is enabled by default and specifies whether any overflow shall be saturated. When enabled, it ensures that the overflow during arithmetic operation is saturated to a minimum or maximum value.
- **Initialize Outputs every time chart wakes up**: This setting is disabled by default, and when enabled, the chart outputs are reset to the specified initial value or value 0 during every execution. This setting ensures that the newly calculated output values are available during every execution.
- **Support Variable-Size Arrays**: This setting enables the usage of data in a chart with varying dimensions. The setting is enabled by default.
- **Export Chart Level Functions**: With this property, the functions from the chart can be called from another part of the Simulink model outside the chart by using the full name of the function as the syntax, for example, as chart **name.function** name. This property is disabled by default.
    - **Treat exported functions as globally visible**: This property is applicable only when Export chart level functions property is enabled. When this property is enabled, the chart functions can be called anywhere in the Simulink model, just with the function name.
- **Enable super step semantics**: The property allows the chart to make multiple transitions in each step to reach a stable state. By default, the property is disabled. The property is not applicable for the **Continuous update** method.
    - **Max iterations in a superstep**: According to its name, the property sets a maximum number of iterations possible in a superstep. The default value is 1,000. After too many iterations, we may choose to proceed or throw an error.
- **Action language**: The property defines the syntaxes for state action and transition action in the chart. There are two possibilities of action language: MATLAB and C. The Action language of the chart can be identified from the symbol at the bottom left corner of the drawing area. By default, the chart action language is MATLAB.

    These are some of the differences between MATLAB and C action languages:
    - MATLAB follows one-bit indexing for vectors and matrices, whereas C follows zero-bit indexing. In MATLAB, it is represented, for example, as X(1,2), whereas in C, it would be defined as *X[1][2]*.

- The syntax is corrected automatically while changing the action language from C to MATLAB. For example, Increment and decrement operators are represented in C as *x++*, whereas in MATLAB as *x=x+1*.
- Assignment operators can be represented in C as *x+=y*, *x-=y*, *x*=y*, and *x/=y*. In MATLAB they are represented as *x=x+y*, *x=x-y*, *x=x*y*, *x=x/y*.
- The evaluation operator in C can be *x!=y* or *x<>=y* or *!x*, in MATLAB, it should be used as *x~=y* or *~x*.
- In MATLAB comments are written with %, in C the comments are written with // and /* */.
- Binary operators %%, >>, << are supported in C, but not in MATLAB. In MATLAB, rem, mod, or bitshift functions are used instead.
- Bit shift operators &, |, and ^ are supported in C; in MATLAB, we shall use functions such as bitand, bitor, and bitxor.
- Conditional and loop statements if, while, for, and so on are supported in MATLAB; in C flow graph is to be used instead.
- MATLAB- transition actions are written in curly brackets ({}); in C, they are not required.
- MATLAB supports datatypes Boolean, **single**, **double**, **int8**, **int16**, **int32**, **uint8**, **uint16**, **uint32**, and so on, whereas C supports Boolean, **single**, **double**, **int8**, int16, int32, int64, **uint8**, **uint16**, **uint32**, **uint64**, **string**, and so on.

- **Enable C-bit operation**: This property is accessible only when the chart action language is set to C. If this property is enabled, then the bitwise operators &, |, and ^ perform a bitwise operation on the operands. If the property is disabled, then & and | perform the logical operation, and ^ works as the power operator.

- **State machine type**: State machine type is derived from finite state machine type. The property represents the available Stateflow semantics. There are three options: Classic, Mealy, and Moore. Classic combines both Mealy and Moore and offers a complete set of semantics, whereas Mealy and Moore offer a subset of semantics. One difference between the Mealy and Moore machines is that the output of the Mealy machine depends on inputs and state, and the output of the Moore machine depends only on the state. The default value is Classic.

- **Use Strong Data Typing with Simulink I/O**: This property is not available in Property Inspector but is available as part of Chart Properties.

It is enabled only when the action language is chosen as C. By default, it is enabled. When enabled, the datatype of Simulink model input must match the input datatype of Stateflow input; else, it causes a mismatch error.

- **Fixed-point properties**: These properties are available only for the chart with MATLAB as an action language. In MATLAB, the **fi** object is used to assign a fixed-point datatype. The property `Treat these inherited Simulink signal types as fi objects` decide whether all fixed-point inputs are treated as fi objects or all fixed-point, and integer inputs are treated as **fi** objects. MATLAB chart **fimath** allows the use of MATLAB default settings or specifies custom settings.

Data properties

Property inspector allows the users to modify properties of data variables when selected in symbols pane. Depending on the scope of the variable chosen, these settings vary accordingly. Stateflow allows us to adjust properties categorized into basic, logging, advanced, and so on. We shall have an overview of some of the essential properties that can be altered using Property Inspector. Alternatively, Model Explorer can be used to update these properties.

- **Constant**: For constant data, the properties such as **Scope**, **Size**, **Type**, and **Constant** value can be adjusted in the **Property Inspector** window. The scope can be changed to **Local**, **Input**, **Output**, **Parameter**, or **Data** stores memory. Size can be any scalar. Similarly, Type can be selected from the drop-down based on the options applicable for chart action language, as explained in the previous section. The default type is double. A constant value can be specified if not already done in the **Symbols** pane. In the **Advanced** properties, Allow the initial value to resolve to a parameter and Lock data type against Fixed-point tools that are disabled by default. Add to watch window option adds the constant to the watch window, which is available for all variables.

- **Input**: Similar to **Constant**, Input offers general properties such as Scope, Port, Size, and Type. Size is −1 by default, and data type is Inherited from Simulink, which can be changed from the drop-down to available types. In Advanced properties, **Variable size** and **Lock data type** are available. Moreover, properties such as Unit, Complexity, Minimum, and Maximum value can be specified as required.

- **Parameter**: Parameter properties are simple. The parameter allows the user to set Scope, Size, and Type properties. Advanced properties have Tunable Parameter enabled by default, Lock data type property, and complexity, which is off by default.

- **Data store memory**: This data has only the Scope property. The other properties are deactivated or non-applicable.
- **Output**: For Output data, General properties consist of Scope, Port, Size, Type, and Initial value. Additionally, logging can be activated for Outputs using the tick box **Log Signal data** or **Test point**. The name can be custom, and data points can be selected to be logged along with its decimation. Different tick boxes are available in Advanced properties, similar to other data variables. It also has properties identical to Input- Unit, Complexity, Minimum, Maximum value, and so on.

Figure 11.8 shows the property inspector parameters available for output:

Figure 11.8: Output data properties with property inspector

- **Local**: Local has General properties Scope, Size, Type, and Initial value. Additionally, it has logging properties the same as output. Advanced properties are also identical, except the Unit property is not applicable for Local.

- **Event**: Event has fixed Scope property that has value Local by default. If the scope is changed to Input from Simulink or Output to Simulink option, then additional properties Port and Trigger become available. Port number is assigned automatically, and Trigger has a default Function call, but it can be changed to Rising, Falling, or Either from the drop-down for input. In the case of output, the Trigger can be a Function call or Either edge. Additionally, the tick box can set breakpoints during the Start of the broadcast or the end of the broadcast. We shall learn more about Events and Messages in *Chapter 14: Event-Based Execution*.

- **Message**: Message offers Scope, Type, Size, Port, and Initial value properties. Depending on chosen Scope—Local, Input, or Output, other properties become available. For example, in the case of Local and Input, Message Queue properties can be set. For Input, Use Internal Queue can be disabled, whereas, for Local, it is enabled by default and cannot be altered. Here Queue capacity, overflow Diagnostic, Queue type—FIFO, LIFO, and Priority can be set. Advanced property has Allow initial value to resolve to a parameter and Complexity properties.

Model Explorer

Model Explorer is a valuable tool in chart and data management. It can be used as an alternative to the symbols pane and property inspector for creating, deleting, and modifying Simulate and Stateflow variables. It is also used for managing Base workspace, Model workspace, and Data dictionary-related data. With the help of model explorer, model properties, chart properties, state properties, data properties, and so on can be updated. Model Explorer can manage the scope and visibility of data variables effectively. Model Explorer is accessible from the **Modeling | Design Data | Model Explorer** button.

For the sake of visualization, the Model Explorer window can be divided into four parts: **Menu** and main **Toolbar**, **Model Hierarchy** pane, **Contents** pane, and **Dialog** pane. The *figure 11.9* shows an example chart data in a Model Explorer window:

Figure 11.9: Model Explorer

- **Menu**: As can be perceived from the preceding image, the Menu bar is available at the top of Model Explorer. Below the menu bar, the main toolbar is located, which has the shortcuts to save, open, cut, paste, and delete data. The icons are also available to add data, events, messages, and so on.

- **Model Hierarchy pane**: Below the Main toolbar, on the left side, the Model hierarchy pane offers a tree view of the model hierarchy from the Simulink root. Along with the Base and model workspace, the Chart name can be seen, expanding which we can navigate to the chart components such as states, subcharts, functions, and so on. Right clicking the elements, such as chart name, shows some menu items; for example, the find referenced variable function can be used from this menu to find variables. Similarly, right-click on workspace has the option to show unused variables.

- **Contents Pane**: Next to the Model hierarchy pane is the **Contents** pane, where the data variables and their properties can be added, removed, or revised. From the **Contents** of option, one can choose to see data from chart level only or chart level along with its children. Users can select any view of choice based on the requirement from the column view drop-down. The Stateflow view is selected by default, which shows Stateflow relevant columns. From the filter, only the objects that should be visible can be chosen, and the rest can be removed. For example, if the transitions are visible in the view but are not required, they can be filtered out. In the pane, one can see different types of data variables—local, input, output, constant, data store, parameter, and their relevant properties—such as name, port, scope, datatype, initial value, and so on.

- **Dialog Pane**: The dialog pane facilitates editing for the detailed properties of the element selected in the Model Hierarchy pane of **Contents** pane. For example, model properties can be updated by clicking the Simulink model name in Model Hierarchy. Similarly, Chart properties or State properties can be modified by selecting the Chart or State name in the Hierarchy pane. If a data element is selected in the **Contents** pane, the data properties concerning that element shall be visible in the **Dialog** pane. In *figure 11.9*, the data variable **Output1** is selected in the contents pane, and the properties of the variable are available for editing in the **Dialog** pane. These properties are the same as discussed in Property Inspector. If any modifications are performed on them, later clicking **Apply** button will save the changes.

Stateflow diagnostics parameters

The Stateflow diagnostics parameter is a list of error-prone situations for which the users can opt for setting an error or warning or ignore the condition. There are multiple ways to access the Diagnostics parameters: such as open **Debug | Diagnostics | Stateflow Diagnostics** operation. Another option is to open **Modeling | Setup | Model Settings** and navigate to the Stateflow page in the **Diagnostics** pane. In case of error occurrence, the simulation stops. In the case of a warning, the warning message is displayed along with additional information links. The *figure 11.10* shows the list of parameters and their default values:

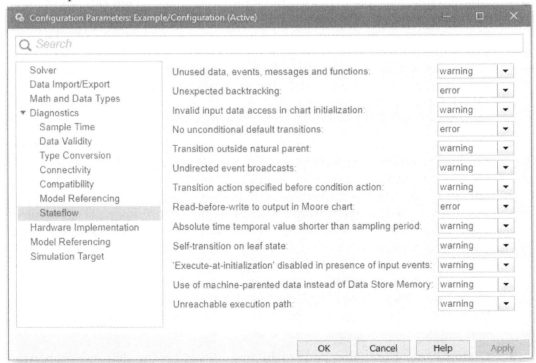

Figure 11.10: *Stateflow diagnostics parameters*

These are the parameters shown in *figure 11.10*:

- **Unused data, events, messages, and functions**: The default value for this parameter is a warning. It indicates all unused data, events, messages, and functions from the chart. Users may choose to delete them or keep them. Clearing the unused data may help the user with model size optimization.

- **Unexpected backtracking**: Stateflow throws an error and stops simulation by default in case backtracking is detected. In the case of backtracking, there are multiple transition paths to a junction, but there is no unconditional path forward to a terminating junction or state; due to that, some actions are unexpectedly executed. To avoid this issue, an unconditional path is added from that junction.

- **Invalid input data access in chart initialization**: The default setting for the parameter is a warning. When Execute at Initialization property is true, the default transition path is executed, and unstable behavior may be observed due to the transient nature during Chart initialization, as some inputs may not be available. To avoid such issues, it is advised not to specify specific actions as part of the default transition path of the chart.

- **No unconditional default transitions**: An error is thrown when no unconditional default transition is available to the state. Add an unconditional default transition to resolve the error.

- **Transition outside natural parent**: A warning is indicated for this situation when a transition loops outside of the parent state or junction.

- **Undirected event broadcasts**: By default, a warning is given for undirected event broadcasts, as it may result in inefficient code generation for the chart.

- **Transition action specified before condition action**: This implementation causes a warning from Stateflow by default. In the case of multiple transition segments, if a transition action is specified on the segment before the one with condition action, this warning indicates the possibility of out-of-order simulation.

- **Read-before-write to output in Moore chart**: This case results in an error, as it violates the design rules of the Moore state machine. Ideally, the output should depend only on the state and not on the previous output value, which may occur during this situation.

- **Absolute time temporal value shorter than the sampling period**: A warning shall be given if the temporal condition requires a shorter time than the Statechart sample time.

- **Self-transition on leaf state**: Self-transition on leaf state generates a warning to indicate the potential of cases where there is no action on the transition or in the state, so such chart execution does not make any difference.

- **Execute-at-Initialization disabled in the presence of input events**: This implementation results in a warning in case of enabled or triggered charts are not running during initialization, as the results may not be reliable.

- **Unreachable execution path**: A warning is shown for the transitions with a dangling transition, or the transition can never be reached.

Conclusion

This chapter has presented the readers well with Stateflow and its key features. Readers can decide when to choose Stateflow for their applications. The readers have been acquainted with various sections of Stateflow Editor. The chapter has briefly explained all the essential functions offered by Stateflow as part of toolstrip. This chapter has presented fundamental Chart properties and Data properties to the users. After studying this chapter, the readers have gained confidence in Stateflow functionalities and have prepared themselves for the hands-on in the upcoming chapters. The reader knows how to use Symbols pane, Property Inspector, and Model Explorer during implementation. The chapter has also introduced the readers to the possible Stateflow Diagnostics warnings or errors. The upcoming chapter introduces Flow Graph, using which the readers shall implement various logical patterns by following simple examples. The chapter also familiarizes the readers with concepts of Junctions, Transitions, Graphical functions, and so on. The reader also understands how to simulate the flow graph with Simulink.

Points to remember

- Stateflow is a graphical design tool that allows control logic development with state transition diagrams, flow charts, state transition tables, and truth tables.

- Stateflow is available as part of the Simulink blockset, or it can work as a standalone Chart with MATLAB.

- Stateflow is chosen over Simulink to effectively implement State-based and conditional or timing-related logic.

- Simulink is preferred over Stateflow in case of continuous changes in a system.

- Statecharts are graphical state diagrams created by placing states, junctions, transitions, and so on in a Chart block.

- Flow charts implement combinatorial logic using junctions and transitions.

- Stateflow Editor is a graphical interface that allows its users to draw and manage graphical as well as non-graphical objects in a chart.

- In the Drawing area, users can see, add, and modify the chart with graphical and non-graphical objects such as states, junctions, transitions, annotations, Images, and so on
- Object palette contains icons of State, Connective Junction, Default transition, Box, Simulink state, Simulink function, MATLAB function, Graphical function, Truth table, History junction, Annotation, Image, and so on.
- Toolstrip consists of five tabs: Simulation, Debug, Modeling, Format, and Apps.
- The symbols pane supports the management of chart data, events, and messages.
- Chart Action language defines the syntaxes for state action and transition action. There are two possible action languages: MATLAB and C.
- There are three types of State machines: Classic, Mealy, and Moore.
- Model Explorer manages model properties and data.
- Stateflow Diagnostics parameter lists error situations with three possible settings- none, warning, and error.

Multiple choice questions

1. **Stateflow can be used only in combination with Simulink.**
    a. True
    b. False

2. **Which of the following options are key features of Stateflow?**
    a. Code generation
    b. Animation
    c. Reusable logic
    d. All of the above

3. **What is the default action language of a Chart?**
    a. C
    b. C++
    c. MATLAB
    d. Java

4. Which of the following tool is helpful for data management?
    a. Property Inspector
    b. Symbols Pane
    c. Model Explorer
    d. All of the above

5. One of the following is not a type of data variable that can be created in Stateflow.
    a. Static
    b. local
    c. Data store memory
    d. Parameter

6. Which of the following datatypes is not available in MATLAB language?
    a. Int64
    b. Uint32
    c. Boolean
    d. None of the above

7. Enable C-bit operation is applicable for MATLAB action language.
    a. TRUE
    b. FALSE

8. Model explorer is used to set one of the following properties.
    a. Chart properties
    b. Model properties
    c. Data properties
    d. All of the above

9. Stateflow Diagnostics parameters throw errors for all situations by default.
    a. TRUE
    b. FALSE

Questions

1. List some of the key features of Stateflow.
2. Explain the different components from the Stateflow layout.
3. What are the options available in Object Palette?
4. List essential functions available in the Simulation tab.
5. Explain Data management options in the Modeling tab.
6. What are the essential functions available in Debug tab?
7. List and describe Chart properties.
8. What are the operations available in the Symbols pane?
9. Explain in brief all panes available in Model Explorer.
10. List down the main differences between MATLAB and C action languages.
11. Give an example of any three Stateflow Diagnostics parameters.

Answers

1. b
2. d
3. c
4. d
5. a
6. a
7. b
8. d
9. b

CHAPTER 12
Flow Graph

Introduction

Flow graph is a powerful graphical modeling tool offered as part of Stateflow. A flow graph is created using simple graphical objects—connective junctions and transitions. Still, it can simplify the implementation of logical functionalities, which would be challenging to implement with other techniques. Flow graph elements are also essential in developing state-based logic, apart from stand-alone use. Therefore, we must understand how to use flow graphs before trying our hands-on state-based logic in the upcoming chapters. This chapter takes the users through a stepwise approach to create a simple flow graph model using basic building blocks—transitions and junctions. This chapter presents basic features of pattern wizards and graphical functions with the help of logic-driven design examples.

Structure

In this chapter, we are going to cover the following topics:

- Overview of flow graph
    - Example: simple If-else condition
- Transitions
    - Transition label notation

- o   Default transition
- Patterns
  - o   Add predefined pattern
  - o   Save As pattern
  - o   Add custom pattern
- Graphical function

Objectives

After studying this chapter, the reader will be able to

- Get a brief overview of the flow graph with a simple example
- Learn more about transitions
- Get to know the use of pattern wizard with various examples
- Be aware of graphical functions

Overview of a flow graph

A flow graph or a flow chart can be defined as a graphical model that is used to implement logic patterns with the help of connective junctions and transitions. A flow graph is a combination of logical comparisons and basic math and loop constructs. Flow charts are preferred to implement decision tree-based combinatorial logic in which the current decision does not depend on any prior states, and the decision is made in real-time without holding any memory. Using multiple junctions interconnected with transitions helps create decision-based logic. Flow graphs also support the modeling of iterative loops, switches, and custom patterns. Flow graphs can also be implemented as graphical functions to be used in a modular and reusable way.

Flow graphs are implemented in the Stateflow chart block. They can be used independently or in combination with state-based logic along with state-to-state transitions. Implementation done with flow graph is readable and easy to maintain. Flow graphs help eliminate or reduce the number of states in the chart, resulting in efficient simulation and optimized memory use in generated code.

We shall start familiarizing ourselves with the flow graph by following a simple example of the **if-else** condition.

Example: simple if-else condition

In this example, the input is **xin**, whereas the output is **xout**. Whenever the value of **xin** exceeds 5, output **xout** shall change to 1; else, **xout** shall hold the value 0.

If our example is represented as a pseudo code,

```
If (xin>5)
    xout=1;
else
    xout=0;
end
```

For simplification, our example can be divided into three different sections:
- Implementation
- Data definition
- Simulation

Implementation

There are two ways to implement such flow graphs in Stateflow as follows:
1. Adding and connecting basic objects—junctions and transitions
2. Using predefined patterns

Using either of these methods, we shall be able to achieve implementation as shown in *figure 12.1*:

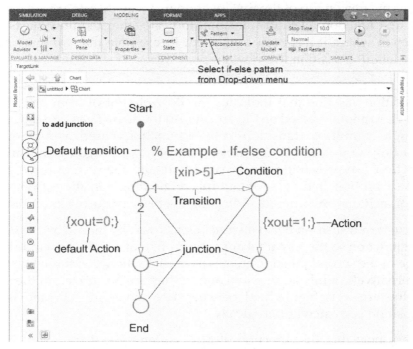

Figure 12.1: Simple flow graph example if-else condition

In the first method, we shall use the basic objects and draw the flow graph manually. The following are the steps to be followed in the blank Stateflow chart:

1. First, we shall add junctions, also known as **connective junctions**. Junctions are used to create multiple variations in the transition paths. Select the junction button from the object palette and then click and place five different junctions on the drawing area as shown in the previous image.

   There are multiple ways to add objects to the drawing area from the object palette as follows:

   - Single-click the object icon (such as a **junction**), move the cursor to the drawing area, and click again to place the object at the desired location.
   - Double-click the object icon, so you can add multiple objects by clicking desired positions of the drawing area.
   - Drag-and-drop the object from the icon to the drawing area. This way, you can add only one instance of the object at a time.

   To duplicate any object, right-click the object and perform drag-and-drop.

2. The next step after adding the junctions shall be adding transitions. To begin with, click on the default transition icon in the object palette and add it to the drawing area on top of the first junction in a way that its arrowhead touches the first junction. Default transition indicates that the flow starts from the junction where it has been connected. Please note that we must have only one default transition in a flow graph.

3. Now it is time to connect all these five junctions with the help of transitions. Transition is a line that indicates the flow of control from one junction or objects to another based on the direction of the arrowhead. We can have either a single or multiple transitions between junctions based on our requirements in a flow graph. In our example, we need two outgoing transitions from Junction 1, representing the `if` condition, and the second representing the `else` condition. In the case of multiple originating transitions from a junction, the transitions are ordered, indicating the priority during execution.

   To create a transition between junctions, hover the mouse on the edge of the first junction so the **+** symbol appears. From that point, drag-and-drop to the edge of the second junction creates a transition between these two junctions. Alternatively, while adding junction, if they are positioned in the same line, a blue arrow is highlighted between two junctions—clicking which, the transition is created automatically.

   Please note that the direction of flow is determined from the direction of the arrow, so ensure the creation of transitions as shown in the image. The usual flow should be so that there is only a junction at the end. To ensure the consistency of the flow, there must not be multiple end junctions, and all transitions must converge to a single terminating junction. The terminating junction does not have any outward transition, and the flow of the state starts from the default transition and ends at the terminating junction.

4. After the four transitions are in place, we shall define the condition, which is, in our case—**xin>5**. The condition shall be given as a transition label. The default label for transition is **?**, which must be changed to the condition. The condition is to be written in square brackets as **[xin>5]**, as shown in *figure 12.1*. The condition in the square brackets specifies that when the condition's result becomes true, only the flow can take the transition path, else not. To write the condition, click the **?** symbol, so the template is highlighted for events, conditions, and actions. We specify a condition on the first transition and action on the consecutive transition as a best practice; as in the flow graph, the transitions are tested but not executed. To ensure the flow from start to end junctions, please make sure to add additional transitions without any conditions. So that when the condition is false, in our case, the else condition transition path toward the terminating junction shall be executed.

5. We shall specify the action on the transition consecutive to the condition. The action is defined in curly brackets. After clicking the transition between Junctions 2 and 3, the **?** symbol appears, clicking which, the template appears, where between the curly brackets you can specify the action, for example **{xout=1;}**. Using the same method, select default action **{xout=0;}** on the else transition between Junctions 1 and 4. Usually, the action is used for applications, such as to set output or event, increment/decrement timers, counters, set/clear flags, and so on.

6. The image shows that the right-side path is executed if the **if** condition is satisfied, and the left side path is executed otherwise. In the end, connect the transition between Junctions 4 and 5. As both transitions converge at Junction 4, you may skip Junction 5. Do not specify any conditions on default and end transitions.

Alternatively, we shall use the predefined pattern template in the second method. As shown in *figure 12.1*, Go to the **MODELING** tab and select the If-else pattern from the pattern drop-down. We can also add the **If**-else pattern by following these steps: right-click on the drawing area | **Add Pattern in chart** | **Decision** | **IF-ELSE** to add the pattern to our chart. After that **Stateflow pattern: IF-ELSE** window pops up, where there are text boxes to specify **Description**, **If** condition, **If** action, and **Else** action. For our example, we have specified **Description** as **Example- If-**

`else condition`; If the condition is specified as **xin>5**; if action is **xout=1** and **Else** action is **xout=0**, as shown in *figure 12.2*:

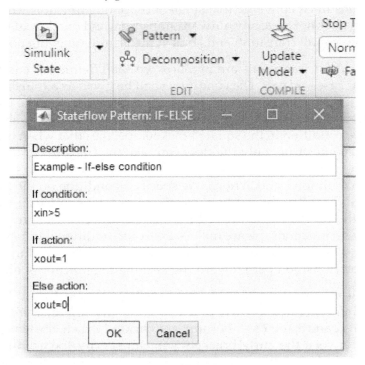

Figure 12.2: Pattern wizard dialog for IF-ELSE pattern

Click **OK**, and the result shall be the same as the flow graph shown in *figure 12.1*.

Data definition

After we implement the desired logic in the flow graph, the next step we shall follow is the data definition, although data can also be defined before starting implementation. Open Model Explorer from the **MODELING** tab, where we have provision to add or modify data, event, trigger, message, function call, and so on, for the charts. For our example, we shall limit it to data. From our flow graph, we can conclude that we need to define input—**xin** and output—**xout**. So, click on Add data button, which adds default data. By changing the column view to Stateflow, we shall be able to see relevant columns. We can change it either here or from the right-side data window, as shown in *figure 12.3*:

Flow Graph ■ 457

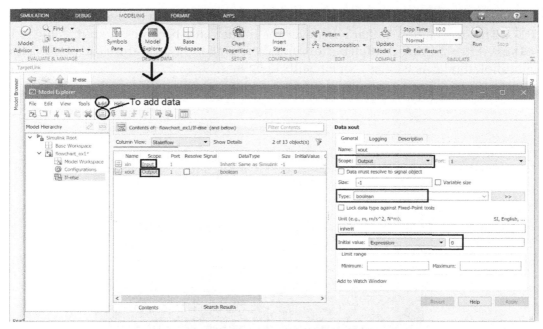

Figure 12.3: Data definition for IF-ELSE chart

In *figure 12.3*, we can observe that the scope of **xin** is set to input. The port number of **xin** is 1, and the datatype of **xin** is inherited from the Simulink input. Similarly, for output **xout**, the scope is set to **Output**. We can specify the datatype explicitly as Boolean; as in the chart, the possible values are 0 and 1. The default action language of the chart is MATLAB, so if you want to keep it the same, the datatype of **xout** can be set to double to support simulation, and in case the action language of the chart is changed to C, then the datatype can be set to Boolean. To change the action language, in model explorer, click chart name, and from the right-side window, select chart action as C from the drop-down. The initial value of the output signal is given as 0. There is also an option to specify minimum and maximum values, unit, and size. The input and output ports are created for the chart, respectively, based on the port number selected in the model browser. The other available data options are local, constant, parameter, and data store memory.

Simulation

After creating data interfaces, we shall observe and validate our implementation with simulation. To simulate **xin**, we have connected the Repeating sequence stair block with the input sequence [0 1 2 3 4 5 6]. We have connected the scope to observe output vs. input on the output side. The fixed sample time of the model is set to 0.5 s. The expectation is that whenever the input value becomes 6, **xout** value is 1, **else** 0. After clicking the **Run** button, simulation takes place, and we can observe the Simulink model as well as scope results in *figure 12.4*:

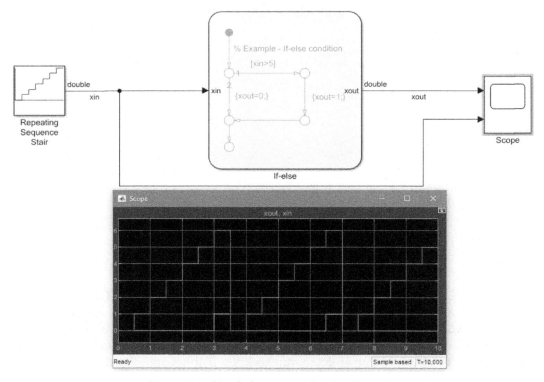

Figure 12.4: Simulink setup and simulation results

The simulation results confirm that when the **xin** input value exceeds 5, output **xout** becomes 1. The following image shows the chart animation during the simulation. When we press run, the complete transition paths taken during simulation time are highlighted in blue, as shown in *figure 12.5*, but the animation speed is fast by default. Therefore, if we are not able to observe the flow properly, we can alter the speed from the drop-down of **DEBUG** tab | **Animation speed**. We shall use the buttons **Step back**, continue, and step forward for the stepwise analysis. Step forward takes the simulation one sample time ahead. In our example, that would be 0.5 seconds. Using **DEBUG** tab option pause time, we can pause the simulation during a specific time. Additionally, it is possible to introduce breakpoints in our flow graph; for example, each time a particular transition is tested or is valid, at that time, we can halt the simulation for better analysis. This way, the users can use chart animation for debugging purposes.

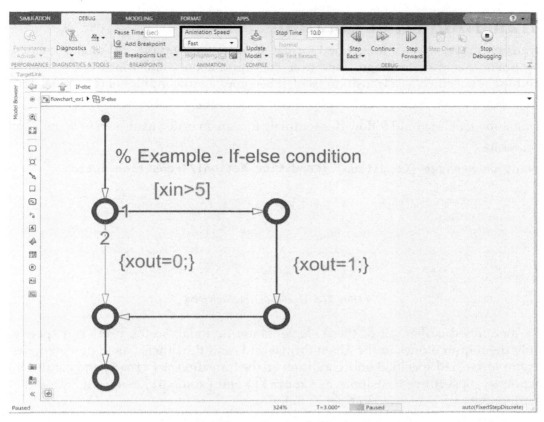

Figure 12.5: Chart animation during simulation

Transitions

A transition is specified as a line with an arrowhead that links one graphical object to another, such as states, junctions, and in the flow chart; these objects are connective junctions. The destination junction is identified where the arrowhead of the transition is, and the starting point is the source junction. In combination with multiple connective junctions, transitions define different transition paths for execution. In Stateflow, these transitions also describe the logic flow between different states that we shall learn in the coming chapters. Sometimes junctions are used in these transitions to introduce segments in the transitions. As explained in the previous example, transitions can be created from mouse click-and-hold operation from one junction to another. A default junction is a junction without any condition or source junction, which defines the starting point of execution.

Transition label notation

Transition labels have a predefined format. It consists of various optional elements: comment, event or message, condition, condition action, and transition action. If nothing is specified as a transition label, it becomes an unconditional transition. The default transition label is **?**, by clicking which the template appears.

Transition labels should follow this template in a given order, as shown in *figure 12.6*:

%comment
event or message [Condition] {Condition Action}/Transition Action

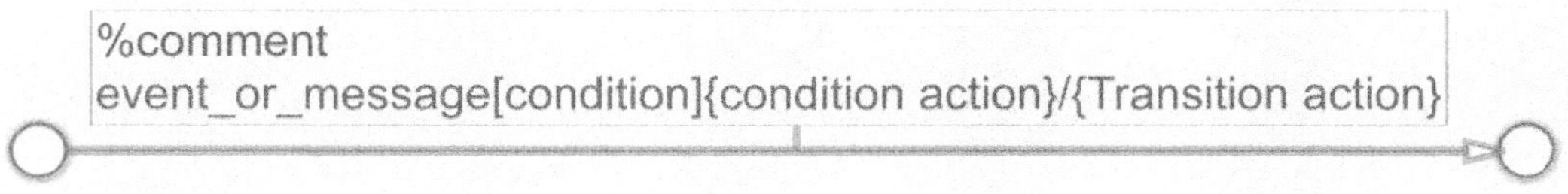

Figure 12.6: Syntax of transition label

As mentioned earlier, all of these elements are optional, so the users can specify only the required ones in the given format and omit the others. As in our previous example, we had specified only condition on the transition as **[xin>5]** and condition action on consecutive transitions as **{xout=1;}** and **{xout=0;}**, respectively. All the components are explained in brief as follows:

- **Event or message name**: If an event or message name is specified, then it means that the condition is true when the specified event occurs; and then only the transition shall be taken. If an event or message name is specified, then the transition can occur on any event. One can combine multiple events with OR (|) operator.

- **Condition**: If a condition is specified, then the Boolean condition mentioned between square brackets (**[]**) must be validated as TRUE for the transition to be taken. The condition may have a Boolean expression to compare data and numeric values. It may also specify any function which could return a Boolean value. Multiple Boolean conditions can be grouped using **&** (AND) and **|** (OR). It cannot have an assignment or unary increment/decrement expressions.

- **Condition action**: Condition action is specified in curly brackets (**{}**) and is executed when the condition is validated as TRUE.

- **Transition action**: Transition action is executed when the conditions on all the segments of the transition path between source and destination are validated as TRUE. Transition action is specified after forwarding slash "**/**". For the flow chart, we use condition actions.

Default transition

Default transition specifies the starting point for execution. In the case of multiple OR states, default transition determines the default state. The default transition shall have a destination junction but no source junction in the flow chart. There must be only one default transition in the flow graph. We may use the default transition to write a description or perform any initial action. The format is the same as condition action, where we can mention the action to be performed (for example, initialization of a local variable) in curly **{}** brackets.

Patterns

Flowchart patterns can be implemented manually, but Stateflow offers a more straightforward possibility to automatically create a flow chart with the help of the pattern wizard utility. Patterns wizard facilitates multiple operations, mainly **Add predefined** decision/loop/switch patterns, **Save a pattern** as a custom pattern, and **Add the custom** pattern. We can reduce the efforts by adding the pattern to the chart or enhancing the existing pattern using these options. We can increase reusability by saving the pattern as a custom pattern and adding it wherever required. Another benefit of the pattern wizard is that the created patterns are geometry and layout-wise in compliance with MAAB guidelines. The pattern wizard can be accessed from the **MODELING** tab | **Edit** | **Pattern** drop-down. *Figure 12.7* shows the menu options available under the drop-down:

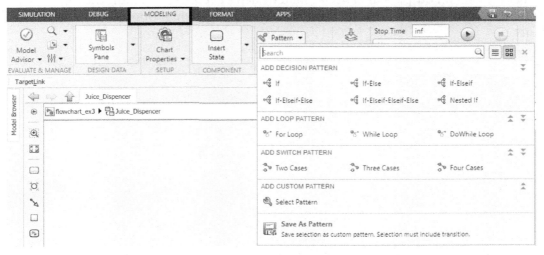

Figure 12.7: Pattern wizard drop-down menu

Add predefined pattern

In this section, we shall discuss the different patterns with the help of some examples. These are the following patterns available in the wizard:

Add decision pattern

Decision pattern offers variations of If-else conditions such as **If**, **If-Else**, **If-Elseif**, **If-Elseif-Else**, **If-Elseif-Elseif-Else**, and Nested If. In the first example, we have already learnt how to add the **If-Else** condition pattern. With the help of the second example, we shall learn how to implement a juice dispenser logic using the **If-Elseif-Elseif-Else** pattern and observe its results. We shall be using a pattern wizard to create the desired flowgraph. As mentioned earlier, go to **Modeling** | **Pattern** | select **If-Elseif-Elseif-Else** pattern or right-click on drawing area, select **Add pattern in chart** | **Decision** | select **If-Elseif-Elseif-Else**. Following either of these steps, a Stateflow pattern window shall pop up, with different fields to help us with pattern generation. For our example, the input can have the values **0** (off), **1**(orange juice), **2** (mango juice), or **3** (pineapple juice). When any of the juices is selected, the Boolean output for that particular juice would be **TRUE**, as shown in *figure 12.8*. So, our first If the condition is **Input==1**, and the corresponding action is **Orange_Juice=1**. Similarly, for **Elseif** condition **Input==2**, action is **Mango_Juice=1**, and the second **Elseif** condition is **Input==3**, whereas action is **Pineapple_Juice=1**. In case Input is 0 or any other value, else action, where all outputs are **FALSE**, shall be activated. In the default transition, too, all the outputs are set to **FALSE**. In this way, the logic shall offer a selection of the juice:

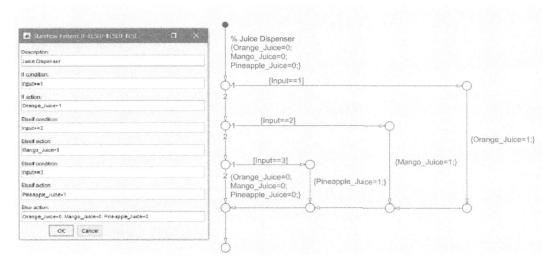

Figure 12.8: Example 2 using pattern—Juice dispenser

To simulate the flow chart, we need to define the data first. In the model explorer, we shall define **Input** as input, and **Orange_Juice**, **Mango_Juice** and **Pineapple_Juice** as outputs. After determining the chart interfaces, we shall prepare a simulation model. For the input, we can connect constant controlled by a rotary switch. We can use lamp block connected to chart outputs to observe the outputs (both rotary switch and lamp blocks are available under the Simulink Dashboard library). The user may also choose similar blocks as per convenience. The expectation is that when we change the rotary switch position, the respective lamp for the juice should turn on, and the remaining lamps should stay off. To make the simulation interactive, increase the simulation time to a higher value, for example, **INF**. The following image shows the simulation results when the **Input** value is 2. As observed in *figure 12.9*, when the rotary switch position is at value 2 corresponding to mango juice, the lamp for mango juice glows:

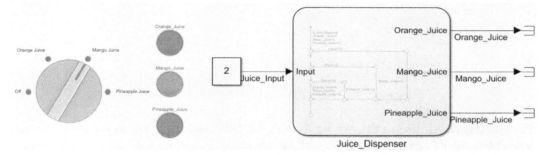

Figure 12.9: Example 2 — Juice dispenser simulation results

Add loop pattern

These patterns offer the creation of iterative loop flowcharts, such as **for** loop, **while** loop, and **do-while** loop. The pattern wizard for the loops can be accessed in the same way. We shall consider the example of Factorial calculation using **For** loop. The input **iMAX** for which we wish to calculate factorial shall be the chart input, whereas **Factorial** shall be the output. Our loop variable **I** shall be incremented by 1 until it reaches **iMAX**, and **numprev** is the temporary variable used for calculating the previous value. In the **For** loop action body, we calculate the Factorial by multiplying the previous Factorial values by the number—1. For example, the factorial value of 5 can be calculated as—$5! = 5 \times 4 \times 3 \times 2 \times 1 = 120$.

Figure 12.10 shows **For** loop pattern window and generated **For** loop pattern. The users can also follow a similar pattern and manually create the flowchart:

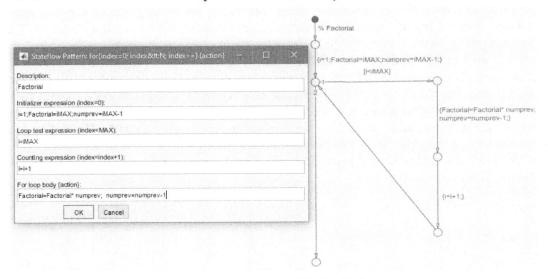

Figure 12.10: *Example 3 — Factorial using For loop pattern*

For the data definition part, we have defined **iMAX** as input, **I** and **numprev** as local variables, and **Factorial** is created as output. For simulation, an edit block from the Dashboard library is connected to a constant to update the input value during the simulation run and observe the results using the display block. As seen in *figure 12.11*, when the input value is **5**, the **Factorial** output shall be **120**. When the output is 6, the output shall be **720**, and so on. In this way, users can input any value and see the results:

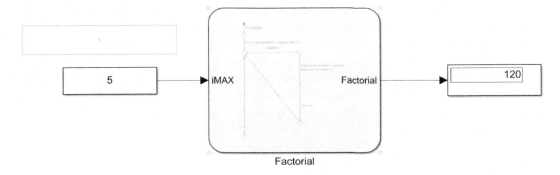

Figure 12.11: *Example 3 — For loop Factorial simulation results*

Add switch pattern

This category offers three types of switch patterns: two cases, three cases, and four cases. We shall demonstrate the usage of the switch pattern wizard with the help of our next example. The body mass index calculator. The body mass index of a person is calculated based on the height and weight of the person. The formula of the calculation is as follows:

$$bmi = weight(kg) / (height(m))^2$$

To simplify the user inputs, height can be considered in cm instead, therefore,

$$bmi = \left(\frac{weight(kg)}{\left(height(cm)\right)^2} \right) \times 10000$$

Based on this calculation, Body Mass Index (BMI) value is derived. As a result, the person can be categorized into one of the four sub-categories: underweight (**<18.5**), normal (**18.5≥** and **<25**), overweight (**25≥** and **<30**), and obese (**≥30**). Based on the **User** inputs **UserHeight** (cm) and **UserWeight** (kg), the output of the flow graph shall be provided as a calculated BMI value and the previously mentioned BMI category. *Figure 12.12* shows the pattern window with the respective values and a generated flow graph with some modifications in the switch case labels:

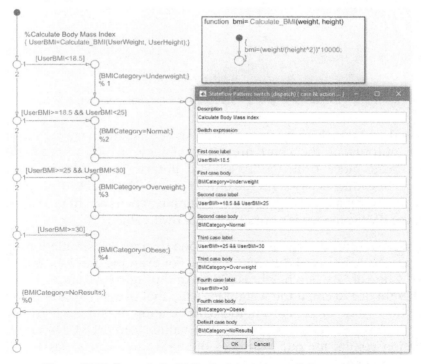

Figure 12.12: *Example 4 — BMI calculator using switch case pattern*

Please note that after generating the **switch** case flow chart, as shown previously, we have also added the graphical function **Calculate_BMI** and the function call as an action on the default transition. We have passed the user input values of **UserWeight** and **UserHeight** as arguments to the function. The function return value is stored in **UserBMI**, used in **switch** case conditions for comparison. We shall discuss the graphical function in the next section. *Figure 12.13* shows the simulation setup for our logic:

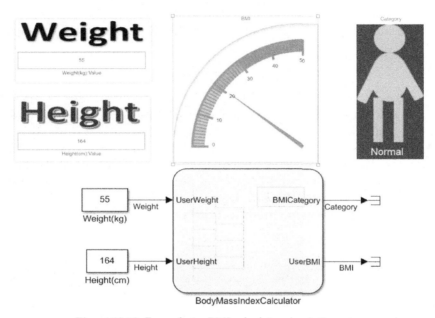

Figure 12.13: Example 4 — BMI calculator simulation setup

We have used edit panels to input weight in kg and height in cm for the simulation setup. The outputs of the chart are **BMICategory**, which is connected to the multistate Image block from the Dashboard library. The multistate image block shows respective images based on the output value. The **UserBMI** output value has been indicated using a quarter gauge. For example, when weight is 55 kg and height is 164 cm, the BMI category is normal, and the BMI value is 20.

Similarly, we have tried various combinations during the simulation of the BMI calculator and have received different results. For example, the user is underweight with a BMI value of 17 when height is 170 cm and weight is 50 cm. For the user with the same height of 170 cm, if the weight is 75 kg, that user is considered overweight due to the BMI value of 26. For another combination of 90 kg weight and 164 cm height, the user is deemed obese, as the BMI value is almost 34. *Figure 12.14* shows the simulation results for our examples of these three categories—underweight, overweight, and obese.

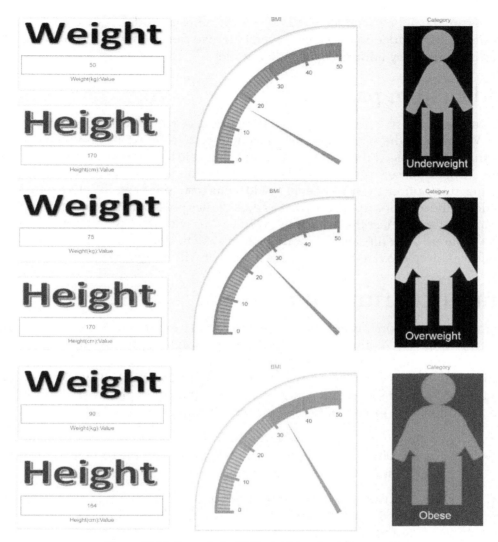

Figure 12.14: Example 4 — BMI calculator simulation results

Save as pattern

Save as pattern option is available in Stateflow under **MODELING** | **Pattern** | **Save as** pattern. This option allows us to reuse the flowchart pattern we have already created. We can either save a complete pattern or a part of it as a pattern reused later. To save a pattern, it is necessary to select the pattern we want to save, which must have transitions. Please note that we can save only a flowchart using this method and not states, functions, or truth tables. Once we select the pattern we wish to save, we shall go to the pattern drop-down menu and click the **Save as** option, so the selection shall be saved as a `.slx` file in the chosen folder. As we advance, all patterns shall be added to the same folder. Later we can open the file and access the pattern or reuse it by adding it to another model.

Add custom pattern

Add custom pattern offers the possibility to reuse a model or a pattern in our chart. We can add the selected pattern as a new pattern or extension to the existing pattern. For example, if the user wants to add multiple loop iterations to the existing loop pattern, the user can extend a vertical transition with a custom pattern. After selecting this option from **Pattern | Add custom pattern |** select pattern, a selection window pops up that displays all `.slx` files present in the folder chosen for a custom pattern. Select the file name saved earlier with the save as pattern option or as a separate `.slx` file, and the same pattern shall be added to the new chart. If no Stateflow pattern is available in the selected file, it will throw an error.

Graphical function

The graphical function introduces the users to another method to reuse the Stateflow flow graph pattern. As the name suggests, a function is created in Stateflow using connective junctions and transitions, the same way any pattern is formed. A graphical function can be implemented anywhere in the Stateflow chart. It works the same way as other functions, except it contains a graphical flow graph. We shall learn how to create and use the graphical function in a flow graph with the following steps:

- **Create function**: To create a graphical function, go to the object palette and click the graphical function icon so after clicking on the drawing area at the desired location, it creates a function box.

- **Declare function**: As per syntax of the function signature, we shall specify function name, formal arguments and return values on top of the box. The syntax is as follows:

    ```
    function [return value1, return value2, ..., return valueM] = function name (arg1, arg2, ..., argN)
    ```

    As suggested, we can have **N** number of return values and arguments in our function. They can be scalar, vector or matrix. If we consider our previous example from *figure 12.12*, the declaration of the graphical function **Calculate_BMI** looks like this:

    ```
    function bmi = Calculate_BMI (weight, height)
    ```

    Here, **bmi** is the return value, **Calculate_BMI** is the function name, and **weight** and **height** are arguments.

- **Create the pattern**: The function box below the signature label creates the desired flow graph pattern using connective junctions and transitions. It is impossible to use states, truth tables, and so on in the function. In our previous example, we have implemented the `bmi` calculation formula in the action of default transition, so in that context, the pattern is simple. Still, users may also implement complex logic based on requirements.

- **Define the data**: In model explorer, under the chart name, we can see a subsection with our function name that will contain all variables. While specifying function declaration, the return values are automatically added with output as scope, and arguments are added with an input scope. These inputs and outputs are not created as chart outputs. Additionally, one may add any required variables and specify data properties for all elements using data explorer. They can also be initialized from the MATLAB workspace.

- **Call the graphical function**: The next step would be to call the function at the desired location. The function can be called in the action of a state or a transition. The signature syntax remains the same to call the function, except we pass actual arguments and store the results in actual return variables. A function can also call another function. If we refer to our example, the function call has been executed in the default transition action. The syntax of this function call is as follows:

    `UserBMI= Calculate_BMI(UserWeight, UserHeight)`

`UserBMI` is the variable used in our main flow graph. In contrast, `UserWeight` and `UserHeight` are chart inputs that receive user input data, which shall be passed as arguments to the graphical function. The function calculates and returns the BMI value stored in `UserBMI`, which is also a chart output.

Conclusion

This chapter has introduced the readers well to flow graphs in Stateflow. We have talked about when to use a flow graph and how to use a flow graph. This chapter has covered all three aspects of the flow graph: implementation, data definition, and simulation, with various examples. It has explained components of transition label notation; this understanding will be helpful while learning state-based logic in upcoming chapters. The reader has been introduced to the patterns available through pattern wizards and their applications with the help of some examples. It also has specified ways to reuse the flow graph; the graphical function is one of these methods. In the end, the chapter has explained how to create and call a graphical function in our chart. The upcoming chapter shall use some of the elements from this chapter and then build the reader's knowledge of the core concepts of State-based modeling using a State chart. It shall also discuss the hierarchies available in Stateflow with the help of examples.

Points to remember

- A flow graph or a flow chart can be defined as a graphical model that is used to implement logic patterns with the help of connective junctions and transitions.
- A flow graph is used to implement decision tree-based combinatorial logic in which the current decision does not depend on any prior states.
- Connective junctions are round-shaped graphical objects used to create multiple variations in the transition paths.
- A transition is a line that has an arrowhead linking one junction to another.
- The direction of flow is determined by the direction of the arrowhead.
- There must be only one default transition in the flow chart.
- There must not be multiple end junctions to the flow chart.
- All transitions must converge to a single terminating junction.
- Except for the terminating junction, all junctions must have one non-conditional transition.
- In a flow graph, one should use condition actions and not transition actions.
- Pattern wizard is used to generate flow graph for decision, switch and loop patterns.
- The graphical function works as a function with a flow graph.
- A graphical function can contain only junctions and transitions.

Multiple choice questions

1. How many default transitions one must have in the flow graph?

    a. 3

    b. 2

    c. 1

    d. As many as required

2. What is the ideal location to specify an action for the condition?

    a. Transition action

    b. Condition action

    c. Default transition

    d. None of the above

3. All the junctions in the flow graph have at least one unconditional out transition.
   a. TRUE
   b. FALSE

4. Is it possible to slow down the Flow chart simulation?
   a. Yes
   b. No

5. In a flow graph, these are the loop details: default transition action is {i=1;}, loop condition is [i>5] and condition action is {i=i+1;}. Model sample time is 200 milli seconds. How much total time would it take to complete all the loop iterations?
   a. 1 second
   b. 1.2 second
   c. 0.8 second
   d. 200 milli seconds

6. Graphical functions are made of states, junctions and transitions.
   a. TRUE
   b. FALSE

Questions

1. Explain the syntax of transition label notation in detail.
2. Provide an overview of the flow graph with an example.
3. When and how do we use pattern wizard?
4. What are the definitions you learnt in this chapter?
5. What is the difference between a graphical function and a Simulink function?
6. Explain the creation of a do-while loop pattern and pattern reuse in another chart with an example.
7. Create flow graph for a simple quiz with five questions.
8. Create a flow graph that outputs the Fibonacci pattern.
9. Create a flow graph that determines vehicle type based on user inputs.

Answers

1. c
2. b
3. b
4. a
5. d
6. b

CHAPTER 13
Statechart and Hierarchical State Model

Introduction

Statechart is an essential part of Stateflow that offers a visual tool-based environment for a finite state-based development. A Statechart can be described as a graphical representation of the finite state machine consisting of graphical objects, non-graphical objects, and their relationship. States represent possible operating modes of a dynamic system. This chapter explores Statechart and its various characteristics with simple examples. In this chapter, the reader will learn about state transition diagrams, state labels, hierarchy, decomposition, and the type of transitions possible in the Statechart. This chapter also introduces the readers to junctions and state grouping techniques.

Structure

In this chapter, we are going to cover the following topics:

- Overview
    - Chart
    - State
- State Labels

- State Name
- State Actions
- Example: Vehicle exterior light control
- State Hierarchy
  - Example: Tax calculator
  - Example: Vehicle exterior light control with State Hierarchy
- State Decomposition
  - OR (Exclusive) decomposition
  - AND (Parallel) decomposition
  - Example: Water dispenser
- Transitions
  - State Transition
  - Default Transition
  - Self-loop Transition
  - Inner Transition
  - Supertransition
- Junctions
  - Connective Junction
  - History Junction
- Group and Subchart
  - Group State
  - Subchart

Objectives

After studying this chapter, the reader will be able to:

- Get a brief overview of States and Statecharts
- Create state transition diagrams
- Know about State Labels, Hierarchy, and Decomposition with examples
- Learn more about different types of transitions
- Be informed about Connective and History junctions
- Be aware of State grouping and subcharts

Overview

As we have already learnt in the previous chapters, Stateflow provides a visual tool environment based on finite state machines. A state machine, also known as a finite state machine, represents reactive systems that work in an event-based manner, which indicates that a dynamic system's operating modes (states) change only on occurrences of the defined events under certain conditions. Stateflow uses state-machine semantics presented by *David Harel*. Along with control systems, state machines are used to implement complex logic in dynamic systems, such as automotive, aviation, industrial, telecommunication, commercial, and so on.

Chart

A chart in a Stateflow is the visual representation of a finite state machine that consists of graphical objects such as transitions, junctions, and states; non-graphical objects such as events and data, and the relationship between them. The chart offers various options to implement combinatorial and sequential logic, such as Flowgraphs, state transition diagrams, state transition tables, and truth tables. In this chapter, we shall learn the techniques to describe event-driven systems with the help of a state transition diagram that is constructed with two elementary building blocks—states and the transitions. In the case of complex systems, state transition diagrams are insufficient; in this case, a state chart combines the usage of hierarchy, parallelism, and broadcasting for complex algorithms of such systems.

Stateflow offers two choices as chart action language: MATLAB and C. In Stateflow, a chart can be built as a standalone chart, that is, executed as a MATLAB object. The Statechart file shall be created with the `.sfx` extension. Additionally, the chart can be created as a Simulink block to be simulated as part of a Simulink model having a `.slx` or a `.mdl` file extension. The Stateflow chart works as a finite state machine in Simulink. The Stateflow chart block is also simulated alongside other Simulink blocks present in the model during simulation. Simulink generates S-Function in the case of a hybrid system. Another exciting aspect of hybrid systems is that it is also possible to use Simulink and MATLAB functions as part of the Statechart. A chart is evoked cyclically, on the event, or based on chart inputs.

Example: State transition diagram

To understand the implementation of a finite state machine using a state transition diagram, we shall consider a simple example of a lamp that glows when the switch is turned on and turns off when the switch is turned off.

We shall start by identifying three behavior characteristics: states, transitions, and interfaces. From the requirement, we can specify that the lamp has two operating modes: On and Off. Therefore, the states in the diagram shall be On and Off. The default machine state shall be Off.

The next step is to identify the transitions. As suggested earlier, the lamp state changes to ON when the input switch status is ON. So, one transition shall be created from Off to On state. Moreover, the lamp output is OFF when the input switch status is OFF. Therefore, that would be our second transition, from ON to OFF state.

Coming to the interfaces, we have one input signal representing switch state and one output representing lamp output. The input, as well as output, has only two states—OFF and ON.

Combining all the points as mentioned earlier, we shall create a state transition diagram, as shown in *figure 13.1*:

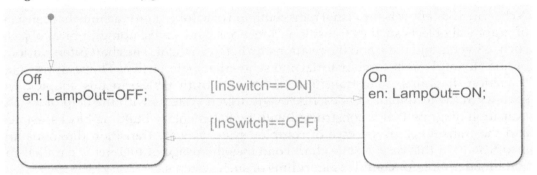

Figure 13.1: Example state transition diagram

We can observe from *figure 13.1* that the diagram consists of two states: Off and On, transition 1 **[InSwitch==ON]** and transition 2 **[InSwitch==OFF]**, and lamp output **LampOut** changing to ON or OFF on the **InSwitch** state change event. We shall learn the stepwise approach to creating such diagrams in this chapter.

State

A state in a Stateflow chart is used to describe the different operating modes of a reactive system. The State is a fundamental building block of the state transition diagram used to describe sequential logic.

A vital characteristic of a state is that a state can be either active or inactive at a given point in time. The State can be active or not shall be decided based on events and conditions applicable to the specific State. The control shall move dynamically from one State to another accordingly.

We shall follow the following steps to create a simple state transition diagram, as shown in *figure 13.1*:

- **Open Chart**: Open a new Simulink model and add a Chart block from the Stateflow library. Double-click and open Chart. Stateflow Editor Window shall be visible.

- **Create States**: Select the **State** icon from the Object palette on the right side of the drawing area. Bring the cursor to the drawing area and click twice to create two states representing our operating modes—Off and On, and place them next to each other, as shown in *figure 13.2*. Resize States when required. Please note that in case no previous default transition is present in the chart, the first State shall be created with a default transition connected to it. Default transition indicates the starting point for execution, similar to what we have already learnt in *Chapter 12: Flow Graph*.

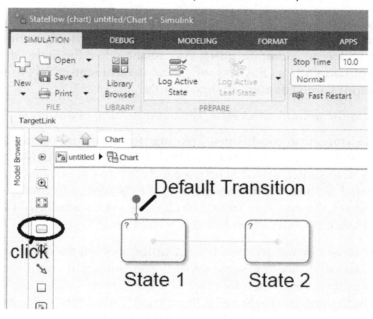

Figure 13.2: Create states

- **Rename State**: A State has a **?** symbol on the top-left corner as its name by default that can be renamed as required. In State 1—click the **?** symbol and rename the state name as Off. Similarly, in State 2—rename this State as On.

- **Create transitions**: As discussed, we require two transitions from one State to the other and vice versa. To create transitions automatically, hover the mouse cursor between these two states, and we shall be able to see blue lines indicating possible transitions. If we click these lines, the transitions are created. Alternatively, click on the right edge of State 1 and drag-and-connect the transition line to the left edge of State 2. Follow the same procedure to create a transition from State 2 to State 1.

- **Update State label**: We want to define output signal states-Off and -On based on the currently active State. There are two ways to achieve this: updating the output signal value within the states or updating the output signal on transitions. The method changes on the chosen state machine type: Classic, Mealy, or Moore. In this chapter, we have retained the state machine type to the default value—Classic.

    We have implemented the output signal **LampOut** in the states in this example. We shall assign the output value in the **entry** action of the State, which is specified after the state name. The general syntax for entry action is as follows:

    en: or entry: <desired entry action> ;

    As shown in *figure 13.1*, we have specified the State entry action for the Off State as **en: LampOut=OFF;**. Similarly, the entry action for the On state can be defined as **en: LampOut=ON;**. As a result, when the State Off is active, the value of **LampOut** is OFF, and when the current state shifts to the On State, the output value **LampOut** changes to ON.

    As Off is the default chart state, the default value of output shall be OFF.

- **Update Transition conditions**: Creating transition and updating state labels can be performed interchangeably. In this step, we shall define the transition condition to switch active State from Off state to On State and vice versa. As illustrated in the example description, the current state changes from Off to On when the input value **InSwitch** changes to ON. Similarly, the active state shifts from On to Off when **InSwitch** changes to OFF.

    As we have already learned the transition label syntax in *Chapter 12: Flow Graph*, we shall use the same syntax. The transition condition is specified in square brackets. Therefore, we shall define the transition condition for transition from State 1 to State 2 (Off->On) as **[InSwitch]** or **[InSwitch==ON]**. The condition must be specified so that the overall result of the condition is Boolean. For the second transition from State 2 to State 1 (On->Off), we shall specify the transition condition as **[~InSwitch]** or **[InSwitch==OFF]**.

- **Define Data**: To be able to compile and simulate the chart, we need to define the data; in our case, that includes input and output interfaces and constant values. We shall navigate to **Simulation | Prepare** drop-down menu, and there we can use the Symbols pane to define our chart data. Alternatively, **Modeling | Model Explorer** can also be used for manual data definition. For ease of use, we shall go with the Symbols pane, as it automatically identifies the unresolved symbols and suggests their names along with possible types, which can be easily changed in the pane if required. Additionally, we also have options to create new data manually. *Figure 13.3* shows the Symbols pane and its essential fields:

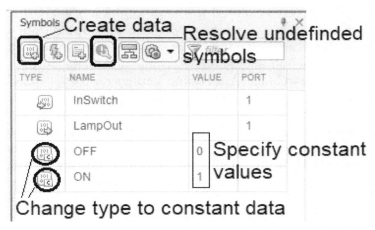

Figure 13.3: Symbols pane

After clicking the Symbols pane icon, symbols appear on the right side of the drawing area. Here, we can already see the suggestions, based on which the input **InSwitch**, output **LampOut** and parameters OFF and ON shall be created when we click the button **Resolve undefined symbols**. It automatically detects that **InSwitch** is input and **LampOut** is an output based on name and usage. We shall change the type of OFF and ON to constants and specify the values 0 and 1, respectively, in the value column.

- **Simulink model interface and Simulation**: In **DEBUG** or **MODELING** menu, click the **Update Chart** icon to identify chart syntax errors. Resolve the errors, if there are any, and then proceed to the next activity of creating simulation interfaces, as shown in *figure 13.4*:

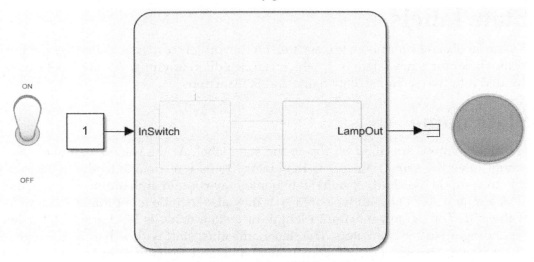

Figure 13.4: Simulink model simulation

As we have already observed in the description, the chart has a Boolean **InSwitch** input interface and one Boolean **LampOut** output interface. For better visualization, on the input side, we have connected the toggle switch block from the Simulink Dashboard library; and on the output side, we have connected the **Lamp** block. After doing settings for these blocks, click **Update model** to identify model issues. Then click the **Run** button, and the simulation begins. By default, the **Lamp** output is **Red**, corresponding to value OFF, but if we change the toggle switch State to ON, the **Lamp** output color changes to green, corresponding to value ON. We can also observe the simulation in the chart, where the transition path and the active State are highlighted in blue, as shown in *figure 13.5*. This feature is beneficial in observing the behavior and debugging:

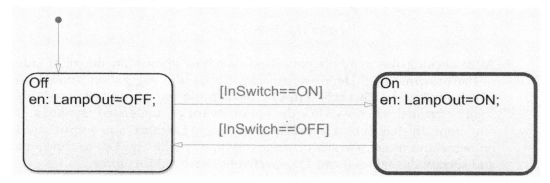

Figure 13.5: Statechart simulation

In the coming sections, we shall learn more about various characteristics of States.

State labels

A state label can be termed a text written on the top-left corner of a state. By default, a state label for a new state is **?**, which can be edited anytime. A state label can be divided into two sections: State name and State actions.

State name

The state name is specified on top of the state label. At the same level, two states cannot have the same name. It is mandatory to assign a name to the State to be able to compile the chart. A valid state name may contain alphanumeric characters (0–9, a–z, and A–Z) and underscore (_). It may also include an optional **/** character at the end. The default maximum length of a state name is 31 characters, further expanding up to 256 characters. The state name must start with a character. Suppose a user tries to use special characters in the name and alphanumeric character, then the first special character is automatically replaced with the character **a**, and the subsequent special characters are replaced by an underscore. A blank space is also replaced with an underscore. If no state name is specified, or a given name contains only special characters, then Stateflow throws an error during compilation.

State actions

State actions are various types of actions performed in an active state which are optional. We can either skip them or specify some or all of them based on our requirements. To describe a state action, we define a predefined keyword prefix in the following line of the state name, followed by a colon, state action, and comma or semicolon. The general format of the state actions are as follows:

```
en or entry: entry action
du or during: during action
ex or exit: exit action
on event_name: on event_name action
on message_name: on message_name action
bind: event
```

In this chapter, we shall learn more about entry, during, and exit state actions, whereas events shall be discussed in the upcoming chapter:

- **entry**: **entry** or **en** keyword is used to specify an action executed once a state becomes active. If no keyword is specified, then the state action is considered as an entry action by default. Another alternative to the prefix is the forward-slash (**/**) symbol. To specify multiple entry actions, we can write them in separate rows or separate them using comma (**,**) or semicolon (**;**). As it can be observed in the previous example of lamp control that the entry action is used to assign the lamp output value as Off or On on the state activation, based on the switch status. The output value is held until the entry action of the subsequent State is executed.
- **during**: **during** or **du** keyword describes a state action that gets executed for an active state whenever an event occurs and no exit condition is true. We can separate multiple during actions with a comma, semicolon, or carriage return similar to entry action. One use case during the action is incrementing the timer or counter on each time step or occurrence of a specific event.
- **exit**: As the name suggests, **exit** or **ex** action is performed just before the exit of the said active State, when a transition out of the State becomes valid. The syntax of **exit** action is similar to entry and during actions; the method to separate multiple actions is also the same. Suppose the State has condition action on the outward transition along with the **exit** condition defined for the State. In that case, the first condition action is executed when

the condition is valid, then the exit action of the first State is executed. After executing the action, the first State becomes inactive, and then the transition to the second State takes place, where the entry action is performed once the second State becomes active.

In case multiple state actions perform similar tasks, we can combine two or all of them in any order by using the following syntax:

entry, during, exit: (or en, du, ex:) task 1, task 2, task 3,….task N;

We shall refer to the following example to understand state actions in exterior light control logic for a vehicle.

Example: Vehicle exterior light control

For the vehicle exterior light control logic example, we shall consider a set of basic exterior light requirements comprising control logic of Position lights and headlights based on positions selected on the rotary light switch and high beam stalk switch:

- When the rotary light switch position is Off, no lights are activated.

- When the position of the switch is changed to Position lights, all four position lights- front left, front right, rear left, and rear right lights are turned on.

- If the Headlight setting is selected on the rotary switch, it allows the headlight to work in either low beam mode or high beam mode, along with position lights. During this time, a high beam control switch comes into consideration, a stalk switch generally connected to the steering wheel.

- When the high beam switch is deactivated and the rotary switch is set to headlights, front left and front right headlights are activated in low beam mode, in addition to all four position lights.

- The high beam switch, when pushed, activates the headlights with a higher trajectory. As continuous activation of high beam lights can blind the oncoming traffic, we have a maximum limit of 15 seconds; after that, the High beam headlights are turned off.

- When the high beam switch is released, then also high beams are turned off, and low beams are turned on.

- From any position, if the rotary switch position is changed back to the Off position, all the lights are turned off.

From the requirements mentioned earlier, we can derive multiple factors required to complete the design, such as the following:

- **States**: desired states of the system are Off, Position Lights, Low beam headlights, and High beam headlights
- **Default state**: Off
- **Inputs**: Lights rotary switch and High beam switch
- **Outputs**: four-position lights, two low beam headlights, and two high beam headlights
- **Transitions**: Among all states, Off ↔ Position lights ↔ Low Beam ↔ High beam, based on the status of both switches and/or a timer

Considering these parameters, we can describe the system in a simplified graphical format, as shown in *figure 13.6*:

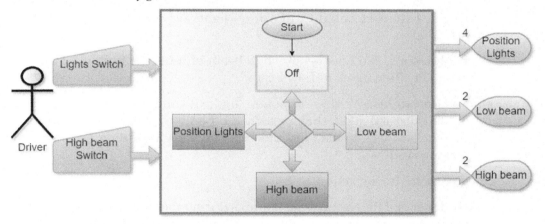

Figure 13.6: Example flowchart

Taking into account the requirements and flowchart; we shall begin a detailed representation of the example logic in Stateflow by following these steps:

1. **Create states:**
    - Create Off State by clicking the state symbol in the object palette and then on the drawing area. The first State created default transition shall be connected to the Off State. One after another, create position lights, headlights low beam, and headlights high beam states.

2. **Specify State entry actions:**

    - **Off State**: Off-state entry action assigns OFF value to all the light outputs

    - **Position Lights**: The entry action assigns the ON value to all four position lights.

    - **Low Beam**: in the entry action, both of the Low beam outputs are assigned ON value, in addition to the four position lamps.

    - **High Beam**: Entry action of this State assigns ON value to both High beam output signals. Additionally, the timer variable is initialized to 0 so that the 15-second timer starts whenever the high beam headlight is requested.

3. **Specify State exit actions:**

    - **Low beam**: Turn off the low beam lights when the switch position is changed from Headlight to Position lights or when the High beam is activated.

    - **High beam**: Like Low beam, High beam outputs are turned off during exit to Position lights or Low beam.

    - **Position lights**: We do not require any exit condition because Position lights, once activated, shall be turned off only when the switch position is switched back to Off, and the Off state entry condition takes care of this scenario.

4. **Specify State during actions:**

    - **High beam**: High beam state requires during the action to increment the High beam timer every sample time until it reaches 15 seconds. We have assumed the model sample time to be 0.1 seconds.

    Figure 13.7 shows the complete Statechart for our example:

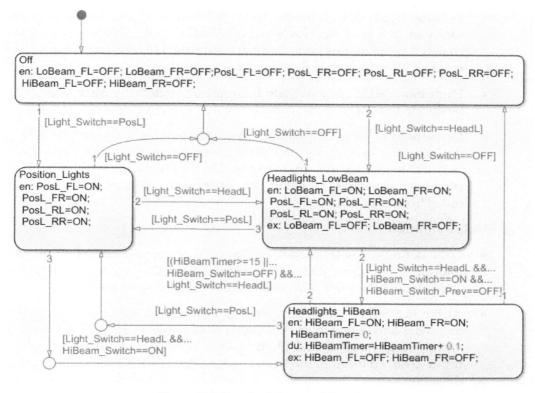

Figure 13.7: Exterior light control Statechart

5. **Specify State transitions among all states:**

    - **Off ↔Position Lights**: The active State shall change from Off to Position lights when the light switch position is chosen as Position Lights. The active State shall change back to Off when the light switch position is shifted to Off.

    - **Off ↔Low beam**: The active State shall change from Off to Low beam when the light switch position is chosen as Headlights. The active State shall change back to Off when the light switch position is shifted to Off. Common transitions can be combined using connective junctions.

    - **Position lights ↔Low beam**: The active State shall change from one State to another based on the position selected on the rotary switch.

    - **Low beam ↔High beam**: The active State shall change from Low beam to High beam when in addition to headlight selection on a rotary switch, the high beam switch is also activated. The active state will change back to low beam when the high beam switch is released, or 15 seconds have passed since high beam lights are on.

- **Position lights↔High beam**: Active State shall be position lights if the rotary switch position is selected as Position lights. If the switch state changes to headlights and simultaneously, the High beam switch status is active, then the active State shall be the High beam.
- **High beam→Off**: Active State becomes Off when the rotary switch is positioned to Off.
- Please note, by default, each transition has a number assigned to it, which describes the execution order during simulation. Based on the desired priority, users have the option to reassign the execution order; to do that- right-click transition | **Execution order** and select desired execution order from the available list.

6. **Data definition:**
   - Data definition with Model Explorer is performed to define all the interfaces, variables, parameters, constants, and so on used within the chart. Model Explorer is accessible from the Modeling menu.
   - At the top level of the chart, we can add desired data blocks from the menu bar and define their attributes; for example- the chart requires two inputs—Light switch and High beam switch. Additionally, one more input- delayed input of the High beam switch is added for signal change detection.
   - The data type of the inputs is set to the default value—inherit, which specifies that whatever datatype shall be assigned to the input signal shall be propagated to the chart.
   - Now coming to the outputs, we shall create four-position lights, two low beam and two high beam outputs. For all the outputs, we have assigned the datatype as double, and the default value of the outputs is specified as 0, which indicates the output OFF State.
   - Next, we shall define a local variable High beam timer to increment the timer. For this variable, too, we have assigned datatype as double and initial value as 0.
   - In the end, we shall define all the constants used in the chart. For example, the light switch positions are each assigned constants for comparison. The high beam signal and the outputs are Boolean, having only two options- OFF and ON, so we have defined them as constants as well.

The *figure 13.8* shows Model Explorer with all the required data definitions for the chart in our example:

Statechart and Hierarchical State Model ■ 487

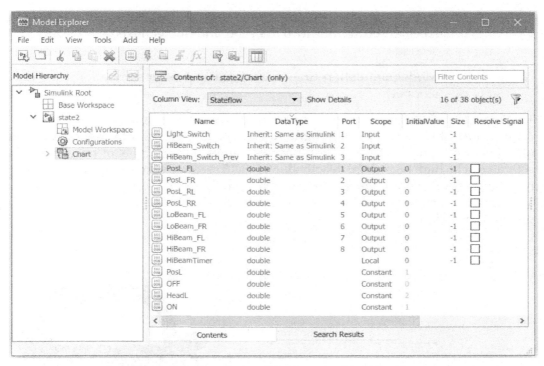

Figure 13.8: Example data definition using Model Explorer

7. **Simulink model creation and simulation:**

    - After creating inputs and outputs in Model Explorer, input and output ports shall appear on the chart block.

    - Create input and output blocks that will help us simulate and validate the functionality. In the case of inputs, we have connected the rotary switch and toggle switch to represent the light switch and high beam switch, respectively.

    - For outputs, we have used dashboard lamps and placed them on the vehicle's front view for better visualization of vehicle exterior lights. With the usage of the Image button on the object palette, any image can be added to the Simulink model.

    - As shown in *figure 13.8*, front position lamps can be placed in the lower part of the vehicle. Low beam headlights are placed on the inner side, and high beam headlights are placed on the outer side of headlights.

    - Please note that we have connected only the front left and front right position lights for simulation purposes.

- In the **Simulink Model Settings** window, we have adjusted the solver type setting to fixed-type and solver Fixed-step size to 0.1 seconds.

- Model simulation time is changed to inf- so simulation runs until stopped.

The *figure 13.9* shows our example chart's dashboard panels and simulation results. As it can be observed, when the light switch position is set to headlights and the high beam switch input is ON, the position lamps and high beam headlights are activated. The high beams are deactivated after 15 seconds of on-time, and low beam headlights are turned on after that. This behavior is in line with our requirements, and similarly, one by one, all transitions can be verified by altering switch positions during simulation:

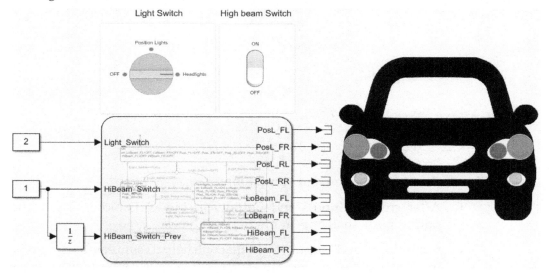

Figure 13.9: Example simulation results

State hierarchy

During Statechart implementation for any complex functionality, if everything is implemented at the same level, the logic becomes less readable and difficult to debug. To resolve this issue, Stateflow offers the opportunity of creating hierarchical states. The state hierarchy feature helps manage multilevel state complexity by organizing the states into multiple parent and child state levels. Such design results in less complexity and better manageable and readable charts. Every State has a parent; if a state is the only State in the chart, then that Statechart would be the parent for this State. We can draw a state within the boundaries of another state; in this case, the parent state is known as a superstate, and the child state is termed substate.

A superstate may contain multiple substates, and a substate can also further have substates within it. A superstate is active when at least one of its children states is active. This structure helps us combine state actions and state transitions, so the overall logic becomes more compact and easier to manage. At a time, only one State can become active at a level, and the rest states shall become passive. State hierarchy can be represented in the textual format using forward-slash (/) followed by superstate name and dot (.) sign followed by substate name. We shall refer to two examples to explore state hierarchy: Tax amount calculator and previously discussed.

Example: Tax calculator

In this example, we shall consider a basic tax calculator on the **point of Sale** (**POS**) terminal. The calculator detects the mode of payment requested by a customer and calculates the total amount of retail payable tax based on the selected method—Cash, Debit card, Credit card, or **Unified Payment Interface** (**UPI**). To keep the explanation simple, we omitted the mathematical tax calculations to focus on the overall structure design. The users can later add inputs, outputs, transitions, and tax calculation formulas as part of each state action and simulate the logic.

As explained in *figure 13.10*, **Tax_Calculator** shall be created as a superstate. We shall consider the State as a Level 1 state for ease of understanding. It has further five states as Level 2 substates- **SelectPaymentMode** (2.a—default state), **Cash** (2.b), **Debit_Card** (2.c), **Credit_Card** (2.d), and **UPI** (2.e). In case all of these substates have any common state actions, we have the option to specify these actions as part of the **Tax_Calculator** superstate so that we can avoid any duplicate work.

We have four distinctive payment modes, and the tax calculation varies for each of them—so we have created them as four distinctive substates, where each of them shall have base tax calculations in the entry actions. Going further, additional components are applicable for debit cards based on their subcategories—Visa, MasterCard, or Maestro. That is why we shall implement tax calculations as part of state actions within each of the individual Level 3 substates located inside **Debit_Card** state- VISA (3.a), MasterCard (3.b), and Maestro (3.c). Similarly, the **Credit_Card** State contains three further Level 3 substates—VISA (3.a), MasterCard (3.b), and `American_Express` (3.c). We can further group states and transitions as required to make the chart more readable and less complex.

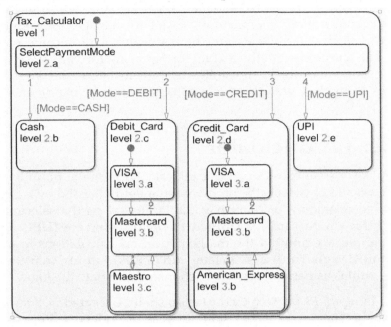

Figure 13.10: Example state hierarchy

Example: Vehicle exterior light control with state hierarchy

In the previous section, we have learnt a stepwise approach to implement vehicle exterior light control. As we can observe in *figure 13.7*, we have some repetitive logic in position lights, low beam, and high beam headlight states. We shall transform this logic into a more simplified logic with the help of hierarchical states:

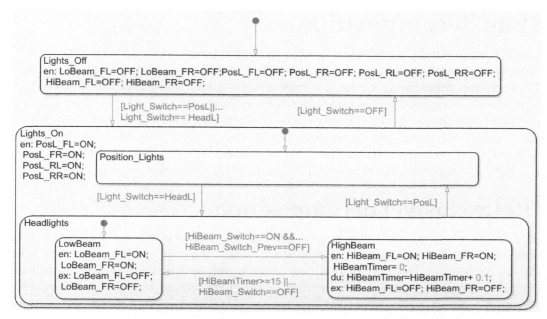

Figure 13.11: Example exterior lights with state hierarchy

The *figure 13.11* shows revamped logic with state hierarchy, and we can observe that the updated logic has lesser transitions and repetitive logic. After cleanup, the logic is more readable, easy to understand, and easy to debug as well.

The first optimization we have done is in the case of position lights activation. In *figure 13.7*, position lights are activated at multiple locations—in the entry action of position lights State and low beam headlights state, and they are turned off only after switching back to the **Lights_Off** State. Therefore, in the new logic, we have created a superstate named **Lights_On**, where only we activate the position lamps in the entry action. We do not have to implement this redundant logic in position lights or low beam states. The creation of the **Lights_On** superstate has also eliminated redundant transitions between the **Off** State and all other states.

The second change is done concerning the headlights substate. Two separate **LowBeam_Headlights** and **HighBeam_Headlights** states have been combined under the newly created **Headlights** state, resulting in the elimination of redundant transitions between position lights and **LowBeam** as well as **HighBeam** states. Moreover, the transition between Low beam and high beam substates is also simplified with this change. Simulation results show that the behavior is identical to the previous example without hierarchy. As a result, we can conclude that state hierarchy effectively helps with the complexity of multilevel designs.

State decomposition

State decomposition specifies the type of substates a superstate can have. There are two possible decompositions for a state: OR (Exclusive) decomposition and AND (Parallel) decomposition. All the substates must have the same type, identical to the superstate decomposition within a superstate. In the case of exclusive decomposition, only one State can be active, whereas, in the case of parallel decomposition, multiple states shall be active simultaneously. State decomposition can be set using right-click-> Decomposition-> Exclusive (OR) or Parallel (AND). This section shall look into both the decomposition types with some simple examples.

OR (exclusive) decomposition

OR decomposition, also known as exclusive decomposition, describes the systems with mutually exclusive operating states. We can say that if a state has OR decomposition, then only one out of its multiple substates will be active at any given time. The state decomposition of a newly created state is by default OR decomposition. It can be observed that the substates within the OR decomposition state are displayed with solid outside borders.

AND (parallel) decomposition

AND decomposition, also known as parallel decomposition, is used to describe the systems with mutually existing operating states. For a state with AND decomposition, all of its substates will be active simultaneously. The substates, as part of AND decomposition state, have dashed borders.

Let us consider a small example, as indicated in *figure 13.12*:

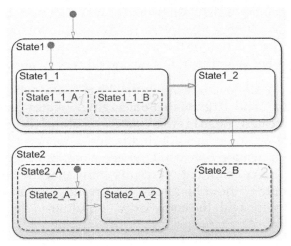

Figure 13.12: OR and AND decomposition example

From *figure 13.12*, we shall discuss various levels of states and their decompositions:

- **Parent chart: OR decomposition**

    State1 and **State2** can be envisioned as mutually exclusive states with solid boundaries, which indicates that at a time, either **State1** or **State2** can be active.

- **State1: OR decomposition**

    State1 substates **State1_1** and **State1_2** can be observed with solid boundaries. Either of them can be active at a time. **State1_1** is the default state.

- **State1_1: AND decomposition**

    State1_1 substates **State1_1_A** and **State1_1_B** can be active in parallel. Both states can be perceived with dashed boundaries.

- **State2: AND decomposition**

    State2 substates **State2_A** and **State2_B** are drawn with dashed boundaries. Both of them can be active at the same time.

- **State2_A: OR decomposition**

    The substates **State2_A_1** and **State2_B_2** are mutually exclusive, and both states have solid boundaries.

The decomposition concept can be elaborated with the following example of a Water dispenser.

Example: Water dispenser

In this example, we shall design a Statechart of a water dispenser that has the capability of dispensing hot, cool, and normal temperature water at the same time via three of its individual outlets. These are further requirements for each operation that we need to consider in this chart:

- **Hot water**: When the **HOT** button is pressed on the dispenser, the first water tap dispenses Hot water and the lamp turns on, respectively. Additionally, a led indicating **Heating** operation glows. When the button is pressed, heating is cyclically turned on for 30 seconds and then turned off for 15 seconds.

- **Normal water**: When the **NORMAL** button is pressed on the dispenser, the second water tap dispenses room temperature water, and a lamp indicating normal operation turns on.

- **Cool water**: When the **COOL** button is pressed on the water dispenser, the cooling water operation begins—glowing the **Cooling** LED, simultaneously turning on the cool water dispensing operation from the third water tap. Additionally, a lamp indicating water dispensing turns on.

From the requirements mentioned earlier, we can conclude that these three water-dispensing operations do not have any interdependency and that they must work concurrently. We will require a simultaneous operation to drive all three outputs simultaneously; hence, it is best to implement this logic using AND decomposition. As shown in figure 13.13, we shall change the decomposition of **Water_Dispenser** superstate to Parallel (AND) decomposition so that its substates **Hot**, **Cool**, and **Normal** shall have dashed boundaries, and each of them shall be active all the time.

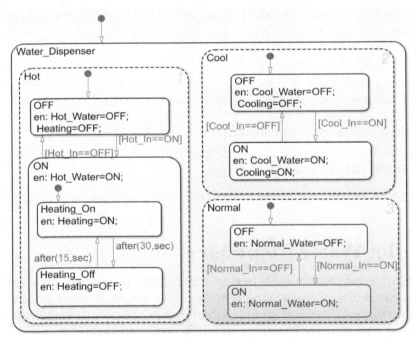

Figure 13.13: Example: Water dispenser Statechart

In *figure 13.13*, the Hot State has OR decomposition, and it has further two substates: OFF and ON. OFF is the default state; when heating is off and when the **HOT** button is pressed, **Heating** and **Hot** water output shall turn on. Heating is turned on with the **Heating_On** substate, from which the transition to **Heating_Off** takes place after 30 seconds. The heating is further turned on after 15 seconds. Both the transitions are implemented using temporal logic with the after keyword so that the transition takes place after a specified time and time unit. We shall learn the usage of temporal logic in detail in the upcoming chapter. Similarly, in the Cool State, cooling and cool water dispensing outputs turn on when the button is pressed. In the Normal State, room temperature water dispensing turns on when the button is pressed and turns off when released:

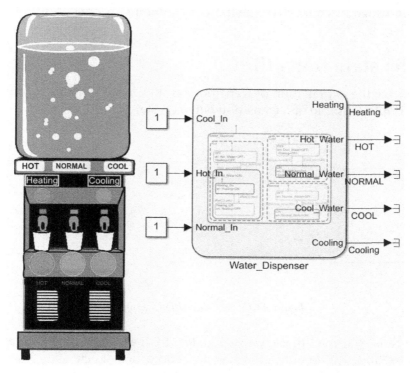

Figure 13.14: Example: Water dispenser simulation results

Transitions

Transitions are the connecting lines with arrowheads created between different objects, such as states and junctions. A transition can be straight or curved. We have already learned about transitions in *Chapter 12: Flow Graph* and the syntax and behavior of transition stay the same for transitions between states. When the transition from the source state to the destination occurs, the control shifts from one State to another. The syntax for state transitions is as follows:

%comment

event or message [Condition] {Condition Action}/Transition Action (Transition action can be specified without {} for C action language, with {} for MATLAB)

All the elements in this syntax are optional. We shall learn about different types of transitions in this section:

State transition

These are the transitions between different exclusive (OR) states. We shall also combine the usage of connective junctions to combine or create different decision paths.

Example: state transition

To reemphasize the explanation of transitions from *Chapter 12: Flow Graph*, we shall observe a simple example of a transition between states:

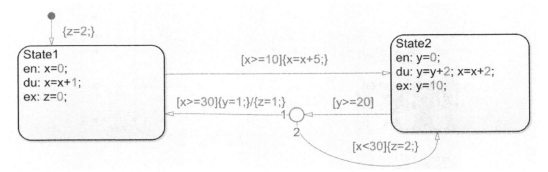

Figure 13.15: State transitions example

In the previous example, there are two states: **State1** and **State2**. **State1** is the default state, and the default state has an action, **z=2**. Each State has the entry, during, and exit conditions.

State1 is an active state. In **State1**, variable x is initialized to 0. Then the out-transition condition **x>=10** is evaluated as false. **State1** has no other valid out transition; therefore, during action shall be executed, and the value of **x** is incremented by **1** every sample time. When the value of x reaches **10**, in the next sample, the out transition is evaluated as true, and the condition action **x=x+5** is executed, so **x** becomes **15**. **State1** exit action is performed, so **z** becomes **0**.

State2 becomes an active state, and **State2** entry action is performed, so **y=0**. In the following sample time, the out transition condition **y>=20** is evaluated as false, so during the action is executed, where variables x and y are incremented by **2** every sample time until the value of **y** reaches **20**. When **y>=20** conditions is true, the following condition **x>=30** is evaluated, and condition action **y=1** is performed.

Please note that when the transition path from **State2** to **State1** is complete, and there will be a definite transition, only at that time is the transition action **z=1** specified after forward slash **/** is performed. The critical difference between condition action and transition action is that the condition action is executed before executing the transition when the respective condition is true. Still, transition action is performed when all the conditions on the transition path from one State to another are true, and the transition to the destination state is possible. After that, **State2** exit action is executed, **State2** is disabled, **State1** is active again, **State1** entry action is executed, and the cycle continues.

A connective junction is used to create an alternate path for the out transition of **State2**. If the condition **y>=20** is evaluated as true, and the first condition **x>=30** is false, in that case, the second condition **x<30** shall be evaluated, and if this condition is true, then the transition from **State2** shall be complete after executing condition action **z=2** and exit condition of **State2**. **State2** shall be reentered during the next cycle time, which means that the entry of **State2** shall be executed, and **State2** is an active state. Such transition originating and ending in the same State is known as **self-transition**.

Default transition

Default transition is a transition to an exclusive (OR) state or a junction without any source. If there are multiple exclusive (OR) states at one level, default transition helps specify the State, which should be active at the start of execution. Please remember that no default transition is required for parallel states, as multiple states shall be active at the same time. There are numerous ways one can implement default transition:

The simplest method is to create the default transition from the object palette and connect it to any desired exclusive (OR) state boundary.

Another way to use default transition is to specify the action(s) as its label, as shown in the example in *figure 13.15*, where we specify action **z=2** upon chart entry.

If the State to be entered must be decided based on the event or condition responsible for the state entry, there can be multiple default transitions with conditions at one level of the hierarchy. Additionally, there should be one unconditional default transition; else, there shall be an error due to the default setting of this diagnostic parameter: No unconditional default transitions. The setting of this parameter can be changed to warning or none, but if none of the conditions is true, it may cause behavioral issues.

Alternatively, an unconditional default transition can be attached to a connective junction, with further conditional transition paths to different states. The default state is decided based on the condition. In this case, too, there shall be no unconditional default path error due to the default value of the diagnostic setting, which can be adjusted based on the requirement.

Self-loop transition

The self-loop transition has the same State as its source and destination. When the transition condition is true, the State exits and reenters the same State. Usually, self-loop transitions are used to implement cases where a reset for the State is required; for example, a reset of a timer/counter can be achieved through a self-loop transition. In *figure 13.15*, we can see a self-loop transition connected to **State2**, which has conditions **y>=20** and **x<30**, and if both conditions are true, then **State2** is exited and reentered, so state entry is executed, which resets the value of **y** back to **0**.

> It is not necessary to have only one transition for a self-loop. Multiple transitions connected with junctions can also form a self-loop transition.

Inner transition

An inner transition is a transition internal to a state that starts within that State but does not leave it. Inner transitions simplify the type of logic in a state, where a specific logic is executed during every instance of an event, condition, or also during every state activation.

Example: inner transition

This example explains the possible use case of inner transition. We require that the timer state is activated only when the switch is pressed once. Two substates, **SwitchA** and **SwitchB**, count the total time elapsed since the last switch press in the timer superstate. Whenever the respective switch is pressed again, the timer must reset to its default value, and the active State must change based on the type of the switch input.

One method is to implement this logic using self-transitions and transitions between these two states. Alternatively, a simplified logic can be implemented with the help of inner transition:

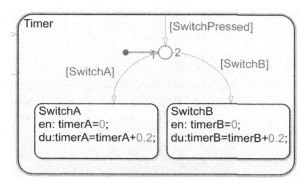

Figure 13.16: Inner transition example

As displayed in *figure 13.16*, we can implement the logic with inner transition, which starts from the state boundary and is connected to the junction, which also has default transition and out transitions based on the type of switch pressed. The timer superstate becomes active during execution when the `SwitchPressed` condition is true. During the first cycle, the default transition path is active, and based on which switch was pressed, Switch A or Switch B, either of the substates will be active and will start incrementing the respective timer. Now, the inner transition path is activated whenever a new `SwitchPressed` condition occurs when no out transitions are valid. Based on the new switch type, the old state exits, the new State becomes active, and the entry action is executed. Even when the newly activated State is the same as the previously active State, exit and entry actions are performed.

If no condition is specified on the inner condition, then the inner transition path is executed every sample time, as long as the State is valid, similar to during action.

Supertransition

Supertransition is a type of transition that supports the connection between different levels of the chart. Irrespective of the current level of the source and destination, Supertransition connects states at any possible levels. Supertransition, in combination with a subchart (chart within a chart), helps efficiently manage the complexity spanned across hierarchy levels. We shall discuss the subchart in the coming section. Supertransition enters or exits the subchart through a slit—a line from where Supertransition originates in the subchart or its arrowhead penetrates the line and exits the subchart.

To create a new supertransition from any object to a subchart, start a transition from the object and bring the arrowhead to the side of the subchart, so a slit shall be created, and the tip of the transition arrowhead seems to penetrate the subchart. The next step is to open the subchart, and the missing tip of the arrowhead is visible at the same position in red color coming out of the slit, drag the arrow and connect it to the desired destination object. In the case of multiple subchart levels, repeat these steps until the desired destination object is connected. In case of supertransition from the subchart to another object, follow the same procedure in reverse order.

Example: supertransition

To understand the application of Supertransition, let us consider Hot State as an example from a Water dispenser *figure 13.13*.

The State has two substates, OFF and ON, and the ON state has two more substates, `Heating_On` and `Heating_Off`. As shown in the first chart of the following figure, the OFF state has out transition to destination substate `Heating_On`, and `Heating_`

Off has a transition to the OFF state, so we can observe that these transitions cross one level of hierarchy to connect to their respective destination states:

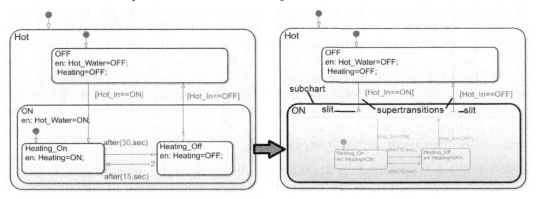

Figure 13.17: Supertransition example

To simplify the logic with multiple levels of hierarchy, we can convert the State into a subchart by performing right-click **Group & Subchart | Subchart** selection. If we convert ON State to Subchart, the resulting chart looks like the second chart in *figure 13.17*. The second chart shows that the transitions are converted into supertransitions, and they enter and exit the ON state through slits. Similarly, if we double-click and open the subchart ON, we shall see these transitions originating and exiting through slits in the subchart. The transition labels of supertransitions are visible at all the respective levels, also in the case of multiple levels of subcharts (subchart in a subchart). When the transition label is altered at any of the hierarchical levels, the change reflects in all of them.

Junctions

In Stateflow, we use two types of junctions: connective junctions and history junctions. We have already seen examples of connective junctions, also called junctions, in *Chapter 12: Flow Graph* and the current chapter. In this section, we shall discuss the applications of both in brief.

Connective junction

Connection junctions are round-shaped graphical objects that are used to create decision points in a Statechart. With the help of connective junctions, users can create multiple alternatives to a transition path in the flow graph as well as in Statechart. These are some of the possible situations where junctions are helpful:

- The transition from a single source object to a single destination object with multiple conditions and/or priorities.

- The transition from a single object to various objects.
- The transition from various objects to a single object.
- To create self-loop transitions.
- To create patterns such as if-else, for loop, switch case, and so on.

Connective junctions can be added from the object palette. To change the size of a connective junction, right-click **Junction size** and select the desired size. In the previous examples, such as figure 13.16, we can see Numbers 1 and 2 on transitions near the junction. These numbers are allocated at source junctions based on implicit ordering, indicating transition evaluation priority. The priority can be modified with explicit ordering by right-clicking **Execution order** and selecting new order operation.

History junction

History junctions are round graphical objects with the letter H written inside them—history junction stores historical state data for the states located at the same level. The history junction can be added from the object palette and placed anywhere in a state to store the history data. In case the history junction is placed inside a state, it will record activities of the State when the State is active, and during reactivation of that State, it resumes the activities from the previous execution. For example, consider a state with a counter, which has been incremented up to 1,600 in the last execution. During the subsequent state activation, instead of reinitializing the counter in entry action, the State will resume the counting from 1,601 onwards.

Example: history junction

We shall consider the example from *figure 13.16*, with the addition of the history junction, as shown in *figure 13.18*. We can add a history junction from the icon available in the object palette to anywhere in the ON state, but typically, it is placed in the top-right corner of the State. When the input signal **Hot_In** is ON, the parent state ON is activated, and the active State toggles between **Heating_On** and **Heating_Off** substates based on the elapsed time. Assume that when **Hot_In** input is turned OFF, before deactivating the State ON, the **Heating_Off** state was activated, and already 10 seconds had elapsed.

When **Hot_In** becomes ON again, in a typical scenario without a history junction, the **Heating_On** state becomes active, as it is the default state, and all timers are reset. Because of the History junction, the execution of **Heating_Off** is resumed from where it was left off, and after completing the remaining 5 seconds, the active state changes to **Heating_On** again.

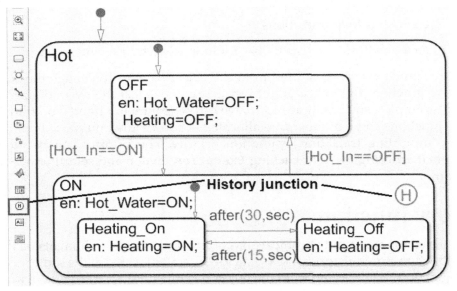

Figure 13.18: History junction example

Group and subchart

To combine the superstate and the implementation within it or to create a hierarchy level, Stateflow provides the option of Group State and Subchart. These options can be accessed by right-clicking **Group & Subchart** and selecting the desired option. In this section, we shall discuss in brief both options.

Group state

State grouping offers virtual grouping and ungrouping of a superstate and its content.

Consider a state with multiple levels of hierarchy. If we require moving the complete State, including all levels of hierarchy, from one place to another in the Statechart, or we need to resize all the states together, in this situation grouping feature becomes helpful. With the help of the group option, we can activate grouping for a superstate, and all states under the superstate are bound together. It is important to note that grouping is performed just for ease of graphical editing of the Statechart; the grouping does not have any impact on the hierarchy or the execution of the Stateflow logic. Compared with the ungrouped State, the grouped State becomes visible in a darker shade.

There are three ways to group/ungroup the states: we can double-click the top area of the State or right-click **Group and Subchart | Group**, or select the state and press shortcut keys *Ctrl + G*. Once the states are grouped, we can treat them as a single state and quickly move or resize them.

Figure 13.19 shows the difference between a grouped state and an ungrouped state:

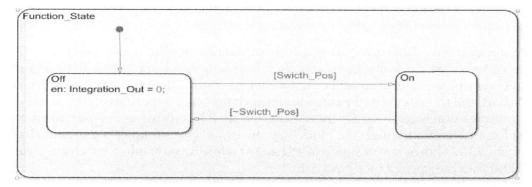

Ungrouped state

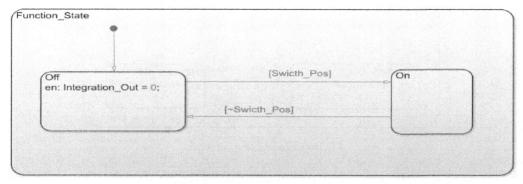

Grouped state

Figure 13.19: *Difference in the appearance of grouped/ungrouped states*

We can observe in *figure 13.19* that when states are grouped, a darker shadow is embedded in the state appearance to distinguish the grouped states from ungrouped states.

Subchart

A subchart is a feature that creates a chart within an existing chart. Subchart behaves the same way as a chart block. Subcharts help reduces the complexity of the Statechart logic with multiple levels of hierarchy. Any superstate can be selected and converted to a subchart either by right-clicking **Group & Subchart | Subchart** operation or by pressing shortcut keys *Ctrl + Shift + G*. When a superstate is converted to a subchart; its content becomes invisible to the higher level, which can be accessed by opening the subchart block. To open the subchart, double-click the subchart, and only the block content becomes visible at a separate level. Subchart does not modify the chart behavior in any way but supports easier chart management with visual separation of the logic. A subchart can contain another subchart within it, and there is no limitation on the possibility of creating subcharts.

The appearance of the subchart is a little different from the usual superstate, the boundary of the block is darker, and there is a horizontal line below the subchart name. As discussed in the earlier section, when a superstate is transformed into a subchart, the transitions to the outside states change into supertransitions. If any in or out transition is required for the subchart, it shall be created as a supertransition. The local transitions within the block stay the same. For example, the second chart in *figure 13.17* shows how a superstate changes while turning into a subchart. *Figure 13.20* shows the opened ON subchart:

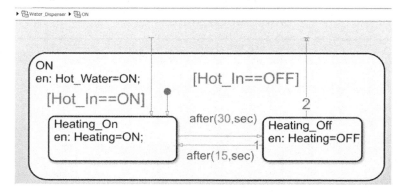

Figure 13.20: Subchart example

We can see in *figure 13.20* that the supertransitions are visible in the subchart entering and exiting through slits, and the subchart name ON is visible under the parent chart **Water_Dispenser**. Subchart provides a better possibility to distribute complex logic into smaller parts. A subchart can also have state actions, similar to a superstate.

Conclusion

This chapter has presented the concept of finite state machines using Statechart to the reader. The readers have been introduced to the states and state transition diagrams. They have learned the stepwise design process of a basic reactive system with definite operating modes. This chapter has also explained the applications of State actions, state hierarchy, and state decomposition in detail. This chapter has effectively used simple examples to introduce the readers to some practical applications of Stateflow.

Built upon the knowledge from the previous chapter, this chapter has taught the readers about different types of transitions and junctions in this chapter. In the end, the chapter introduces the readers to the concept of subchart and state grouping. In the upcoming chapter, the readers shall learn Implicit and explicit events, temporal logic, and functions such as graphical function, Simulink function, MATLAB function, and custom C-code function. The chapter shall also introduce the readers to the truth table and Simulink state.

Points to remember

- Statechart is a graphical representation of a finite state machine consisting of graphical objects such as transitions, junctions, states, and non-graphical objects such as events and data and their relationship.
- The state transition diagram is constructed with two elementary building blocks- states and the transitions.
- Stateflow chart can be built as a standalone chart that is executed as a MATLAB object.
- Statechart can be created as a Simulink block to be simulated as part of the Simulink model.
- A state in a Stateflow chart is used to describe the different operating modes of a reactive system.
- At a given time, a state can be either active or inactive.
- A state label can be described as a text written on the top-left corner of a state.
- State label has two parts: state name and state actions.
- The state name is specified on top of the state label. At the same level, two states cannot have the same name.
- A valid state name may contain alphanumeric characters (0–9, a–z, and A–Z) and underscore ("_").
- State actions are entry, during, and exit actions, all of which are optional.
- Data definition with Model Explorer is performed to define all the interfaces, variables, parameters, constants, and so on used within the chart.
- State hierarchy helps manage multilevel state complexity by organizing the states into multiple parent and child state levels.
- The parent state is known as a superstate, and the child state is termed a substate.
- State decomposition specifies the type of substates a superstate can have.

- There are two possible decompositions for a state: OR (Exclusive) decomposition and AND (Parallel) decomposition.
- All the substates must have the same type, identical to the superstate decomposition within a superstate.
- In the case of exclusive decomposition, only one State can be active.
- In the case of parallel decomposition, multiple states shall be active simultaneously.
- OR decomposition substates have solid borders, whereas AND decomposition substates have dashed borders.
- Transitions are the connecting lines with arrowheads created between different objects, such as states and junctions.
- Default transition is a transition to an exclusive (OR) state or a junction without any source.
- The self-loop transition has the same State as its source and destination.
- An inner transition is a transition internal to a state that starts within that State but does not leave it.
- Supertransition is a type of transition that supports the connection between different levels of the chart.
- Connective junctions are round-shaped graphical objects used to create multiple variations in the transition paths.
- History junction stores historical state data for the states located at the same level.
- State grouping is a virtual grouping and ungrouping of a superstate and its content.
- A Subchart is a graphical object that creates a chart within an existing chart.

Multiple choice questions

1. **What is the extension of the standalone chart file?**
    a. .mdl
    b. .slx
    c. .sfx
    d. None of the above

2. A state name can start with an alphanumeric character.
    a. TRUE
    b. FALSE

3. In Stateflow, two states cannot be active at a time.
    a. TRUE
    b. FALSE

4. Which of the action languages are available in Stateflow?
    a. MATLAB
    b. C
    c. Fortran
    d. Both a & b

5. Which of the following is not a state action?
    a. at
    b. entry
    c. exit
    d. during

6. A substate can also be a superstate.
    a. TRUE
    b. FALSE

7. Which of the following is not a type of transition?
    a. Supertransition
    b. Self-transition
    c. Subtransition
    d. Inner transition

8. Are subcharts and substates identical?
    a. TRUE
    b. FALSE

9. Grouping of the State creates a level of hierarchy.
    a. TRUE
    b. FALSE

10. **What type of data can be added using Model Explorer?**
    a. Inputs
    b. Events
    c. Locals
    d. All of the above

Questions

1. Explain the rules for State name.
2. Explain applications of State actions with an example.
3. What are the types of transitions in Stateflow?
4. What is the significance of a superstate?
5. When are parallel states used?
6. Explain the process to switch the states from OR decomposition to AND decomposition and vice versa.
7. When are the history junctions used in a Statechart?
8. Explain the benefits of the subchart with an appropriate example.
9. What are the different fields available in the symbols pane?
10. Create a Statechart of a traffic light logic and describe the steps.

Answers

1. c
2. b
3. b
4. d
5. a
6. a
7. c
8. b
9. b
10. d

CHAPTER 14
Event-Based Execution

Introduction

In the previous chapters, the readers have gone through the basic features of the Stateflow graphical editor, flow graph, Statechart, and its hierarchical model. They have educated themselves about the basic properties of Stateflow and its advantages over Simulink. They have learnt the creation of simple Stateflow logic using transitions and junctions. They have received adequate knowledge to implement a statechart hierarchical model to simplify and optimize the algorithm. They have educated themselves about some advanced concepts of statechart such as Superstate, Substate, Subcharts, Super transition, composition, and so on. In this chapter, we shall learn some more advanced concepts of Stateflow, such as event-based execution. These concepts will help us understand Stateflow in-depth to efficiently implement edged-/trigger-based logic.

Structure

In this chapter, we are going to cover the following topics.

- Events
    - Implicit events
    - Explicit events

- Temporal logic
- Stateflow function or Graphical function
- Simulink Function
- MATLAB function
- Truth table
- Simulink state
- Calling of custom "C" code functions

Objectives

After studying this chapter, the reader will be able to:

- Work with different types of events
- Understand internal timers using temporal logic
- Use Simulink logic in Stateflow using the Simulink function and Simulink state
- Apply MATLAB code in Stateflow using the MATLAB function
- Handle combination of different conditions using truth table
- Use custom "C" code in Stateflow

Events

One of the essential functions of the Stateflow is the event. Based on generated events, we can perform actions accordingly. These events help to execute certain functions at a specific instance. Stateflow contains two types of events. Implicit events and explicit events. Implicit events are built-in events that are not required to be defined in the data explorer. Explicit events are user-defined events that must be defined in the data explorer.

Implicit events

The implicit events can be categorized based on whether they are data-based or state-based events. The implicit events are always local events that cannot be accessed outside the Stateflow. *Table 14.1* explains some of the implicit events available in Stateflow:

Event	Syntax	Description

`Enter`	`enter(state)`
	
	 `en(state)`
		This event is a state-based event. When execution control enters the specified "state", this event occurs. This event is used in the parallel (AND) states.

`Exit`	`exit(state)`
	
	 `ex(state)`
		This event is also state based. This event occurs when the execution control exits from the specified "state". This event is also used in a parallel (AND) state.

`In`	`in(state)`	It is also a state-based event. This event occurs when the execution control is inside a specified "state". This event is also used in a parallel (AND) state.

`change`	`change(data)`
	
	 `chg(data)`
		This event is a data-based event. When the value to "data" is assigned, this event occurs. We can use this event in both parallel (AND) or non-parallel states.

`hasChanged`	`hasChanged(data)`	This event is a data-based event. This event is used to detect a change in input data value.
`hasChangedFrom`	`hasChangedFrom(data, value)`	This event is a data-based event. It is used to detect the change in the value of input data from a specific value.
`hasChangedTo`	`hasChangedTo(data, value)`	This is a data-based event. This is used to detect a change in the value of input data to a specific value.

`tick`	`after(10,tick)`
	
	 `on(10,tick)`
	
	 `before(10,tick)`
	
	 `every(10,tick)`
	
	 `at(10,tick)`
	
	 `temporalCount(tick)`
		This event is neither data nor state-based event; the tick specifies each execution cycle of the Statechart. Tick is used in temporal logic. We shall look into temporal logic in upcoming sections.

Table 14.1: Implicit events

Figure 14.1 shows these implicit events in the Statechart:

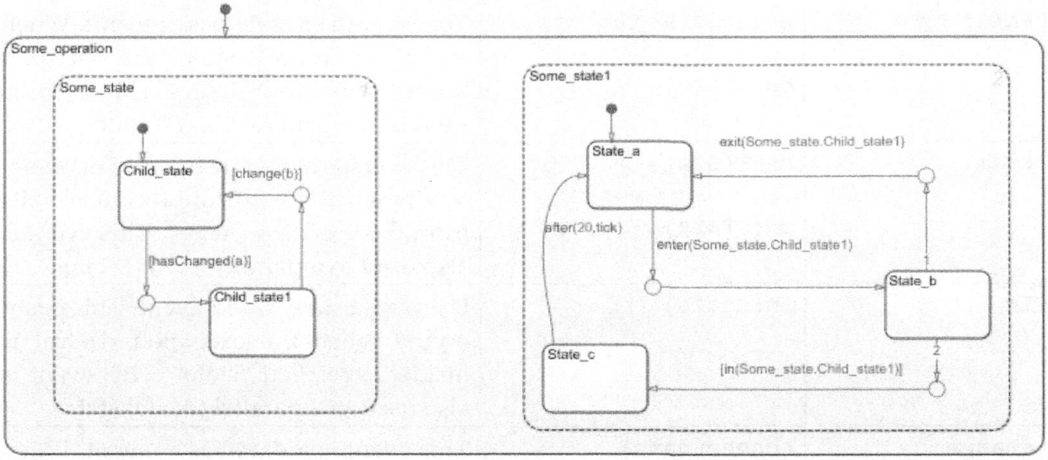

Figure 14.1: *Implicit events in Stateflow*

Explicit events

Explicit events are required to be defined in the data explorer. They can be either Input events, Output events, or Local events. Before getting into details of explicit events, first, we need to see how they are defined in the data explorer. *Figure 14.2* shows how to open the explorer. Right-click anywhere on Statechart and select explorer from the menu. Then click on the flashing symbol to add the event. By default, it will create the local event:

Figure 14.2: *Add events using explorer*

There is a window on the right-hand side of the explorer; using that, we can change the type of event. *Figure 14.3* shows how to change the scope of the event:

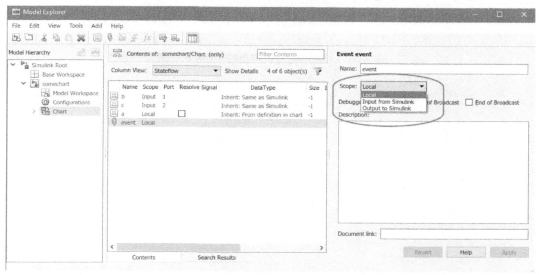

Figure 14.3: *Change event scope*

Now, let us see these events in detail:
- Input event: The scope of this event is **Input from Simulink**. The scope itself suggests that these events are coming to the state chart. They are used to execute the Statechart when input events are active. When we do not have input events, the statechart executes at every cycle when the parent subsystem is active. Input events can be of two types, Edge trigger or Function call.

Users can configure the edge trigger to the rising, falling, or edge. *Figure 14.4* displays different options available for an input event:

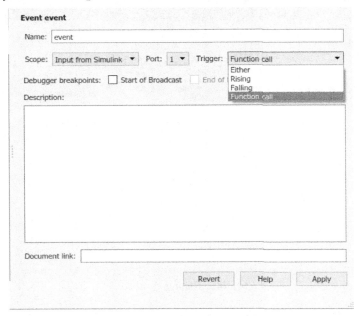

Figure 14.4: *Input event options*

Input event port is always added at the top side of the Statechart. We can add multiple input events. However, it is required that all input events must be of the same type; either they can be edge triggers or function call triggers. To feed these events to the Statechart, we must mux them before connecting. Muxing is required only if there are more than one input event; otherwise, we can directly connect the required event to the trigger port. In our example, we have two events; both of them are function call events. In *figure 14.5*, let us observe how muxing is used to feed input events:

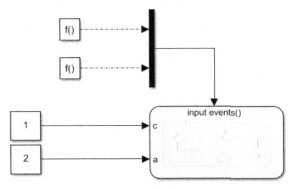

Figure 14.5: *Muxing of the input events*

It is important to note that we cannot use the *tick* implicit event in that statechart when we use input events.

- **Output event**: The scope of the output event is **Output to Simulink**. These events are the outputs of the Statechart. Which are used to control Simulink blocks execution. Most of the time, output events are used in the schedulers. Output events can also be of either edge trigger or function call. *Figure 14.6* shows the options available for the output event:

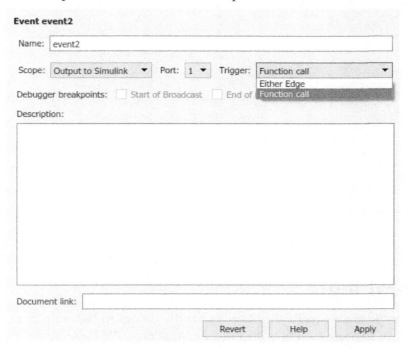

Figure 14.6: Options for output events

Output events are triggered using the **send** keyword. This command can be used at any of the actions. In our example, we have added **event2** as a function call, which we are sending when execution control enters the state **State_a**. *Figure 14.7* depicts the same:

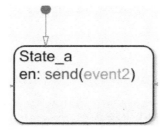

Figure 14.7: Trigger output event

- **Local event**: These are local to the Statechart. These events are sent to other parallel states in the Statechart. Similar to the output events, they are also triggered using the **send** command. In our example, we are sending event **local_event** from **Some_state** to **Some_state1**. *Figure 14.8* shows that the local event **local_event** is triggered from **Some_state** to **Some_state1**. So, when **local_event** is triggered by **Some_state**, the execution control changes from **Child_state** to **Child_state1** in **Some_state1**:

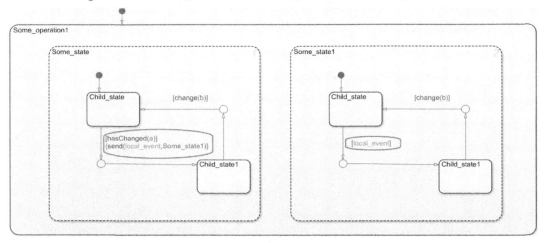

Figure 14.8: Local event triggered locally in the statechart

Temporal logic

Simulink provides an excellent option to handle timers in the statechart. Temporal Logic helps to execute timers with built-in functions. We have already seen some of the temporal functions in the *tick* implicit event. With tick, additional commands such as sec, msec, or usec also are used with these functions. Now, let us learn these functions or temporal logic operators in detail.

- **After**: This operator is used to perform the timer operation. It returns true when the timer is elapsed. So, this operator can be used with some other conditions, which are required to be checked after timer is elapsed. The syntax of **after** function is given as follows:

```
after(10,tick)
after(10,sec)
after(10,msec)
after(10,usec)
after(10,explicit_Input_event)
local_event[after(10,sec)]
```

In the preceding lines of code, we can see, **after** returns **true** if execution control remains in the respective state for more than 10 ticks, 10 execution cycles of explicit input event or 10 seconds, or 10 milliseconds or 10 microseconds. In addition, we can use the **after** operator to trigger events when conditions are true. Let us realize the usage of the **after** operator in the actual statechart using *figure 14.9*:

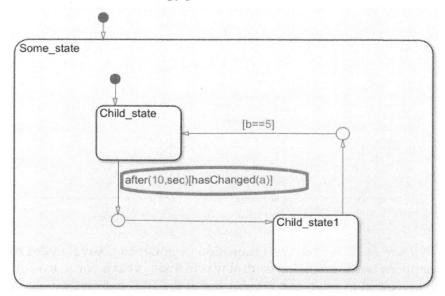

Figure 14.9: *Use of "after" temporal logic operator*

In *figure 14.9*, we can see that a transition from **Child_state** to **Child_state1** occurred when execution control was in **Some_state** for 10 seconds, and after 10 seconds, input **a** changes its value.

- **At**: This operator also performs the timer operation; it returns true only for one sample time when the timer elapses. We can use this operator to perform actions exactly when the timer has elapsed. With the **at** operator, we can also add other conditions. The syntax of this operator is given as follows:

```
at(10,tick)
at(10,explicit_Input_event)
local_event[at(10,tick)]
```

In the preceding lines of code, we can see **at** returns **true** if execution control remains in the respective state for 10 ticks or 10 execution cycles of the explicit input event. Also, the **at** operator can trigger events when conditions are **true**; unlike the **after** operator, we cannot use **sec**, **msec**, or **usec** keywords for the **at** operator. In our example, we have explicit input events. Let us realize the usage of the **at** operator in the actual statechart using *figure 14.10*:

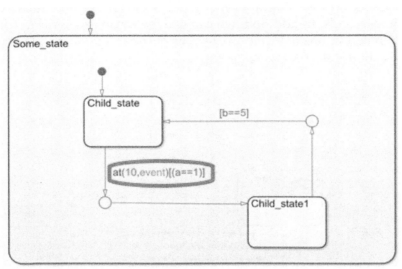

Figure 14.10: Use of "at" temporal logic operator

In *figure 14.10*, we can see a transition from **Child_state** to **Child_state1** happens when execution control was in **Some_state** for 10 execution cycles when input event **event** is valid and at the 10th cycle if the value of input **a** is **1**.

- **Before**: This operator returns true before the mentioned timer value elapses. We use this operator when specific actions must be performed before the timer elapses. Similar to other temporal logic operators, with the **before** operator as well, we can add other conditions. This operator is the opposite of the **after** operator. The syntax of the **before** operator can be used like the following:

```
before(10,tick)
before (10,sec)
before (10,msec)
before (10,usec)
before (10,explicit_Input_event)
local_event[before (10,sec)]
```

In the preceding lines of code, we can see **before** returns **true** for every execution cycle if execution control remains in the respective state for less than 10 ticks, or 10 execution cycles of explicit input event or 10 seconds, or

10 milliseconds or 10 microseconds. Also, the **before** operator can trigger events when conditions are true. Let us see the usage of the **before** operator in the actual statechart using *figure 14.11*:

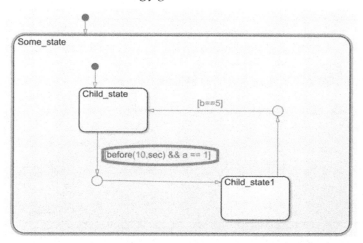

Figure 14.11: *Use of "before" temporal logic operator*

In *figure 14.11*, we can see a transition from `Child_state` to `Child_state1` happens when execution control was in `Some_state` for less than 10 seconds, and before 10 seconds, input **a** attains its value to **1**.

- **Every**: This operator returns **true** at every specified cycle. Like the **at** operator, we can also not use **sec**, **msec**, **usec** keywords. With this operator as well, we can use other conditions. The syntax of **every** operator is mentioned as the following:

`every(10,tick)`

`every(10,explicit_Input_event)`

`local_event[every(10,tick)]`

In the preceding lines of code, as we can see, **every** returns **true** if execution control for every 10th tick or every 10th execution cycle of the explicit input event. Also, the **every** operator can trigger events when conditions are **true**.

In our example, we have explicit input events. Let us understand the usage of the **every** operator in the actual statechart using *figure 14.12*:

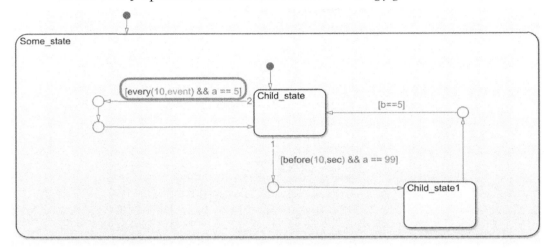

Figure 14.12: Use of "every" temporal logic operator

In *figure 14.12*, we can see self-transition from **Child_state** occurs every 10th execution cycle when input event **event** is valid and input **a** is **5**.

- **Temporal Count**: We have seen temporal logic operators used to handle timers until now. However, we may have a requirement to monitor the elapsed time. The temporal count is used for the same. The **temporalCount** operator returns the number of ticks or execution cycles of explicit input events till the execution control is active in the specified state. The syntax of the **temporalCount** is given as follows:

temporalCount(tick)

temporalCount(explicit_Input_event)

In our example, we have explicit input events. So **temporalCount** gives the number of execution cycles when **event** was triggered. Let us check the use of **temporalCount** in *figure 14.13*:

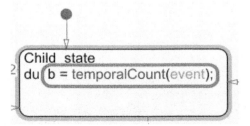

Figure 14.13: Use of "temporalCount" temporal logic operator

In *figure 14.13*, variable **b** holds the number of cycles when the state `Child_state` is active.

Stateflow functions or graphical functions

Suppose we have a logic pattern used at multiple places in the Stateflow/statechart. We can implement this pattern in a graphical function and call the function wherever required. We can add a graphical function from the left side of the toolbar and then at the empty place in the statechart. *Figure 14.14* displays the option for graphical function selection:

Figure 14.14: *Add graphical function from the toolbar*

It simplifies Stateflow logic up to a bigger extent. Imagine we have three inputs **a**, **b**, and **c**. All of them are required to be classified concerning some thresholds. We have two thresholds, `threshold_1` and `threshold_2`. They can have different values for input **a**, **b**, and **c**. If the input value is lesser than `threshold_1`, it is `class_1`. When the value is in-between `threshold_1` and `threshold_2`, then it is `class_2`. And when the value is greater than **threshold_2**, it is **class_3**. The pseudo-code of this logic will look like the following:

```
class = function Classify_signal(signal, threshold_1, threshold_2)
{
    if (signal < threshold_1)
    {
        class = 1;
    elseif (signal < threshold_2)
        class =2;
    else
        class = 3;
    }
}
```

As this classification must be done for every input signal, we can create a graphical function to implement the previously mentioned pseudo code. The *figure 14.15* illustrates the **classify_signal** function in Stateflow:

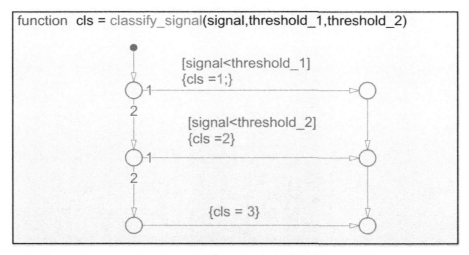

Figure 14.15: Graphical function

We call graphical function separately for three signals **a**, **b**, and **c**. In our example, we use three parallel states to classify input signals. Control goes to the respective class states based on the determined class execution. Certainly, the use of the graphical function simply helps the Stateflow logic. We call the function **classify_signal** for each place and save lots of graphical space. This approach also helps in maintenance. Therefore, whenever there is a change in the logic of the graphical function, we need to make the change only in one place. We can directly realize it with **C** functions. The *figure 14.16* helps to understand the use of graphical functions in state-based logic:

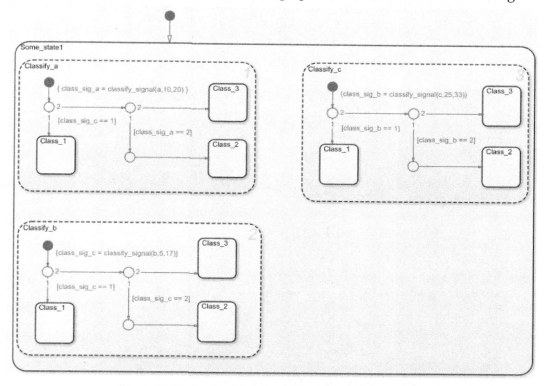

Figure 14.16: *Graphical function calling syntax in a statechart*

As we can see in *figure 14.16*, at every reset transition, we check the class of input signal, and based on the return value of the graphical function, and the target state is activated.

Simulink function

Suppose there is already a pattern or library block available that we need to use in Stateflow. Using the *Simulink function*, we can use the already existing pattern or library from Simulink in Stateflow. We can select the `Simulink function` option from the left side toolbar. In addition, add it to the Stateflow at an empty place. *Figure 14.17* shows the toolbar option for the **Simulink function**:

Figure 14.17: Add the Simulink function from the toolbar

Let us consider the same example mentioned in the graphical function. We need to classify the input signals based on the thresholds. In addition, we already have a Simulink logic available for the same. Then, we can use the Simulink function and implement the Simulink logic in it. Simulink function has a similar signature (pattern for inputs, outputs, and function name) as graphical function. The syntax of the Simulink function definition is as follows:

[Output1, Output2,…OutputN] = Function_name(Arg1,Arg2,Arg3…, ArgN)

Figure 14.18 shows how the Simulink function looks in the Stateflow:

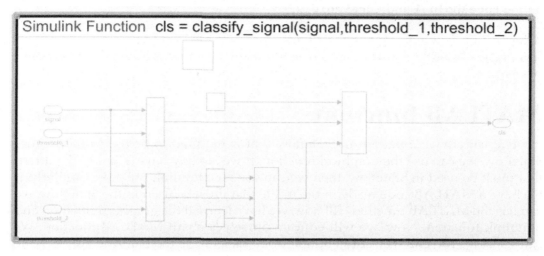

Figure 14.18: Simulink function view from parent Stateflow

Simulink function is a function-call subsystem, and we cannot change the subsystem type. The Simulink function is called similarly to the graphical function. Input ports and output ports are automatically added as inputs and outputs in the signature of the Simulink function. Unlike a Simulink library block, the Simulink function works like a C function. Whenever the Simulink function is called, execution control goes to the Simulink function and returns to the caller after execution. The Simulink logic for classifying inputs can be implemented as per *figure 14.19*:

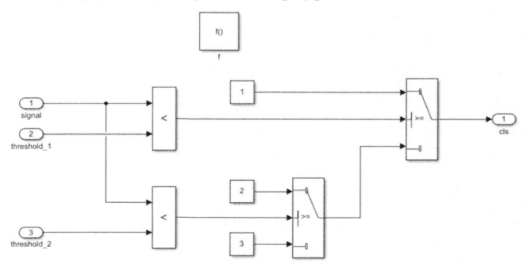

Figure 14.19: Simulink function logic for classification of input

As we can see in *figure 14.19*, the `signal` is the input signal, which we classify, based on the `threshold_1` and `threshold_2`.

> Check box `Execute (enter) Chart at Initialization` from Stateflow properties should be unchecked if the Simulink function is being called at reset transition.

MATLAB function

If we already have a pattern in Stateflow that is required to be used in any other Stateflow, we can use the graphical function. If we already have a Simulink pattern that must be used in Stateflow, then we can use the Simulink function. Similarly, if we have a MATLAB code ready in the m-file that must be used in the Stateflow, we can use the MATLAB function. Till now, we have learned the graphical function and Simulink function. Now, we will educate ourselves about MATLAB function. We can select the `MATLAB function` option from the left side toolbar. And add it in the Stateflow at an empty place. *Figure 14.20* shows the toolbar option for the `MATLAB function`:

Figure 14.20: Add MATLAB function from the toolbar

Let us consider the same example. We need to classify the input signals based on the thresholds. In addition, we already have a MATLAB code available for the same, or we want to use a MATLAB code in Stateflow. Then we can use the MATLAB function and write MATLAB code in it. MATLAB function has a similar signature (pattern for inputs, outputs, and function name) as the graphical function and Simulink function. *Figure 14.21* shows how the MATLAB function looks in Stateflow:

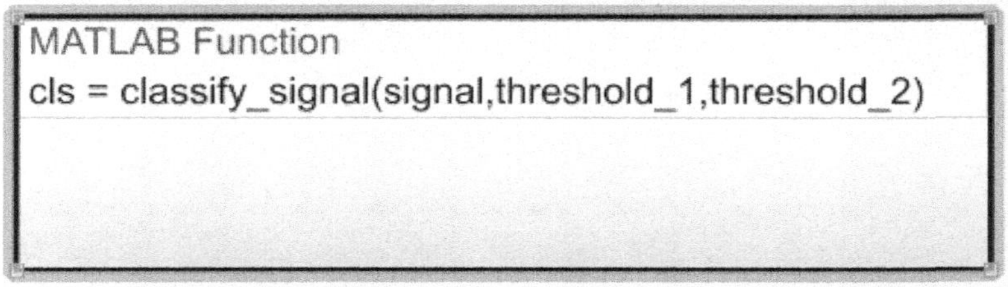

```
MATLAB Function
cls = classify_signal(signal,threshold_1,threshold_2)
```

Figure 14.21: MATLAB function view from parent stateflow

MATLAB function is called in a way similar to graphical function and Simulink function. MATLAB function is the same as the m-function, where we can use all possible MATLAB commands. The MATLAB code for classifying inputs can be written as mentioned in *figure 14.22*:

```
classify_signal
1    function cls = classify_signal(signal,threshold_1,threshold_2)
2        if (signal < threshold_1)
3            cls = 1;
4        elseif (signal < threshold_2)
5            cls = 2;
6        else
7            cls = 3;
8        end
9
10
11
```

Figure 14.22: MATLAB function code for classification of input

As we can see in *figure 14.22*, the **signal** is the input signal that we classify based on the **threshold_1** and **threshold_2**.

Truth table

When we have many conditions with different combinations and based on these conditions, we need to take action; the truth table is the best option available in Stateflow. Unlike functions, the truth table does not have an option for input/output arguments. We can use all data elements declared in explorer in the truth table. Therefore, if we use a truth table to classify the inputs, then we need to use explicit conditions. We can either use a separate truth table for each input or add all conditions in the single truth table with the **don't care** option. We can select the **Truth table** option from the left side toolbar and add it to the Stateflow at an empty place. *Figure 14.23* shows the toolbar option for the **Truth table**:

Figure 14.23: Add a truth table from the toolbar

Let us consider the same example. We need to classify the input signals based on the thresholds. Now, we implement the conditions and their combinations for inputs **a**, **b**, and **c**. Nevertheless, before that, let us see what the truth table looks like in Stateflow in *figure 14.24*:

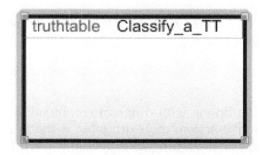

Figure 14.24: Truth table view from parent Stateflow

The truth table contains two tables, the condition table, and the action table. We have columns for description, condition, and decision in the condition table. The number of rows it contains is as many as its conditions. Additionally, there is one more row to select the action from the action table. It is the last row from the condition table. Column description is optional; it can be kept empty. However, we can add a description to have better readability. In the action table, we can perform the actions. It is a must to have a default column with don't care conditions that can perform default actions. *Figure 14.25* illustrates the use of the Truth table to classify the input a concerning **threshold_1** and **threshold_2**. Here, we have used hardcoded thresholds:

	DESCRIPTION	CONDITION	D1	D2	D3	D4
1	a is less than threshold_1	a < 10	T	F	F	-
2	a is inbetween threshold_1 and threshold_2	a >= 10 && a < 20	F	T	F	-
3	a is greater than or equal threshold_2	a >= 20	F	F	T	-
		ACTIONS: SPECIFY A ROW FROM THE ACTION TABLE	1	2	3	1

Action Table

	DESCRIPTION	ACTION
1	Set Class = 1	class_sig_a = 1;
2	set Class = 2	class_sig_a = 2;
3	set Class = 3	class_sig_a = 3;

Figure 14.25: Truth table for classification of input

In *figure 14.25*, we can see a condition table with different conditions required for input classification with the necessary description. We also have decision columns D1, D2, D3, and D4, where individual cells are configured with either true or false. The last column, D4, is mandatory for **don't care** conditions. "-" indicates **don't care**. **T** indicates true, and "F" indicates false. In the last row, we have mentioned the row number of the action table required when combinations of conditions as per the decision column are true. It is important to note that combinations in the column for a decision must be unique among other columns. Else, we get the model compilation error. From the condition table, we can see combinations from column **D1** results in Class 1, combinations from column **D2** results in Class 2, and combinations from column **D3** results in Class 3. These results are formed based on actions mentioned in the action table. The action table has two columns, one for the description and the other for action. As we have three inputs, a, b, and c, classified based on thresholds, we have three truth tables: `Classify_a_TT`, `Classify_b_TT`, and `Classify_c_TT`. These truth tables are called similar to the functions. *Figure 14.26* shows the calling procedure of truth tables:

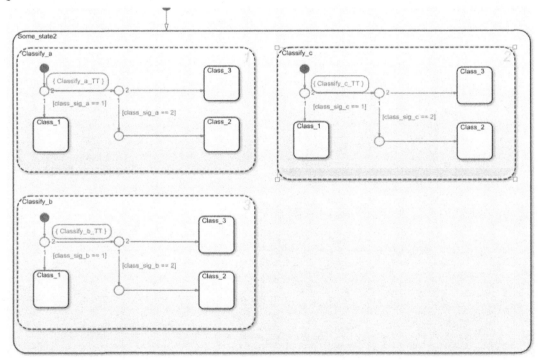

Figure 14.26: Truth table for classification of input

Simulink state

Like the `Simulink function`, state flow has a `Simulink state`. Simulink state can be used as a state in place of a state flow state. Imagine we already have some Simulink libraries that must be executed when execution control goes to a particular state. Simulink state acts as an action subsystem whenever it is activated. First, let us learn how to add Simulink state in the statechart. To do that, we have to select the `Simulink state` option from the left side toolbar. *Figure 14.27* depicts the same:

Figure 14.27: Add Simulink state from the toolbar

Suppose we have two states, **On** and **Off**. When a state **On** is activated, we need to perform an integration operation on an input. We can use the Simulink state for the **On** state. When the switch changes its position from Off to On, the On state gets activated, and when it changes from On to Off, the Off state gets activated. *Figure 14.28* shows the design of On/Off states using Simulink state:

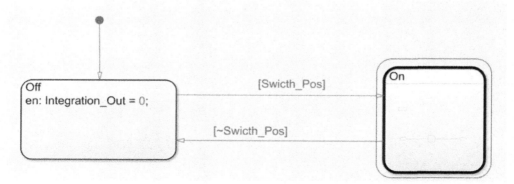

Figure 14.28: Simulink state view from parent Stateflow

When the **Off** state is active output, **Integration_Out** is set to 0. Under on state, we are doing the integration operation for input **a**. **On** state is a Simulink state, which is nothing but an **action** subsystem. *Figure 14.29* shows the implementation for the state **On**:

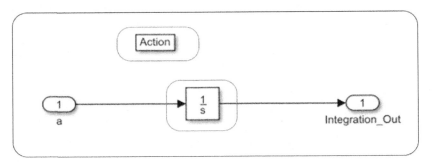

Figure 14.29: Simulink state implementation for integration operation

All inputs/outputs for the statechart are accessible from the Simulink state. In our example, **a** is the input, and **Integration_Out** is the output of the statechart. To realize the use of the Simulink state, let us simulate the preceding logic. We feed sinewave to the input **a**, and **Switch_Pos** changes between 0 and 1 and 0. Let us observe the output **Integration_Out** concerning inputs **Switch_Pos** and **a** in the scope. The following image shows the waveform we get for **Integration_Out**, **a**, and **Switch_Pos**, respectively. Cannot change the type of subsystem. The Simulink function is called similarly to a graphical function. Input ports and output ports automatically get added as inputs and outputs in the signature of the Simulink function. Unlike a Simulink library block, the Simulink function works like a **C** function. That means, Whenever the Simulink function is called, execution control goes to the Simulink function and returns to the caller after execution. The Simulink logic for classifying inputs can be implemented as per *figure 14.30*:

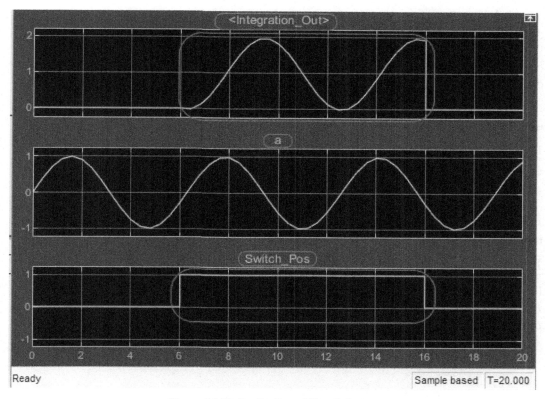

Figure 14.30: Realization of Simulink state

Therefore, we can see, Integration of signal **a** happens only when `Switch_Pos` is 1. That is between 6 and 16 in the waveform for `Integration_Out`.

Calling external "C" function from statechart

We have seen different functions such as graphical function, Simulink function, and MATLAB function. All these functions are part of MATLAB modeling. Statechart supports calling the external **C** function. Suppose we already have some optimized **C** code that is required to use in the statechart, then we can do that. So, we save lots of effort for converting those **C** functions in Simulink or Statechart logic. First, we need to add the required header files and source files in the `Simulink Target` pane inside the model settings. We have a **C** file that performs an optimized multiplication operation. This file contains a function **custom_mul**, which we call from the statechart. We have **sf_cutom_mutiplication.h** and **sf_cutom_mutiplication.c** that contains the required multiplication function. The header file contains an extern declaration of the "**custom_mul**" function. The following code is part of the content of the header file:

```
extern int custom_mul(int Arg1, int Arg2);
```

The following code is part of .c file:

```
#include "sf_cutom_mutiplication.h"
int custom_mul(int Arg1, int Arg2)
{
return Arg1*Arg2;
}
```

It is necessary to have all required files directly where model files are located. *Figure 14.31* shows the declaration of header files in source files in the **Simulation Target** pane:

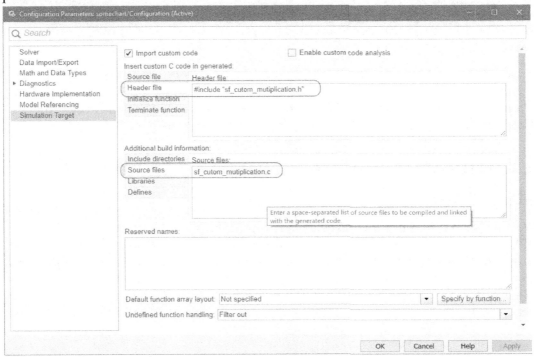

Figure 14.31: Simulation target pane

To call the custom **C** function, we need to use its signature similar to other functions. *Figure 14.32* depicts the same:

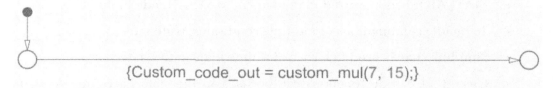

Figure 14.32: Call custom C function

Wherever we can perform the actions in a statechart, we can call the custom **C** code function from all those places.

> **MATLAB function uses the m-script, whereas the external c function uses the c code.**

Conclusion

In this chapter, we have learnt about event-based execution in Stateflow. We have also gone through the concepts of different built-in events and their usage in parallel states. These built-in events are called implicit events. After implicit events, the chapter takes the reader to explicit events, which must be defined in the model explorer. The reader has been educated on the handling of timers using temporal logic. After temporal logic, the reader has been introduced to various functions such as graphical function, Simulink function, and MATLAB function. The reader has understood the usage of the truth table and Simulink state. At the end of the chapter, the reader has learned how to use custom "C" code functions in Stateflow. In the upcoming chapter, the reader will learn various parsing and debugging techniques for Stateflow. The reader will get familiar with Breakpoints, Stateflow animation, and Data displays.

Points to remember

- The events built-in in the Stateflow are called implicit events.
- Implicit events are not required to be added in the model explorer.
- Explicit events are classified as input, output, and local events.
- Explicit events are required to be defined in model explorer.
- Timer handling in the Stateflow is done using temporal logic operators.
- To reuse the existing Stateflow logic, graphical functions are implemented

- Simulink logic or libraries can be reused in Stateflow using the Simulink function.
- MATLAB function is used to implement MATLAB code in the statechart.
- To handle combinations of multiple conditions, truth tables are used.
- Simulink state is used to have a Simulink logic in the statechart.
- Custom "C" code functions can be used in the statechart after declaring header files and source files in the Simulation Target pane in the model setting.
- It is required to keep source files and header files at the exact location of the model file.

Multiple choice questions

1. "tick" is the implicit event.
    a. True
    b. False

2. "tick" can be used in a statechart where explicit input events are used.
    a. True
    b. False

3. "enter" implicit event used in parallel states.
    a. True
    b. False

4. Which type of data "hasChanged" is used for?
    a. Input
    b. Local
    c. Event
    d. None of the above

5. Are events triggered from statechart using the "send" keyword?
    a. False
    b. True

6. Which of the following temporal logic operator is used to check conditions on execution of the timer?

    a. before

    b. after

    c. at

    d. both B & C

7. Which of the following can be used to implement similar Stateflow logic at multiple places in the statechart?

    a. Graphical function

    b. Simulink function

    c. Custom "C" code function

    d. All of the above

8. Simulink functions are function call subsystems.

    a. True

    b. False

9. Simulink state is used to implement MATLAB code in the statechart.

    a. True

    b. False

10. Which of the following value can the decision column cell have in the truth table?

    a. T

    b. F

    c. –(don't care)

    d. All of the above

11. To use Custom "C" code functions in Statechart, it must declare headers and source files in the Simulation target pane in model properties.

    a. False

    b. True

Questions

1. Explain the difference between implicit and explicit events.
2. Explain the temporal logic.
3. List different types of functions available in Statechart.
4. Explain graphical function with its advantages.
5. What is the Simulink function?
6. What is the difference between the Simulink function and Simulink state?
7. Explain the MATLAB functions.
8. Explain the condition and action tables in the truth table.
9. Explain the process of calling the custom "C" code function.
10. Create a statechart logic to implement a car's roof lamp functionality. When a door is opened, the roof lamp shall turn on. It shall turn off after 60 seconds or all doors are closed. Use temporal logic to implement the 60-second timer.

Answers

1. a
2. b
3. a
4. a
5. b
6. d
7. a
8. a
9. b
10. d
11. a

CHAPTER 15
Stateflow Parsing and Debugging

Introduction

Brian Kernighan says *"Debugging is twice as hard as writing the code in the first place. Therefore, if you write the code as cleverly as possible, you are, by definition, not smart enough to debug it"*. Debugging is the most critical phase of any software development, and the same applies to Stateflow. Stateflow provides us with many ways to debug, which helps pinpoint exactly the defective part of Stateflow logic. This chapter takes the reader to different ways of Stateflow parsing. This chapter also introduces the reader to various debugging options.

Structure

In this chapter, we are going to cover the following topics.

- Stateflow parsing
    - Update Chart
    - Live Parsing
- Debugging options in Stateflow
    - Breakpoints
        - Breakpoint on transition when transition condition is valid

- Breakpoint on transition when transition condition is tested
- Breakpoint on state
  o Stateflow animation
  o Data displays

Objectives

After studying this chapter, the reader will be able to:

- Understand Stateflow parsing techniques such as "Update Chart."
- Use parsing with Stateflow model configuration settings
- Use different debugging options such as "Breakpoints."
- Handle Stateflow animation
- Use data displays during simulation

Stateflow parsing

We need parsing techniques to detect errors—such as syntax errors or variable use before declaring, and so on. Similarly, the Stateflow parser is used to see these kinds of errors.

Update Chart

The **Update Chart** option is available in the **DEBUG** context menu of Stateflow. **Update Chart** parses the Stateflow for the syntax errors. First, navigate the debug context menu and click the dropdown arrow near the **Update Model** option to perform the update chart operation. Then select the **Update Chart** option. *Figure 15.1* shows the **Update Chart** option:

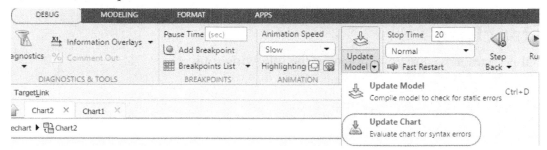

Figure 15.1: Update Chart option

To understand the use of the **Update Chart** in detail, let us consider an example where we introduce an intentional error. We do not declare the variable **Button** in the Model Explorer and directly use it. *Figure 15.2* shows the Stateflow logic. When the Button is pressed, the control goes from the "**OFF**" state to the "**ON**" state:

Figure 15.2: *State logic ON–OFF*

Now, we hit the **Update Chart** option. *Figure 15.3* shows the result after parsing:

Figure 15.3: *Parse results*

Since variable **Button** is not declared, we get Parse error as **Unresolved data**. With this error, Stateflow Editor launches the **Symbol Wizard** where we can configure the **Class** and **Scope** of the variable **Button** and add it directly to the Model Explorer. *Figure 15.4* shows **Symbol Wizard**:

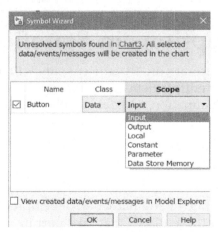

Figure 15.4: *Symbol Wizard*

Live Parsing

Stateflow parses the implemented logic live, based on the model configuration settings for Stateflow, so that we do not always need to **Update Chart** for syntax errors. By default, the configuration setting for **Unexpected backtracking** is set to **error**. When we encounter the same scenario, Stateflow highlights the junction error, where unexpected backtracking is detected. *Figure 15.5* shows the Stateflow logic when **Unexpected backtracking** occurs with highlighted parsed error:

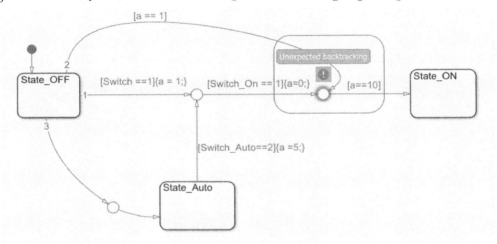

Figure 15.5: Unexpected backtracking detected

There are two paths to reach the highlighted junction from **State_OFF**. Additionally, there is a conditional transition to get **State_ON** from the highlighted junction. Therefore, in this case, it is difficult for Stateflow to backtrack to the correct path if the condition mentioned on the transition is not valid.

Debugging options in Stateflow

Any development tool becomes highly efficient only with better-debugging options. Stateflow also provides multiple debugging options. We can debug Stateflows with the help of breakpoints, animation, and data display. Let us learn about these options in detail.

Breakpoints

Breakpoints are used to break the simulation at particular conditions. We add a breakpoint on a specific line in any hardcode development tool. Stateflow gives us options to apply it at all those places that take part in Stateflow simulation. In the following sections, let us educate ourselves about breakpoints in Stateflow.

Breakpoint on transition when transition condition is valid

We can apply breakpoint on every transition. To set the breakpoint on any transition, right-click on the transition and then set the breakpoint. *Figure 15.6* shows how to set the breakpoint on transition:

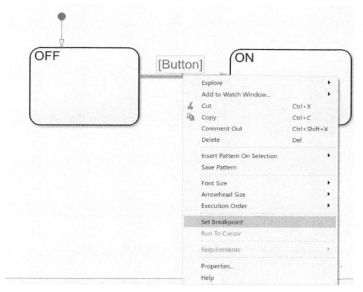

Figure 15.6: Set breakpoint to the transition

Once the breakpoint is applied to the transition, then a red color bubble appears on the transition. It indicates that a breakpoint is already set for the transition. When the cursor is placed on the red bubble, a tooltip appears with the information. This information is about the event when this breakpoint shall hit. Similarly, when the breakpoint is cleared, this red bubble disappears. *Figure 15.7* displays the transition after applying the breakpoint with tooltip information about when the breakpoint will hit:

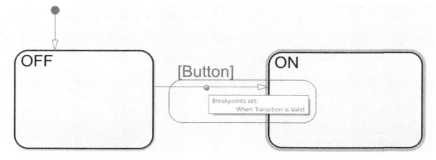

Figure 15.7: Red bubble on the transition to indicate breakpoint is active on the transition

We have set a breakpoint on transition, which connects state **OFF** and state **ON** when the value of the variable **Button** is received as true. The simulation pauses precisely at that time when the transition condition is valid. To realize this function of the Stateflow, first, we use a Signal Editor to change the value of the input **Button** at a specific time. *Figure 15.8* shows the logic we used for Signal Editor:

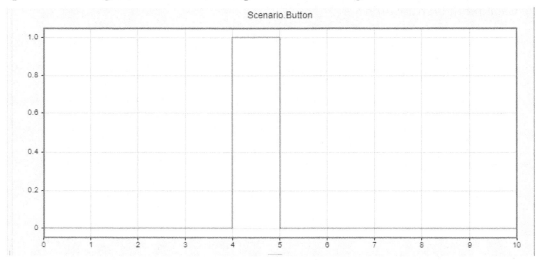

Figure 15.8: Signal Editor to set the value of "Button"

We are setting the value of **Button** as **1** between time intervals of 4 seconds to 5 seconds. Therefore, when we run the simulation, we expect simulation should pause at 4 seconds when the transition from state **OFF** to state **ON** is valid. *Figure 15.9* depicts the top view of the connections between Signal Editor and Stateflow:

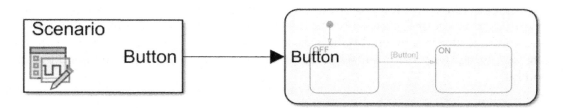

Figure 15.9: Signal Editor — Stateflow connection

Now, we shall move towards simulation. As soon as the breakpoint hits, the Stateflow window containing the transition appears to the front with a zoomed-in view. *Figure 15.10* displays how it looks when the simulation pauses at the breakpoint:

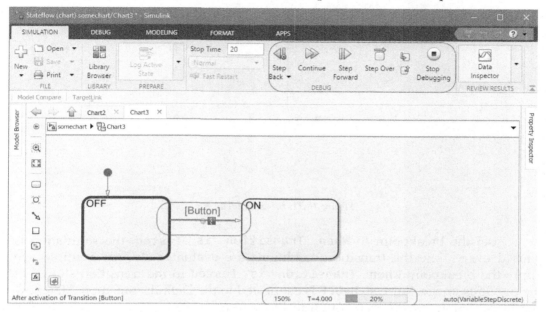

Figure 15.10: Breakpoint hit: simulation paused

We can see in figure 15.10 that the transition is highlighted with green color. Simulation is paused at 4.000. Simulations options such as **Step forward**, **Continue**, and so on are enabled. This debugging feature is very advantageous in the complexed Stateflows where we want to verify the intended paths taken by the simulation as per the valid conditions.

Breakpoint on transition when transition condition is tested

By default, a breakpoint is set to **when transition is valid**. However, sometimes, we may need to check whether the transitions are being tested or not. The transition conditions may not be valid, but they are tested or evaluated by Stateflow during simulation. To do so, we need to click on a breakpoint, that is, a red bubble then a small window pops up to configure the breakpoint options. Then we need to select an option **when transition is tested**. *Figure 15.11* shows the popup window that appears when we click on the breakpoint.

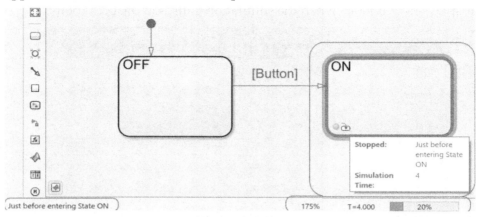

Figure 15.11: Breakpoint editor

As we set the breakpoint to **When Transition is Tested**, the simulation is paused every time the transition conditions are evaluated. In our example, we apply the breakpoint **When Transition is tested** to the transition shown in the previous image. Since state **OFF** is connected to the Default transition, Stateflow starts evaluating conditions on out transitions from the second execution cycle. The sample time of our model is 1 second. *Figure* 15.12 displays the scenario when the simulation pauses when the mentioned transition condition is evaluated:

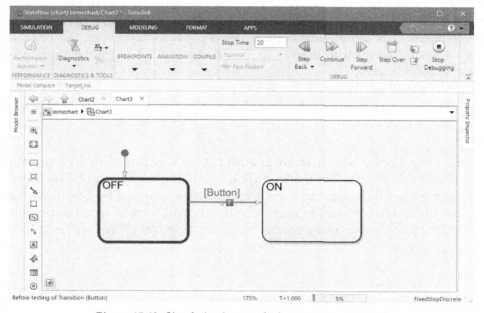

Figure 15.12: Simulation is paused when transition is tested

The first execution cycle happens at the 0th second and the second one at the 1st second. We can see in *figure 15.12* that the simulation has been stopped at 1st second, which is the second execution cycle of the simulation. The debugging option **When Transition is Tested** is valuable for complex and bigger Stateflow.

Breakpoint on state

Similar to the transition, we can also assign breakpoints to the state. When a breakpoint is set on the state, it is applied for entry and during the state by default. The simulation pauses precisely at the time when control goes to the respective state. After that, it hits at every during the state. Here, a red bubble appears on the state to indicate the breakpoint is set. When we take the cursor on the red bubble, a tooltip appears, mentioning when this breakpoint will hit. *Figure 15.13* displays the same with the tooltip:

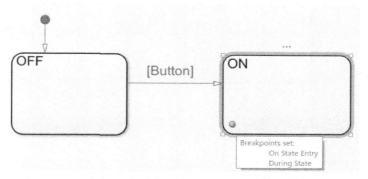

Figure 15.13: Set breakpoint on state

Similar to transition, we can also configure breakpoint for different conditions such as Entry, During, or Exit. When we click the red bubble, a similar breakpoint editor appears where we can set/clear breakpoints for these state conditions. *Figure 15.14* shows the breakpoint editor for the state:

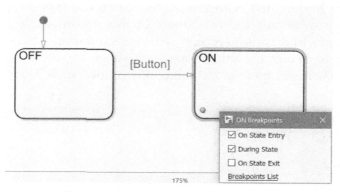

Figure 15.14: Breakpoint editor for the state

We have set the breakpoint on the state **ON** for `On State Entry` and for `During State`. When control goes from state **OFF** to state **ON**, the `On State Entry` breakpoint is hit, which pauses the simulation. We have also selected breakpoint for `During State`, and simulation pauses at every sample time until control is in the **ON** state. Let us use the same Signal Editor to provide the **Button** signal as **1** at the 4th second. When we run the simulation, it will pause 4th second onwards for every sample time till the end of the simulation. When *figure 15.15* simulation pauses due to breakpoint, we can also see why the simulation paused when we take the cursor near the breakpoint. *Figure 15.15* depicts the scenario when simulation pauses due to the `On State Entry` Breakpoint:

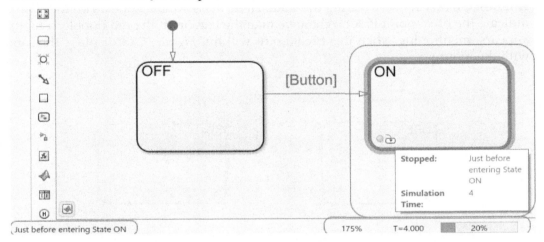

Figure 15.15: Simulation paused at state entry

Stateflow animation

Stateflow animation is a worthwhile debugging tool that realizes the Stateflow execution flow. In the previous section of breakpoints, we have seen that state boundaries are highlighted with blue when control is inside the state. Similarly, when Stateflow evaluates the conditions of the transitions, transitions are also highlighted with a blue color to recognize the execution flow. In debug window, we have an option to change the animation speed. When we select the animation speed as slow, then whenever there is a change in execution flow, Stateflow slows down the simulation to realize the change. *Figure 15.16* shows different options available for **Animation Speed**:

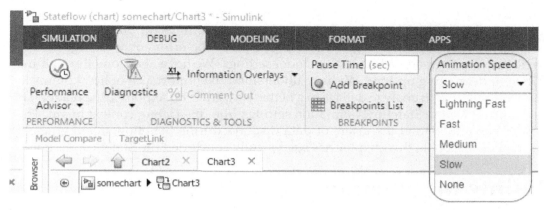

Figure 15.16: Change Stateflow animation speed.

Data display

Unlike other debugging options we have observed, data display is a powerful debugging tool. Using data display, we can see the values of the variables in Stateflow when the simulation is paused. The live display of the variable values helps the users understand the Stateflow execution flow. To visualize the variable values during live simulation, we need to take the cursor on the variables wherever they are used in Stateflow. In our example, we have used only one variable, **Button**, so when we take the cursor to the variable **Button**, the tooltip Stateflow displays its value. *Figure 15.17* displays how to use the data display option to check variable values:

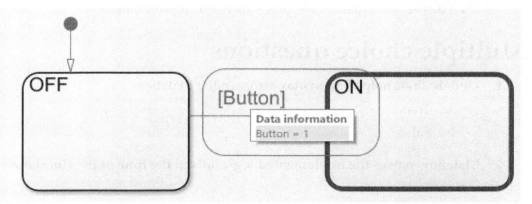

Figure 15.17: data display for variable "Button"

Conclusion

This chapter has taught us different parsing techniques, such as "Update Chart". We have also realized how the model configuration settings for Stateflow are used to have efficient Stateflow logic. Stateflow displays the errors or warnings during logic development according to the model settings. We have also gone through the different debugging options. We have understood the importance of breakpoints to pause simulation to analyze defects in a better way. After breakpoints, the reader has been introduced to Stateflow animation settings from the Debug context menu. The reader has understood the usage of data displays during Stateflow debugging. At the end of this book, this chapter has successfully concluded the Stateflow section.

Points to remember

- Update Chart is used to detect syntax errors in the Stateflow
- The variables are declared in Model Explorer using Symbol Wizard
- According to the model settings, Stateflow displays the error and warnings during Stateflow development.
- Breakpoints are set on transitions as well as on states.
- The red bubble indicates breakpoints on transitions and states.
- After clicking on the red bubble, the breakpoint editor pops up, which is used to configure breakpoints.
- Stateflow animation helps realize the execution control flow of the Stateflow.
- Data displays are used to monitor values during simulation.

Multiple choice questions

1. **Update chart helps find syntax errors in the Stateflow.**
    a. True
    b. False

2. **Stateflow parses the implemented logic only at the time of the simulation.**
    a. True
    b. False

3. Which of the following technique is not applicable for Stateflow debugging?
   a. Symbol Wizard
   b. Breakpoints
   c. Animation
   d. Data Display

4. Symbol Wizard automatically launches at the Update Chart if unresolved data is present in the Stateflow.
   a. True
   b. False

5. Stateflow displays errors or warnings according to the model settings.
   a. False
   b. True

6. Which of the following options are available for states breakpoints?
   a. When transition is valid
   b. When transition is tested
   c. During state
   d. None of the above

7. Which of the following options are available for transition breakpoints?
   a. When transition is valid
   b. When transition is tested
   c. On state entry
   d. Both A & B

8. Simulation aborts after hitting the breakpoint.
   a. True
   b. False

9. Stateflow animation speed is adjusted in Debug context menu
   a. True
   b. False

10. Data Displays do not support checking the values of variables.
    a. True
    b. False

Questions

1. Explain the process of the update chart.
2. Explain unexpected backtracking.
3. Explain the use of Symbol Wizard.
4. List different debugging options.
5. Why do we need breakpoints?
6. How can we identify breakpoints in Stateflow?
7. Explain the importance of Stateflow Animation.
8. Explain the process to monitor variable values during Simulation

Answers

1. a
2. b
3. a
4. a
5. b
6. c
7. d
8. b
9. a
10. b

Index

Symbols

1-D lookup table 289, 290
2-D lookup table 291
2-D plot
  bar graph 158
  pie chart 157
  scatter plot 157
  stem 158
3-D plot
  mesh surface plot 160
  surface plot 160

A

action
  options 371
additional output 311
advanced parameter sub-pane 332, 333
AND decomposition 492

apps tab 44
arithmetic array operator
  on matrices 85
arithmetic operator 116
array
  about 78
  arithmetic operator 78-80
  creating 78
  element, accessing 81
array command 80
array function
  combining 103, 104
  creating 97-102
  order 106, 107
  reshape 107, 108
  resize 107, 108
  shape 106, 107
  size 106, 107

array function, type and properties
    about 113
    is function 113
    strlength function 114
Automotive Open System Architecture (AUTOSAR) 14
AUTOSAR XML (ARXML) file 14

B

block callbacks
    about 377
    block compilation and simulation callbacks 379, 380
    block editing-related callbacks 379
    block opening-related callbacks 378
    block save and close callbacks 380
    subsystem-related callbacks 380
block parameters
    gain block 196
    integrator block 196
    scope block 196
    Sine wave generator block 195
breakpoint on state 547, 548
breakpoint on transition
    setting, when transition condition is tested 545-547
    setting, when transition is valid 543-545
breakpoints 542
break statement 136
built-in commands
    about 88
    desktop environment command 88
built-in functions
    about 88
    array function 97
    matrices function 97
    vector function 97

C

case statement 132
catch statement 133, 134
cell array 74
character array
    about 73
    cell array 74
    logical type 73
    structure 75, 77
character array function
    about 111
    creating 111-113
chart properties
    settings 436-440
classes, variable classification
    numeric type 70-72
code generation 417
code section, home tab
    operations 38-40
column wise concatenation 87, 88
command history panel 34
command window
    used, for accessing variables 49
command Window panel 32
command window shortcuts
    about 66
    working tips 66-68
compatibility pane
    about 338
    frame status of signal 339
    s-function upgrade 339
    SimState object 339

component menu, options
  insert component 217
  subsytem, converting 218
  subsytem, creating 218
  subsytem, expanding 218
conditionally executable subsystems 392, 393
connection junctions 500, 501
connective junctions 454
connectivity pane
  about 336
  bus signal treated as vector 337
  context-dependent inputs 338
  element name mismatch 337
  invalid function-call connection 338
  non-bus signals treated as bus signals 337
  repair bus selection 337, 338
  signal label mismatch 336
  unconnected block input ports 336
  unconnected block output ports 337
  unconnected line 337
  unspecified bus object, at outport block 337
constants
  in MATLAB 126
containers
  options 371
continue statement 137
continuous library
  about 267, 268
  delays 279
  integrators 268
  PID controller 279
continuous model 180

control programming flow
  about 131
  break statement 136
  case statement 132
  catch statement 133, 134
  continue statement 137
  elseif statement 131
  else statement 131, 132
  for loop 134, 135
  if statement 131, 132
  otherwise statement 132
  return statement 138
  switch statement 132
  try statement 133, 134
  while loop 135
current folder browser panel 33
current folder browser toolbar 47
custom libraries, with mask options
  block callbacks 377, 378
  creating 362
  library mask, creating 362-368
  mask editor options 368
  model callbacks 374, 375
custom library creation
  basics 348

D
data display 549
Data Import/Export
  about 308, 309
  additional parameters 311
  advanced parameters 311
  load from workspace 309
  save to workspace or file 310
  simulation data inspector 310

data properties 440-442
dataset signal format
  about 311
  time series 312
  time table 312
data type
  about 314
  default for underspecified
      data type 314
  division for fixed-point net slope
      computation, using 314
  floating-point multiplication, using
      to handle net slope correction 315
  gain parameterinherit 315
  reference link 77
data type propagation 314
data validity pane
  about 325
  advanced parameter
      sub-pane 332, 333
  compatibility pane 338
  connectivity pane 336
  diagnostic model referencing pane 340
  diagnostic stateflow pane 342
  parameters sub-pane 328
  signals sub-pane 325, 326
  Type Conversion pane 334
data viewers, Sinks library
  about 258
  display block 260
  floating scope 259, 260
  scope 259
  XY Graph block 259

debug tab
  about 220, 430
  animation section 432
  breakpoint section 432
  compile section 432
  debug section 432, 433
  diagnostics & tools section 431
  menu 221-224
  performance section 431
decision pattern
  adding 462, 463
default transition 461, 497
delays
  about 279
  transport delay 280
derivative block 281
design validation 417
desktop environment command
  about 88
  help command 96
  session command 93
  system command 89
details panel 33
detect read before write
  values 331
detect write after read
  values 331, 332
deterministic model 180
diagnostic model referencing pane
  about 340
  invalid root inport/outport block
      connection 341
  model block version mismatch 340
  no explicit final value for model
      arguments 341

port and parameter mismatch 340, 341
unsupported data logging 341
diagnostics
  about 315, 316
  advanced parameters 320-323
  data validity pane 325
  sample time pane 323
diagnostics, Solver section
  about 316
  algebraic loop 316, 317
  automatic solver parameter selection 320
  block priority violation 318, 319
  consecutive zero-crossing violation 319, 320
  extraneous discrete derivative signal 320
  minimize algebraic loop 317
  min step size violation 319
  operating point interface checksum mismatch 320
  state name clash 320
diagnostic stateflow pane 342
discrete library
  about 281-284
  delay block example 285
  discrete-time integrator example 284, 285
discrete model 180
display
  options 371
division operator 116
documentation pane 374
dot product
  abs block 262

assignment block 263
complex vector conversion block 264
math function block 262
matrix oncatenate block 263
minmax block 262
rounding function block 262
sign block 262
trigonometric function block 262
unary minus block 262
vector concatenate block 263
double integrator 272
dynamic model 179

E

editor tab 45
editor window 34, 35
elseif 132
elseif statement 131
else statement 131, 132
Embedded coder 14
environment section, home tab
  operations 40-42
events
  about 510
  explicit event 512
  implicit event 510
  temporal logic 516
event scope
  input event 513, 514
  local event 516
  output event 515
exclusive decomposition 492
execution order of blocks 386, 387
explicit event 512
explicit model 180

external C function
  calling, from statechart 533-535

F

Fast Fourier Transform (FFT) 6
file section, home tab
  operations 36-38
finite state machine 475
fixed-point designer 14
fixed-step type solver
  about 299
  auto (Automatic Solver detection) 300
  discrete (no continuous states) 300
  ode1be (Backward Euler) 300
  ode1 (Euler) 300
  ode2 (Heun) 300
  ode4 (Runge-Kutta) 300
  ode5 (Dormand-Prince) 300
  ode8 (Dormand-Prince RK8(7)) 300
  ode14x (extrapolation) 300
  versus variable-step type
    solver 306-308
flowcharts 415
flow graph
  data definition 456, 457
  if-else condition 452, 453
  implementing 453-456
  overview 452
  simulation 457, 458
for loop 134, 135
format tab
  about 433
  align section 434
  content section 434

copy & size section 433
copy & style section 433
distribute section 434
layout section 433
match section 434
menu 220
function 124, 127
function methods
  2-D line function plot, creating 140
  2-D line plot, creating 139, 140
  2-D plot 157
  2-D plot, creating with line
    specification 144
  2-D plot line properties, creating 146
  2-D plot line properties,
    modifying 146
  3-D plot 160
  3-D plot, creating 158, 159
  about 139
  area plot, creating 153, 154
  axis limits, adding 150
  function plot, creating 154
  grid, adding 151
  legend, adding 150
  logarithmic plot, creating 155-157
  matrix plot, creating 143, 144
  multiple line plot, creating with
    different axes 142, 143
  multiple line plot, creating
    with same axes 141, 142
  plot axes label, adding 148, 149
  plot title, adding 149
  stairstep plot, creating 153
  two y-axes, adding to plot 151, 152

G

graphical function
  about 468, 521-523
  calling 469
  creating 468
  data, defining 469
  declaring 468
  pattern, creating 469
grayscale image 164
grid function
  creating 105, 106
Group state 502, 503

H

hardware implementation 342, 405
hardware implementation, parameters
  device type 406
  device vendor 405
  hardware board 405
Hardware-in-Loop (HIL) 187
help command
  about 96
  demo 97
  doc 96
  help 96
  lookfor 97
history junctions
  about 501
  example 501, 502
home tab
  about 36
  code section 38, 39
  environment section 40-42
  file section 36, 37
  resources section 42, 43
  Simulink section 40
  variable section 38

I

identified library block
  methods 249, 250
if statement 131
image functions
  im2double 167
  image 164
  imagesc 164
  imfinfo 167
  imread 165
  imresize 166
  imshow 165
  imwrite 166
  ind2rgb 167
  rgb2gray 167
  rgb2ind 167
images
  about 163
  grayscale image 164
  indexed image 164
  RGB image 163
implicit event 510, 511
implicit model 180
indexed image 164
Infinite Impulse Response (IIR) 283
infinite number (Inf) 328
inner transition
  about 498
  example 498, 499
insert component
  about 217
  area 218

bus 218
chart 218
library browser 218
subsystem 217
integrator block
  about 269, 270
  parameters 271, 272
integrator limited block 272
integrators
  about 268
  integrator block 269, 270
  integrator limited block 272
  second-order integrator block 272-275
  second-order limited block 276
  transfer function block 276-278
intensity image 164
interactive method 161, 188
interactive tool
  figure palette 162
  plot browser 162
  property editor 163
is function 113, 114

J

junctions
  about 500
  connection junctions 500, 501
  history junctions 501

L

library link
  about 358
  operations 359-362
library mask
  properties 365

license options
  reference link 18
line and marker-related properties
  color 146
  LineStyle 147
  LineWidth 147
  Marker 147
  MarkerEdgeColor 147
  MarkerFaceColor 147
  MarkerIndices 147
  MarkerSize 147
  XData 147
  YData 147
  ZData 147
linear algebra matrix function
  about 109
  cross function 110
  det function 110
  dot function 109
  eig function 111
  inv function 109
  mpower function 109
  mtimes function 109
  rank function 110
  sqrtm function 109
  trace function 110
linear model 179
line specification options
  color specification 145
  line style specification 144
  marker symbol specification 145
live editor 35
live editor tab 45
Live Parsing 542

live script 129, 130
load from workspace
  input options 309
logical operator 117
logical type 73
lookup tables library
  1-D lookup table 289, 290
  2-D lookup table 291
  about 288
loop pattern
  adding 463, 464

M

Main attributes
  parameters 253
manual activation
  reference link 23
mask editor options
  about 368
  documentation 374
  Icon & Ports 368, 369
  initialization 372, 373
  Parameters & Dialog 370
math
  about 313
  algorithm optimized for row-major array layout 314
  simulation behavior for denormal numbers 313
math and data types
  about 312
  advanced parameters 315
mathematical model types
  about 178, 179
  continuous model 180
  deterministic model 180
  discrete model 180
  dynamic model 179
  explicit model 180
  implicit model 180
  linear model 179
  nonlinear model 179
  static model 179
  stochastic model 180
Math operations library
  about 261
  add block 262
  divide block 262
  dot product block 262
  gain block 262
  product block 262
  product of elements block 262
  slider gain block 262
  subtract block 262
  sum block 262
  sum of elements block 262
MathWorks
  about 7
  URL 19
MathWorks, license options
  education 18
  home 18
  standard 18
  student 18
MATLAB Academy
  reference link 43
MATLAB applications
  about 10-12
  reference link 12
MATLAB-based programming
  challenges 16

MATLAB central
　reference link　43
MATLAB desktop
　about　30, 31
　panels　31
　toolbars　31, 32
MATLAB function　526, 527
MATLAB functions
　reference link　118
MATLAB installation
　about　18
　license options　18
MATLAB installation process
　about　19, 20
　offline installation　19
　online installation　19
　on Windows OS　20, 21
MATLAB key users　10
MATLAB modeling
　advantages　15
　versus traditional programming approach　15
MATLAB products
　about　12
　activating　21
　AUTOSAR blockset　14
　Embedded coder　14
　fixed-point designer　14
　for development　13
　for model-based design　13
　for validation　13
　offline activation　22, 23
　online activation　21, 22

Simulink　13
Simulink coverage　14
Stateflow　13
MATLAB program
　debugging　128, 129
MATLAB search path setting　57-61
MATLAB toolboxes　12-15
MATLAB user guide
　reference link　6
MATLAB versions
　about　7-10
　reference link　10
MATLAB workspace parameter
　data store memory block sub-pane　331
　detect downcast　330
　detect loss of tunability　330, 331
　detect overflow　330
　detect precision loss　330
　detect read before write　331
　detect underflow　330
　detect write after read　331
　detect write after write　332
　duplicate data store names　332
　multitask data store　332
matrices
　about　85
　arithmetic array operator　85
matrix
　about　82
　arithmetic operator　82
　creating　82
　element, accessing　83, 84
　matrix arithmetic operator　85, 86

matrix concatenation
  column wise concatenation 87, 88
  performing 86
  row wise concatenation 87
MATrix LABoratory (MATLAB)
  about 5
  overview 5, 6
  system requirements 16, 17
  version development 5, 6
maximum step size 303
minimum step size
  about 304
  absolute tolerance 304
  algorithm 304
  auto scale absolute tolerance 304
  higher priority value 305
  initial step size 304
  number of Consecutive min steps 304
  number of consecutive zero
      crossings 305
  rate transition, handling automatically
      for data transfer 305
  relative tolerance 304
  sharp preservation 304
  signal threshold 305
  time tolerance 305
  zero crossing control 304
model and subsystem outputs, Sinks
    library
  about 256
  out bus element block 258
  outport block 257
  terminator block 258
  To File block 258
  To Workspace block 258

model and subsytem input,
    Sources library
  about 251
  From File block 254
  From Spreadsheet block 254
  From Workspace block 254
  Ground block 254
  in bus element block 253, 254
  inport block 252
  Signal generator block 254-256
model-based design
  about 182
  advantages 183
  versus traditional system design 181
  workflow 183, 184
model-based design process
  about 184
  model results, simulating 186
  model results, verifying 186
  production code automatically,
      generating 186, 187
  simulation methods 187
  Simulink model behavior,
      defining 186
  system architecture, designing 186
  system, defining 185
  system requirement, deriving 185
  validation 187
  verification 187
Model Browser 208
model callbacks
  about 374, 375
  model load/close callbacks 376
  model save callbacks 376
  model simulation callbacks 376, 377

model configuration parameter 296, 297
Model Data Editor 208
Model Explorer
  about 442
  contents pane 443
  dialog pane 443, 444
  menu 443
  model hierarchy pane 443
modeling 188
modeling tab
  about 214
  compile menu 219
  component menu 217
  component section 428, 429
  design data section 426, 427
  design menu 216, 217
  edit section 430
  evaluate & manage menu 214, 215
  evaluate & manage section 425
  setup menu 217
  setup section 427
  simulate menu 219
Model-in-Loop (MIL) 187
model referencing
  about 342, 393, 394, 397
  advantages 393
  parameters 398-400

N

nonlinear model 179
non-virtual signal bus 402-404
non-virtual subsystems 390-392
Not a Number (NaN) 328

numeric type
  about 70-72
  double (double-precision floating-point) 70
  int8 (8-bit signed integer) 71
  int16 (16-bit signed integer) 71
  int32 (32-bit signed integer) 71
  int64 (64-bit signed integer) 71
  single (single-precision floating-point) 70
  uint8 (8-bit unsigned integer) 70
  uint16 (16-bit unsigned integer) 70
  uint32 (32-bit unsigned integer) 70
  uint64 (64-bit unsigned integer) 70

O

operator precedence 118
operators
  about 85
  arithmetic array operator 85
  matrix arithmetic operator 85
operator types
  about 115
  arithmetic operator 116
  division operator 116
  logical operator 117
  operator precedence 118
  relational operator 117
  rounding operator 116
OR decomposition 492
Ordinary Differential Equation (ODE) 6
otherwise statement 132

P

Palette 209

panels, in MATLAB desktop
　about 32
　command history panel 34
　command Window panel 32
　current folder browser panel 33
　details panel 33
　editor window 34, 35
　live editor 35
　variables editor panel 35
　workspace browser panel 35
parallel decomposition 492
parameters
　options 370
parameters sub-pane
　about 328
　properties 329
patterns
　about 461
　custom pattern, adding 468
　predefined pattern, adding 462
　save as pattern 467
PC-MATLAB 7
periodic sample time constraint
　ensure sample time-independent 301
　specified 301
　unconstrained 301
PID controller 224-229, 279
plots
　about 139
　function methods 139
plots tab 43, 44
ports library 288
predefined pattern
　adding 462
　decision pattern, adding 462, 463

loop pattern, adding 463, 464
　switch pattern, adding 465, 466
processor-in-the-loop (PIL) 14, 187
programmatic method 188
Property Inspector
　about 208, 436
　chart properties 436
　data properties 440
Proportional-Integral-Derivative
　(PID) 224

Q
quick access toolbar 46, 47

R
refine output 311
relational operator 117
resources section, home tab
　operations 42, 43
return statement 138
RGB image 163
rounding operator 116
row wise concatenation 87

S
sample time pane, of diagnostics
　enforce sample times, by Signal
　　Specification block 324
　equal priority tasks 324
　multitask conditionally executed
　　subsytem 324
　multitask rate transition 323
　sample hit time adjusting 324
　single task rate transition 324
　source block specifies 323
　unspecified inheritability 324
save as pattern 467

save figure 163
save to workspace or file
  output options 310
scalars 77
script
  about 124-126
  constants, in MATLAB 126
second-order integrator block 272-275
second-order limited block 276
self-loop transition 498
Service Pack (SP) 7
session command
  about 93
  ans 94
  clc 93
  clear 93
  diary 94
  echo 95
  exist 94
  format 95, 96
  home 94
  more 94
  who 95
  whos 95
Signal attributes
  parameters 253
signal bus
  about 400, 401
  non-virtual signal bus 402-404
  signal conversion block 404
  virtual signal bus 401, 402
signal conversion block 404
signal loading techniques
  about 229, 230
  Dashboard block, using 231

From File block, using 232
From Spreadsheet block, using 233
From Workspace block, using 231, 232
Root Inport mapper, using 234, 235
Signal Editor, using 233, 234
Simple Source block, using 230, 231
signal logging techniques
  about 229, 236
  Dashboard block, using 240
  Outport block, using 240
  scope, using 236
  Signal logging, using 238
  Simulation Data Inspector, using 239
  To File block, using 237
  To Workspace block, using 237
signal routing library
  about 285, 286
  bus creator block 287
  bus selector block 287
  Data Store Memory block 288
  Data Store Read block 288
  Data Store Write block 288
  demux block 287
  From block 288
  Goto block 288
  merge block 287
  multiport switch block 287
  mux block 287
  switch block 287
signals sub-pane
  about 325
  division by singular matrix 327
  Inf or NaN block output 328
  prefix for identifiers 328
  properties 326

saturate on overflow 328
signal resolution 327
simulation range checking 327
string truncation checking 327
underspecified data types 327
underspecified dimensions 328
wrap on overflow 327, 328
signal visualization techniques
  about 229, 236
  Dashboard block, using 240
  Outport block, using 240
  scope, using 236
  Signal logging, using 238
  Simulation Data Inspector, using 239
  To File block, using 237
  To Workspace block, using 237
simulation behavior for denormal numbers
  Flush to Zero (FTZ) 313
  Gradual underflow 313
Simulation model
  running 198-200
simulation tab
  about 209
  file menu 209, 210
  file section 420, 421
  library menu 211
  prepare menu 211
  prepare section 422
  review results menu 214
  review results section 424
  simulate menu 212, 213
  simulate section 423, 424
Simulation Target 342
simulation time 298

simulation time, parameters
  start time 298
  stop time 298
Simulink
  about 13
  overview 176, 177
Simulink coverage 14
Simulink Editor
  about 206
  canvas 190
  features 206, 207
  model browser 190
  palette 191
  property inspector 191
  quick access toolbar 190
  toolstrip 190
Simulink Editor components
  Toolstrip 208
Simulink function 523-525
Simulink, key features
  about 177
  automatic code generation 178
  modeling 177
  simulation 177
  testing 177, 178
  validation 177, 178
  verification 177, 178
Simulink library
  creating 352-358
Simulink library browser
  about 248-250
  continuous library 267, 268
  discrete library 282-284
  logic and bit operations library 264-267

lookup tables library 288
Math operations library 261
methods 248
ports library 288
signal routing library 285, 286
Sinks library 256
Sources library 250, 251
subsystems library 288
Simulink logic
  creating 349-352
Simulink model
  block parameters, configuring 195
  blocks, adding 192-194
  blocks, connecting 196, 197
  creating 188
  model configuration parameters, defining 198
  Simulink Editor, opening 190
  Simulink library browser, opening 191, 192
  starting 189
Simulink model behavior
  controller model 186
  plant model 186
Simulink modeling
  shortcuts 241, 242
Simulink section, home tab
  operations 40
Simulink state 530-533
Sinks library
  about 256
  data viewers 258
  model and subsystem outputs 256
  simulation control 260

sizes, variable classification
  array 78
  matrix 82
  scalars 77
software-in-the-loop (SIL) 14, 187
solver details
  about 300
  discrete rate, executing 301
  fixed-step size (fundamental sample time) 301
  higher priority value 301
  periodic sample time constraint 301
  tasks, executing concurrently on target 301
Solver pane configuration parameter
  reference link 305
solver selection
  about 298
  type 299
Solver settings
  about 297
  advanced setting 305
  simulation time 298
  solver details 300
  solver selection 298
  variable-step type solver 301, 302
Sources library
  model and subsytem input 251
  specified output 311
state 476
state actions
  about 481, 482
  during 481
  entry 481

Index

exit 481
vehicle exterior light
    control, example 482-488
statechart
  about 415
  used, for calling external
    C function 533-535
state decomposition
  about 492
  AND decomposition 492
  OR decomposition 492
  water dispenser, example 493
Stateflow 13, 414, 415
Stateflow animation 548, 549
Stateflow chart
  about 475
  debugging 416
  executing 416
  state 476
Stateflow, debugging options
  about 542
  breakpoints 542
Stateflow diagnostics parameter
  about 444
  parameters 445, 446
Stateflow Editor
  about 417
  drawing area 419
  explorer bar 419, 420
  model browser 419
  object palette 419
  Property Inspector window 436
  status bar 420
  Symbols pane 434

title bar 418
tootlstrip 420
stateflow function 521
Stateflow, key features
  about 415
  chart execution 416
  control logic, designing 415
  debugging 416
  reusable logic, developing 416
  validation and code generation 417
Stateflow parsing
  about 540
  Live Parsing 542
  Update Chart option 540, 541
state hierarchy
  about 488, 489
  tax calculator, example 489-491
  vehicle exterior light
    control, example 490
state label
  about 480
  state actions 481
  state name 480
state name 480
state transition
  about 496
  example 496, 497
state transition diagram
  about 475, 476
  chart, opening 477
  data, defining 478, 479
  simulation 479
  simulink model interface 479, 480
  state label, updating 478

state, renaming 477
states, creating 477
transition condition, updating 478
transition, creating 477
static model 179
stochastic model 180
string array function
  about 111
  creating 111-113
  erase operator 115
  find operator 114
  strcmp operator 115
  strfind, count operator 115
  strrep operator 115
strings 73
strlength function 114
structure 75, 77
subchart 503, 504
subsystem
  about 386
  conditionally executable subsystems 392, 393
  execution order of block 386, 387
  model referencing 393, 394
  non-virtual subsystems 390-392
  variant model 397
  variant subsystem 395, 396
  virtual subsystems 388-390
subsystems library 288
supertransition
  about 499
  example 499, 500
switch pattern
  adding 465, 466
switch statement 132

Symbols pane
  about 434, 435
  operations 435, 436
system command
  about 89
  cd 92
  dir 92
  exit 90
  finish 90
  license 91
  matlab 89
  matlabroot 89
  path 91, 92
  pwd 91
  quit 89
  startup 90
  type 93
  version 90, 91
  what 92
  which 93
system under test (SUT) 187

T

temporal logic 516
temporal logic, function
  after function 516, 517
  at function 517, 518
  before function 518, 519
  every function 519, 520
  temporal count function 520
toolbar types
  about 35
  current folder browser toolbar 47
  quick access toolbar 46, 47
  toolstrip 35

toolstrip
  about 35, 208, 209, 420
  apps 208
  apps tab 44
  canvas 208
  debug tab 208, 220, 430
  editor tab 45
  format tab 208, 220, 433
  home tab 36
  live editor tab 45
  modeling tab 208, 425
  plots tab 43, 44
  quick access toolbar 208
  simulation tab 208, 209, 420
  view tab 46
traditional programming approach
  versus MATLAB modeling 15
traditional system design
  about 181
  versus model-based design 181
  workflow 181, 182
Transfer Fcn 276
transfer function block 276, 277
transition
  about 459, 495
  default transition 461, 497
  inner transition 498
  self-loop transition 498
  state transition 496
transition label notation
  about 460
  condition 460
  condition action 460

event or message name 460
transition action 460
transport delay 280
trial license
  reference link 19
truth table 415, 416, 527-530
try statement 133, 134
Type Conversion pane
  32-bit integer to single-precision float conversion 335
  about 334
  detect overflow for fixed-point constant 335
  detect precision loss for fixed-point constant 335
  detect underflow for fixed-point constant 335
  unnecessary type conversion 334
  vector/matrix block input conversion 334
type, solver selection
  fixed-step type solver 299
  variable-step type solver 299

U
Update Chart option 540, 541

V
variable
  overview 69
variable accessing, with command window
  about 49
  creating 49
  deleting 49, 50
  modifying 50, 51

variable accessing, with workspace browser
  about 51
  creating 51, 52
  deleting 52, 53
  modifying 53
  modifying, with open selection 54
  workspace durability 54-56
variable classification
  about 69
  character array 73
  matrix concatenation, performing 86
  operators and matrices 85
  sizes 77
  strings 73
  types or classes 70
variable naming convention 69
variable section, home tab
  operations 38
variables editor panel 35
variable-step type solver
  about 301, 302
  auto 302
  daessc (Solver for Simscape) 303
  discrete (no continuous states) 302
  ode15s (stiff/NDF) 303
  ode23 (Bogacki-Shampine) 303
  ode23s (stiff/Mod. Rosenbrock) 303
  ode23tb (stiff/TR-BDF2) 303
  ode23t (Mod. stiff/Trapezoidal) 303
  ode45 (Dormand-Prince) 302
  ode113 (Adams) 303
  odeN (fixed step with zero crossings) 303
  versus fixed-step type solver 306-308

variable-step type solver, parameter
  maximum step size 303
  minimum step size 304
variant model 397
variant subsystem 395, 396
view tab 46
virtual signal bus 401, 402
virtual subsystems 388-390
visualization
  about 139
  images 163
  plots 139

W

water dispenser
  example 493-495
while loop 135
Windows OS
  used, for MATLAB installation process 20, 21
workspace browser
  about 47
  concept 47-49
  used, for accessing variable 51
  variables, accessing with command window 49
workspace browser panel 35